Story and Art by **Arina Tanemura**

SAKURA HIME
Princess Sakura

4

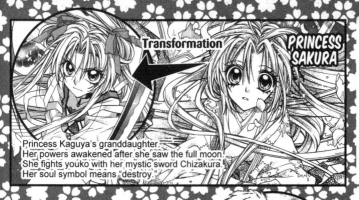

Characters

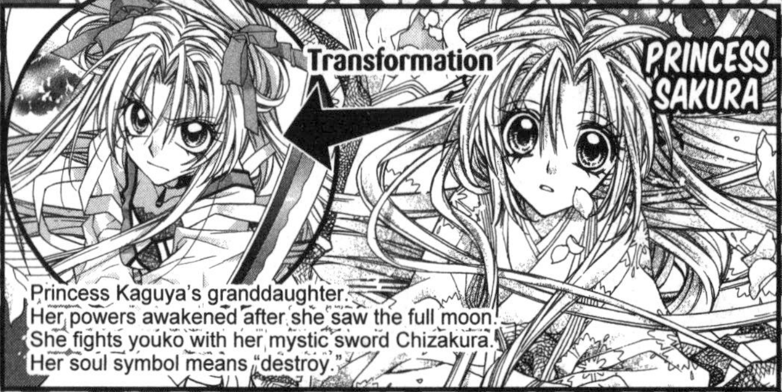
PRINCESS SAKURA
Transformation
Princess Kaguya's granddaughter.
Her powers awakened after she saw the full moon.
She fights youko with her mystic sword Chizakura.
Her soul symbol means "destroy."

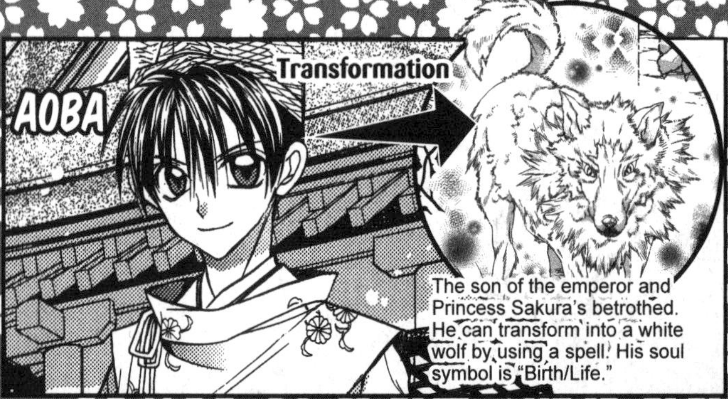
Transformation
AOBA
The son of the emperor and Princess Sakura's betrothed. He can transform into a white wolf by using a spell. His soul symbol is "Birth/Life."

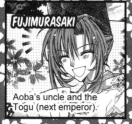

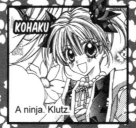

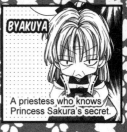

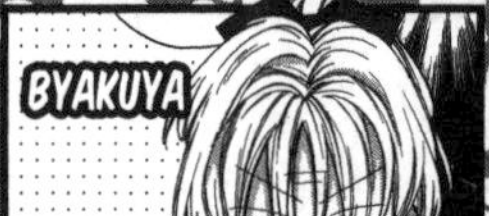
BYAKUYA
A priestess who knows Princess Sakura's secret.

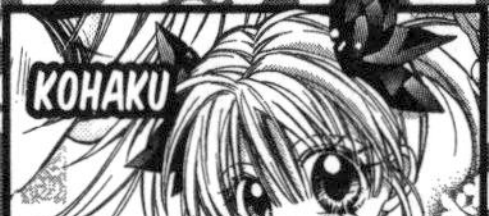
KOHAKU
A ninja. Klutz.

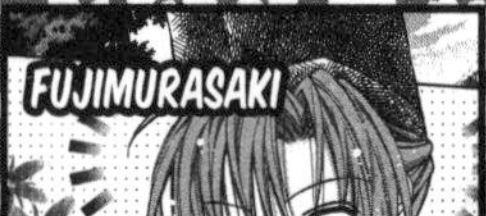
FUJIMURASAKI
Aoba's uncle and the Togu (next emperor).

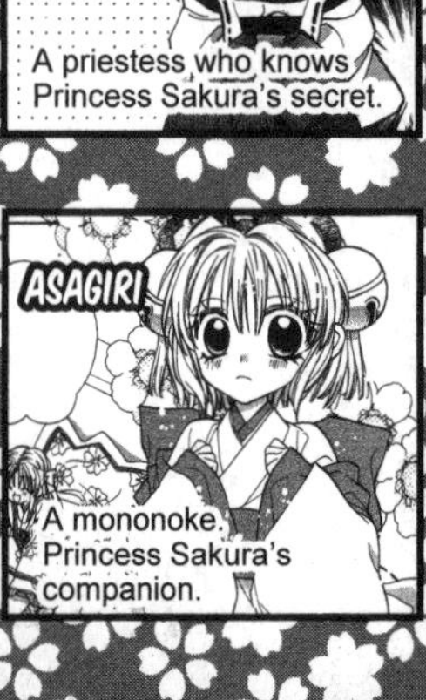
ASAGIRI
A mononoke. Princess Sakura's companion.

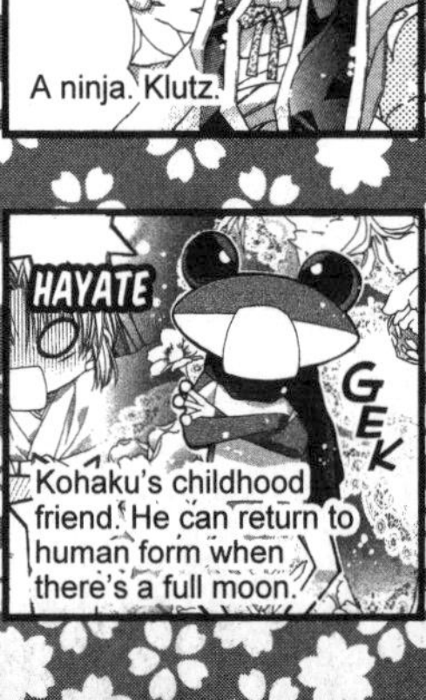
HAYATE
GEK
Kohaku's childhood friend. He can return to human form when there's a full moon.

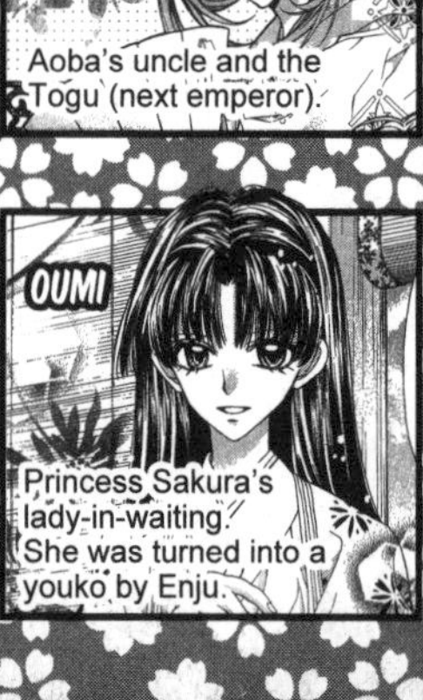
OUMI
Princess Sakura's lady-in-waiting. She was turned into a youko by Enju.

RURIJO

MAIMAI

ENJU

Princess Sakura's older brother. He used to be kind, but he has a deep hatred of humans now.

SHURI

UKYO

SAKURA HIME
The Legend of Princess Sakura

Story Thus Far

Heian era. Princess Sakura is 14 years old and learns from Byakuya that she is the granddaughter of Princess Kaguya, a princess from the moon. She is the only person able to wield the mystic sword Chizakura that can kill the demon youko. And at the same time, she finds out that her fated soul symbol is "destroy"...

Aoba discovers this and captures Sakura, intending to kill her. Fujimurasaki arrives and Sakura is given orders from the Emperor to officially hunt down a youko.

Sakura travels to Uji where she is told by her lady-in-waiting, Oumi, that the councilor is a traitor. But then Oumi turns into a youko and attacks Sakura...! The person behind the treachery is a mysterious man named Enju, who kills both Oumi and the councilor. He tells Sakura that they'll meet again and leaves...

After the battle, Sakura starts living with Aoba, who is now kind to her. But Enju reappears and tells Sakura that he is her older brother Kai, whom she thought had died. He holds a deep hatred for the emperor who betrayed him. Enju and his followers from the moon kidnap Sakura to get revenge...?!

SAKURA HIME
The Legend of Princess Sakura

....

CONTENTS

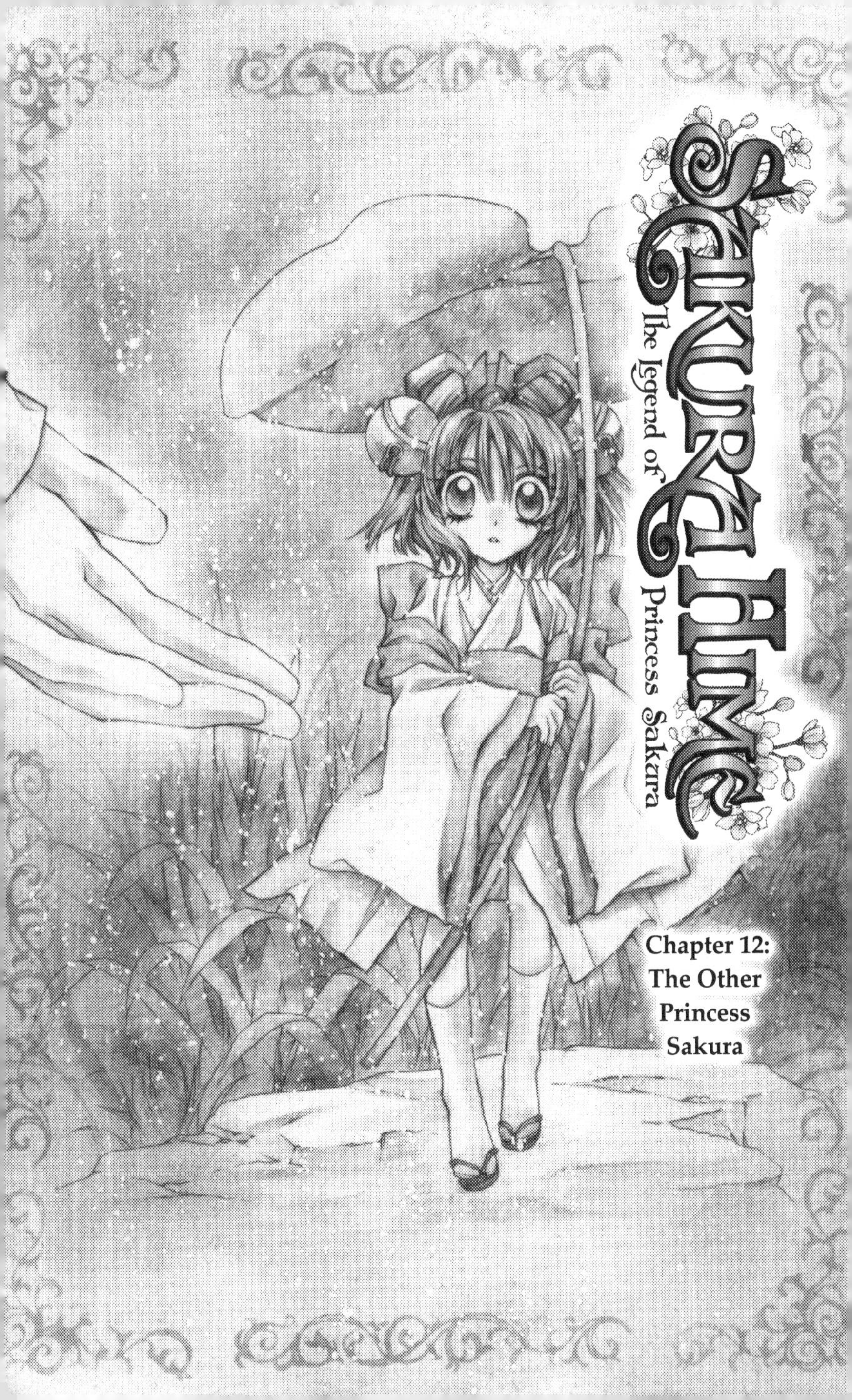
Sakura Hime
The Legend of Princess Sakura
Chapter 12:
The Other
Princess
Sakura

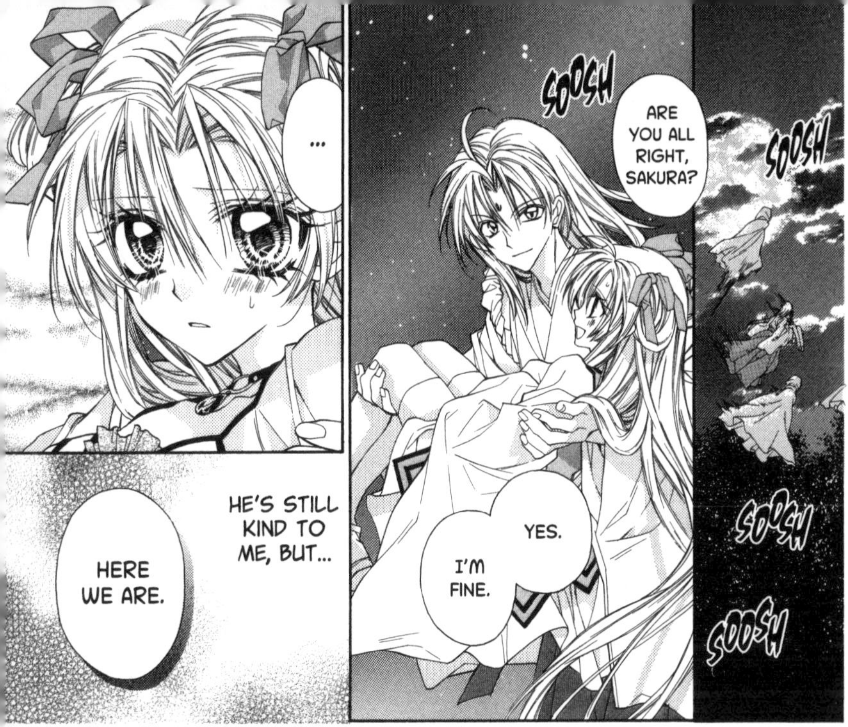
SOOSH
SOOSH
ARE YOU ALL RIGHT, SAKURA?
SOOSH
SOOSH
YES.
I'M FINE.
...
HE'S STILL KIND TO ME, BUT...
HERE WE ARE.

Chapter 12: The Other Princess Sakura

※ I'm giving away the story.

The chapter page illustration is of Asagiri. When I was in elementary school, I always felt a little disappointed when a chapter illustration in *Ribon* was not of the main character. But I was in a slump when I drew it and decided on Asagiri for a change of pace.

The story is now entering the Shura Yugenden (Mysterious Battle Palace) arc. This is my very first series that I decided to draw serious battles for, so I need to think a lot about how to build the chapters.

I've stuffed a lot in this chapter, so I hope you read it again after you finish this volume, or after the Yugenden arc is over.

You finally get to meet my favorite character at the end of this chapter. I'm talking about Rurijo, and I was glad to see the readers kindly accept her as well. It's the first time I've added designs like that to the face, so I feel slightly strange, as if I'm doing something bad. But then again, I can also draw her naked because of those marks all over her body... (It lessens my embarrassment of drawing her like that. ;) Yes, drawing a naked body embarrasses me. ////;

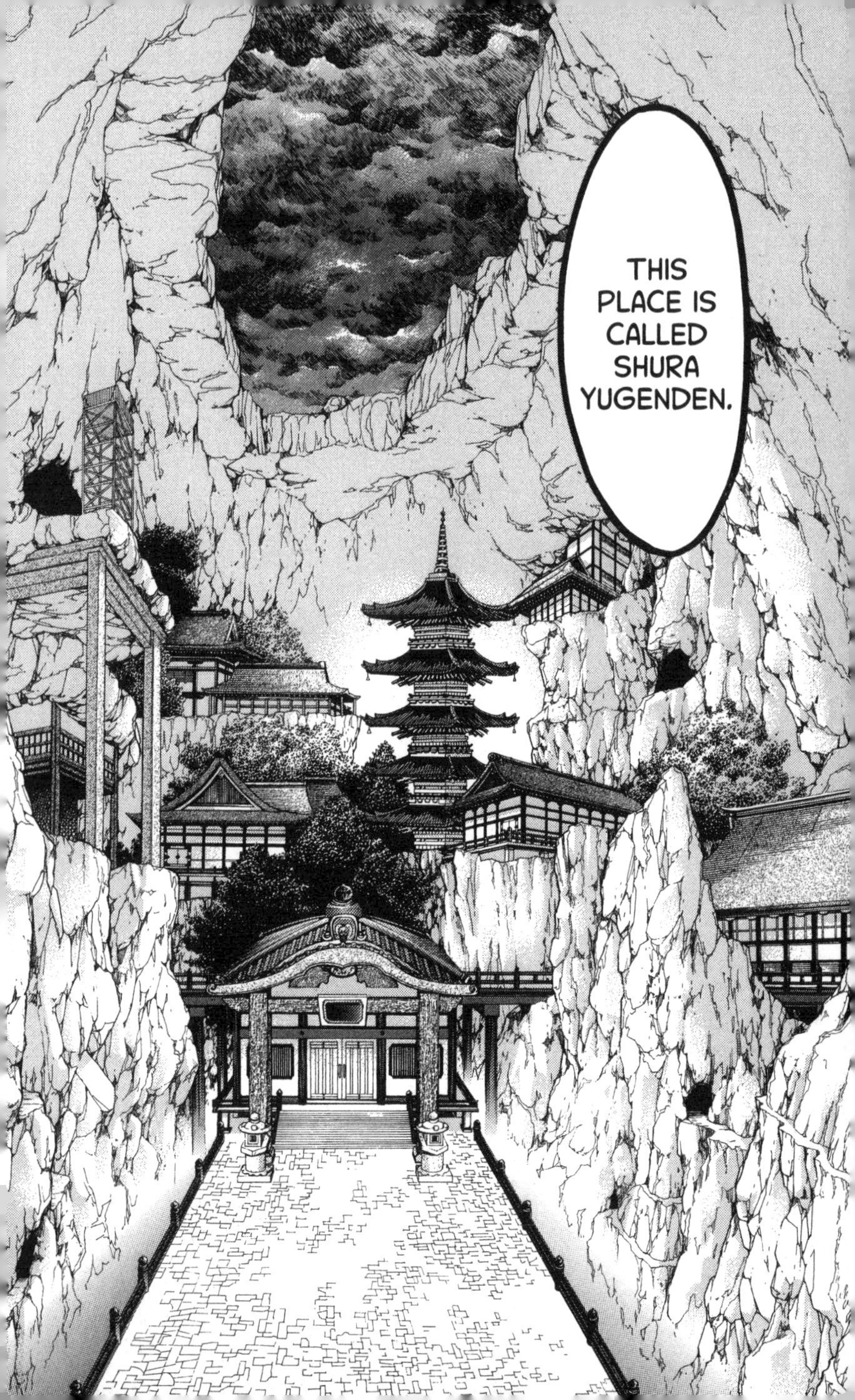
THIS PLACE IS CALLED SHURA YUGENDEN.

HELLO.

Hi there! It's Arina Tanemura.
This is *Sakura Hime* volume 4.

The spring wind took me by surprise, and I caught a terrible cold. I wasn't able to draw an illustration for the character card (I'm sorry), but I'm better now.

I can't write a lot in the sidebars in this volume, but my Saint☆ Assistants have drawn short manga in the back, so please enjoy those.

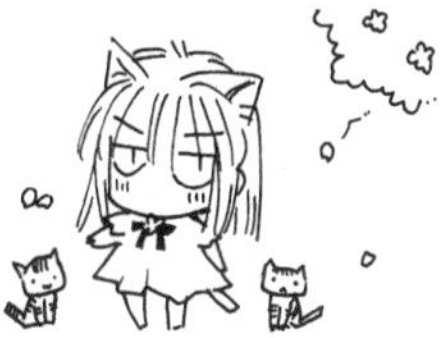

Blog Arina's Diary
http://rikukai.arina.lolipop.jp/

Twitter arinacchi
Please feel free to follow me.
If there is anyone in the same business, or any voice actors out there among my followers, please tell me about yourselves. I'd like to follow you too.
(I'm sorry... I don't keep track of my followers, so I often don't notice you following me...)

Twitter is a lot of fun.
Let's increase our circle of friends. ♪

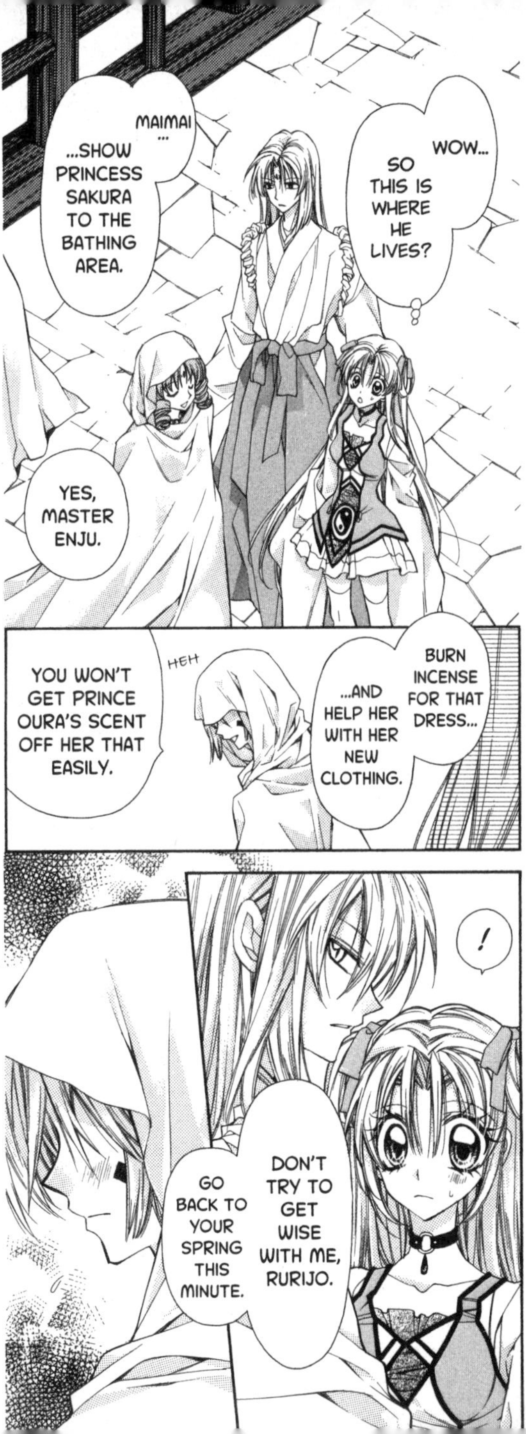
WOW... SO THIS IS WHERE HE LIVES?
MAIMAI... ...SHOW PRINCESS SAKURA TO THE BATHING AREA.
YES, MASTER ENJU.
BURN INCENSE FOR THAT DRESS...
...AND HELP HER WITH HER NEW CLOTHING.
HEH
YOU WON'T GET PRINCE OURA'S SCENT OFF HER THAT EASILY.
!
DON'T TRY TO GET WISE WITH ME, RURIJO.
GO BACK TO YOUR SPRING THIS MINUTE.

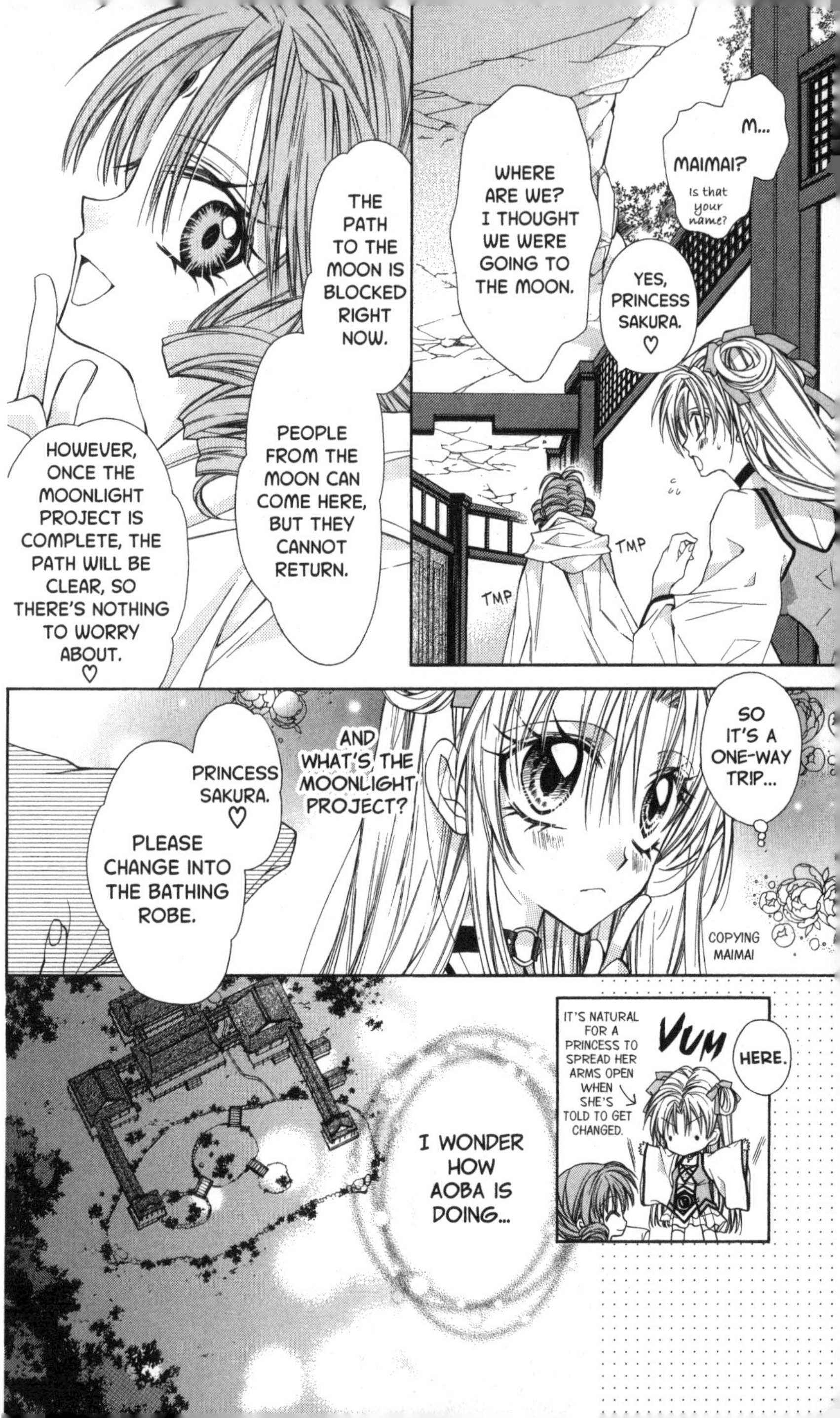
M...
MAIMAI?
Is that your name?
YES, PRINCESS SAKURA. ♡
WHERE ARE WE? I THOUGHT WE WERE GOING TO THE MOON.
TMP
TMP
THE PATH TO THE MOON IS BLOCKED RIGHT NOW.
PEOPLE FROM THE MOON CAN COME HERE, BUT THEY CANNOT RETURN.
HOWEVER, ONCE THE MOONLIGHT PROJECT IS COMPLETE, THE PATH WILL BE CLEAR, SO THERE'S NOTHING TO WORRY ABOUT. ♡
SO IT'S A ONE-WAY TRIP...
COPYING MAIMAI
AND WHAT'S THE MOONLIGHT PROJECT?
PRINCESS SAKURA. ♡
PLEASE CHANGE INTO THE BATHING ROBE.
HERE.
VUM
IT'S NATURAL FOR A PRINCESS TO SPREAD HER ARMS OPEN WHEN SHE'S TOLD TO GET CHANGED.
I WONDER HOW AOBA IS DOING...

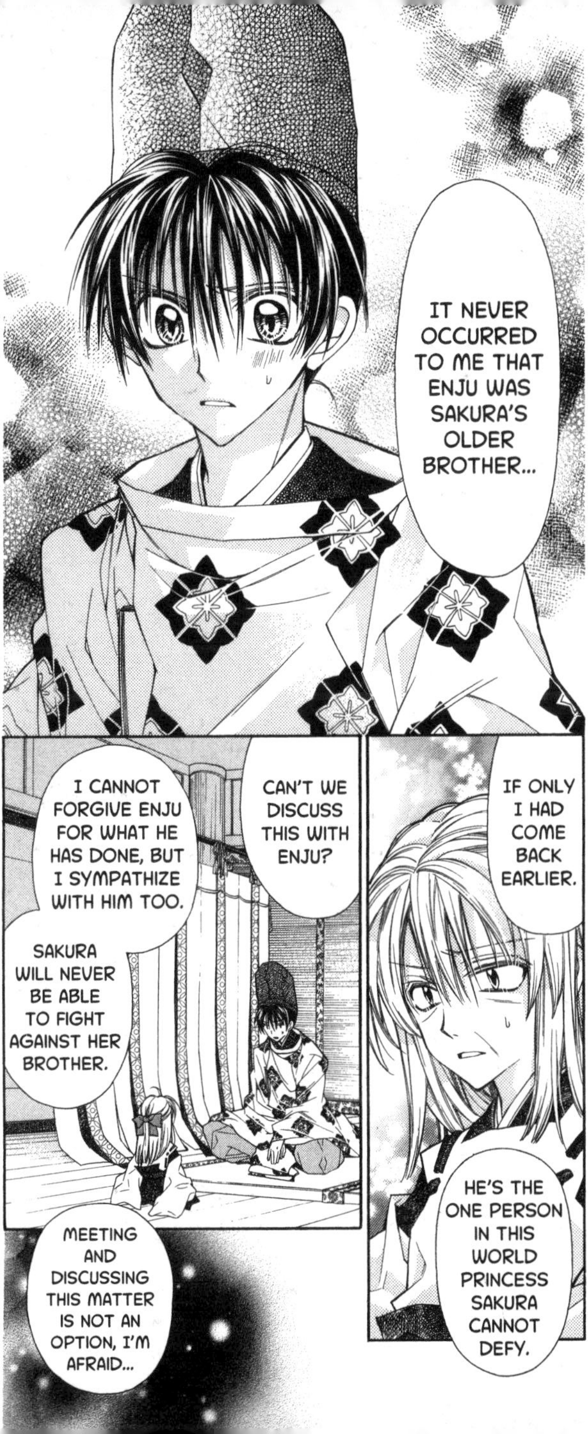
IT NEVER OCCURRED TO ME THAT ENJU WAS SAKURA'S OLDER BROTHER...
IF ONLY I HAD COME BACK EARLIER.
HE'S THE ONE PERSON IN THIS WORLD PRINCESS SAKURA CANNOT DEFY.
CAN'T WE DISCUSS THIS WITH ENJU?
I CANNOT FORGIVE ENJU FOR WHAT HE HAS DONE, BUT I SYMPATHIZE WITH HIM TOO.
SAKURA WILL NEVER BE ABLE TO FIGHT AGAINST HER BROTHER.
MEETING AND DISCUSSING THIS MATTER IS NOT AN OPTION, I'M AFRAID...

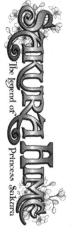

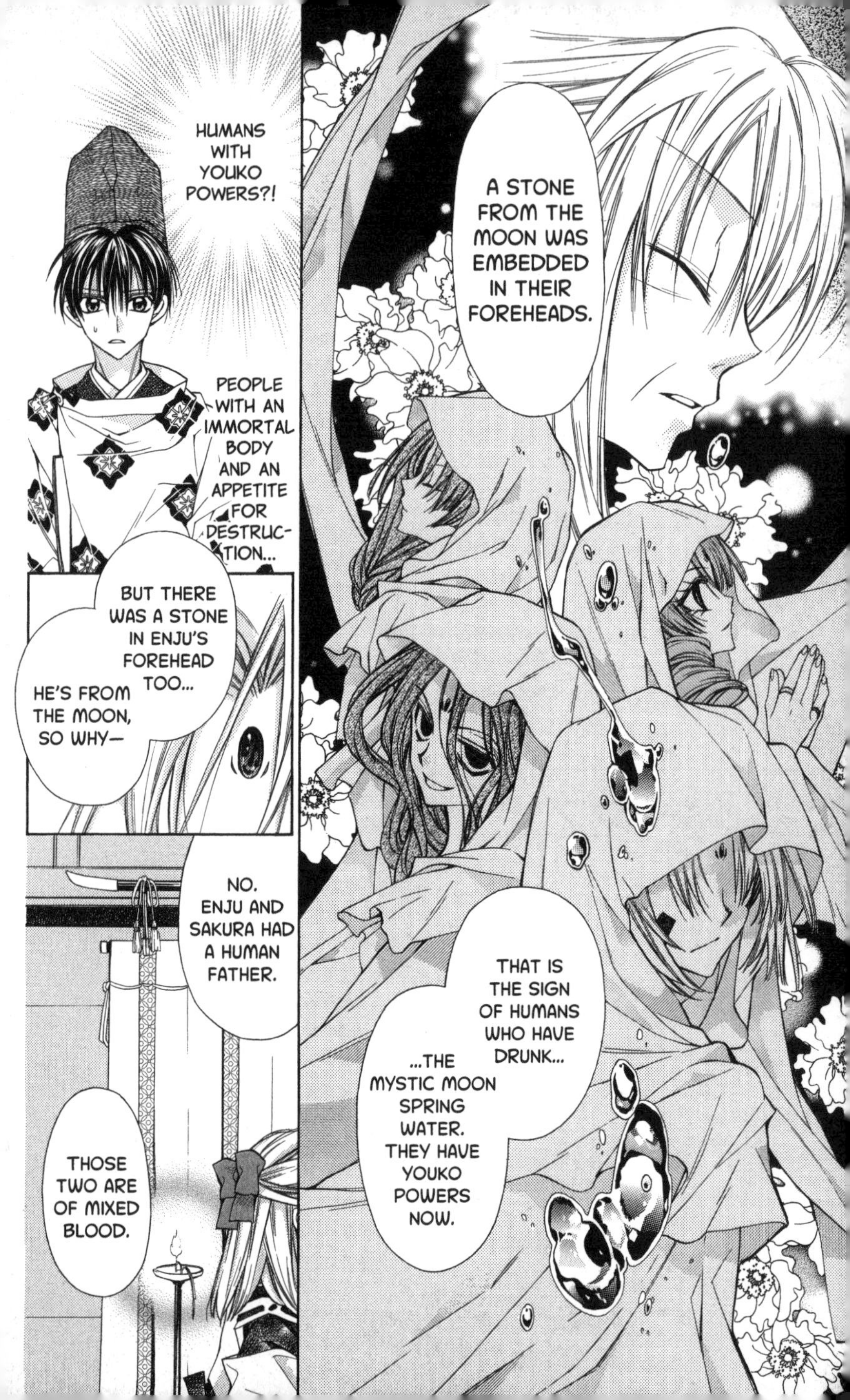
A STONE FROM THE MOON WAS EMBEDDED IN THEIR FOREHEADS.
THAT IS THE SIGN OF HUMANS WHO HAVE DRUNK...
...THE MYSTIC MOON SPRING WATER. THEY HAVE YOUKO POWERS NOW.
HUMANS WITH YOUKO POWERS?!
PEOPLE WITH AN IMMORTAL BODY AND AN APPETITE FOR DESTRUCTION...
BUT THERE WAS A STONE IN ENJU'S FOREHEAD TOO...
HE'S FROM THE MOON, SO WHY—
NO. ENJU AND SAKURA HAD A HUMAN FATHER.
THOSE TWO ARE OF MIXED BLOOD.

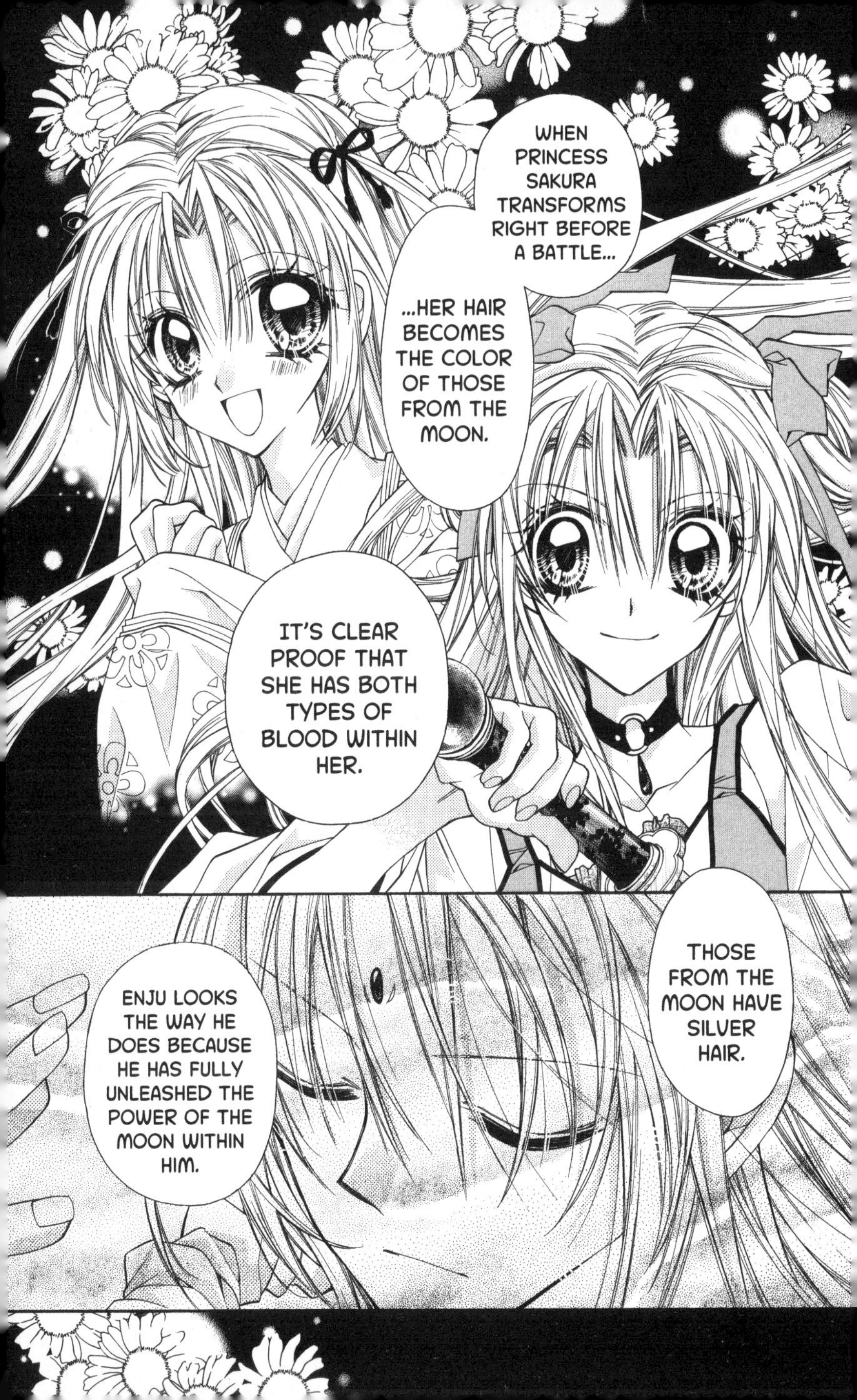
WHEN PRINCESS SAKURA TRANSFORMS RIGHT BEFORE A BATTLE...
...HER HAIR BECOMES THE COLOR OF THOSE FROM THE MOON.
IT'S CLEAR PROOF THAT SHE HAS BOTH TYPES OF BLOOD WITHIN HER.
THOSE FROM THE MOON HAVE SILVER HAIR.
ENJU LOOKS THE WAY HE DOES BECAUSE HE HAS FULLY UNLEASHED THE POWER OF THE MOON WITHIN HIM.

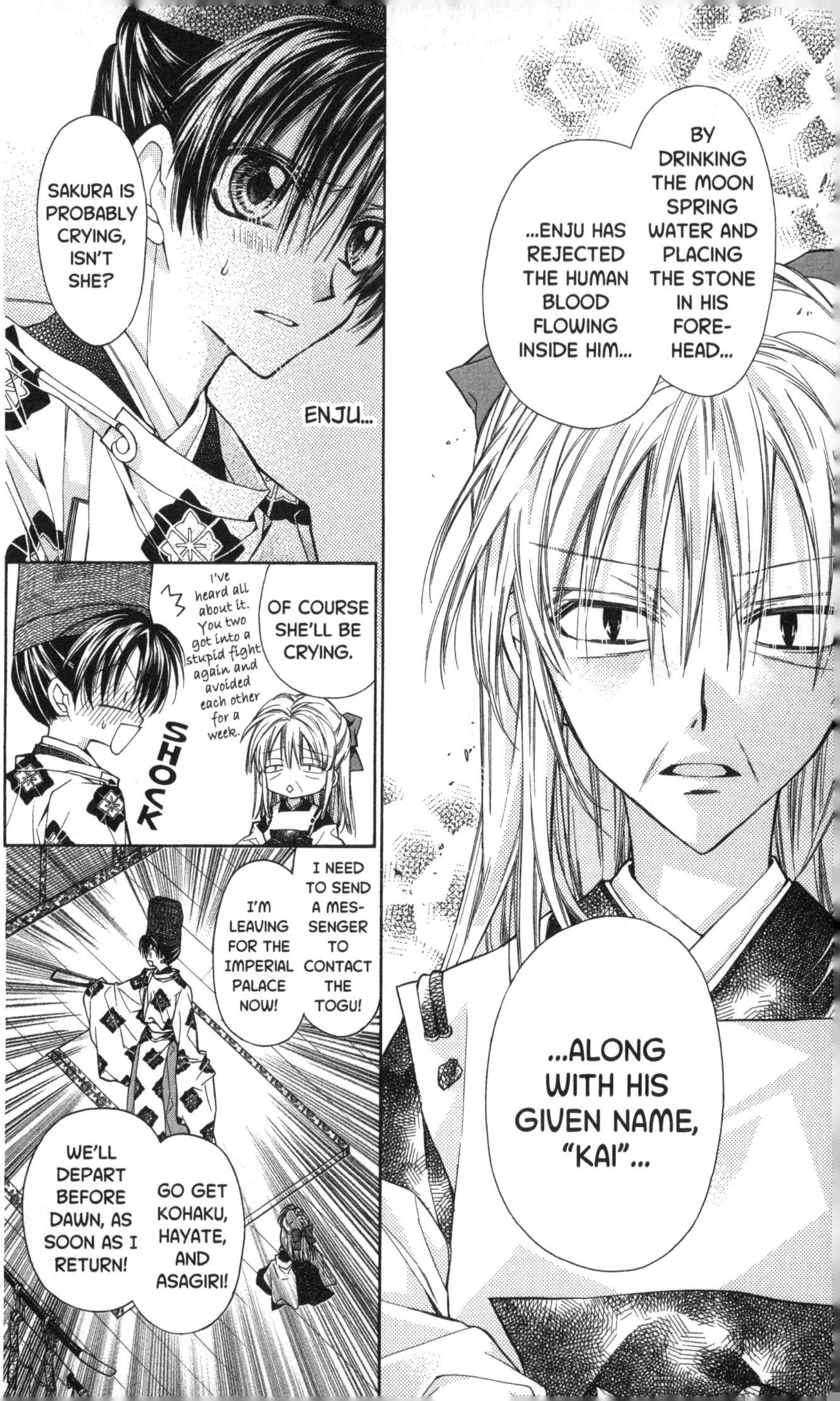
BY DRINKING THE MOON SPRING WATER AND PLACING THE STONE IN HIS FOREHEAD...
...ENJU HAS REJECTED THE HUMAN BLOOD FLOWING INSIDE HIM...
...ALONG WITH HIS GIVEN NAME, "KAI"...
ENJU...
SAKURA IS PROBABLY CRYING, ISN'T SHE?
OF COURSE SHE'LL BE CRYING.
I've heard all about it. You two got into a stupid fight again and avoided each other for a week.
SHOCK
I NEED TO SEND A MESSENGER TO CONTACT THE TOGU!
I'M LEAVING FOR THE IMPERIAL PALACE NOW!
GO GET KOHAKU, HAYATE, AND ASAGIRI!
WE'LL DEPART BEFORE DAWN, AS SOON AS I RETURN!

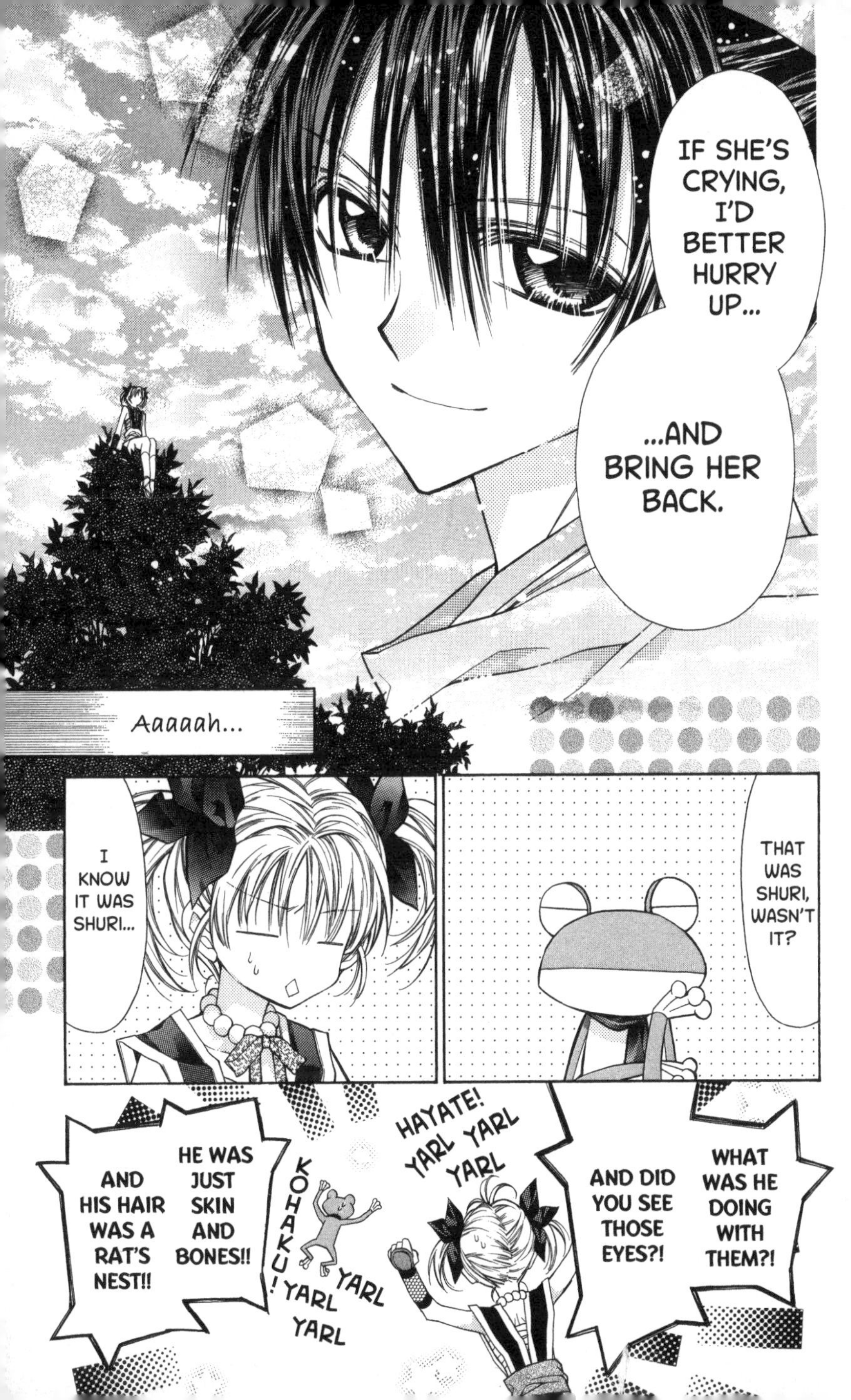

IF SHE'S CRYING, I'D BETTER HURRY UP...
...AND BRING HER BACK.
Aaaaah...
THAT WAS SHURI, WASN'T IT?
I KNOW IT WAS SHURI...
WHAT WAS HE DOING WITH THEM?!
AND DID YOU SEE THOSE EYES?!
HAYATE! YARL YARL YARL
KOHAKU!
YARL YARL YARL
HE WAS JUST SKIN AND BONES!!
AND HIS HAIR WAS A RAT'S NEST!!

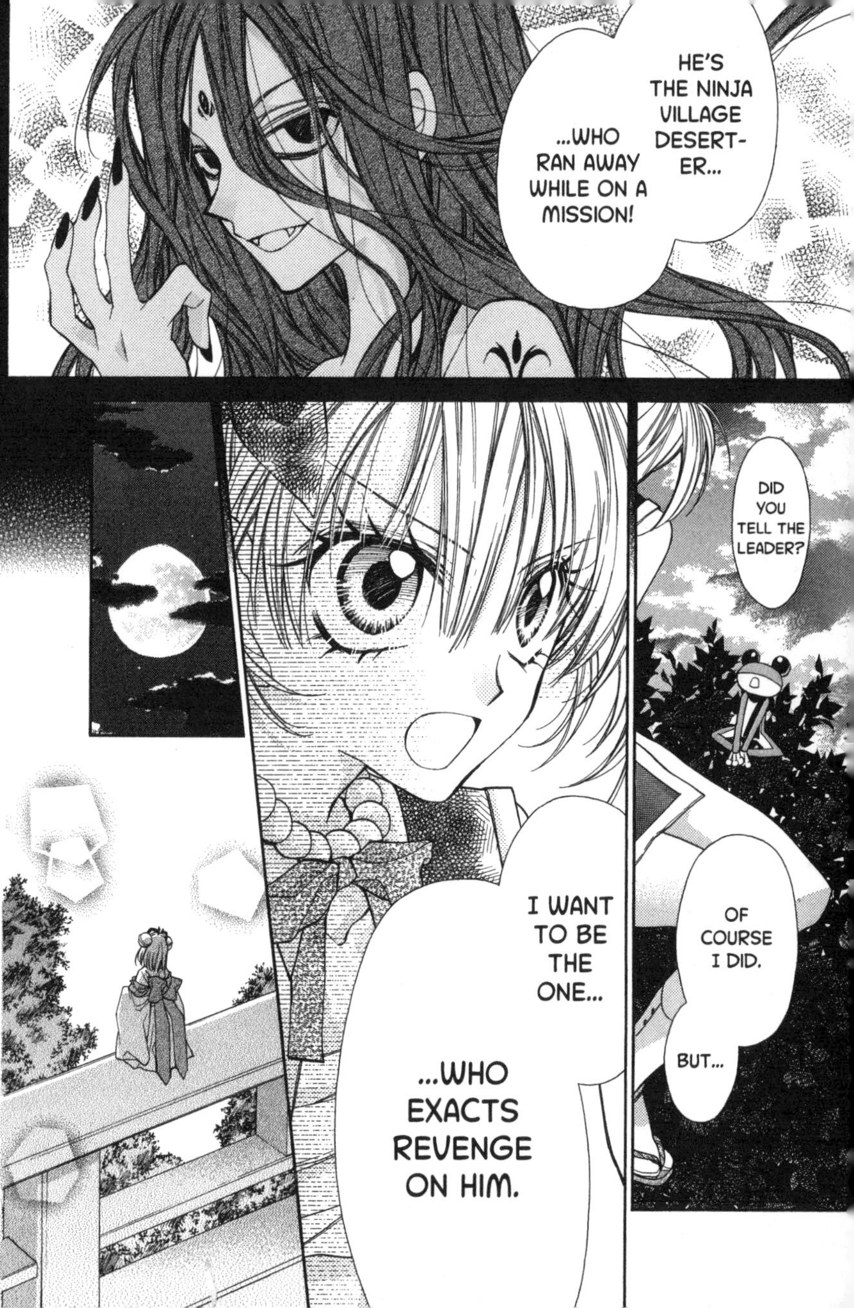
HE'S THE NINJA VILLAGE DESERTER...
...WHO RAN AWAY WHILE ON A MISSION!
DID YOU TELL THE LEADER?
OF COURSE I DID.
BUT...
I WANT TO BE THE ONE...
...WHO EXACTS REVENGE ON HIM.

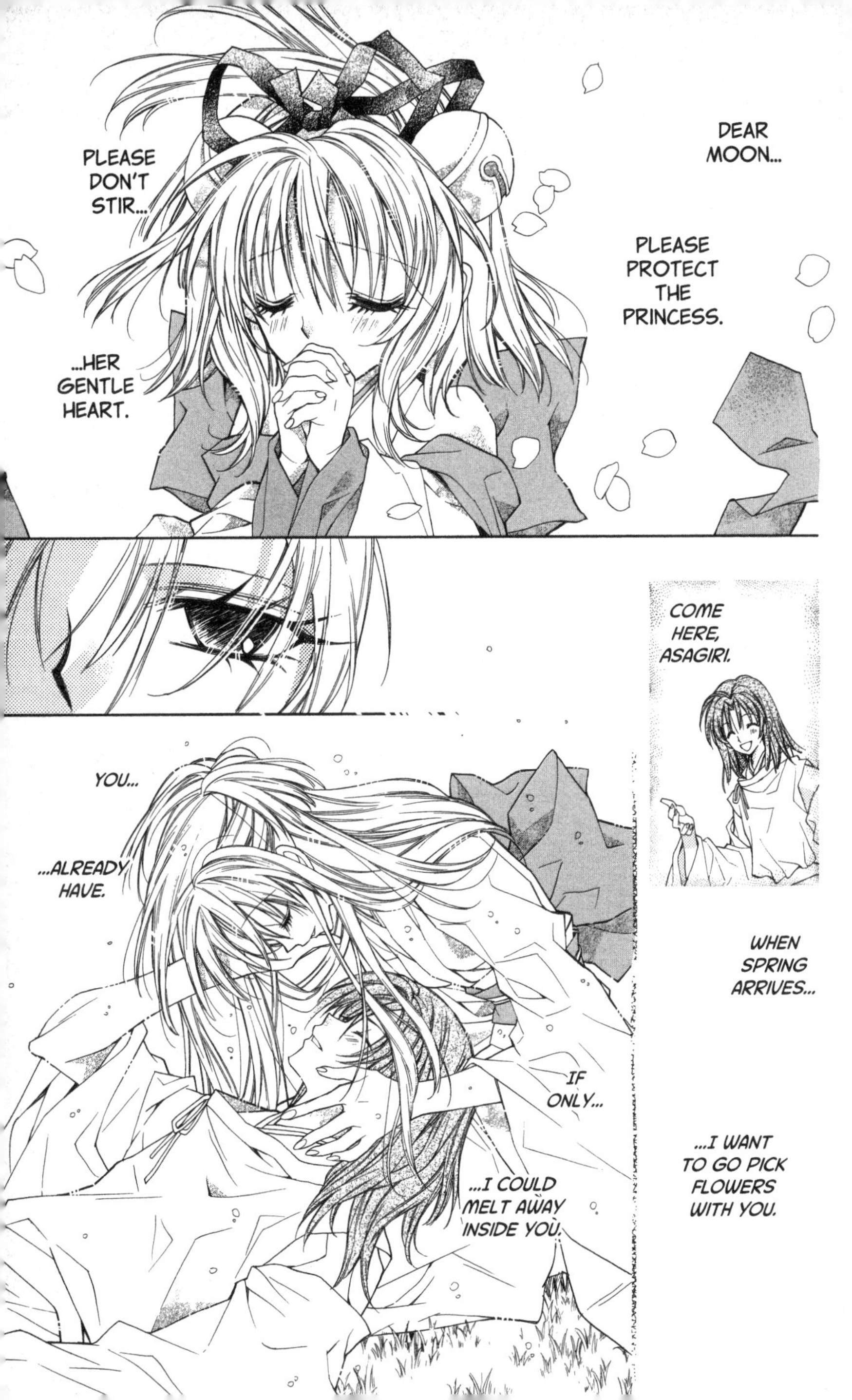
DEAR MOON...
PLEASE PROTECT THE PRINCESS.
PLEASE DON'T STIR...
...HER GENTLE HEART.
COME HERE, ASAGIRI.
WHEN SPRING ARRIVES...
...I WANT TO GO PICK FLOWERS WITH YOU.
YOU...
...ALREADY HAVE.
IF ONLY...
...I COULD MELT AWAY INSIDE YOU.

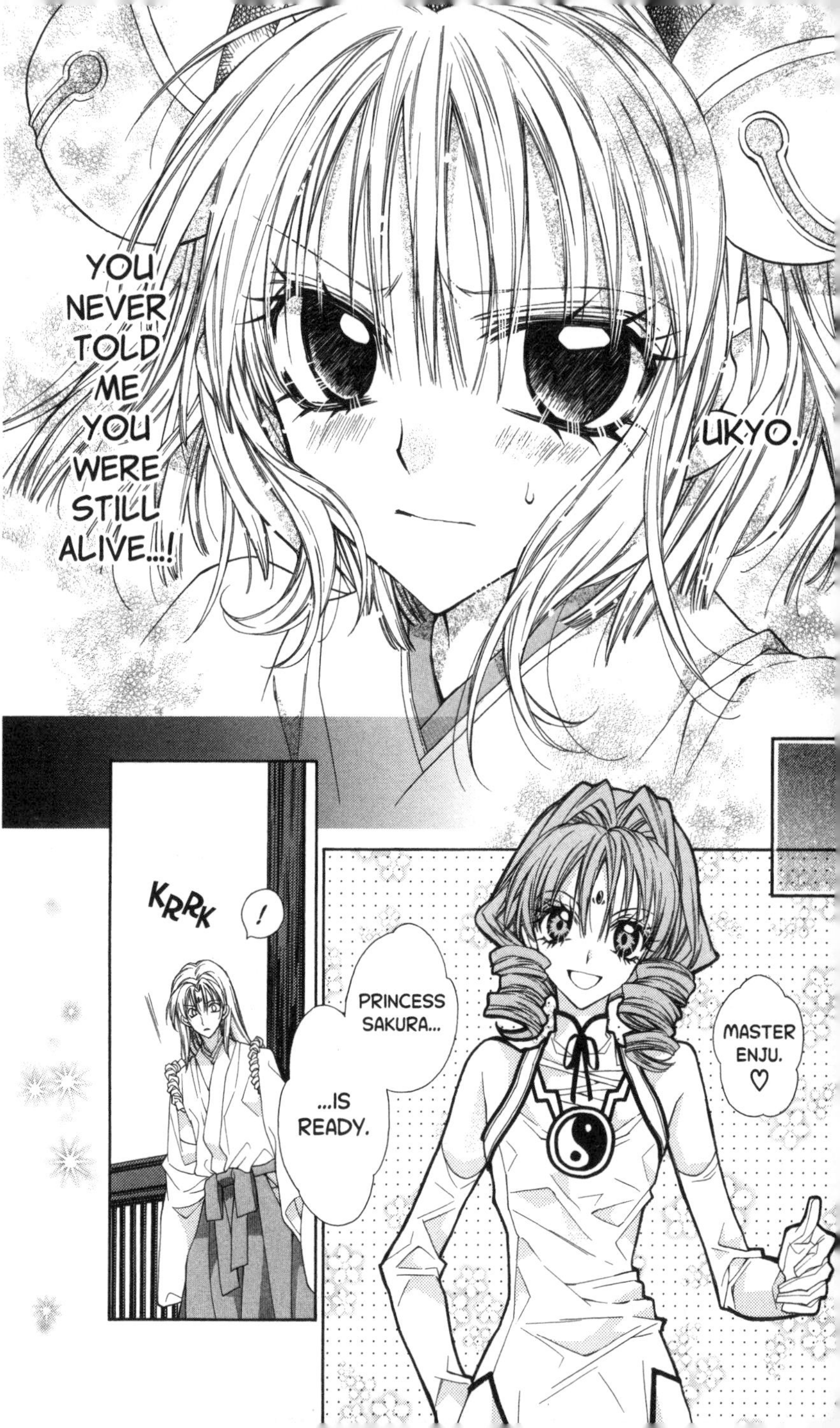
UKYO.
YOU NEVER TOLD ME YOU WERE STILL ALIVE...!
MASTER ENJU. ♡
PRINCESS SAKURA...
...IS READY.
KRRK
!

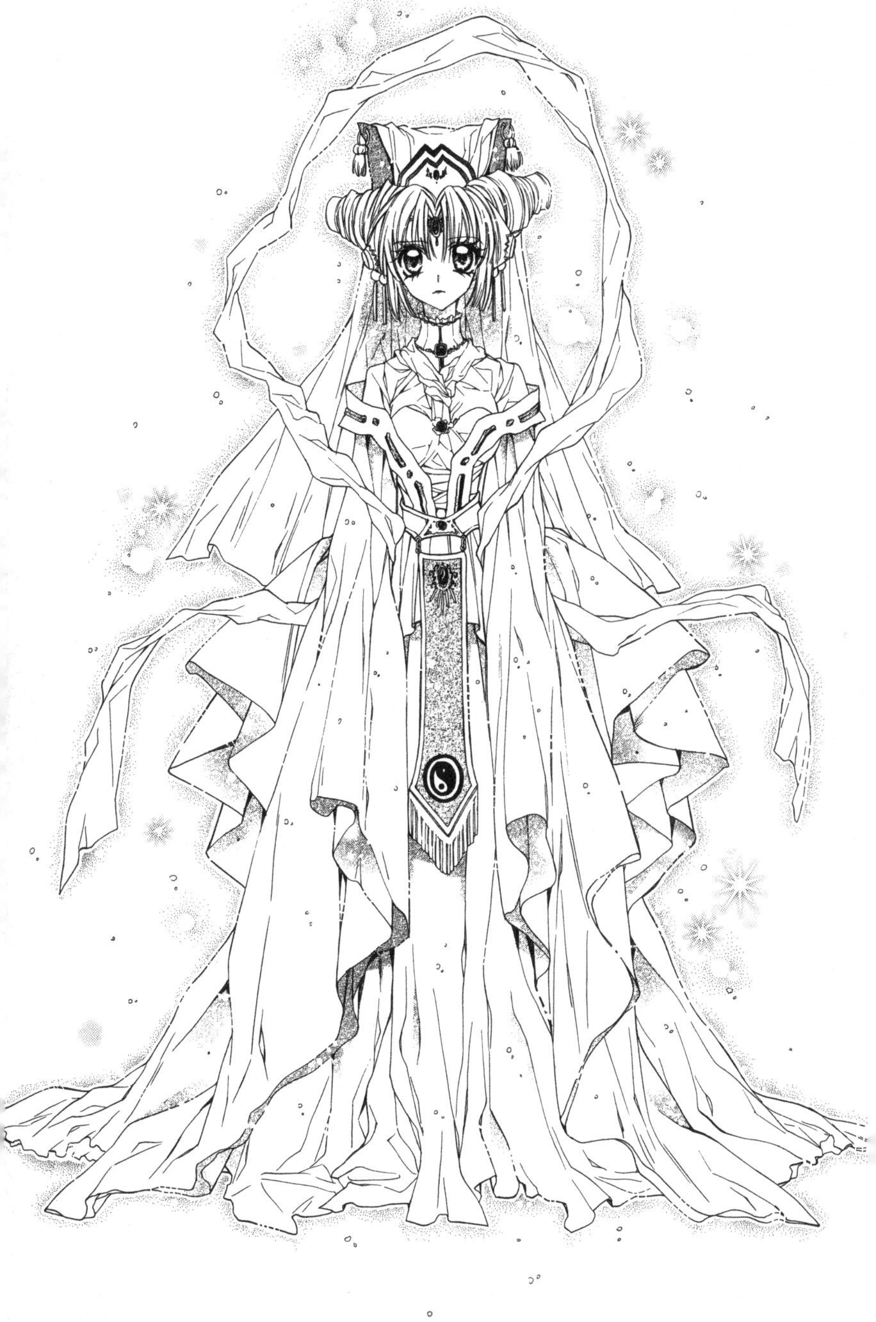

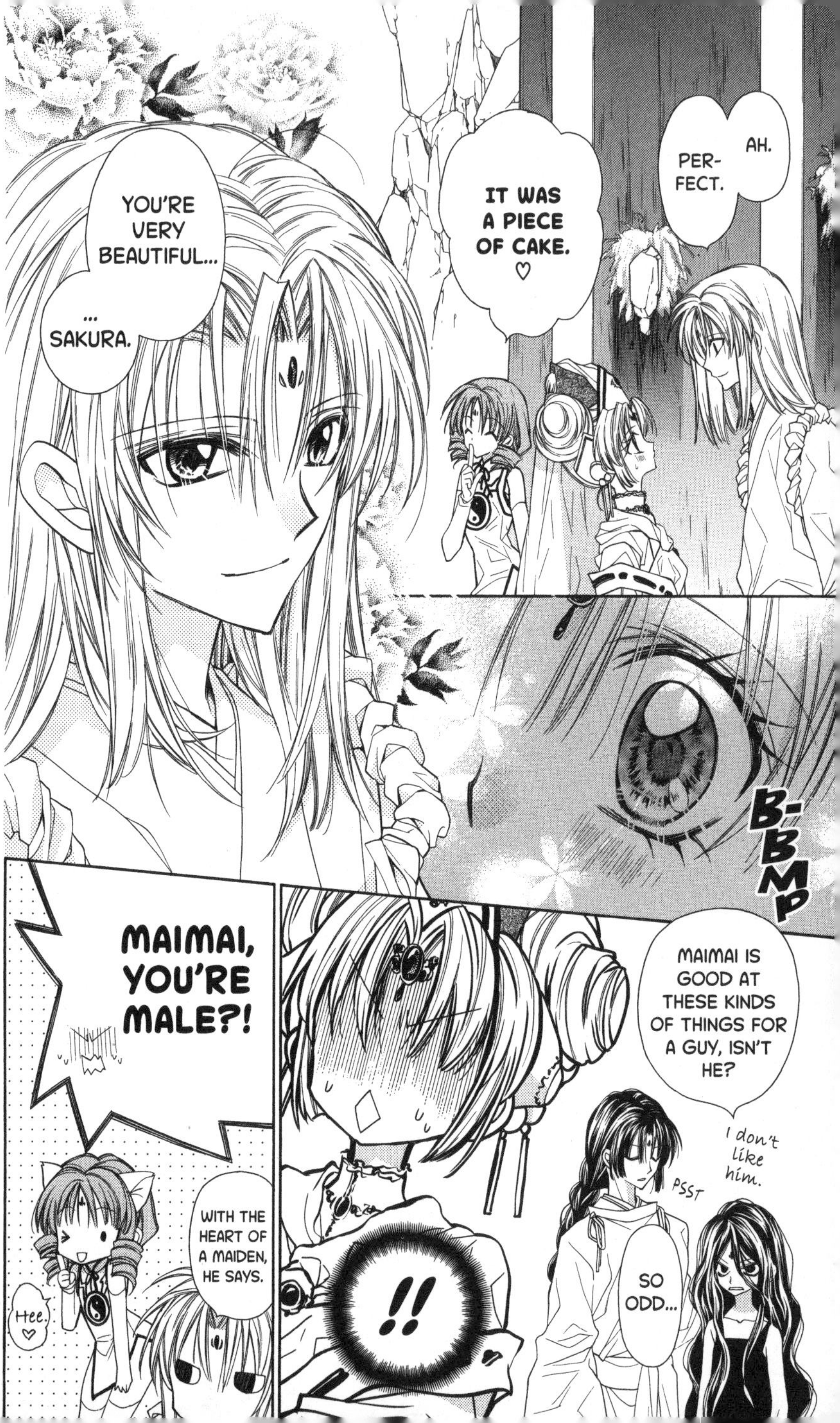
AH. PER-FECT.
IT WAS A PIECE OF CAKE. ♡
B-BMP
YOU'RE VERY BEAUTIFUL...
... SAKURA.
MAIMAI IS GOOD AT THESE KINDS OF THINGS FOR A GUY, ISN'T HE?
I don't like him.
PSST
SO ODD...
!!
MAIMAI, YOU'RE MALE?!
WITH THE HEART OF A MAIDEN, HE SAYS.
Hee. ♡

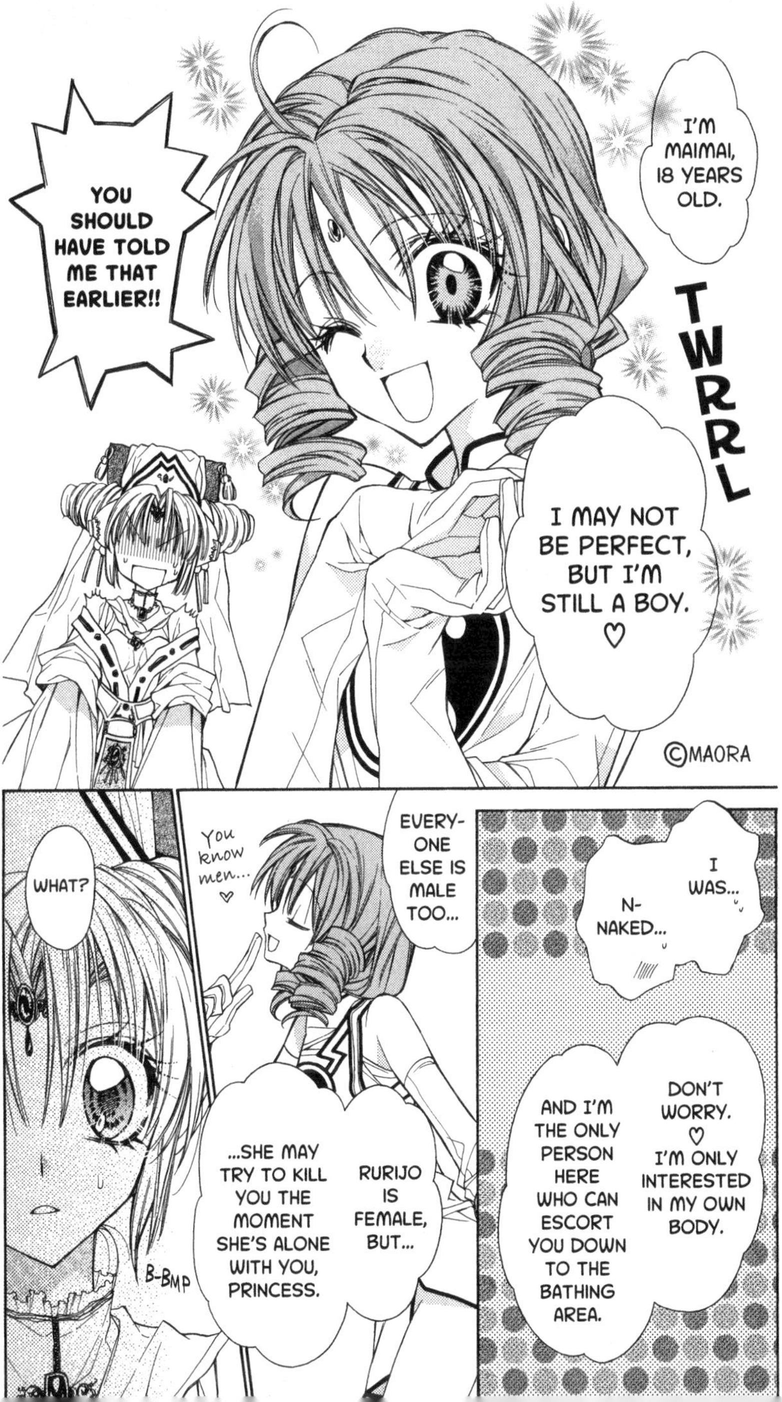
I'M MAIMAI, 18 YEARS OLD.
TWRRL
I MAY NOT BE PERFECT, BUT I'M STILL A BOY. ♡
YOU SHOULD HAVE TOLD ME THAT EARLIER!!
©MAORA
I WAS...
N-NAKED...
DON'T WORRY. ♡ I'M ONLY INTERESTED IN MY OWN BODY.
AND I'M THE ONLY PERSON HERE WHO CAN ESCORT YOU DOWN TO THE BATHING AREA.
EVERY-ONE ELSE IS MALE TOO...
You know men... ♡
RURIJO IS FEMALE, BUT...
...SHE MAY TRY TO KILL YOU THE MOMENT SHE'S ALONE WITH YOU, PRINCESS.
WHAT?
B-BMP

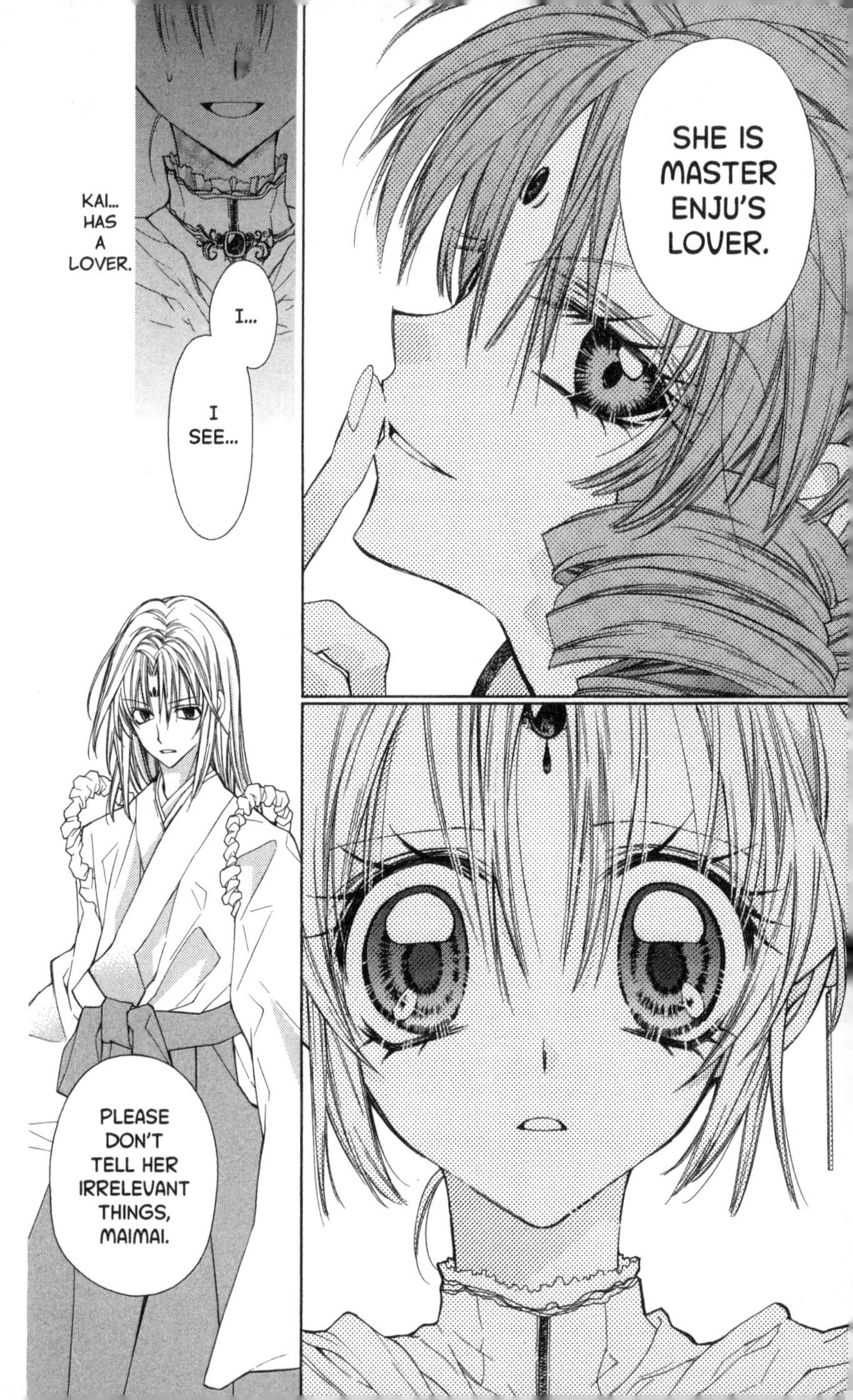
SHE IS MASTER ENJU'S LOVER.
KAI... HAS A LOVER.
I...
I SEE...
PLEASE DON'T TELL HER IRRELEVANT THINGS, MAIMAI.

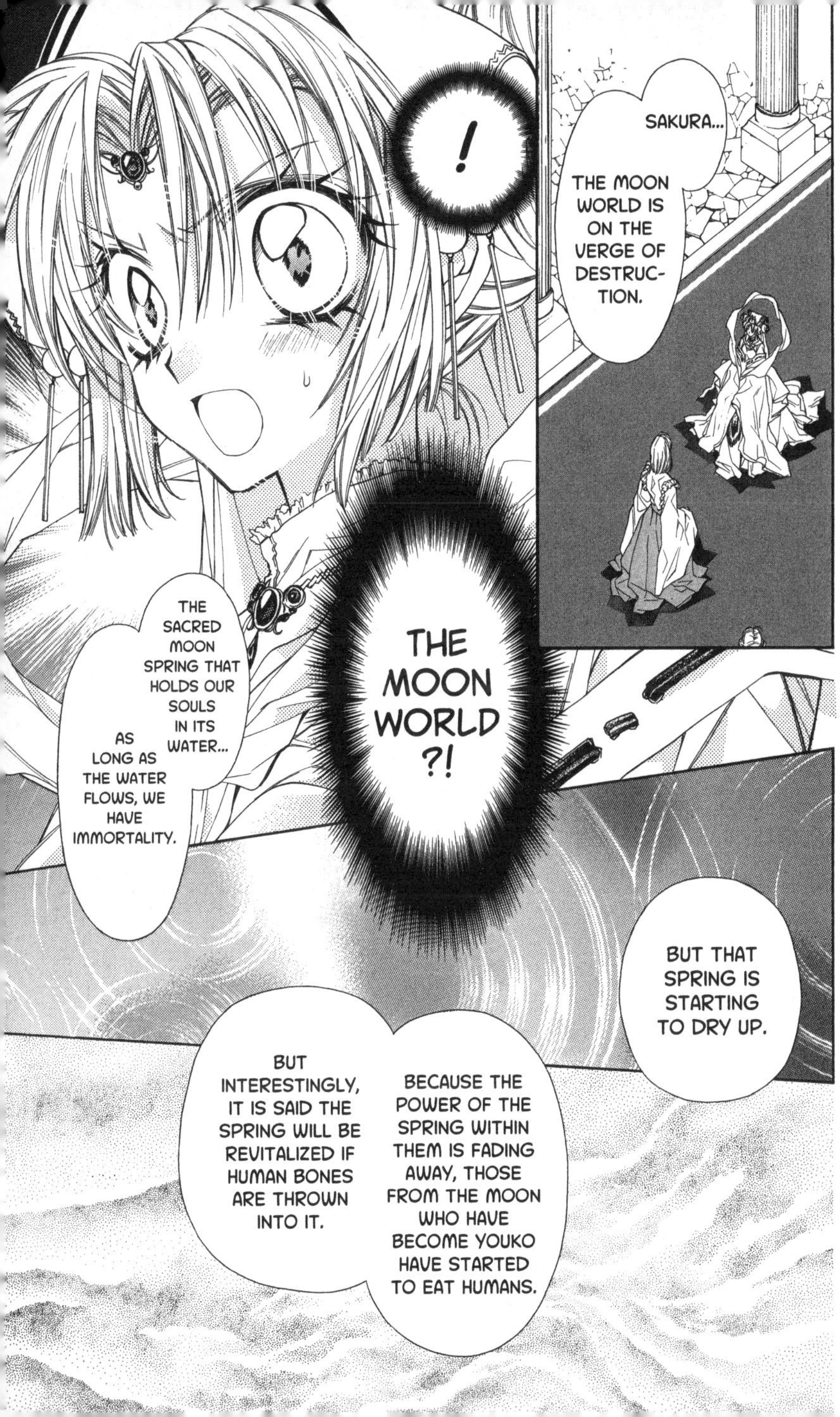
SAKURA...
THE MOON WORLD IS ON THE VERGE OF DESTRUCTION.
!
THE MOON WORLD ?!
THE SACRED MOON SPRING THAT HOLDS OUR SOULS IN ITS WATER... AS LONG AS THE WATER FLOWS, WE HAVE IMMORTALITY.
BUT THAT SPRING IS STARTING TO DRY UP.
BECAUSE THE POWER OF THE SPRING WITHIN THEM IS FADING AWAY, THOSE FROM THE MOON WHO HAVE BECOME YOUKO HAVE STARTED TO EAT HUMANS.
BUT INTERESTINGLY, IT IS SAID THE SPRING WILL BE REVITALIZED IF HUMAN BONES ARE THROWN INTO IT.

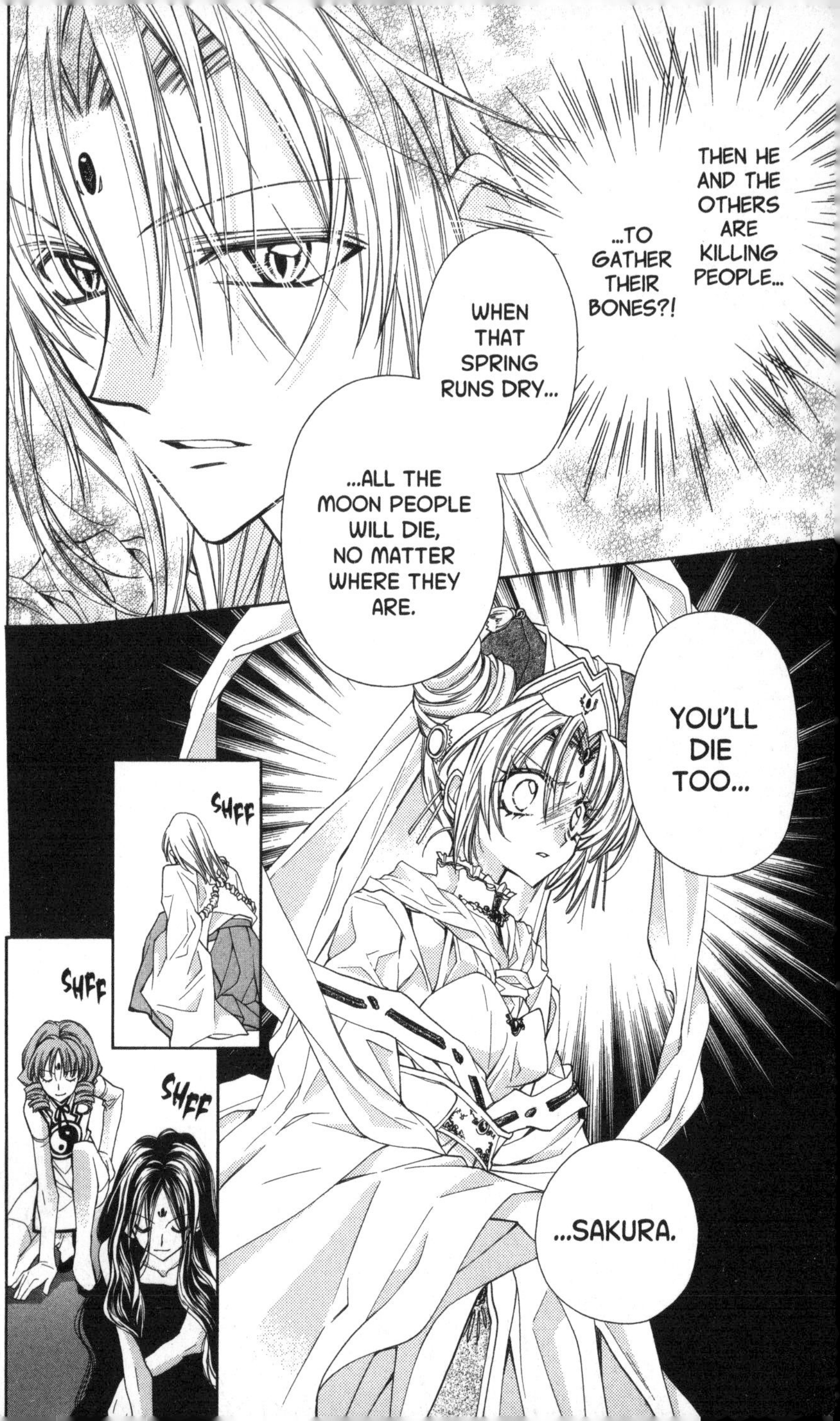
THEN HE AND THE OTHERS ARE KILLING PEOPLE...
...TO GATHER THEIR BONES?!
WHEN THAT SPRING RUNS DRY...
...ALL THE MOON PEOPLE WILL DIE, NO MATTER WHERE THEY ARE.
YOU'LL DIE TOO...
...SAKURA.
SHFF
SHFF
SHFF

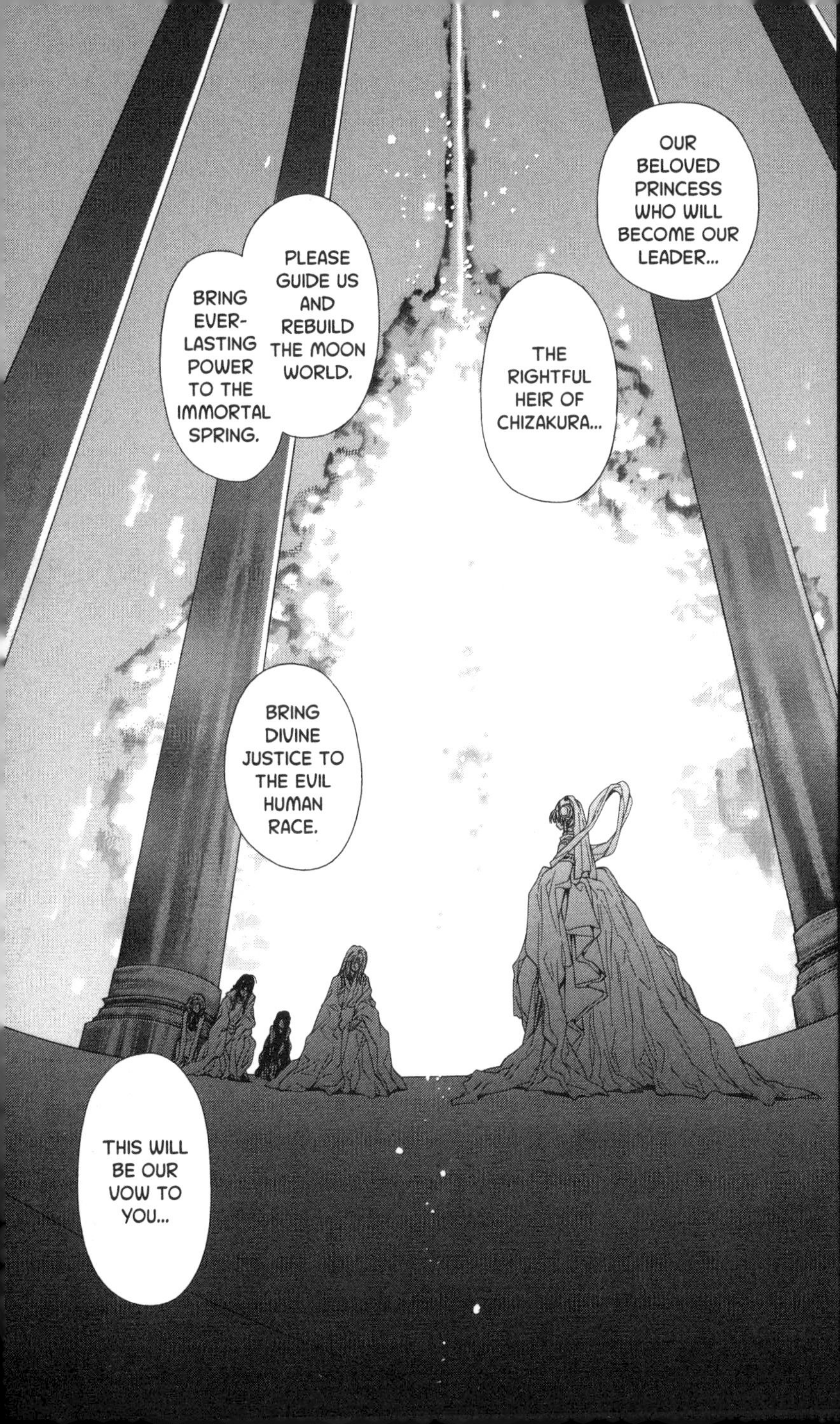
OUR BELOVED PRINCESS WHO WILL BECOME OUR LEADER...
THE RIGHTFUL HEIR OF CHIZAKURA...
PLEASE GUIDE US AND REBUILD THE MOON WORLD.
BRING EVER-LASTING POWER TO THE IMMORTAL SPRING.
BRING DIVINE JUSTICE TO THE EVIL HUMAN RACE.
THIS WILL BE OUR VOW TO YOU...

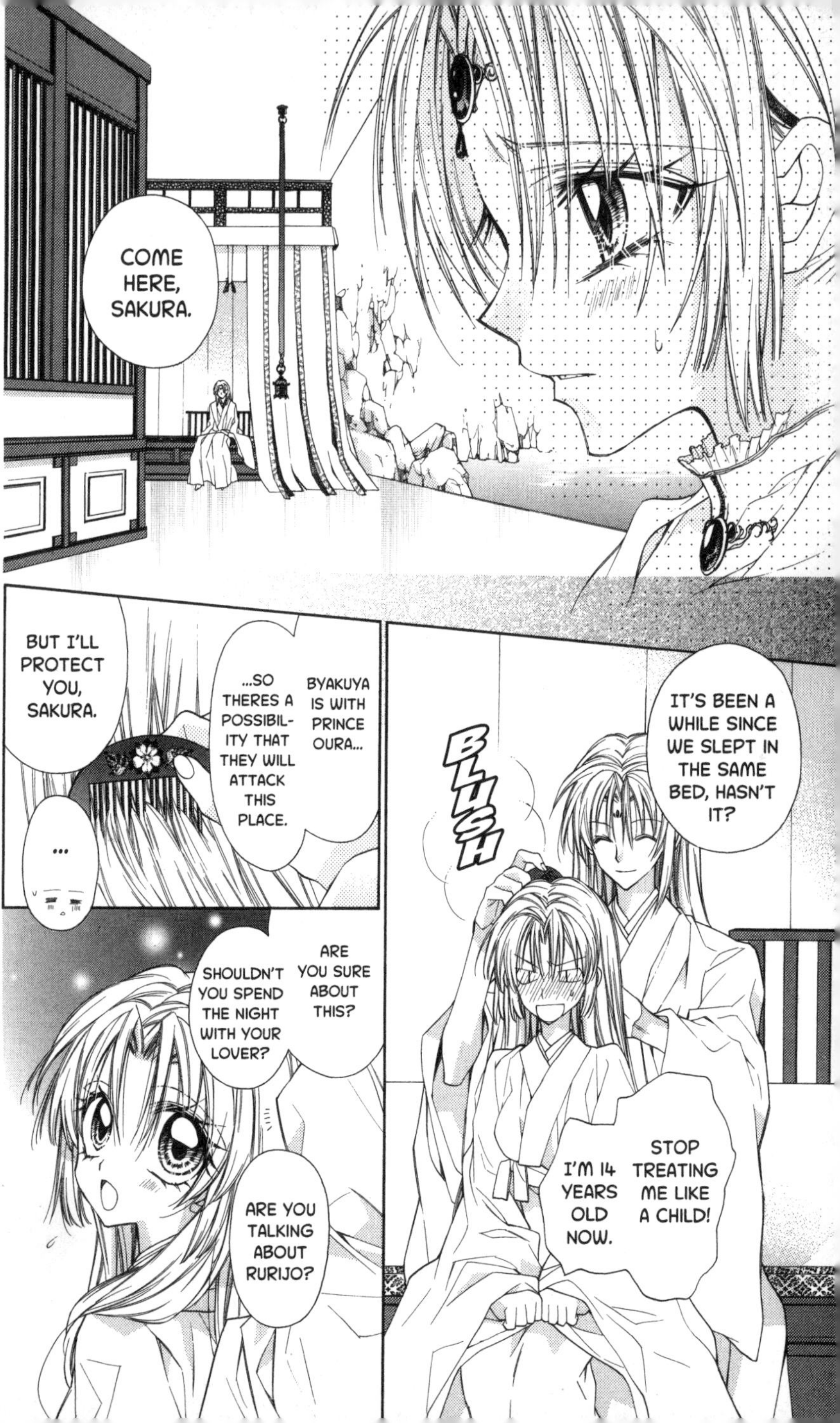
COME HERE, SAKURA.
IT'S BEEN A WHILE SINCE WE SLEPT IN THE SAME BED, HASN'T IT?
BLUSH
STOP TREATING ME LIKE A CHILD!
I'M 14 YEARS OLD NOW.
BYAKUYA IS WITH PRINCE OURA...
...SO THERES A POSSIBILITY THAT THEY WILL ATTACK THIS PLACE.
BUT I'LL PROTECT YOU, SAKURA.
...
ARE YOU SURE ABOUT THIS?
SHOULDN'T YOU SPEND THE NIGHT WITH YOUR LOVER?
ARE YOU TALKING ABOUT RURIJO?

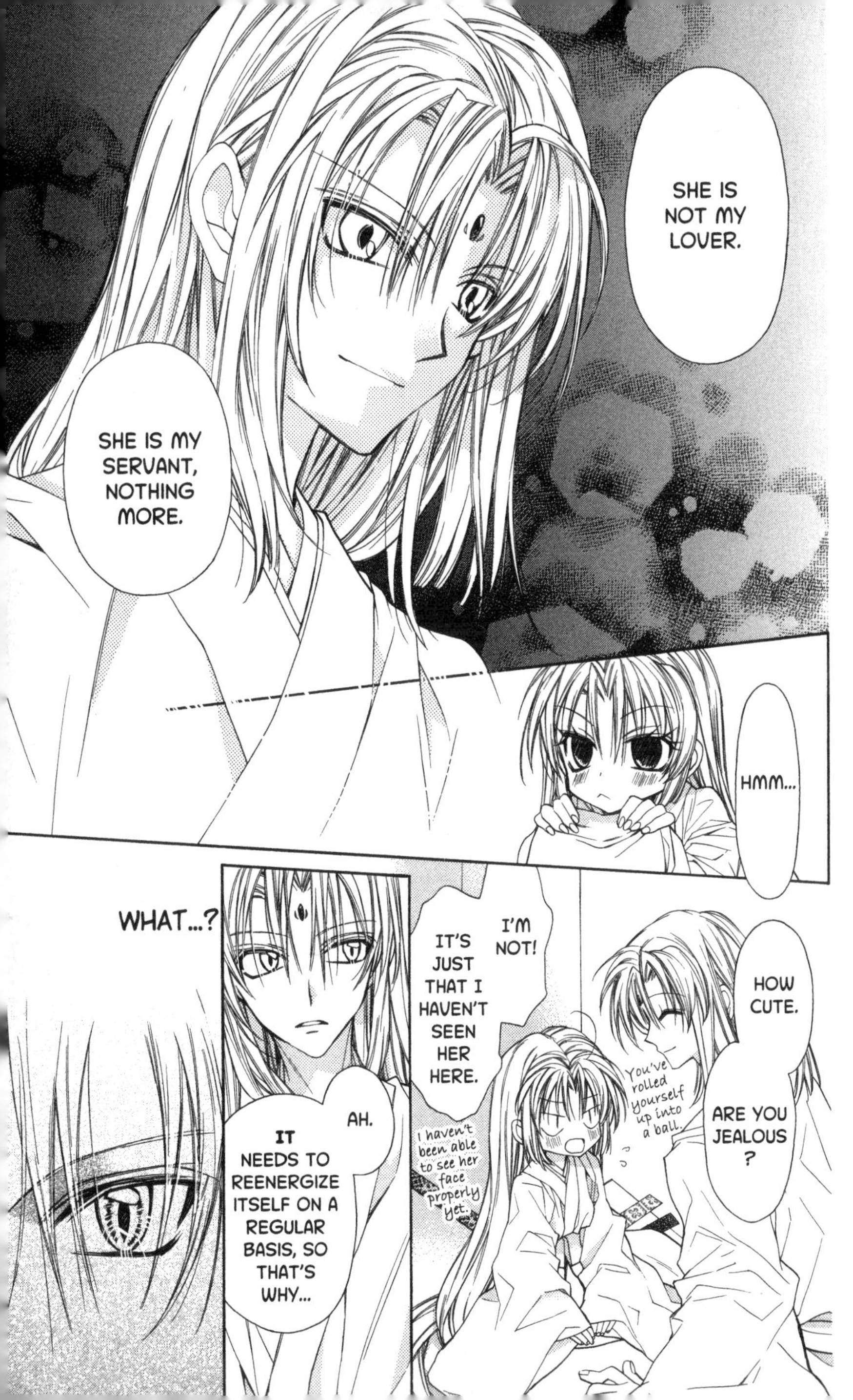
SHE IS NOT MY LOVER.
SHE IS MY SERVANT, NOTHING MORE.
HMM...
HOW CUTE.
ARE YOU JEALOUS?
You've rolled yourself up into a ball.
I'M NOT!
IT'S JUST THAT I HAVEN'T SEEN HER HERE.
I haven't been able to see her face properly yet.
AH.
IT NEEDS TO REENERGIZE ITSELF ON A REGULAR BASIS, SO THAT'S WHY...
WHAT...?

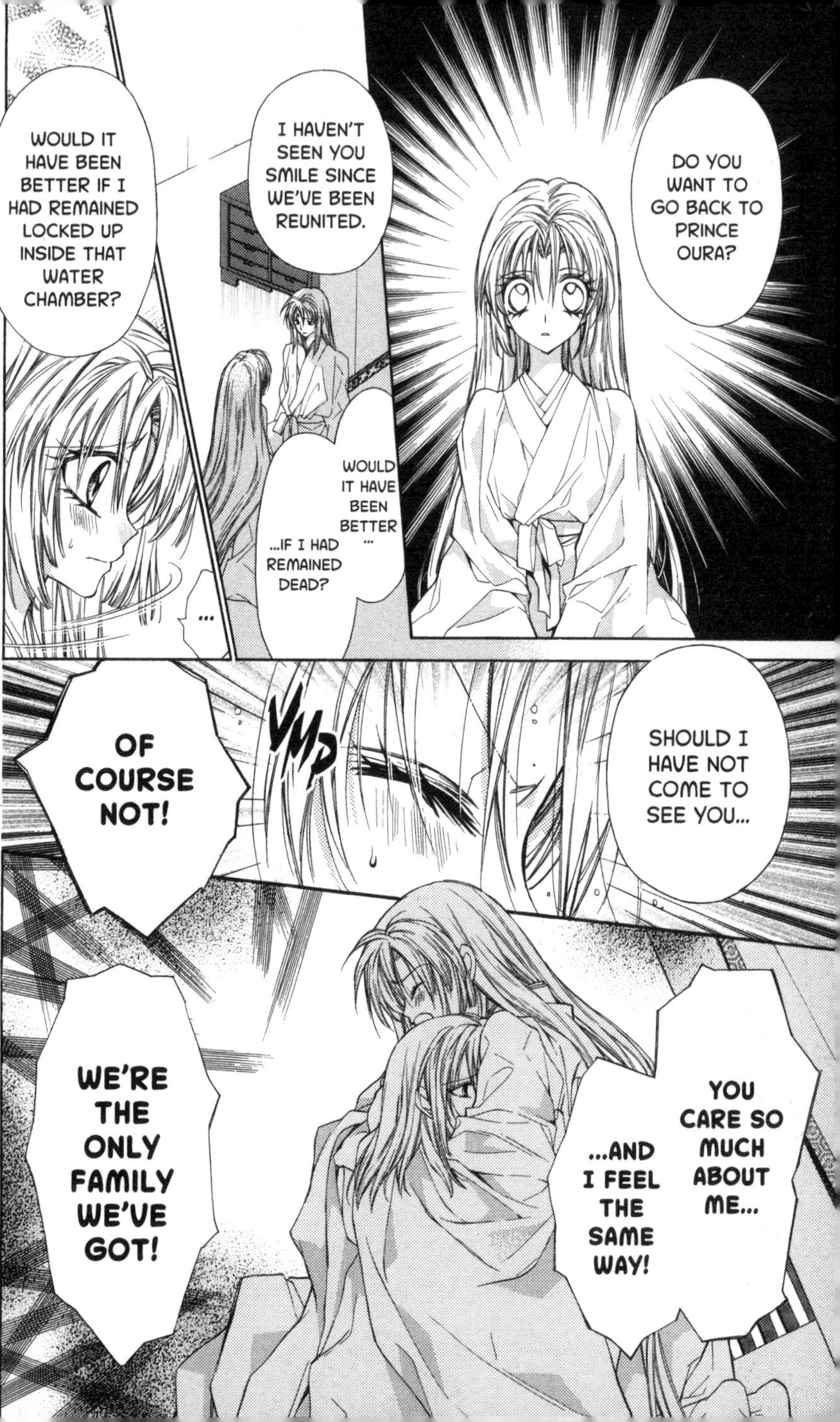
DO YOU WANT TO GO BACK TO PRINCE OURA?
I HAVEN'T SEEN YOU SMILE SINCE WE'VE BEEN REUNITED.
WOULD IT HAVE BEEN BETTER ...
...IF I HAD REMAINED DEAD?
WOULD IT HAVE BEEN BETTER IF I HAD REMAINED LOCKED UP INSIDE THAT WATER CHAMBER?
...
SHOULD I HAVE NOT COME TO SEE YOU...
VMP
OF COURSE NOT!
YOU CARE SO MUCH ABOUT ME...
...AND I FEEL THE SAME WAY!
WE'RE THE ONLY FAMILY WE'VE GOT!

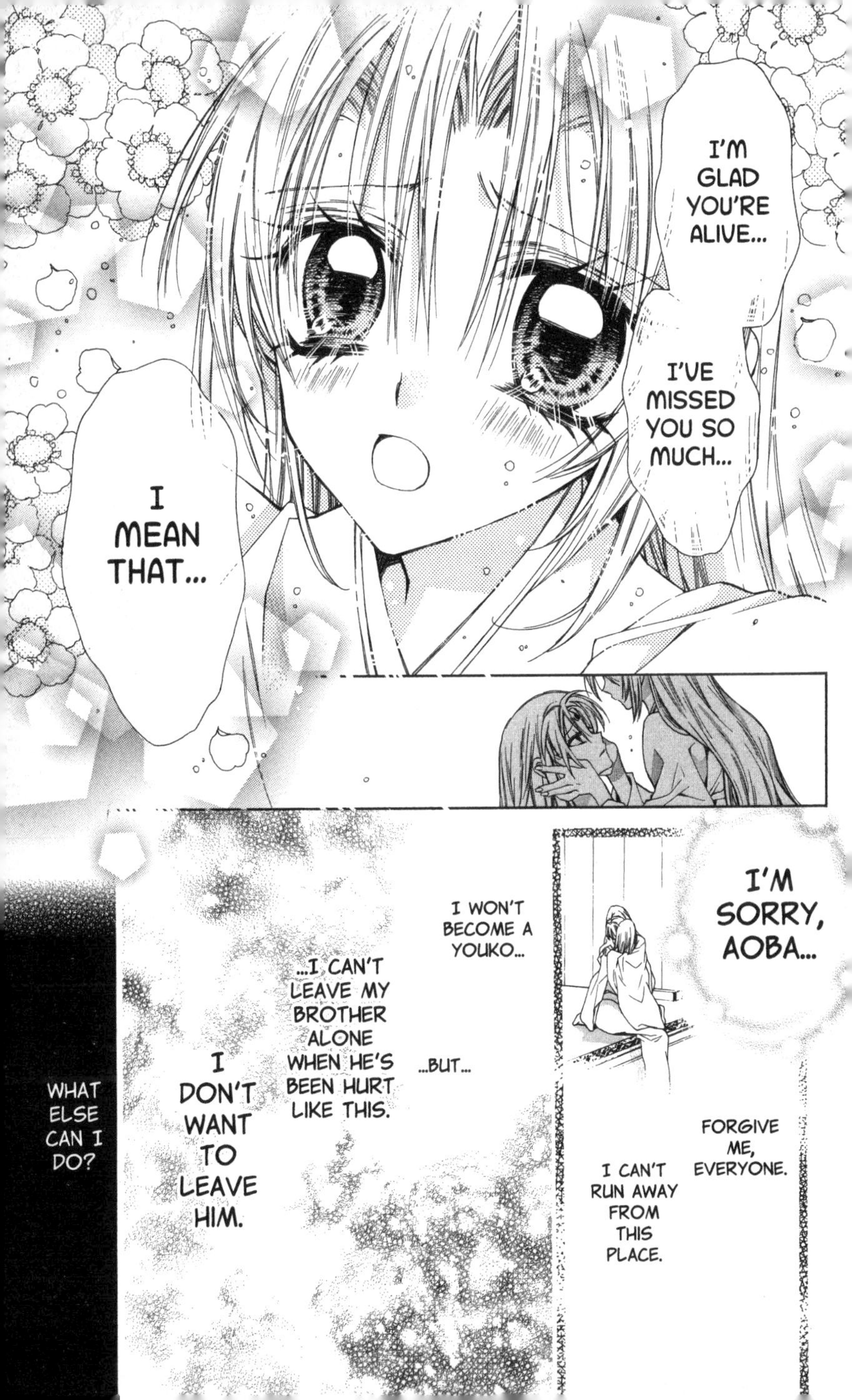
I'M GLAD YOU'RE ALIVE...
I'VE MISSED YOU SO MUCH...
I MEAN THAT...
I'M SORRY, AOBA...
FORGIVE ME, EVERYONE.
I CAN'T RUN AWAY FROM THIS PLACE.
I WON'T BECOME A YOUKO...
...BUT...
...I CAN'T LEAVE MY BROTHER ALONE WHEN HE'S BEEN HURT LIKE THIS.
I DON'T WANT TO LEAVE HIM.
WHAT ELSE CAN I DO?

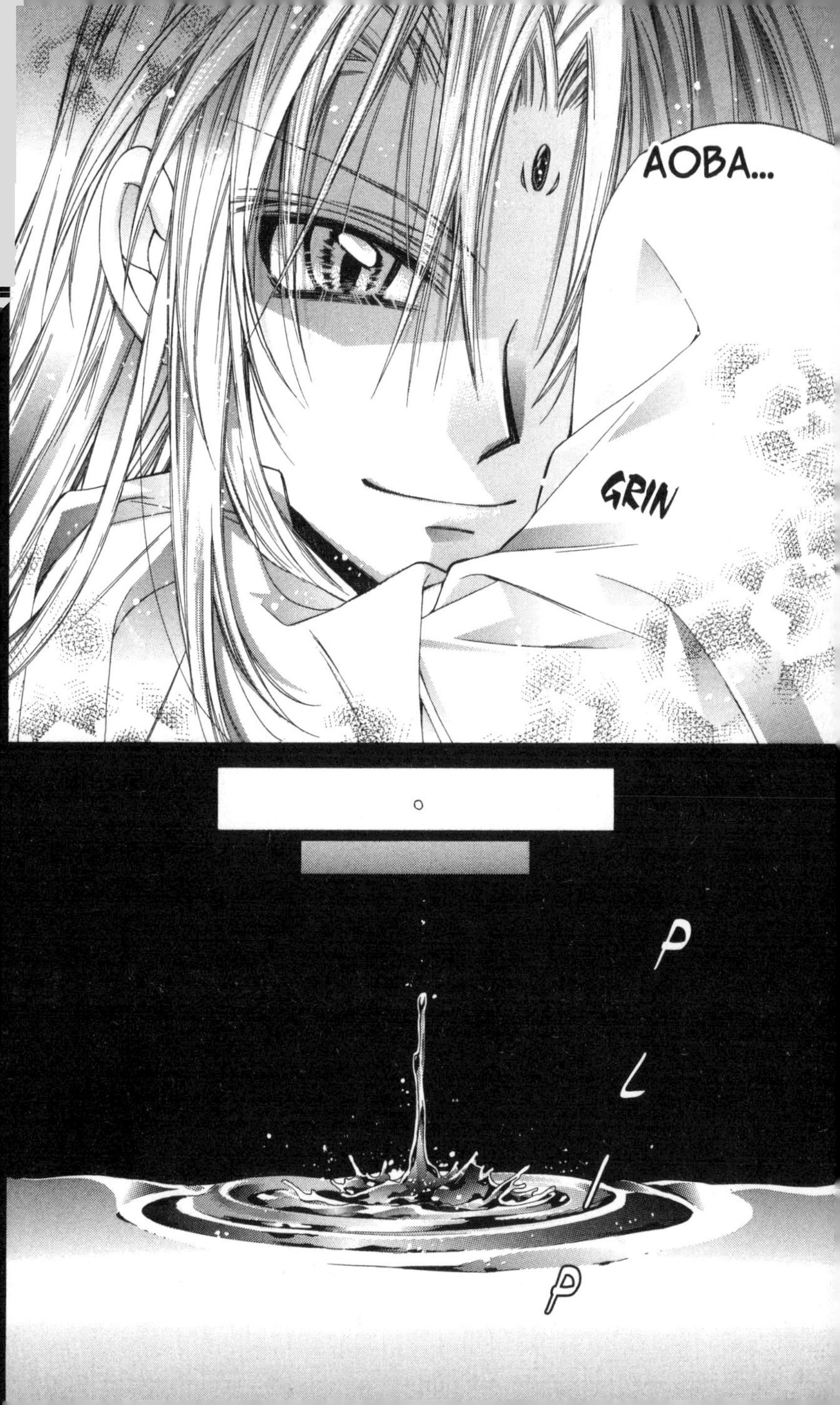
AOBA...
GRIN
PLIP

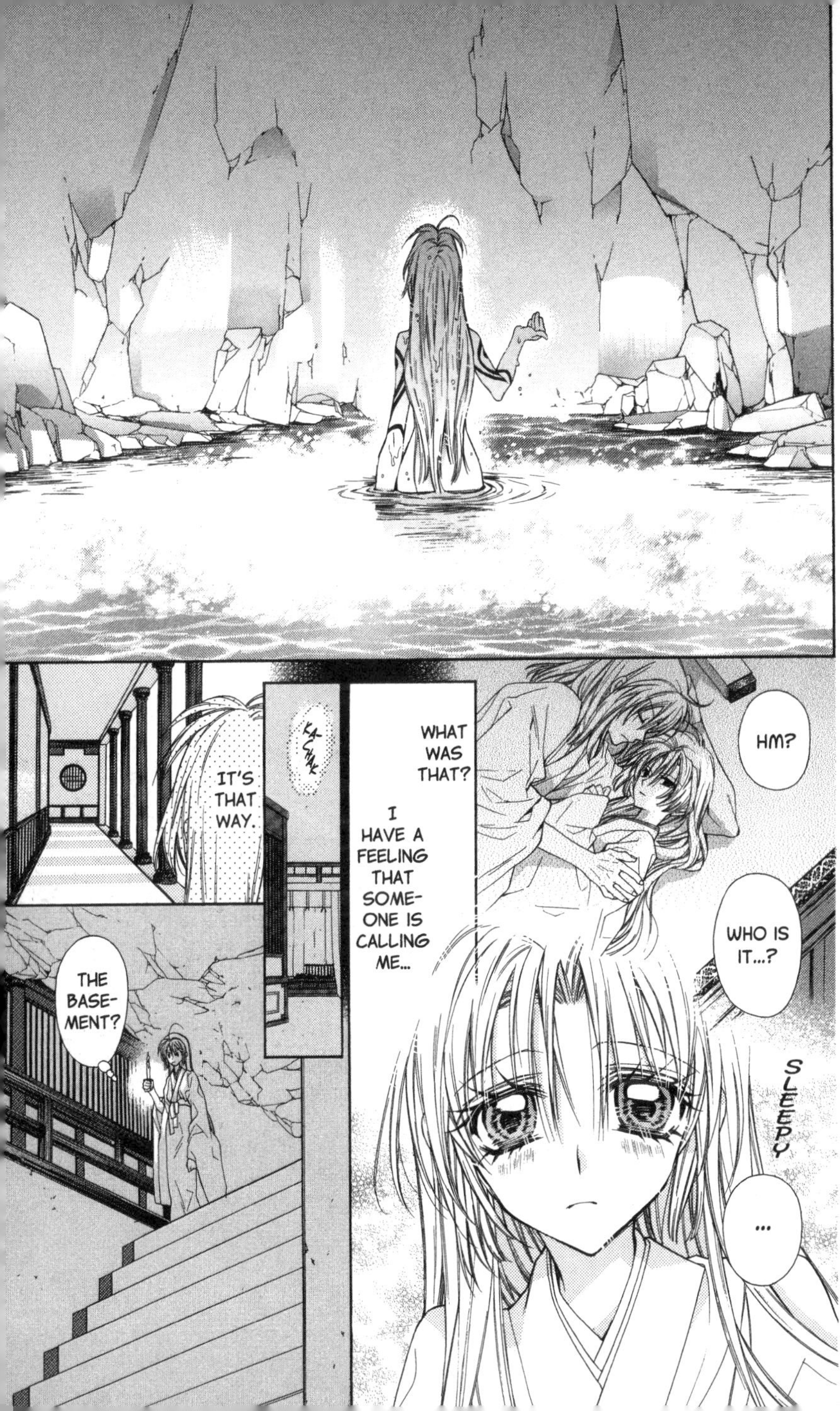
HM?
WHO IS IT...?
SLEEPY
...
WHAT WAS THAT?
I HAVE A FEELING THAT SOME-ONE IS CALLING ME...
KA-CHAK
IT'S THAT WAY.
THE BASE-MENT?

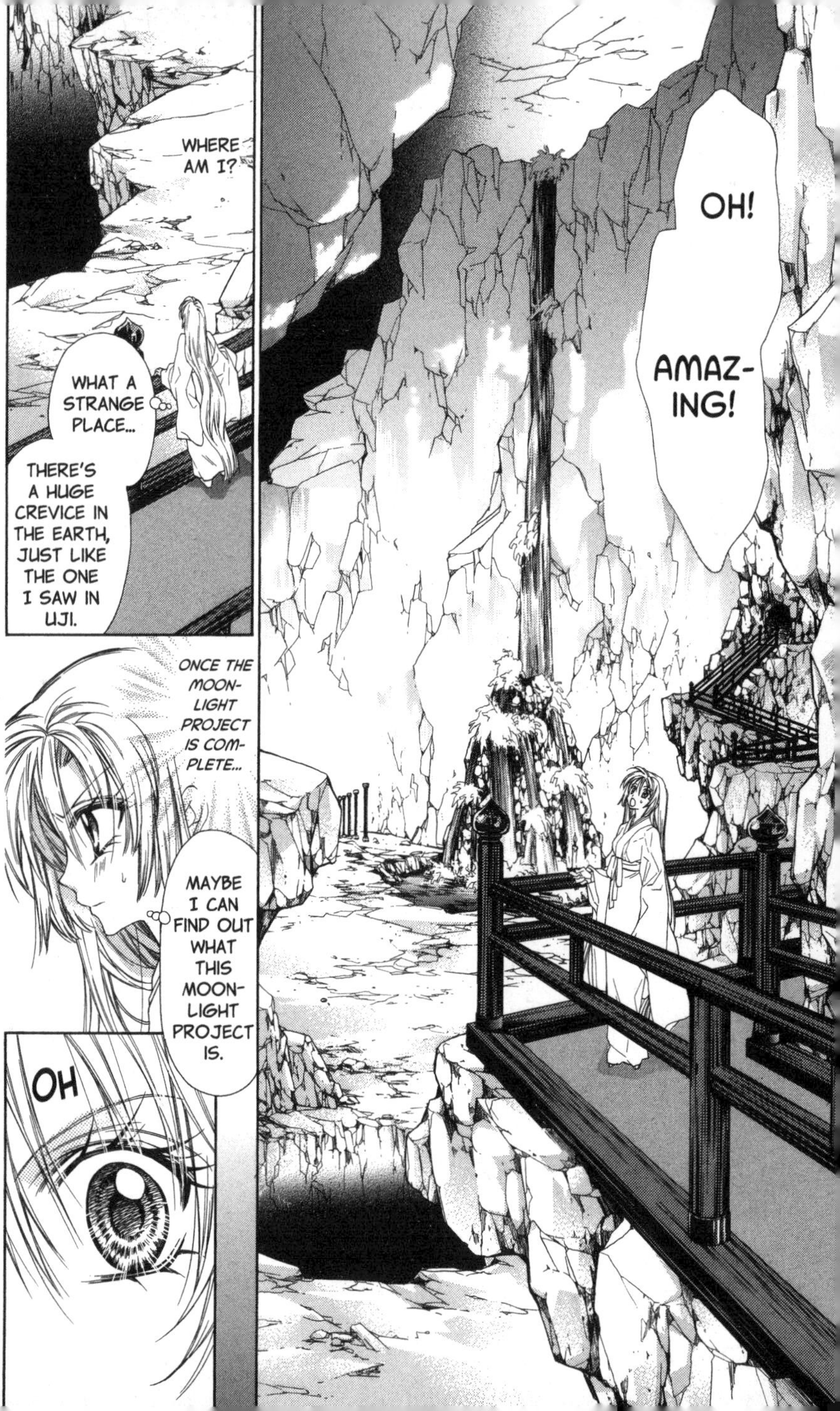
OH!
AMAZ-ING!
WHERE AM I?
WHAT A STRANGE PLACE...
THERE'S A HUGE CREVICE IN THE EARTH, JUST LIKE THE ONE I SAW IN UJI.
ONCE THE MOON-LIGHT PROJECT IS COM-PLETE...
MAYBE I CAN FIND OUT WHAT THIS MOON-LIGHT PROJECT IS.
OH

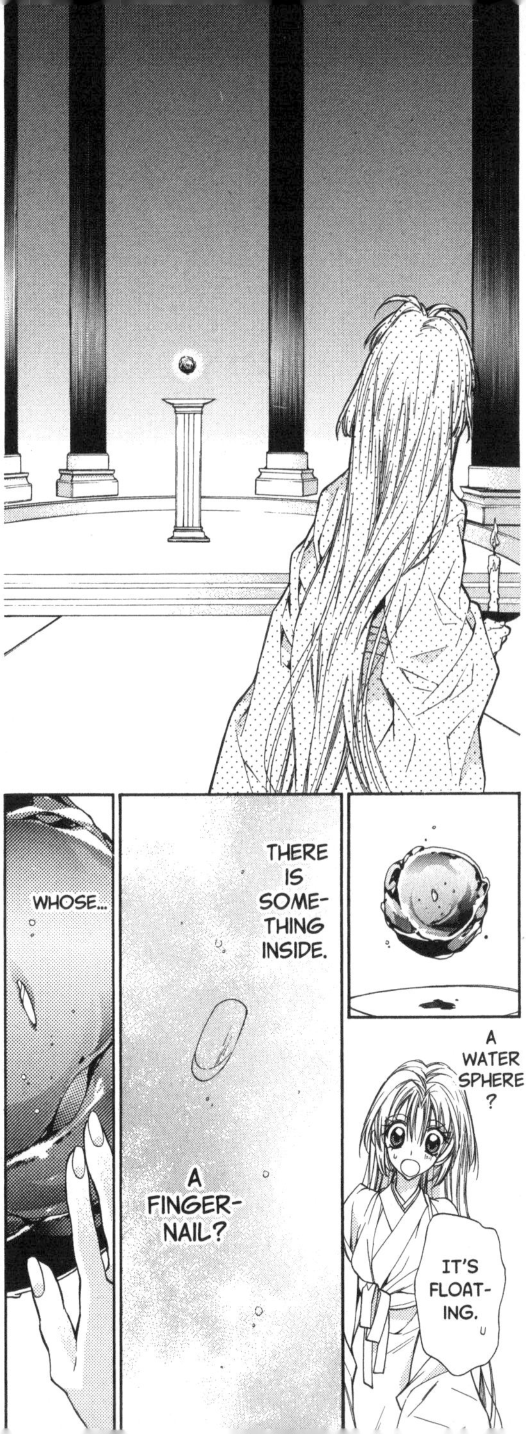
A WATER SPHERE?
IT'S FLOATING.
THERE IS SOMETHING INSIDE.
A FINGERNAIL?
WHOSE...

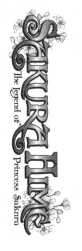

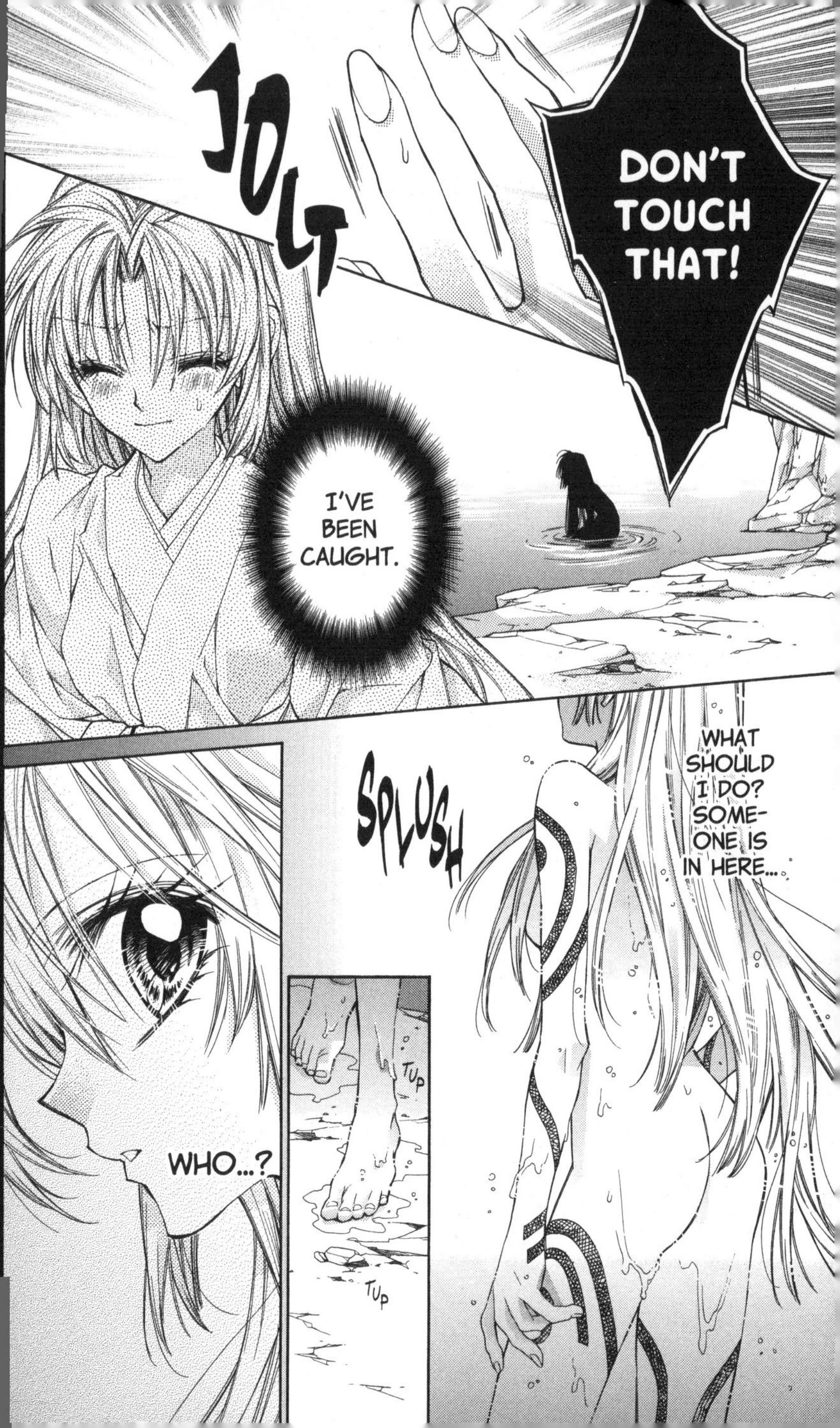
DON'T TOUCH THAT!
JOLT
I'VE BEEN CAUGHT.
WHAT SHOULD I DO? SOME-ONE IS IN HERE...
SPLUSH
TUP
TUP
WHO...?

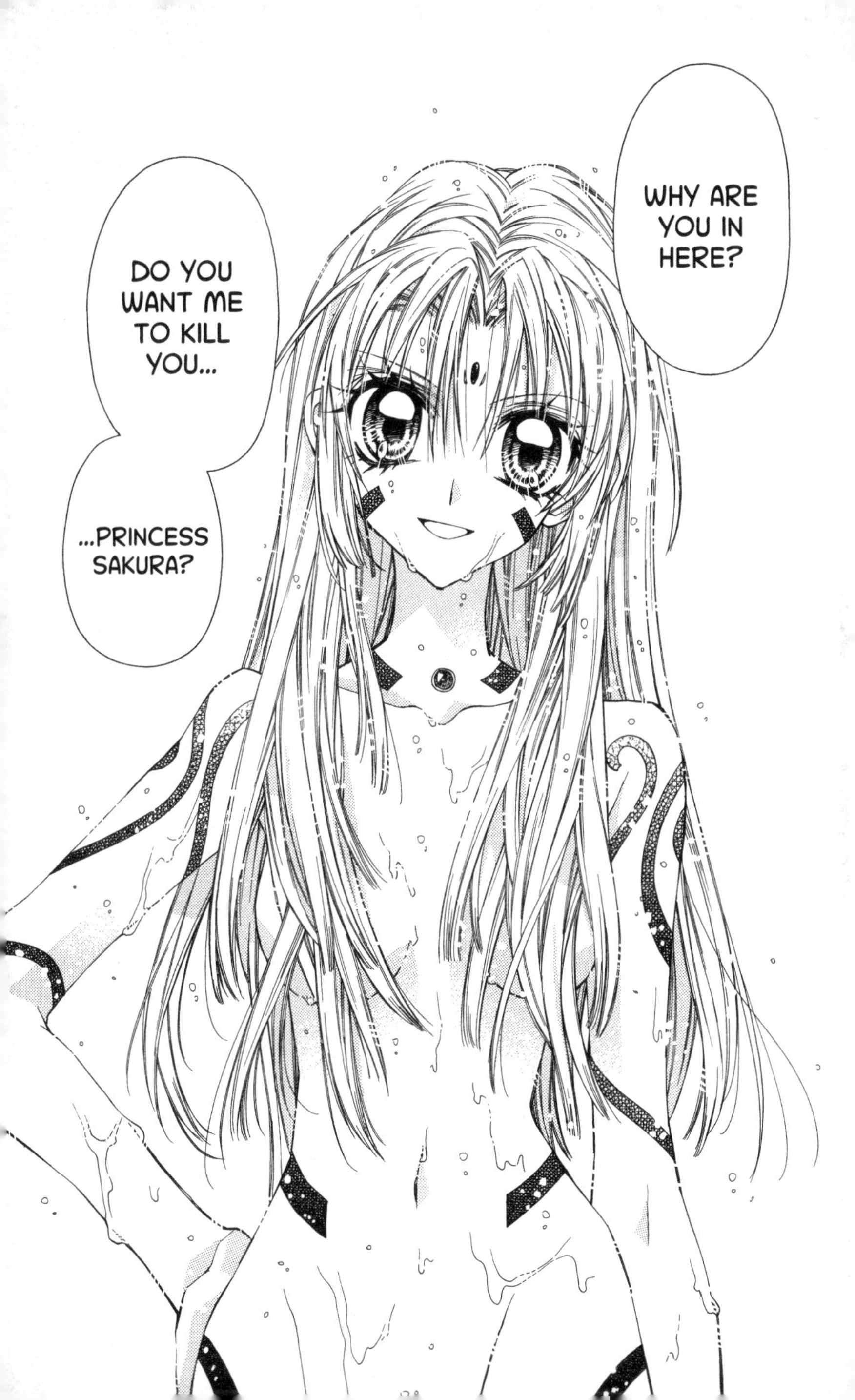
WHY ARE YOU IN HERE?
DO YOU WANT ME TO KILL YOU...
...PRINCESS SAKURA?

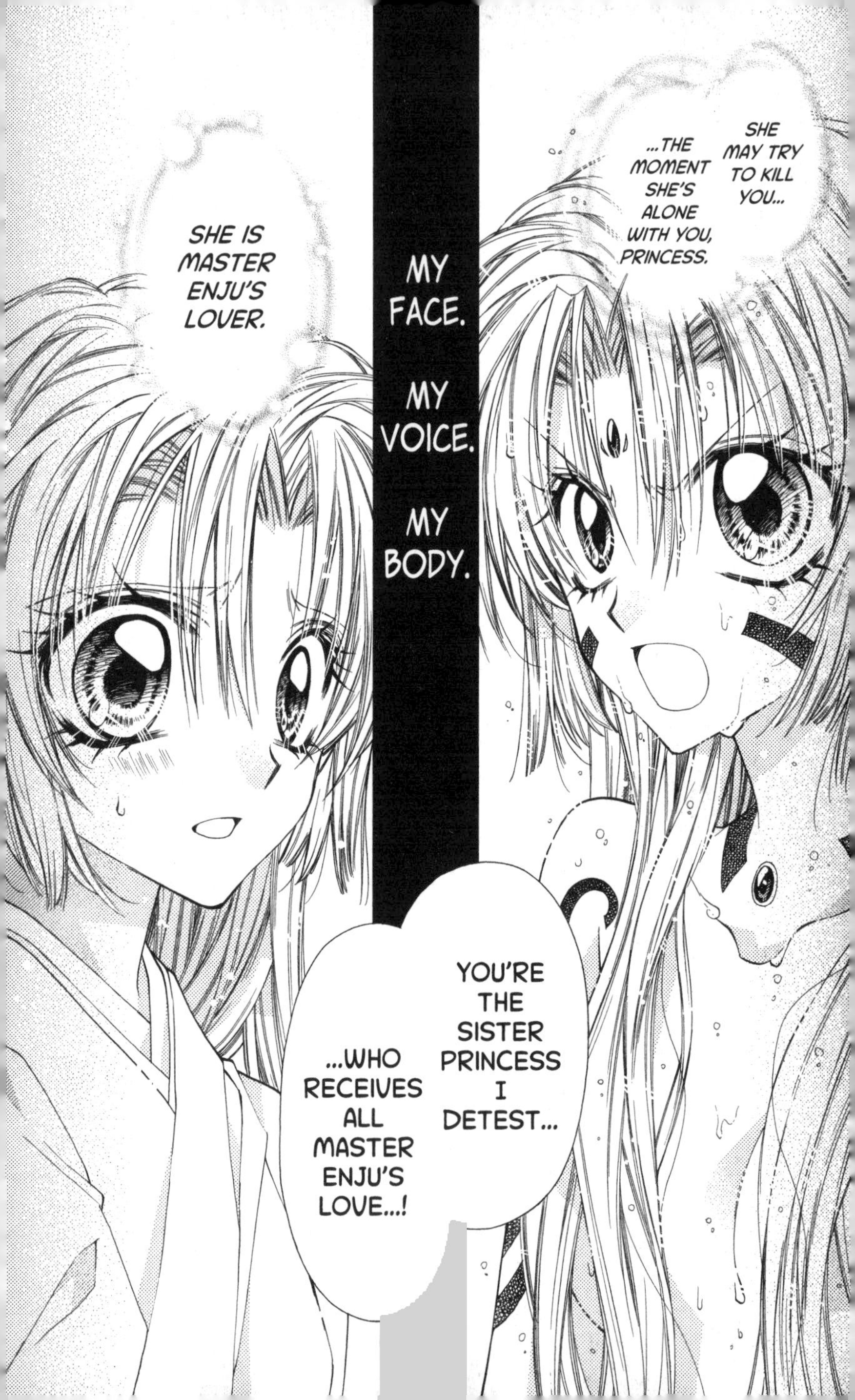
SHE MAY TRY TO KILL YOU...
...THE MOMENT SHE'S ALONE WITH YOU, PRINCESS.
MY FACE.
MY VOICE.
MY BODY.
SHE IS MASTER ENJU'S LOVER.
YOU'RE THE SISTER PRINCESS I DETEST...
...WHO RECEIVES ALL MASTER ENJU'S LOVE...!

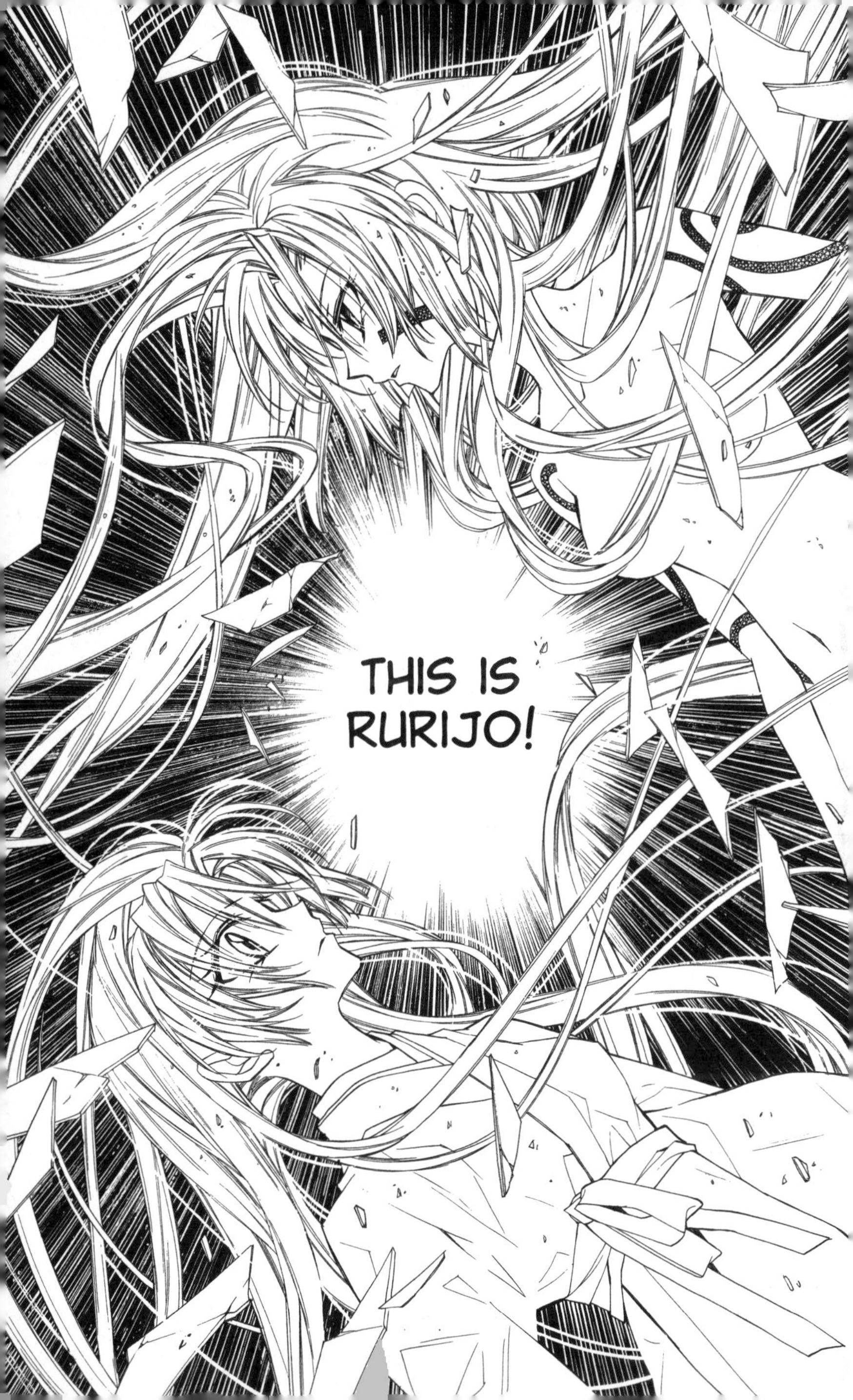
THIS IS RURIJO!

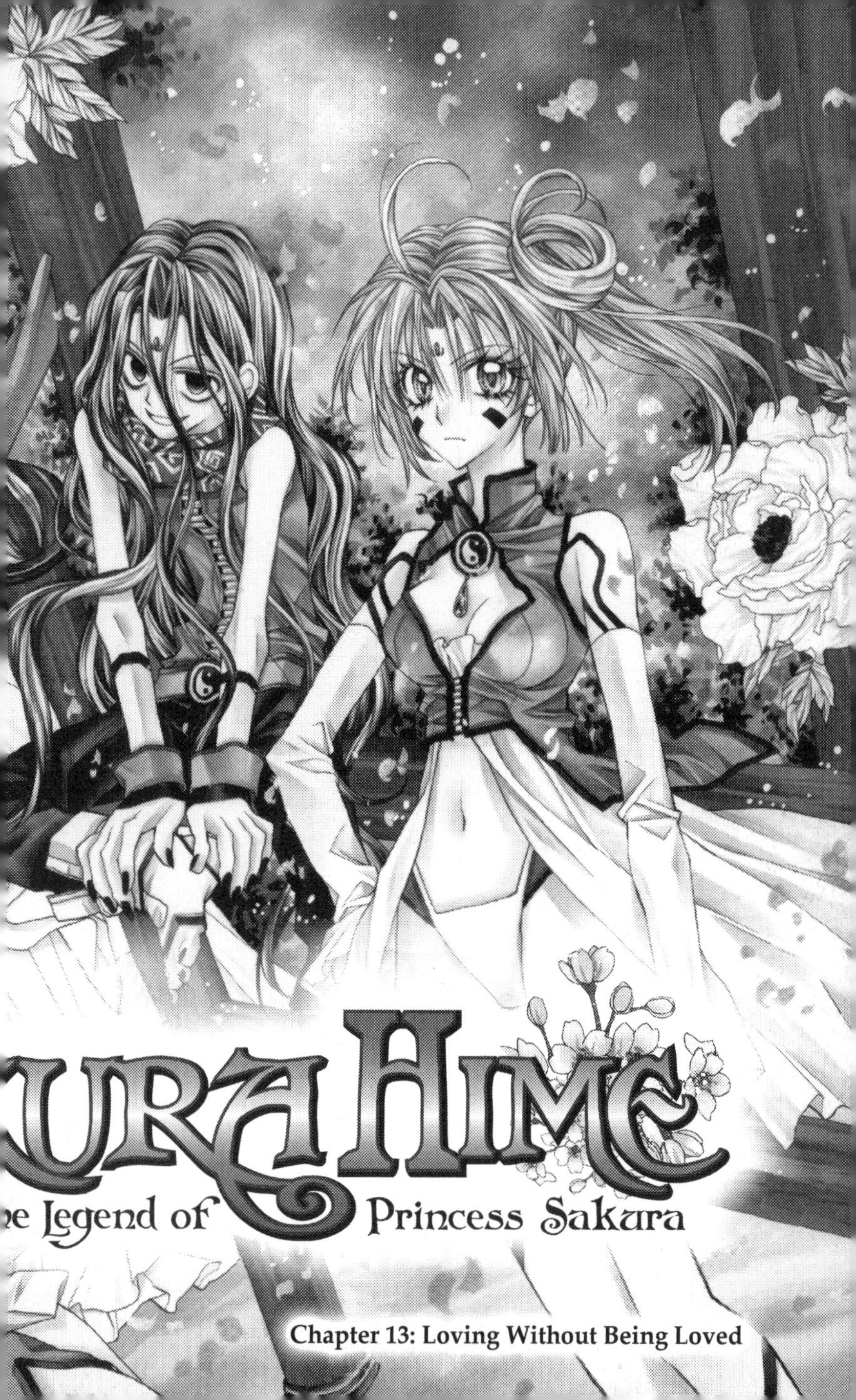
URA HIME
e Legend of Princess Sakura

Chapter 13: Loving Without Being Loved

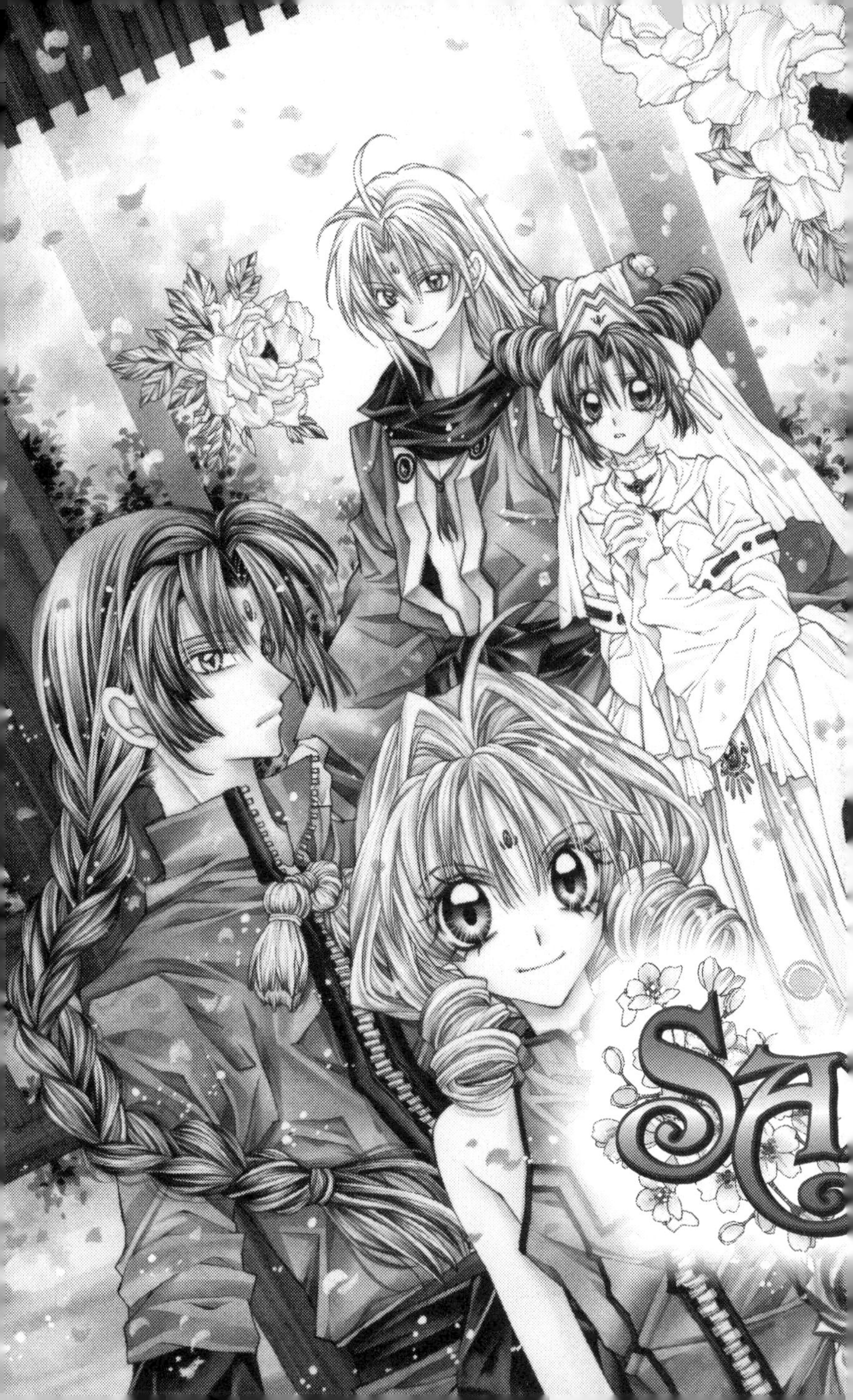

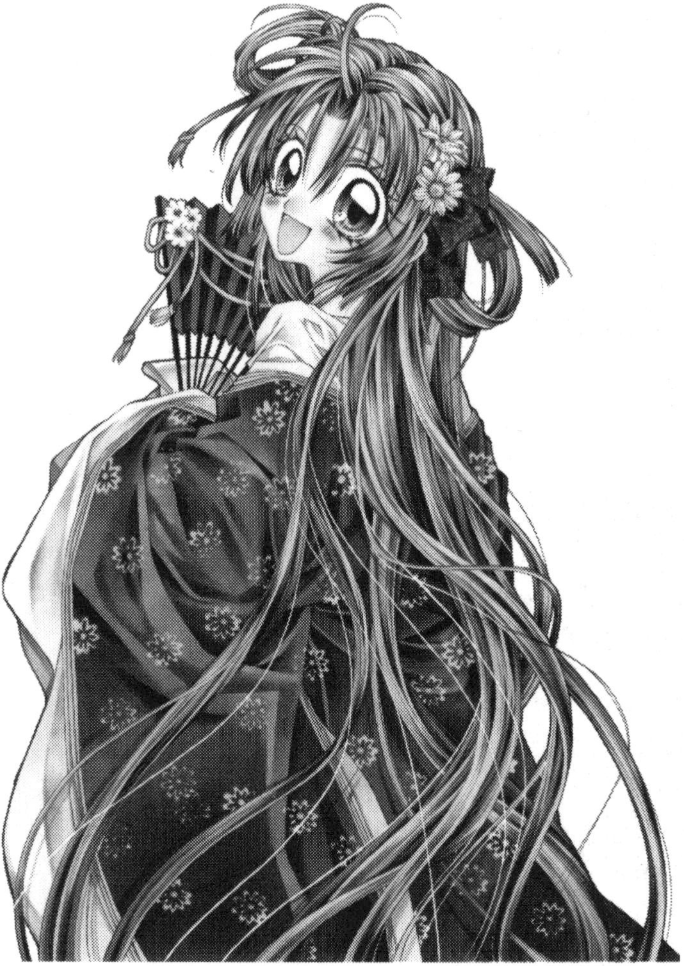

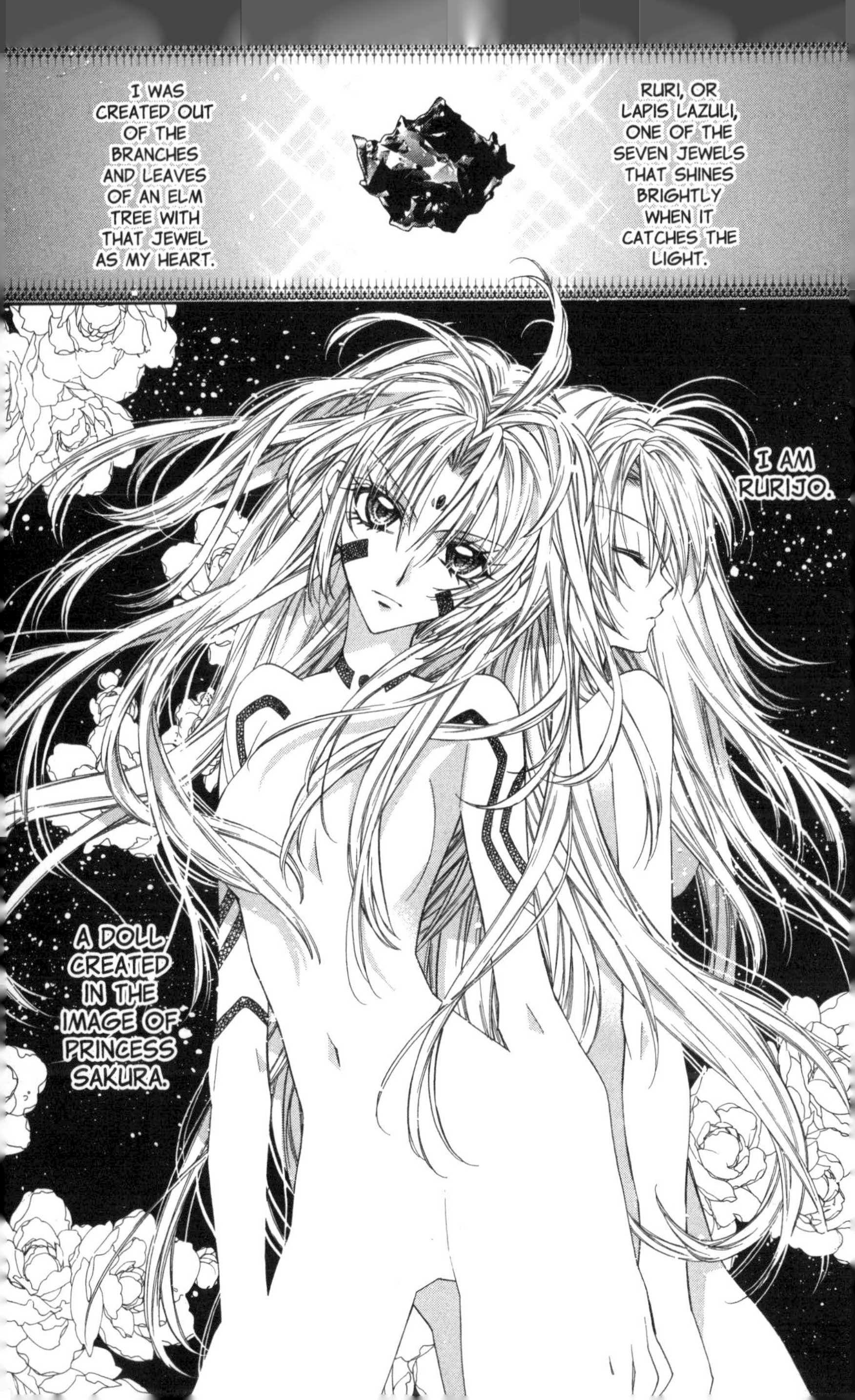
RURI, OR LAPIS LAZULI, ONE OF THE SEVEN JEWELS THAT SHINES BRIGHTLY WHEN IT CATCHES THE LIGHT.
I WAS CREATED OUT OF THE BRANCHES AND LEAVES OF AN ELM TREE WITH THAT JEWEL AS MY HEART.
I AM RURIJO.
A DOLL CREATED IN THE IMAGE OF PRINCESS SAKURA.

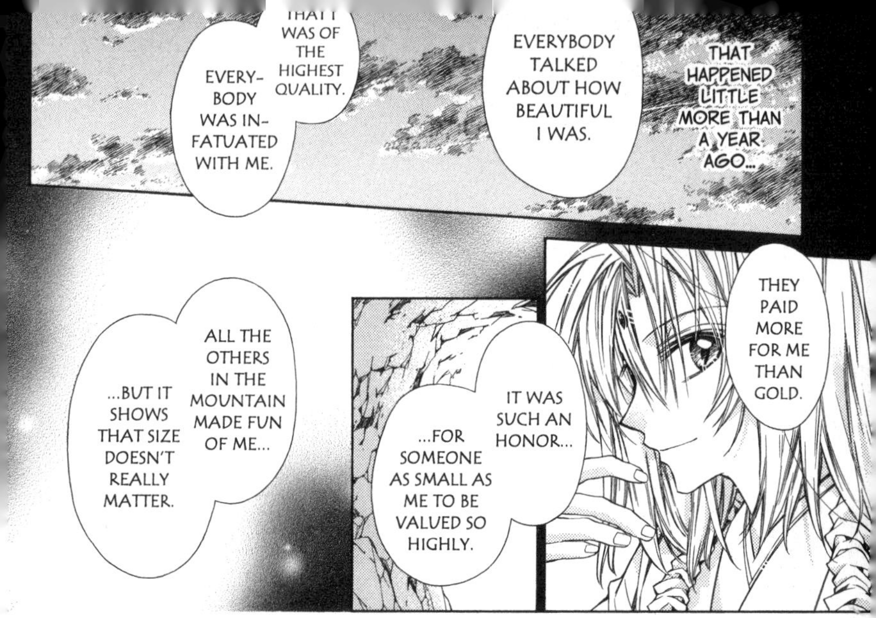
THAT HAPPENED LITTLE MORE THAN A YEAR AGO...
EVERYBODY TALKED ABOUT HOW BEAUTIFUL I WAS.
THAT I WAS OF THE HIGHEST QUALITY.
EVERY-BODY WAS IN-FATUATED WITH ME.
THEY PAID MORE FOR ME THAN GOLD.
IT WAS SUCH AN HONOR...
...FOR SOMEONE AS SMALL AS ME TO BE VALUED SO HIGHLY.
ALL THE OTHERS IN THE MOUNTAIN MADE FUN OF ME...
...BUT IT SHOWS THAT SIZE DOESN'T REALLY MATTER.

Chapter 13: Loving Without Being Loved

※ I'm giving away the story.

The moon people are on the title page. The one I enjoy drawing the most because of the way he looks is Shuri. (He looks so afflicted...)

Everyone on Aoba's team wears different clothes, so I had these characters wear similar garments.

Rurijo symbolizes instinct, and Sakura symbolizes rationality. Rurijo isn't rational(?). How can I put it... She's very impulsive and indelicate... She's easy to draw because she has such a straightforward personality.

I drew lots of naked bodies in this chapter too. To be honest, drawing them made me feel embarrassed. //// And to top it off, she even tries to fight with Sakura when she's naked... (laugh) I'm so sorry she's such an uncouth girl.

I've drawn Sakura and Rurijo as a type of twins. (Or as the two sides of a person's heart). They'll continue to have a rather delicate relationship, so I hope you enjoy it.

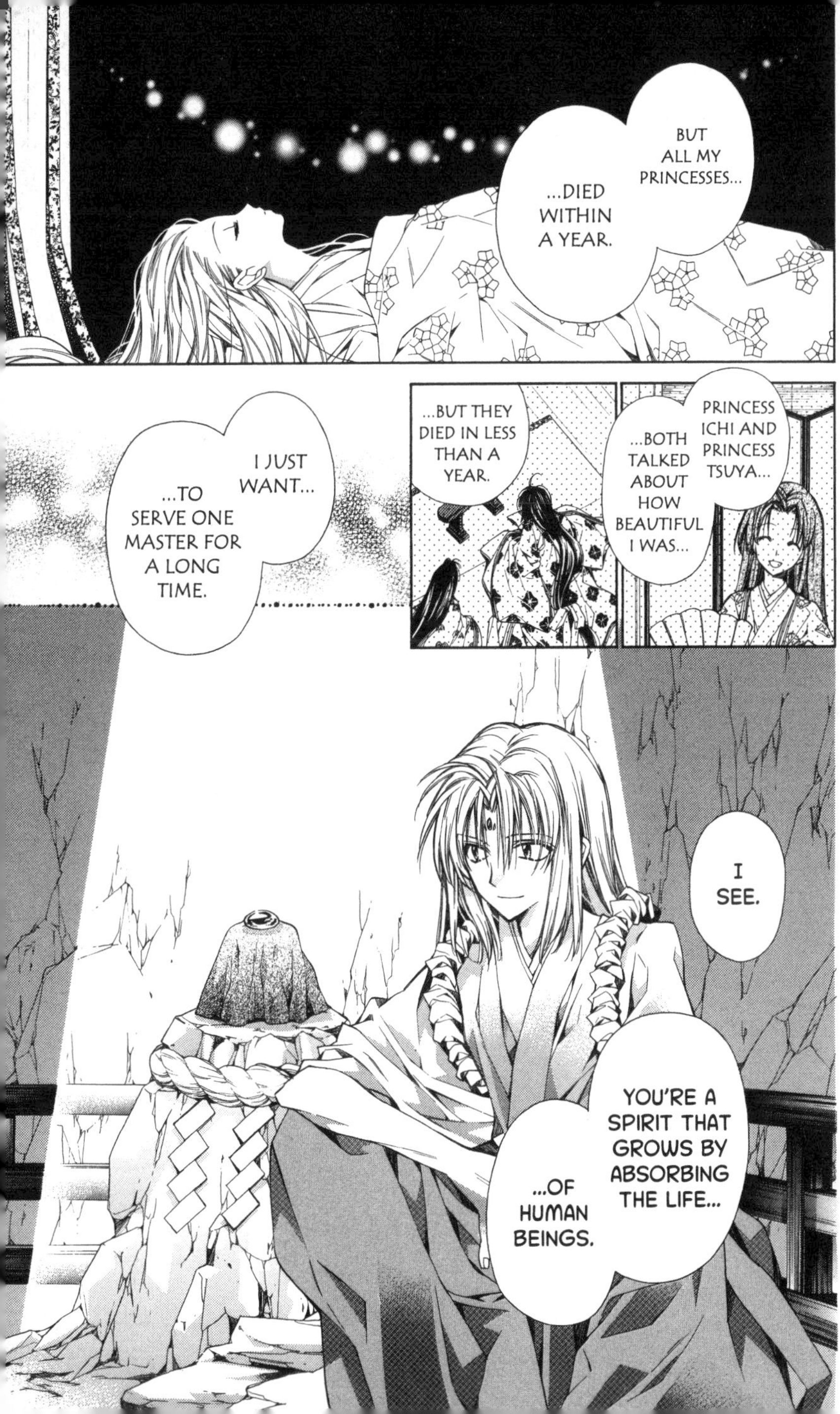
BUT ALL MY PRINCESSES...
...DIED WITHIN A YEAR.
PRINCESS ICHI AND PRINCESS TSUYA...
...BOTH TALKED ABOUT HOW BEAUTIFUL I WAS...
...BUT THEY DIED IN LESS THAN A YEAR.
I JUST WANT...
...TO SERVE ONE MASTER FOR A LONG TIME.
I SEE.
YOU'RE A SPIRIT THAT GROWS BY ABSORBING THE LIFE...
...OF HUMAN BEINGS.

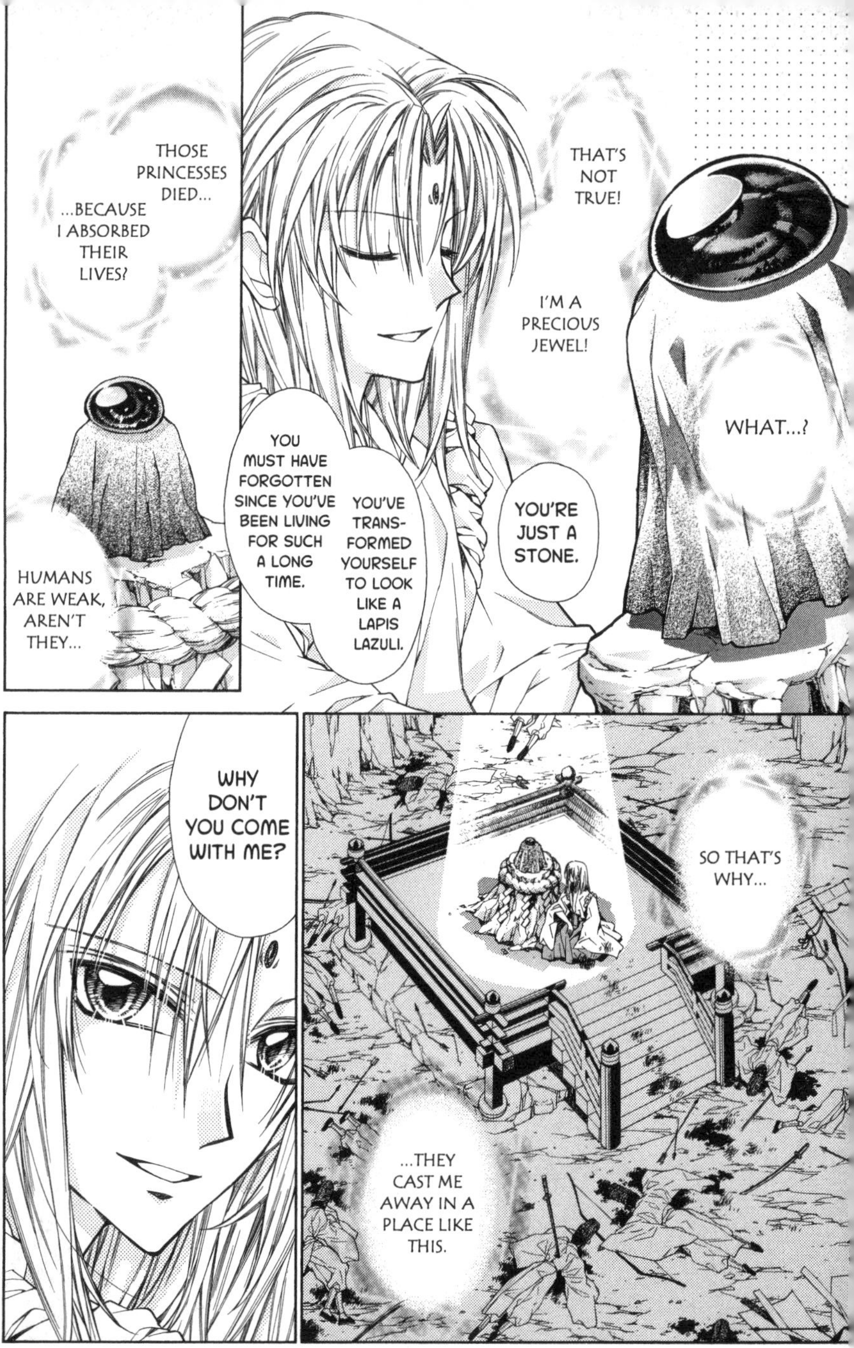

THAT'S NOT TRUE!
I'M A PRECIOUS JEWEL!
WHAT...?
YOU'RE JUST A STONE.
YOU'VE TRANS-FORMED YOURSELF TO LOOK LIKE A LAPIS LAZULI.
YOU MUST HAVE FORGOTTEN SINCE YOU'VE BEEN LIVING FOR SUCH A LONG TIME.
THOSE PRINCESSES DIED...
...BECAUSE I ABSORBED THEIR LIVES?
HUMANS ARE WEAK, AREN'T THEY...
SO THAT'S WHY...
...THEY CAST ME AWAY IN A PLACE LIKE THIS.
WHY DON'T YOU COME WITH ME?

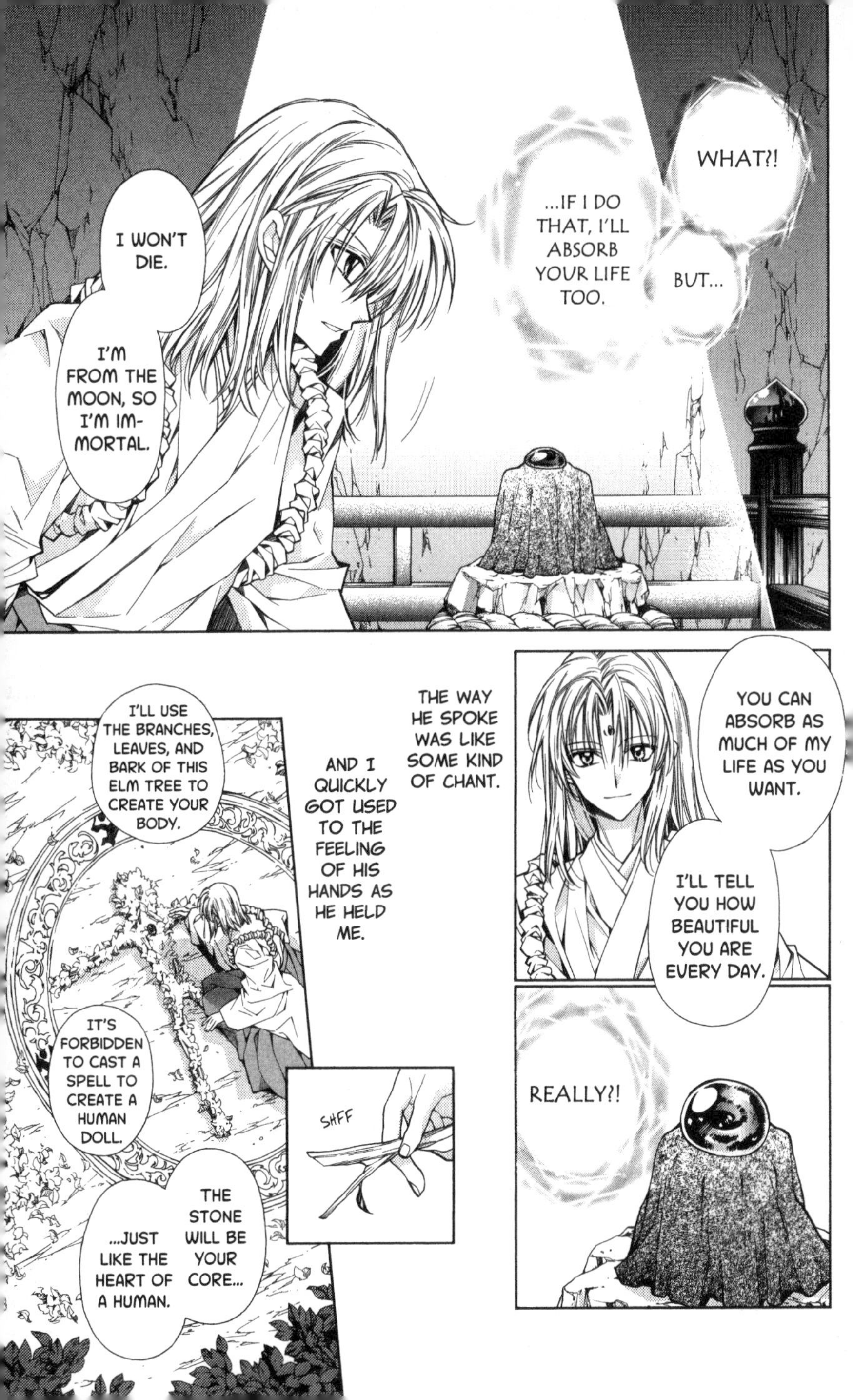
WHAT?!
BUT...
...IF I DO THAT, I'LL ABSORB YOUR LIFE TOO.
I WON'T DIE.
I'M FROM THE MOON, SO I'M IM-MORTAL.
YOU CAN ABSORB AS MUCH OF MY LIFE AS YOU WANT.
I'LL TELL YOU HOW BEAUTIFUL YOU ARE EVERY DAY.
REALLY?!
THE WAY HE SPOKE WAS LIKE SOME KIND OF CHANT.
AND I QUICKLY GOT USED TO THE FEELING OF HIS HANDS AS HE HELD ME.
SHFF
I'LL USE THE BRANCHES, LEAVES, AND BARK OF THIS ELM TREE TO CREATE YOUR BODY.
IT'S FORBIDDEN TO CAST A SPELL TO CREATE A HUMAN DOLL.
THE STONE WILL BE YOUR CORE...
...JUST LIKE THE HEART OF A HUMAN.

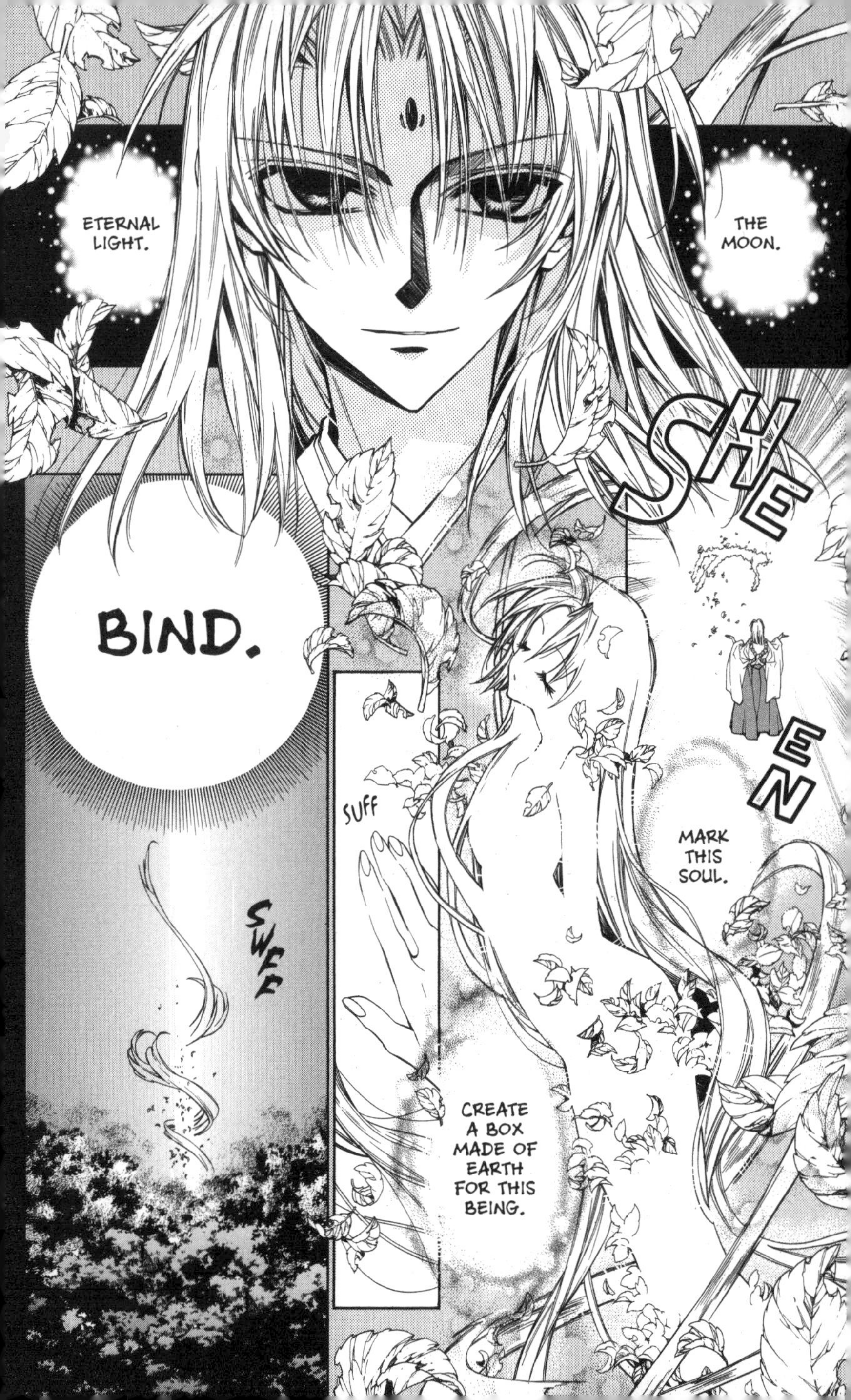
THE MOON.
ETERNAL LIGHT.
SHEEN
MARK THIS SOUL.
CREATE A BOX MADE OF EARTH FOR THIS BEING.
SUFF
BIND.
SWFF

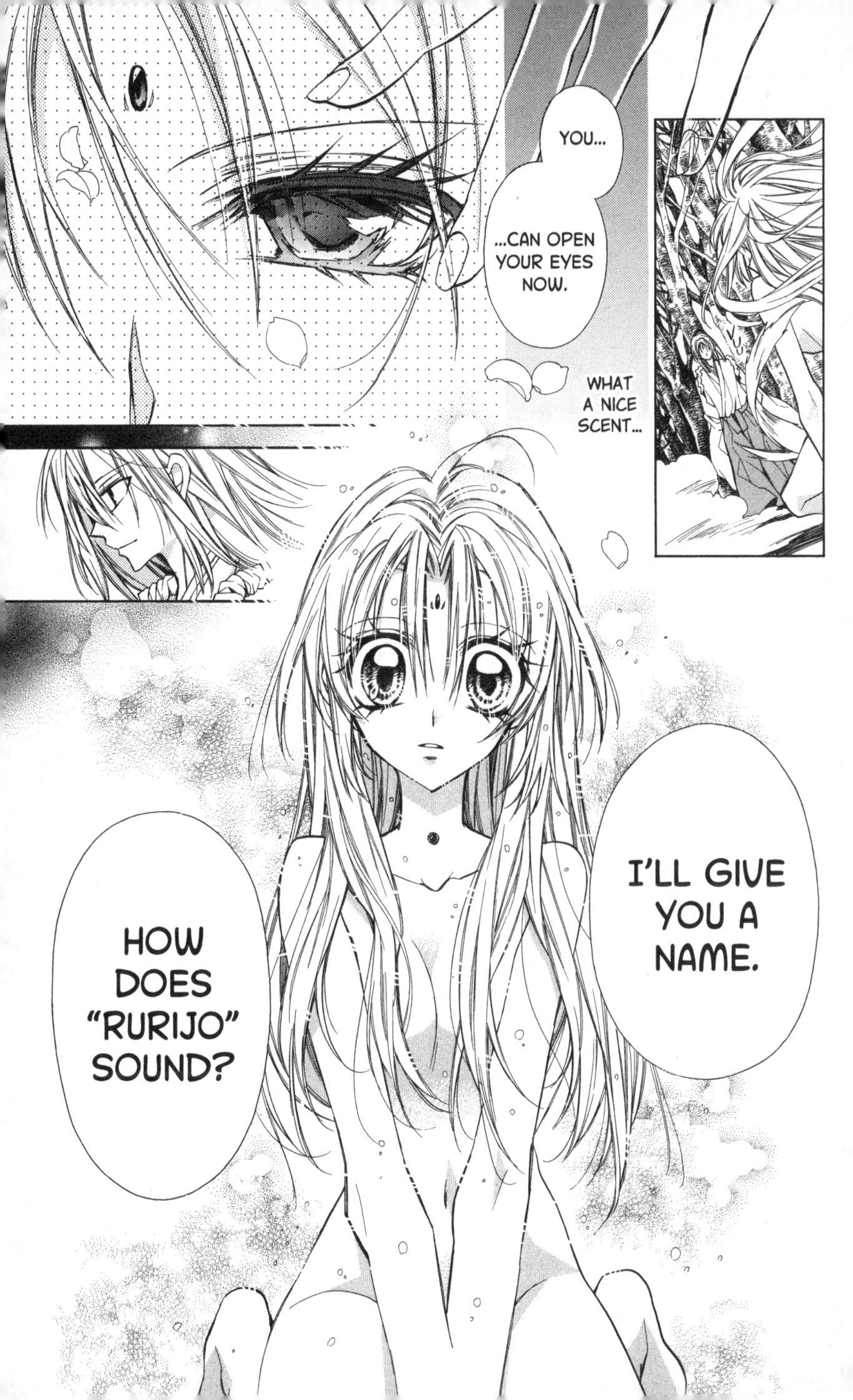
YOU...
...CAN OPEN YOUR EYES NOW.
WHAT A NICE SCENT...
I'LL GIVE YOU A NAME.
HOW DOES "RURIJO" SOUND?

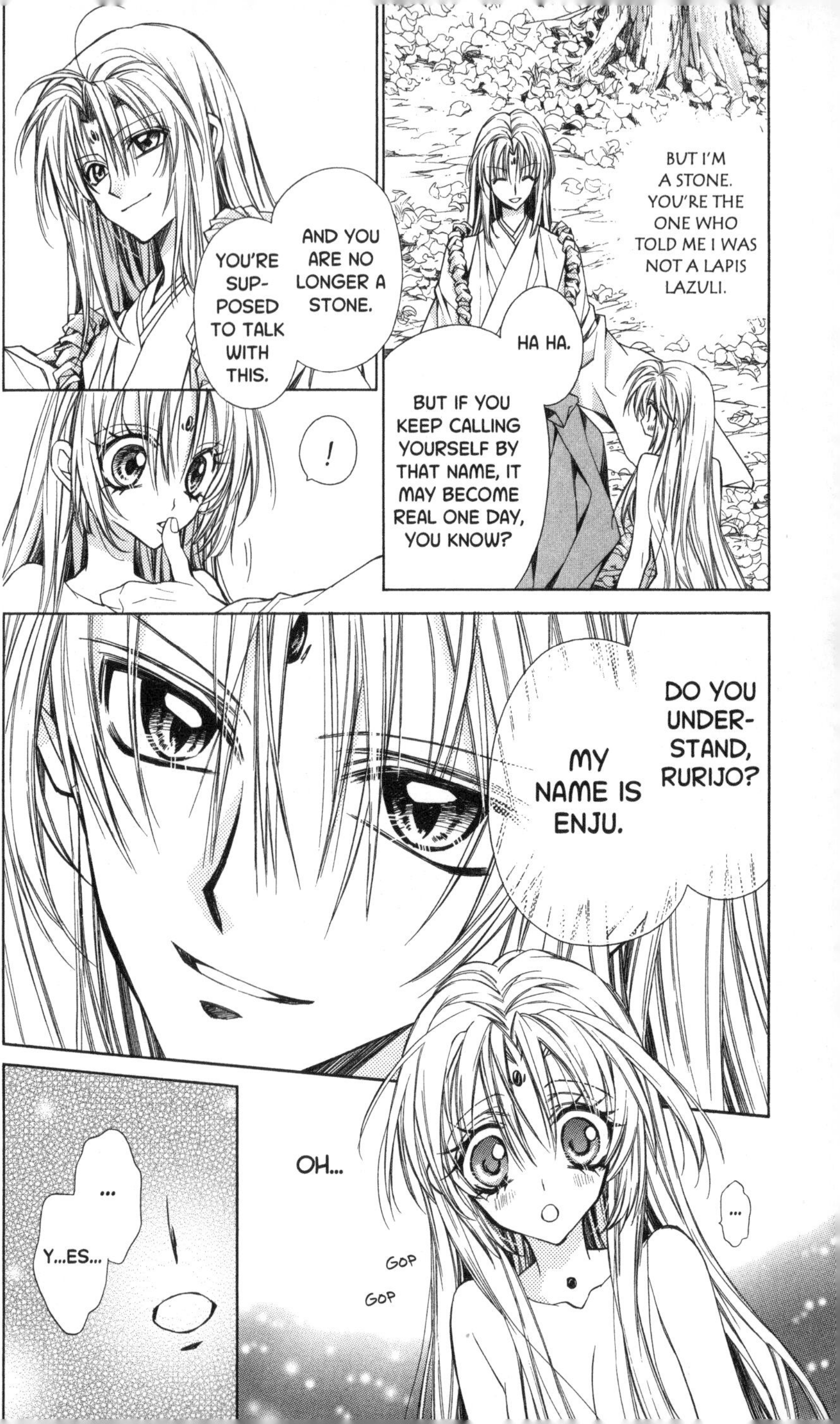
BUT I'M A STONE. YOU'RE THE ONE WHO TOLD ME I WAS NOT A LAPIS LAZULI.
HA HA.
BUT IF YOU KEEP CALLING YOURSELF BY THAT NAME, IT MAY BECOME REAL ONE DAY, YOU KNOW?
AND YOU ARE NO LONGER A STONE.
YOU'RE SUP-POSED TO TALK WITH THIS.
!
DO YOU UNDER-STAND, RURIJO?
MY NAME IS ENJU.
...
OH...
GOP
GOP
...
Y...ES...

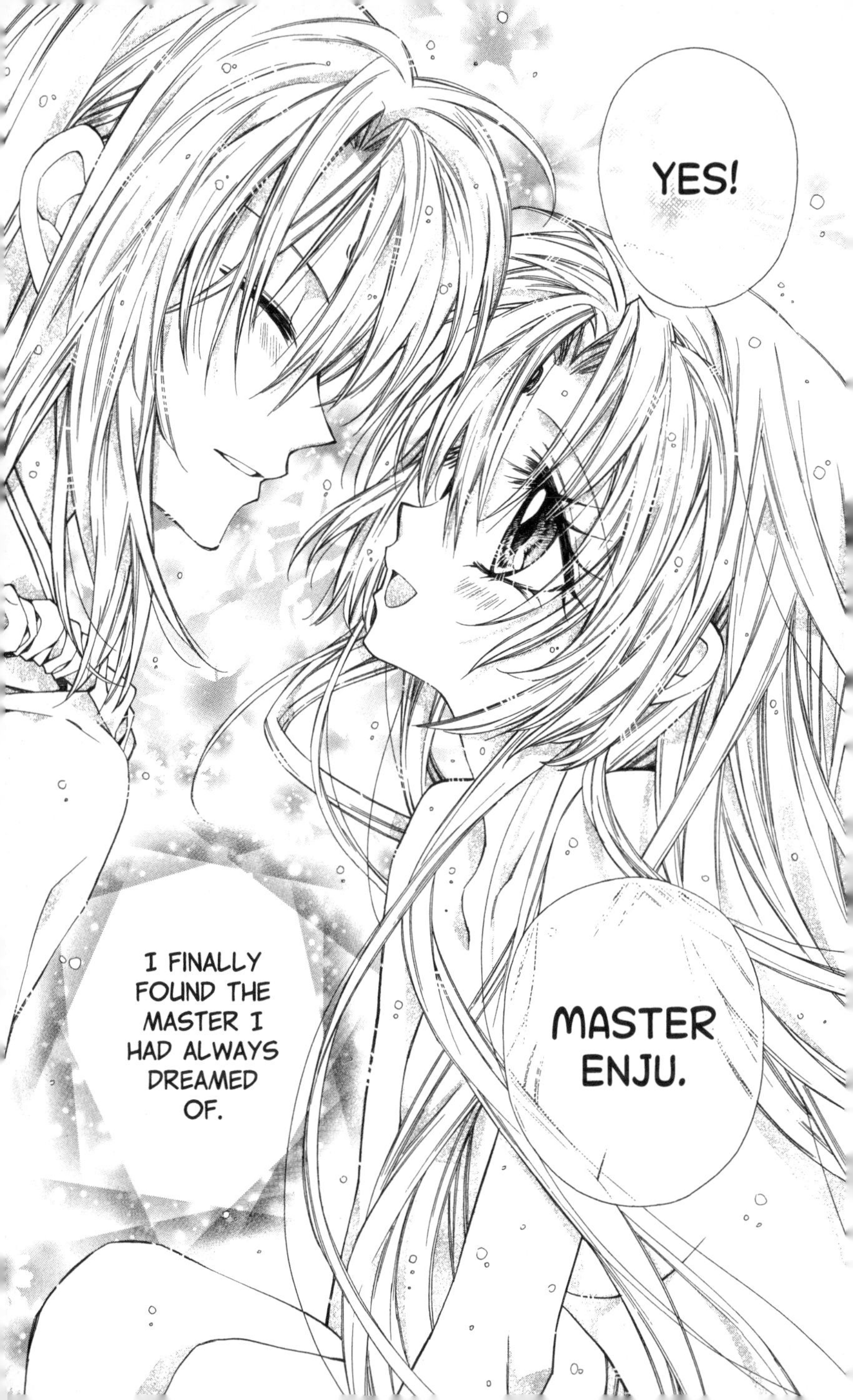
YES!
MASTER ENJU.
I FINALLY FOUND THE MASTER I HAD ALWAYS DREAMED OF.

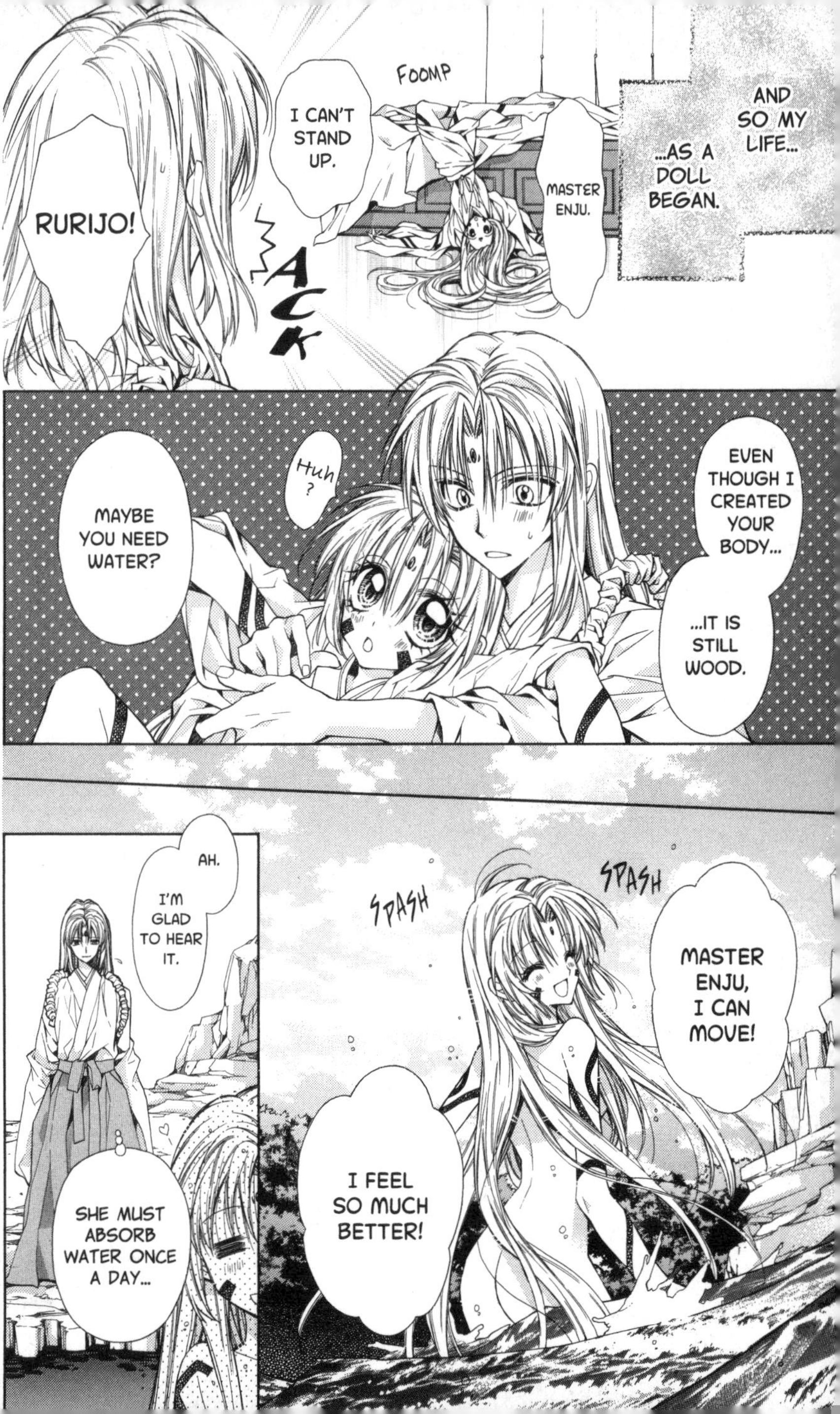
AND SO MY LIFE...
...AS A DOLL BEGAN.
MASTER ENJU.
FOOMP
I CAN'T STAND UP.
WACK
RURIJO!
EVEN THOUGH I CREATED YOUR BODY...
...IT IS STILL WOOD.
Huh?
MAYBE YOU NEED WATER?
SPASH
MASTER ENJU, I CAN MOVE!
SPASH
I FEEL SO MUCH BETTER!
AH.
I'M GLAD TO HEAR IT.
SHE MUST ABSORB WATER ONCE A DAY...

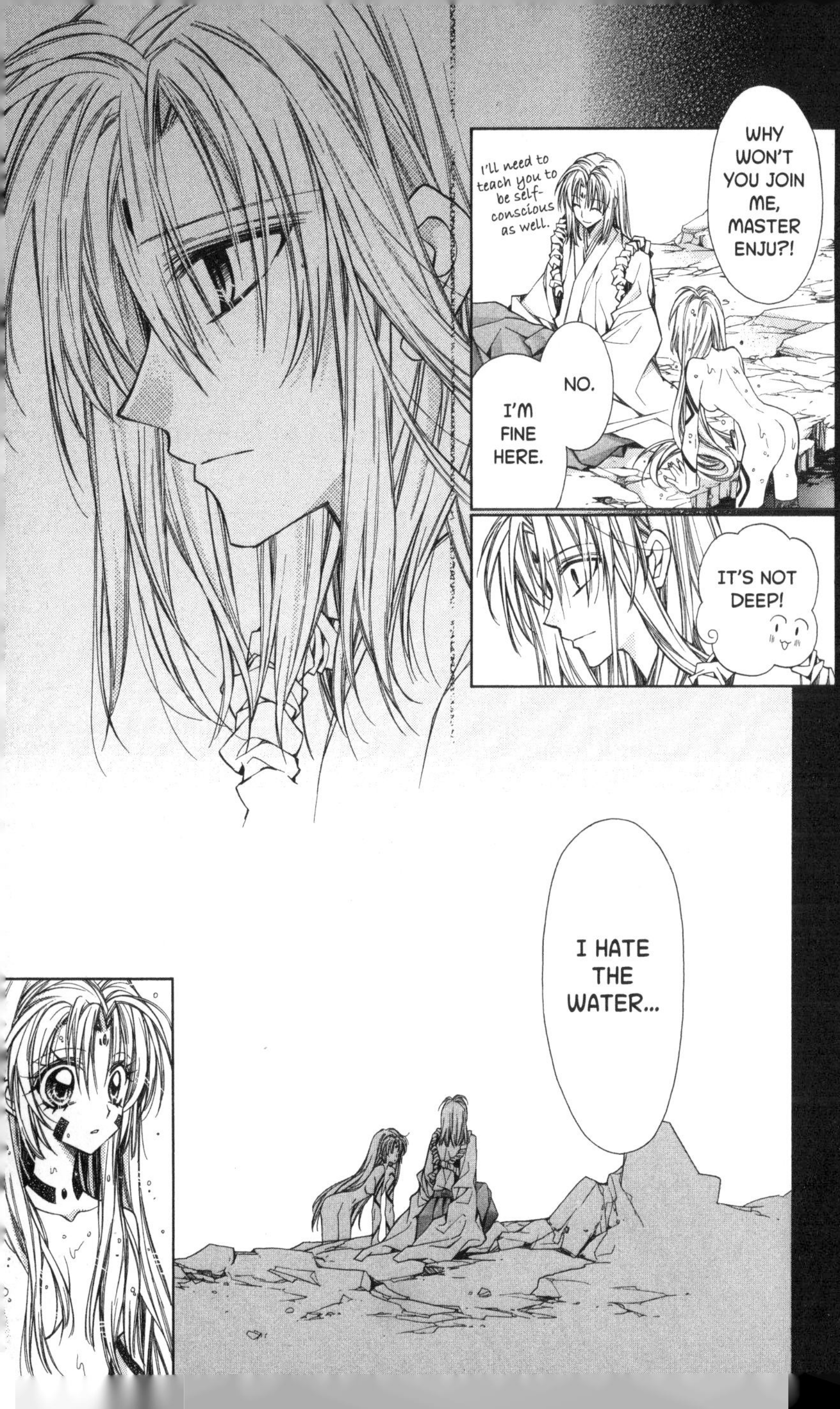
WHY WON'T YOU JOIN ME, MASTER ENJU?!
I'll need to teach you to be self-conscious as well.
NO.
I'M FINE HERE.
IT'S NOT DEEP!
I HATE THE WATER...

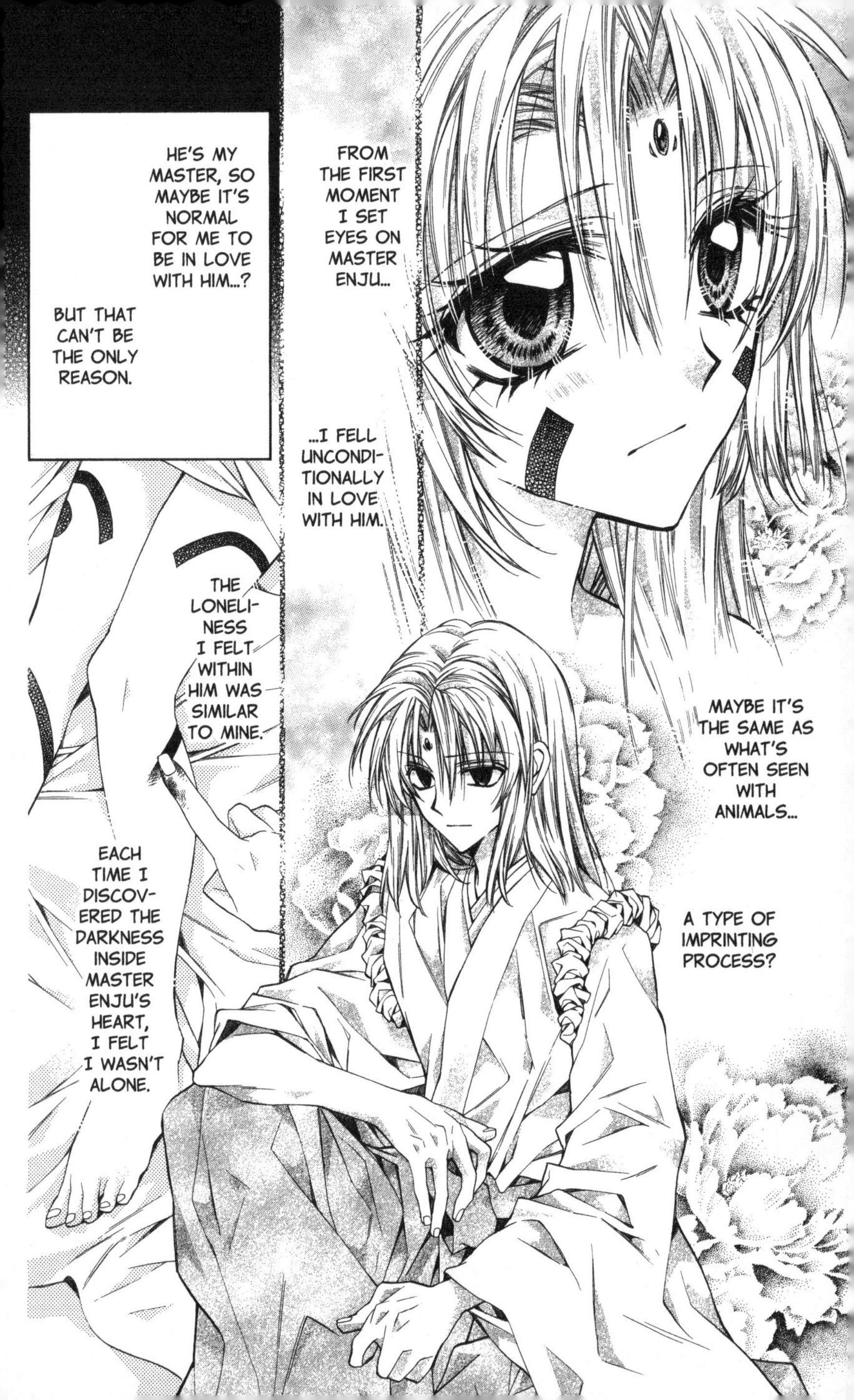
FROM THE FIRST MOMENT I SET EYES ON MASTER ENJU...
...I FELL UNCONDITIONALLY IN LOVE WITH HIM.
MAYBE IT'S THE SAME AS WHAT'S OFTEN SEEN WITH ANIMALS...
A TYPE OF IMPRINTING PROCESS?
HE'S MY MASTER, SO MAYBE IT'S NORMAL FOR ME TO BE IN LOVE WITH HIM...?
BUT THAT CAN'T BE THE ONLY REASON.
THE LONELINESS I FELT WITHIN HIM WAS SIMILAR TO MINE.
EACH TIME I DISCOVERED THE DARKNESS INSIDE MASTER ENJU'S HEART, I FELT I WASN'T ALONE.

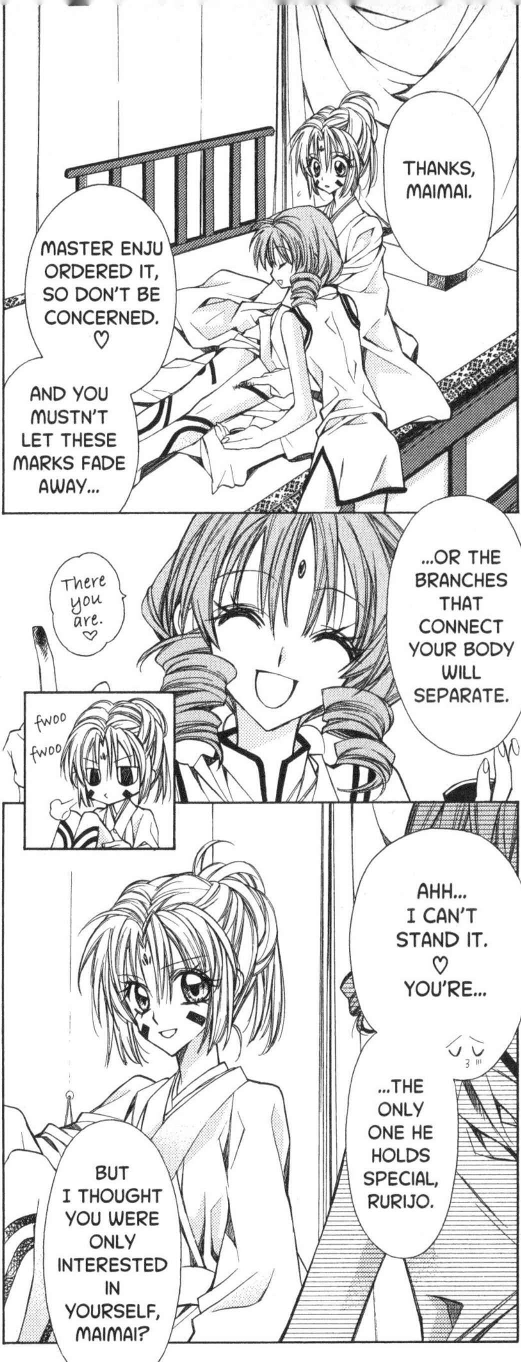
THANKS, MAIMAI.
MASTER ENJU ORDERED IT, SO DON'T BE CONCERNED. ♡
AND YOU MUSTN'T LET THESE MARKS FADE AWAY...
...OR THE BRANCHES THAT CONNECT YOUR BODY WILL SEPARATE.
There you are. ♡
fwoo
fwoo
AHH... I CAN'T STAND IT. ♡ YOU'RE...
...THE ONLY ONE HE HOLDS SPECIAL, RURIJO.
BUT I THOUGHT YOU WERE ONLY INTERESTED IN YOURSELF, MAIMAI?

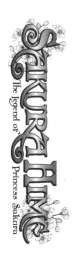

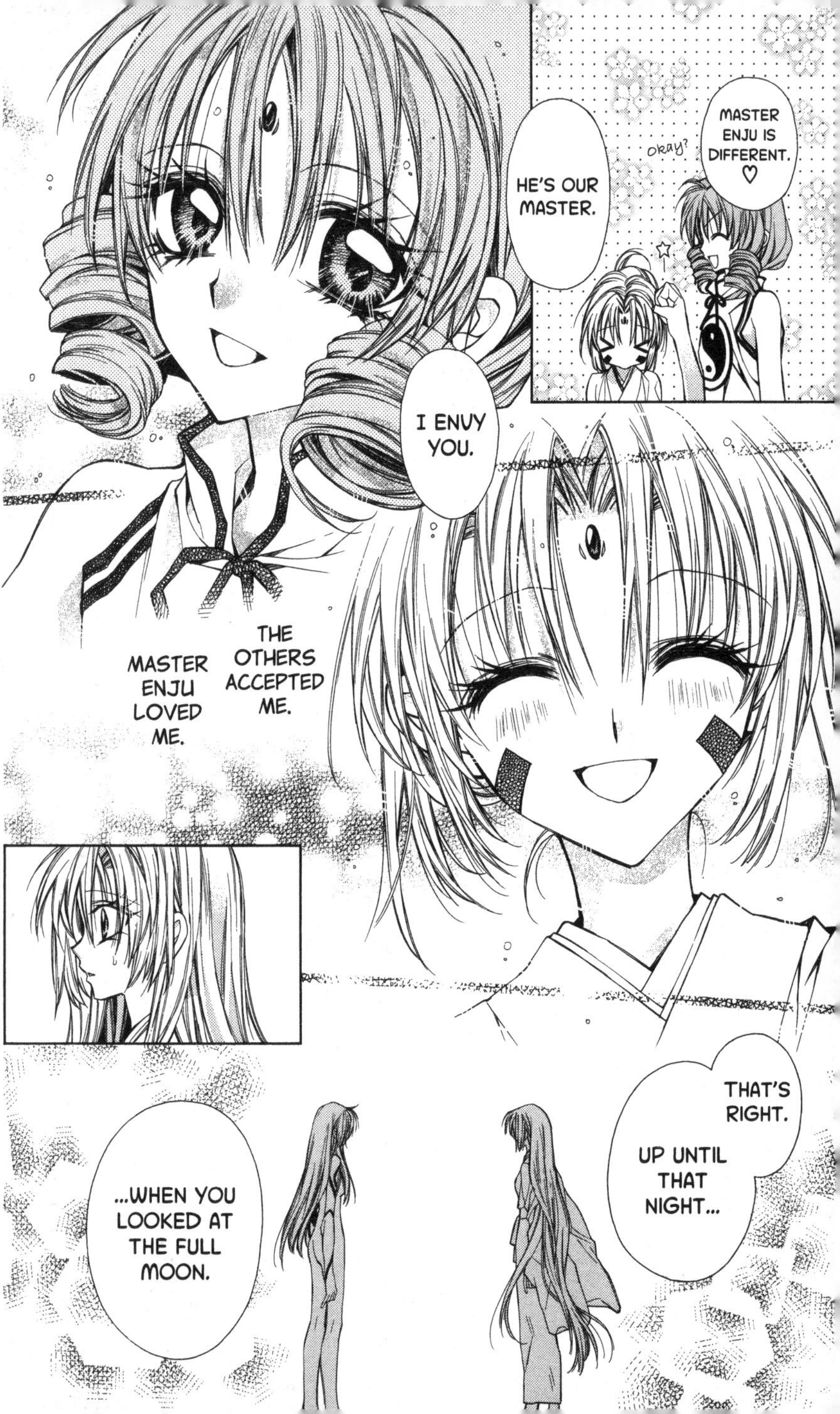
MASTER ENJU IS DIFFERENT. ♡
Okay?
HE'S OUR MASTER.
I ENVY YOU.
THE OTHERS ACCEPTED ME.
MASTER ENJU LOVED ME.
THAT'S RIGHT.
UP UNTIL THAT NIGHT...
...WHEN YOU LOOKED AT THE FULL MOON.

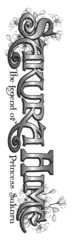

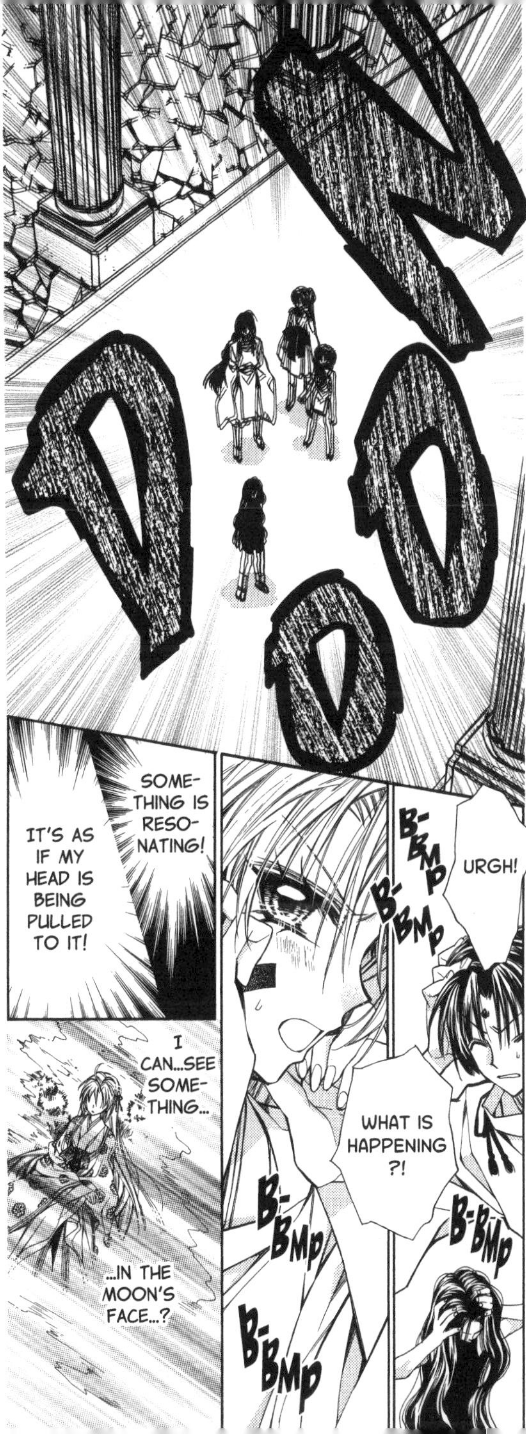
DOON
B-BMP
URGH!
B-BMP
B-BMP
WHAT IS HAPPENING ?!
B-BMP
B-BMP
SOME-THING IS RESO-NATING!
IT'S AS IF MY HEAD IS BEING PULLED TO IT!
I CAN...SEE SOME-THING...
...IN THE MOON'S FACE...?

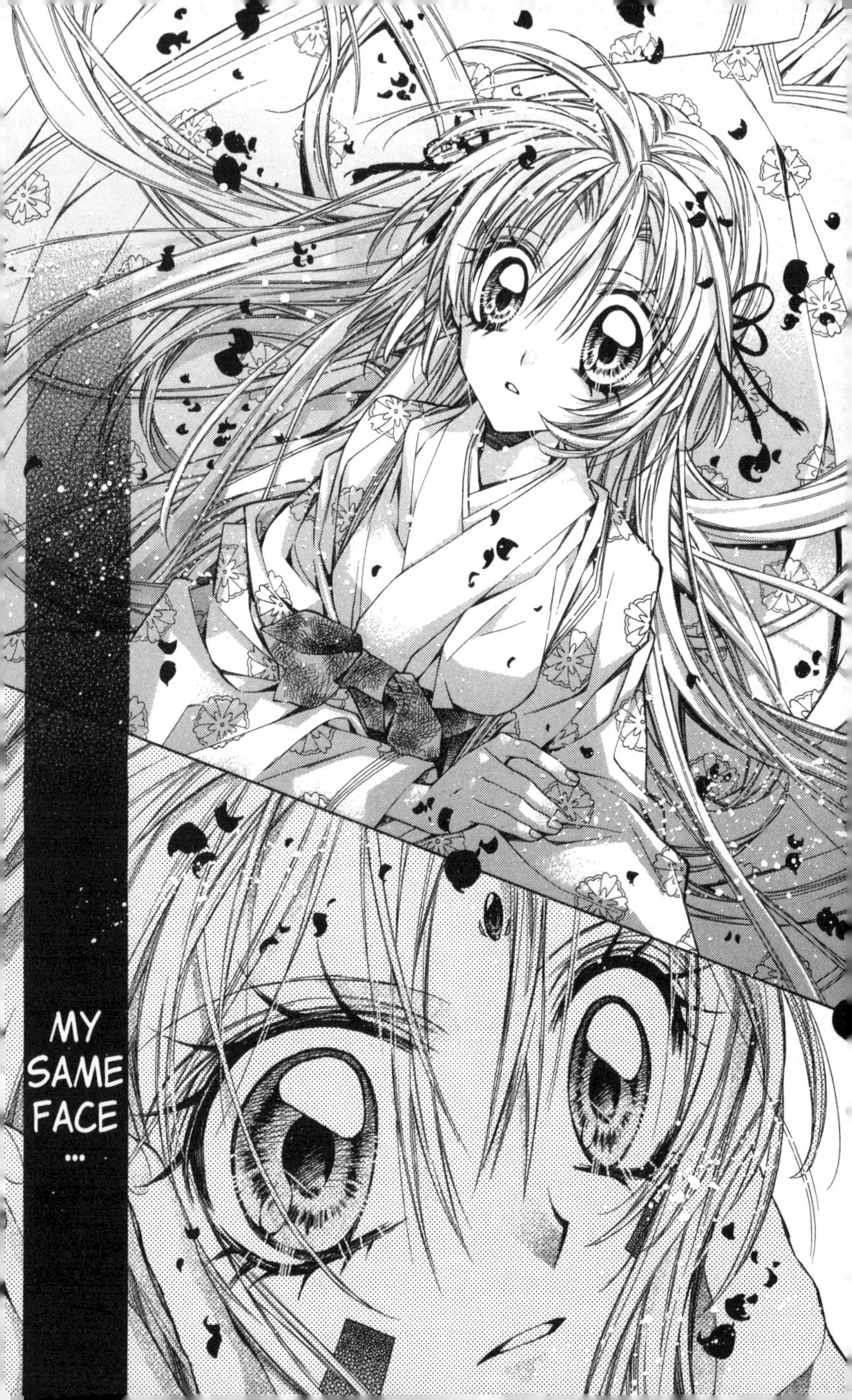
MY SAME FACE ...

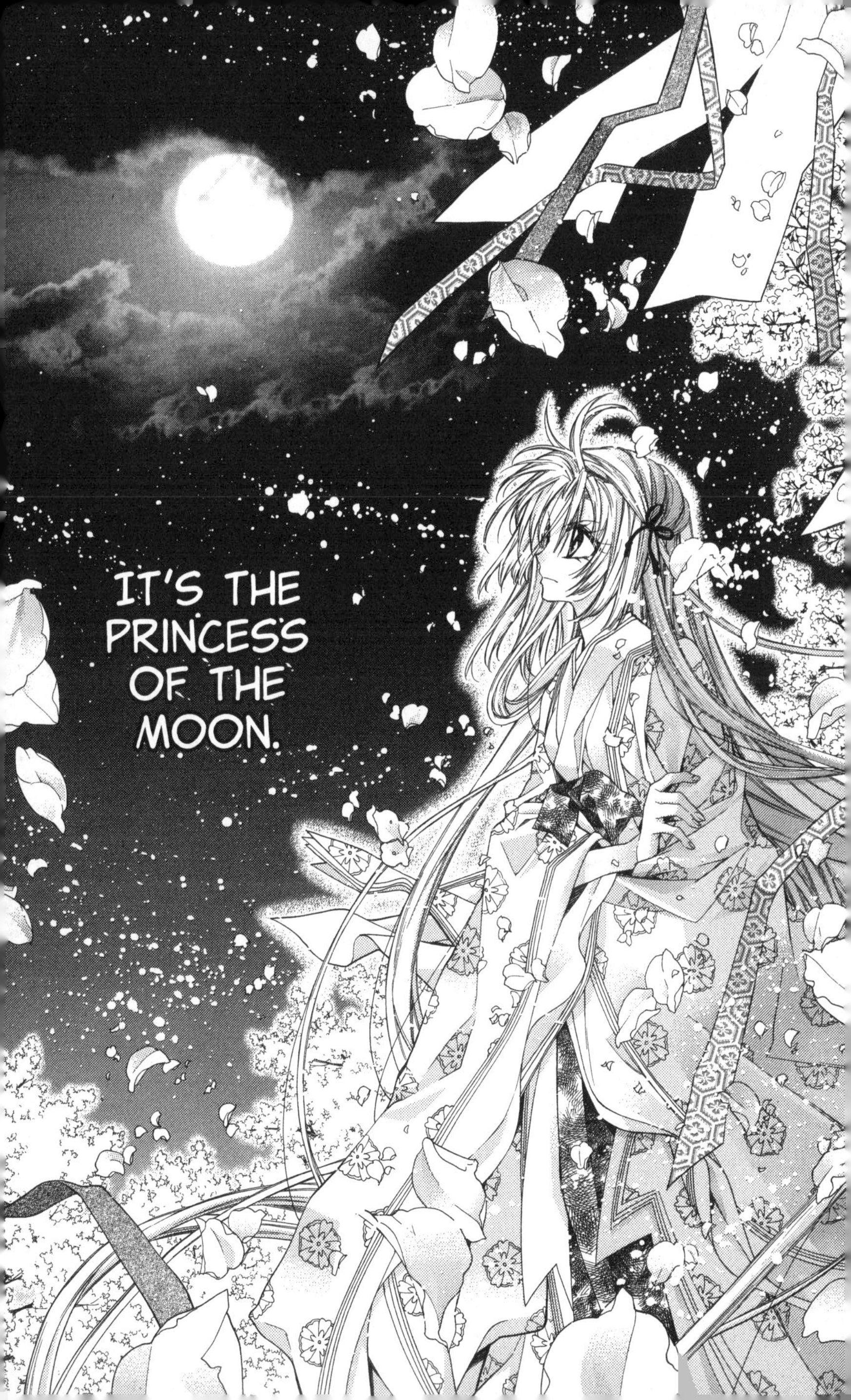
IT'S THE PRINCESS OF THE MOON.

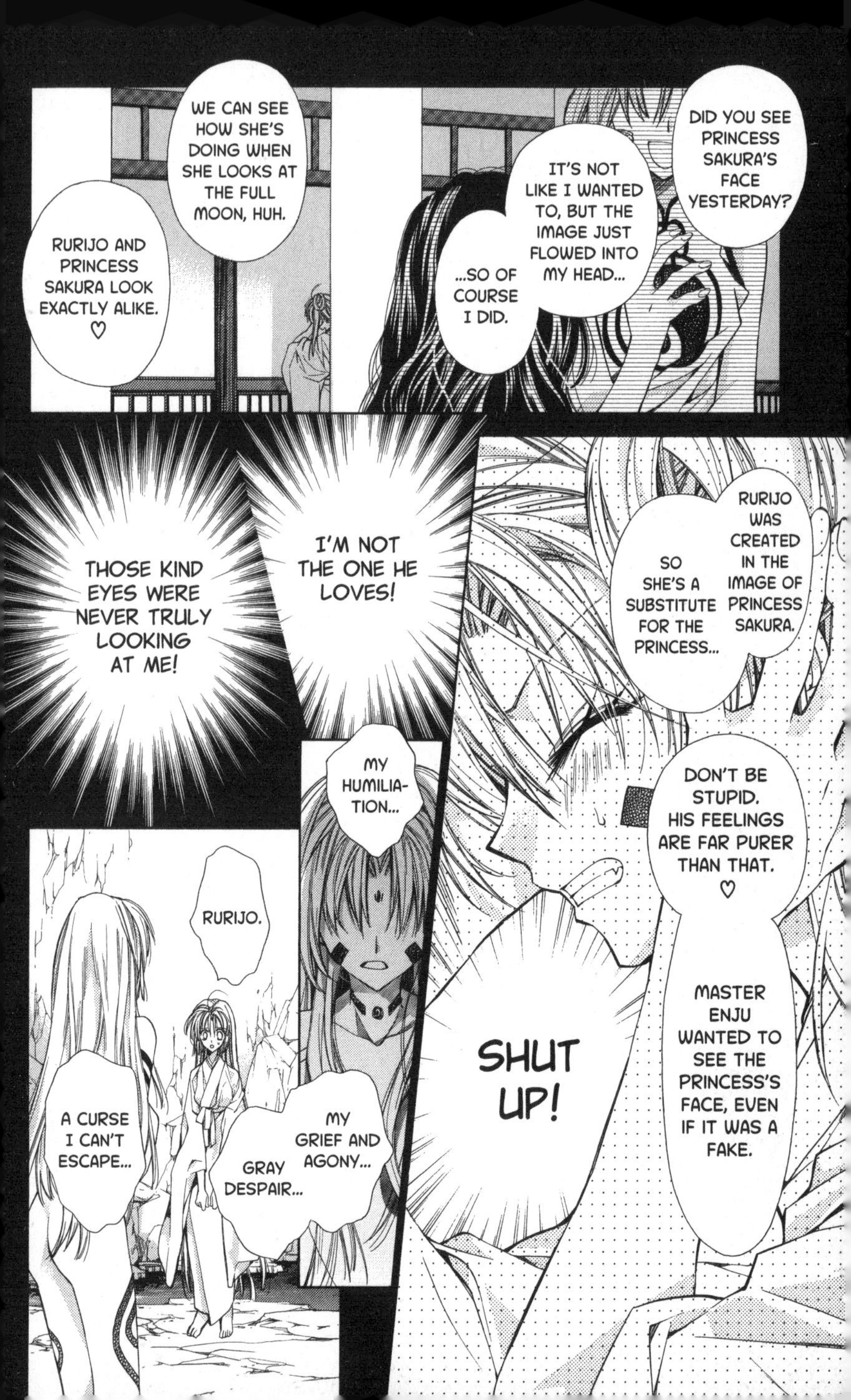
DID YOU SEE PRINCESS SAKURA'S FACE YESTERDAY?
IT'S NOT LIKE I WANTED TO, BUT THE IMAGE JUST FLOWED INTO MY HEAD...
...SO OF COURSE I DID.
WE CAN SEE HOW SHE'S DOING WHEN SHE LOOKS AT THE FULL MOON, HUH.
RURIJO AND PRINCESS SAKURA LOOK EXACTLY ALIKE. ♡
RURIJO WAS CREATED IN THE IMAGE OF PRINCESS SAKURA.
SO SHE'S A SUBSTITUTE FOR THE PRINCESS...
DON'T BE STUPID. HIS FEELINGS ARE FAR PURER THAN THAT. ♡
MASTER ENJU WANTED TO SEE THE PRINCESS'S FACE, EVEN IF IT WAS A FAKE.
SHUT UP!
I'M NOT THE ONE HE LOVES!
THOSE KIND EYES WERE NEVER TRULY LOOKING AT ME!
MY HUMILIATION...
MY GRIEF AND AGONY...
GRAY DESPAIR...
RURIJO.
A CURSE I CAN'T ESCAPE...

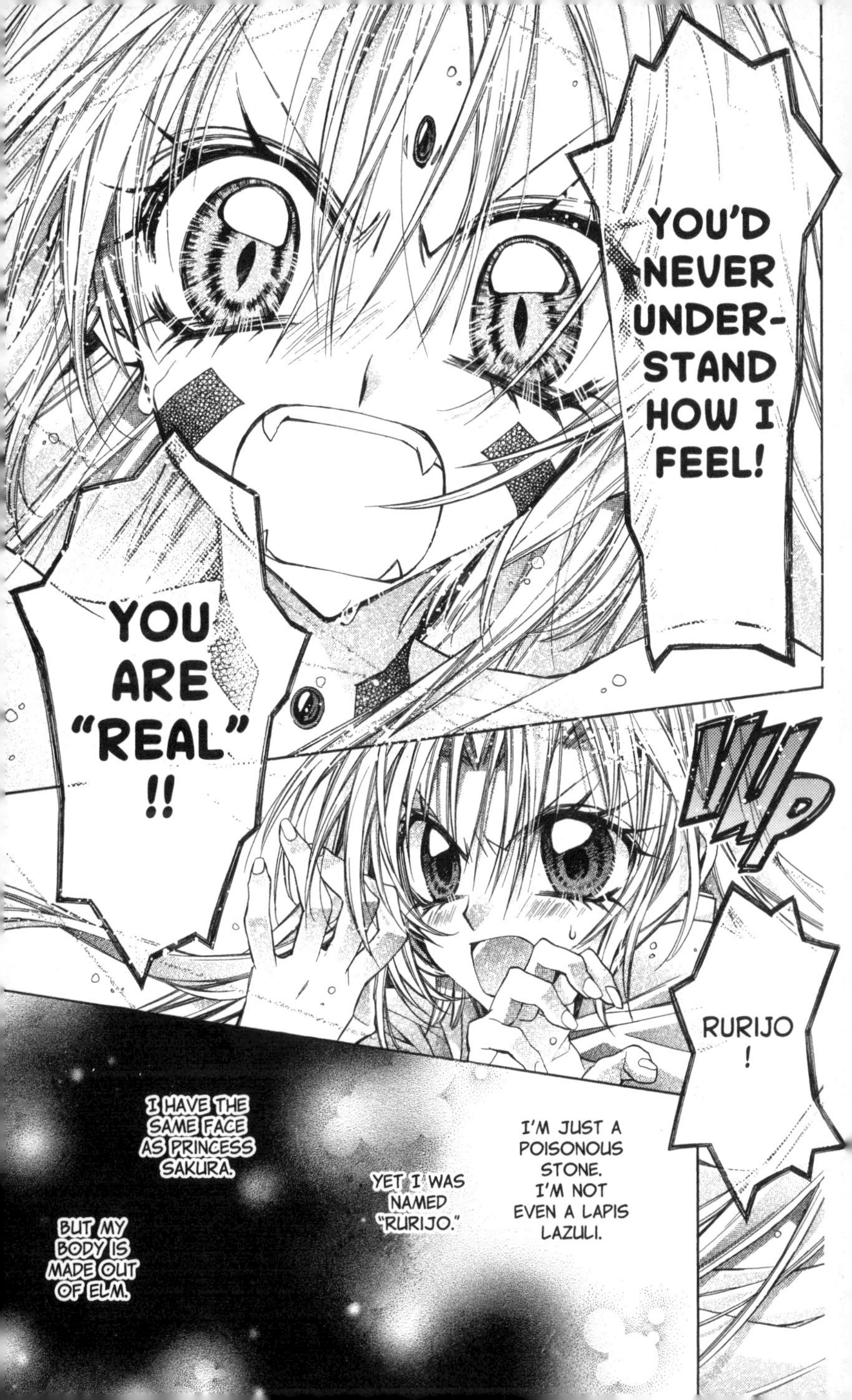
YOU'D NEVER UNDERSTAND HOW I FEEL!
YOU ARE "REAL"!!
WHAP
RURIJO!
I'M JUST A POISONOUS STONE. I'M NOT EVEN A LAPIS LAZULI.
YET I WAS NAMED "RURIJO."
I HAVE THE SAME FACE AS PRINCESS SAKURA.
BUT MY BODY IS MADE OUT OF ELM.

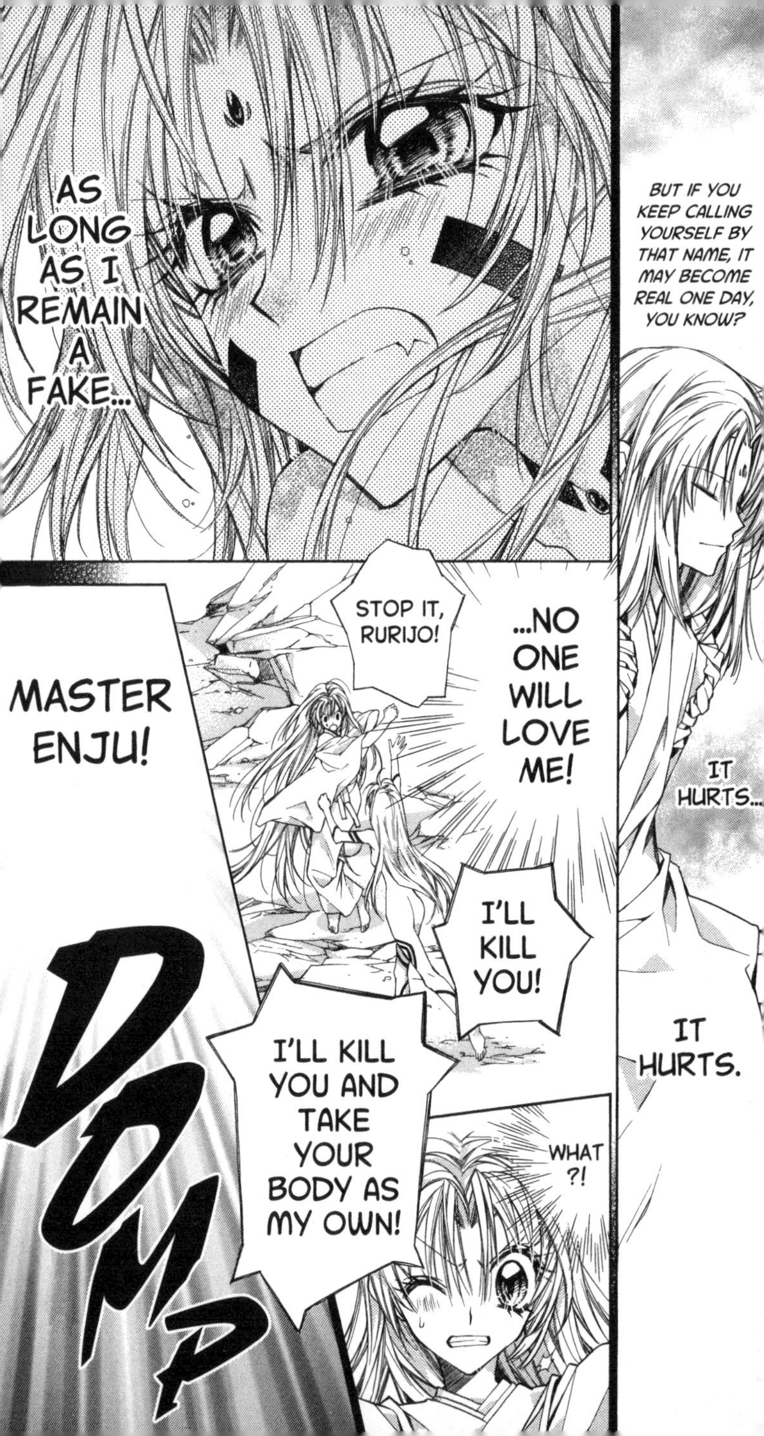
BUT IF YOU KEEP CALLING YOURSELF BY THAT NAME, IT MAY BECOME REAL ONE DAY, YOU KNOW?
IT HURTS...
IT HURTS.
AS LONG AS I REMAIN A FAKE...
...NO ONE WILL LOVE ME!
STOP IT, RURIJO!
I'LL KILL YOU!
I'LL KILL YOU AND TAKE YOUR BODY AS MY OWN!
WHAT?!
MASTER ENJU!
DOMP

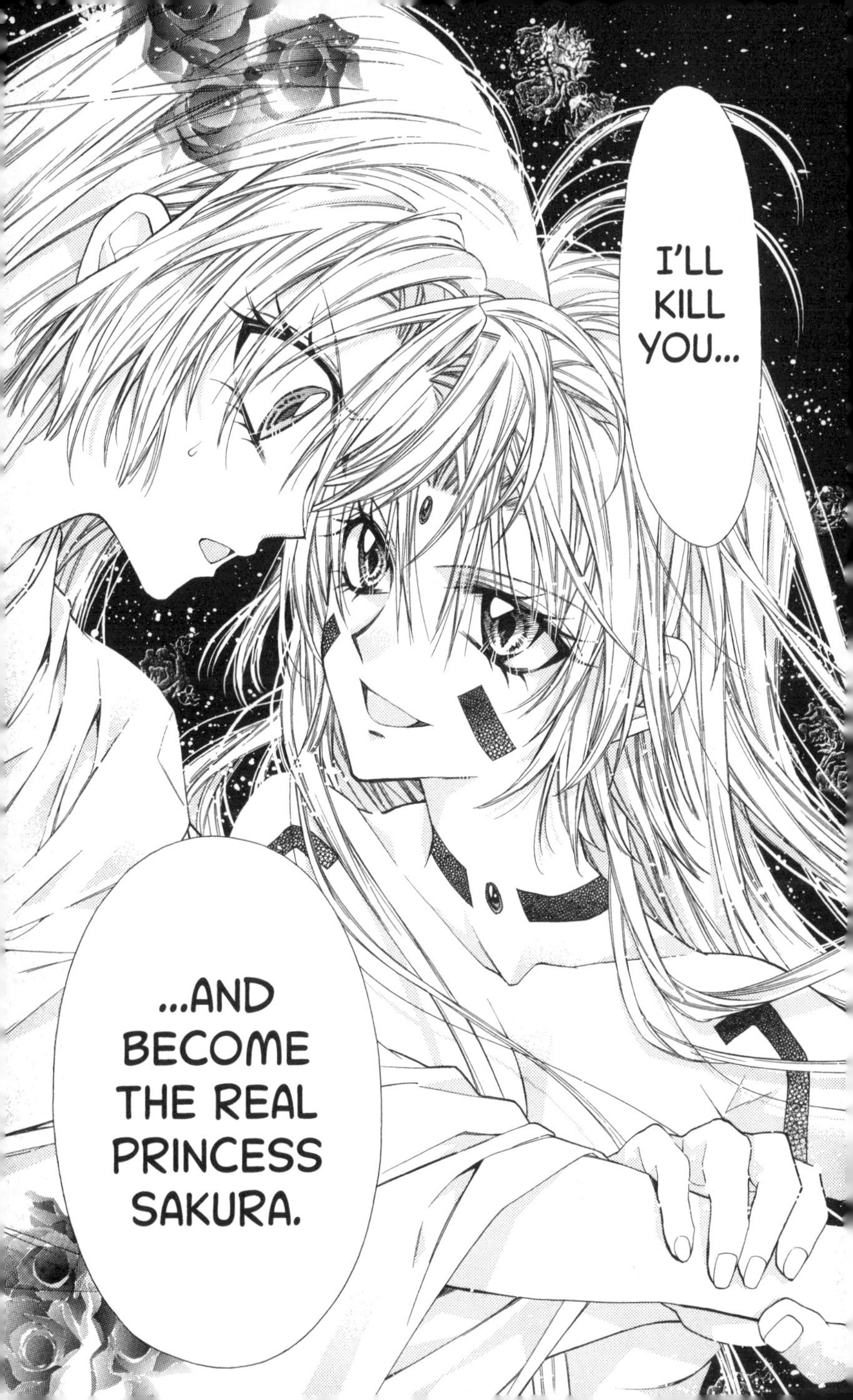
I'LL KILL YOU...
...AND BECOME THE REAL PRINCESS SAKURA.

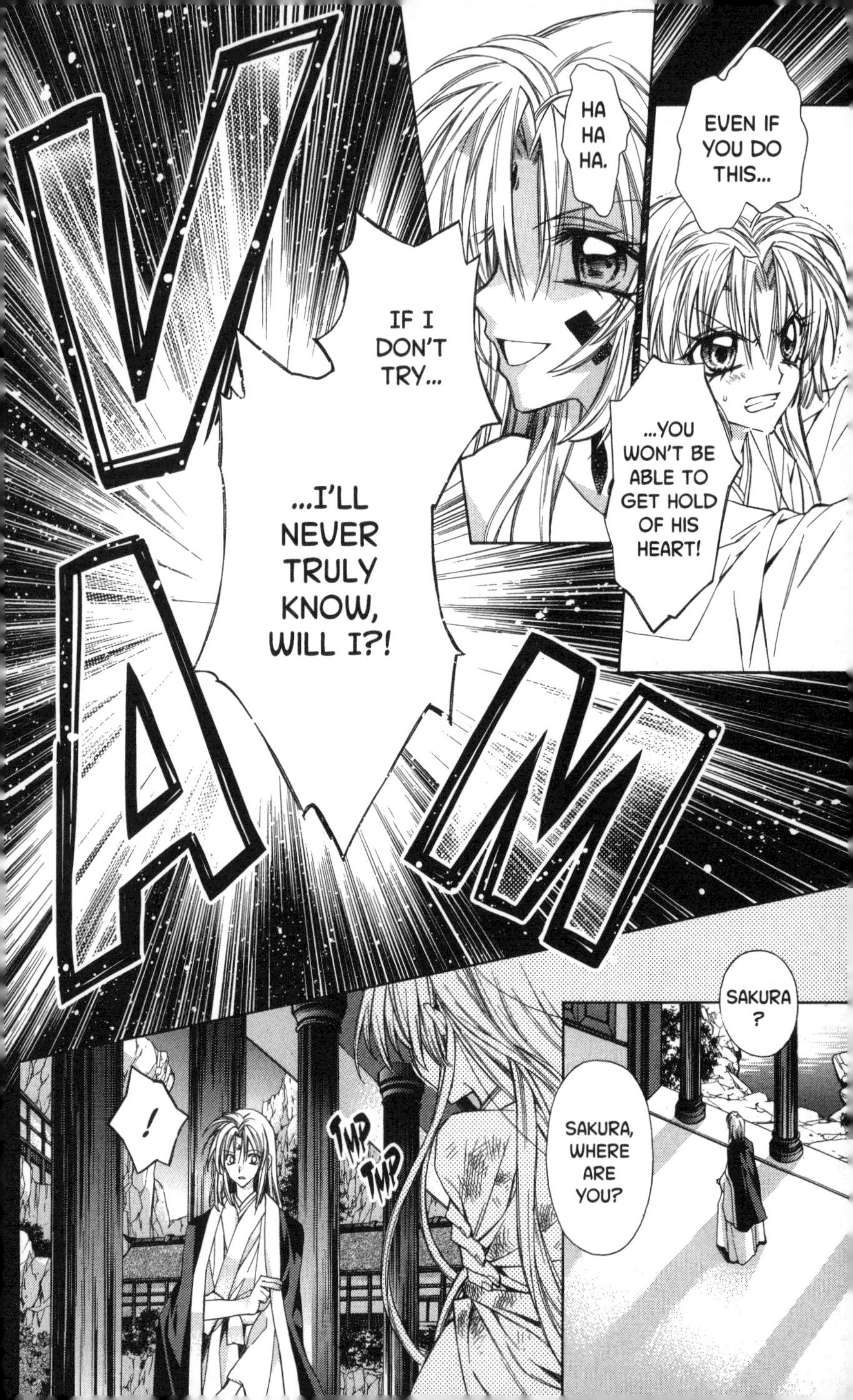
EVEN IF YOU DO THIS...
...YOU WON'T BE ABLE TO GET HOLD OF HIS HEART!
HA HA HA.
IF I DON'T TRY...
...I'LL NEVER TRULY KNOW, WILL I?!
WAM
SAKURA?
SAKURA, WHERE ARE YOU?
TMP TMP
!

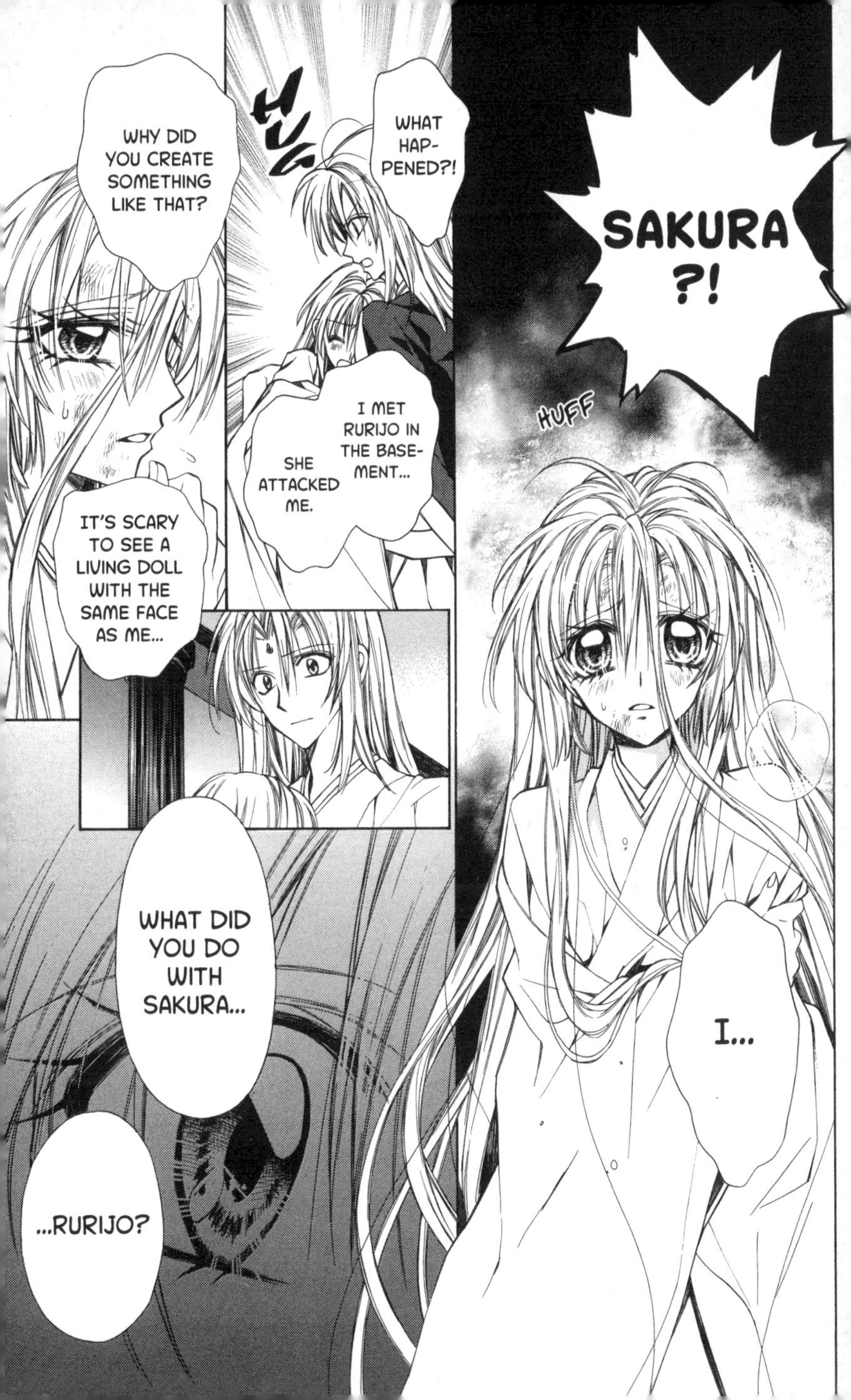
SAKURA ?!
HUFF
I...
HUG
WHAT HAPPENED?!
I MET RURIJO IN THE BASEMENT...
SHE ATTACKED ME.
WHY DID YOU CREATE SOMETHING LIKE THAT?
IT'S SCARY TO SEE A LIVING DOLL WITH THE SAME FACE AS ME...
WHAT DID YOU DO WITH SAKURA...
...RURIJO?

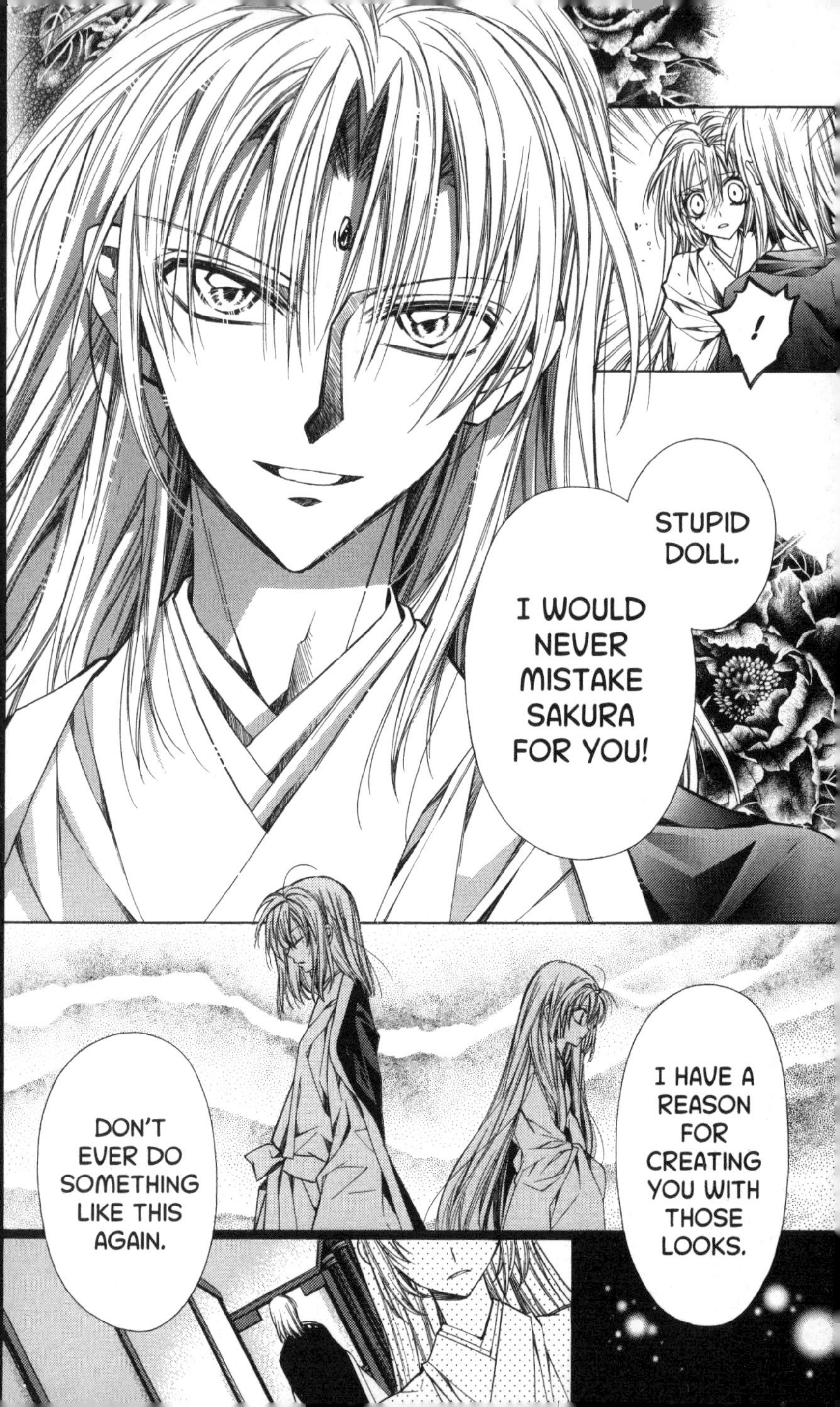
!
STUPID DOLL.
I WOULD NEVER MISTAKE SAKURA FOR YOU!
I HAVE A REASON FOR CREATING YOU WITH THOSE LOOKS.
DON'T EVER DO SOMETHING LIKE THIS AGAIN.

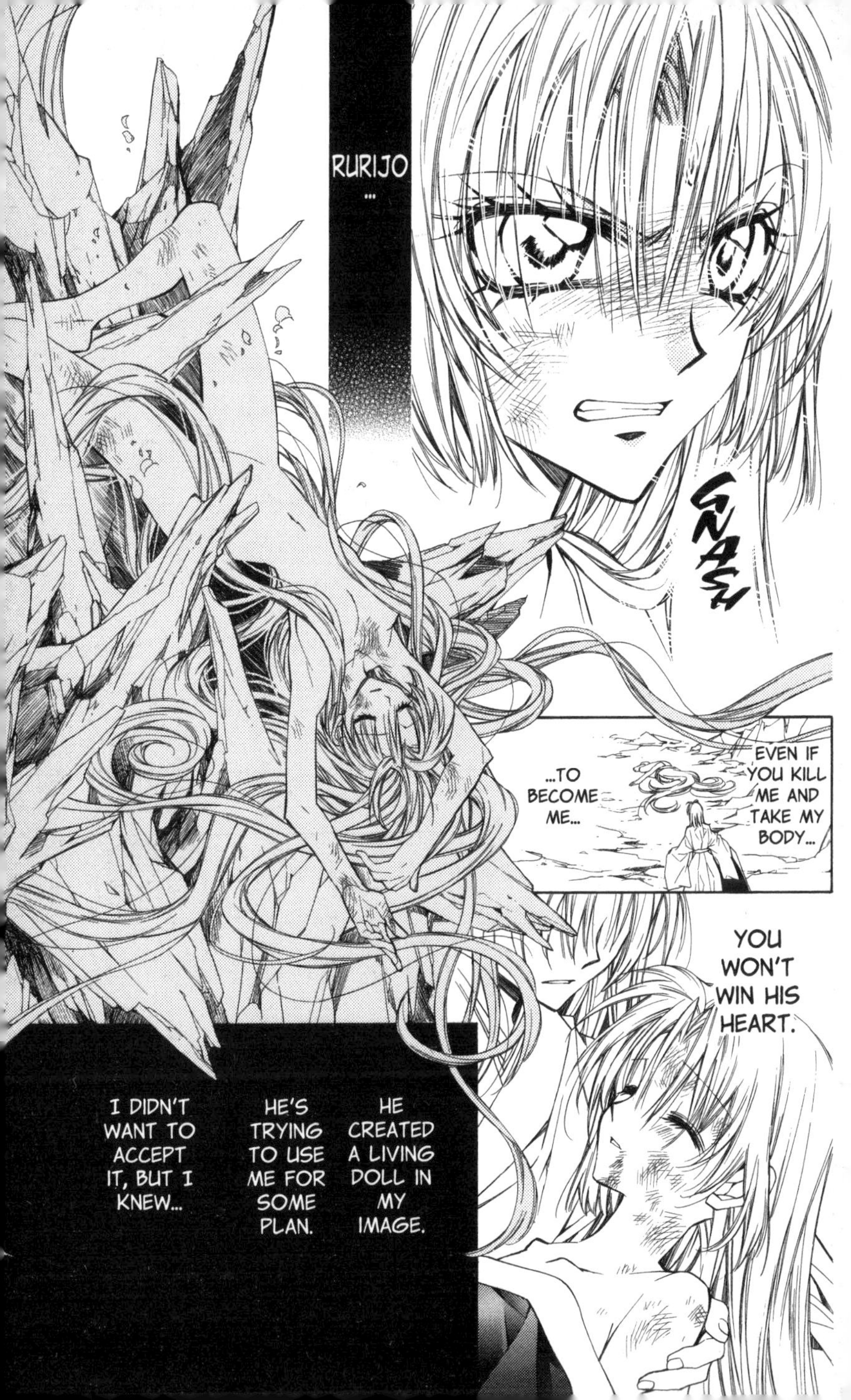
RURIJO...
GNASH
EVEN IF YOU KILL ME AND TAKE MY BODY...
...TO BECOME ME...
YOU WON'T WIN HIS HEART.
HE CREATED A LIVING DOLL IN MY IMAGE.
HE'S TRYING TO USE ME FOR SOME PLAN.
I DIDN'T WANT TO ACCEPT IT, BUT I KNEW...

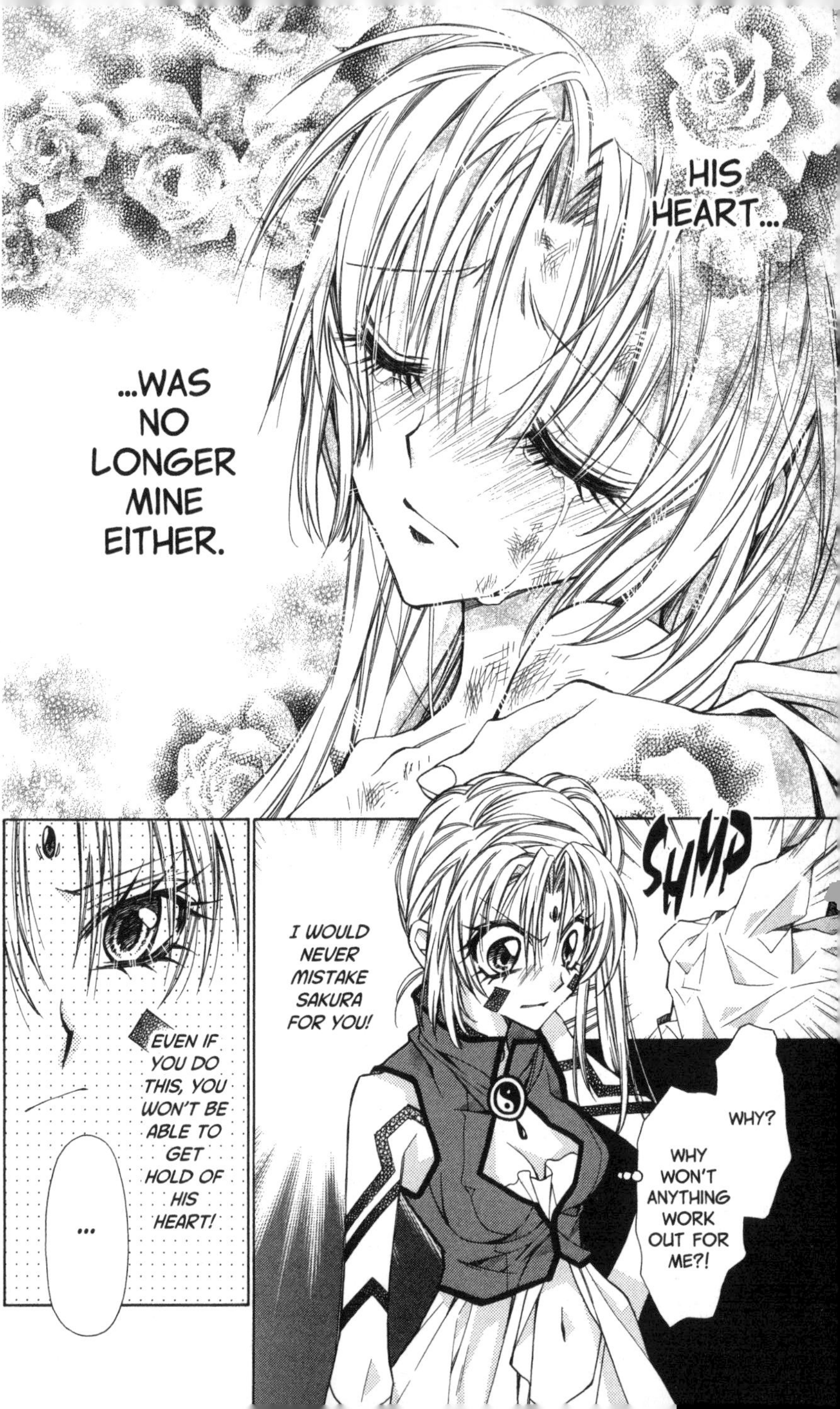
HIS HEART...
...WAS NO LONGER MINE EITHER.
SHMP
I WOULD NEVER MISTAKE SAKURA FOR YOU!
WHY?
WHY WON'T ANYTHING WORK OUT FOR ME?!
EVEN IF YOU DO THIS, YOU WON'T BE ABLE TO GET HOLD OF HIS HEART!
...

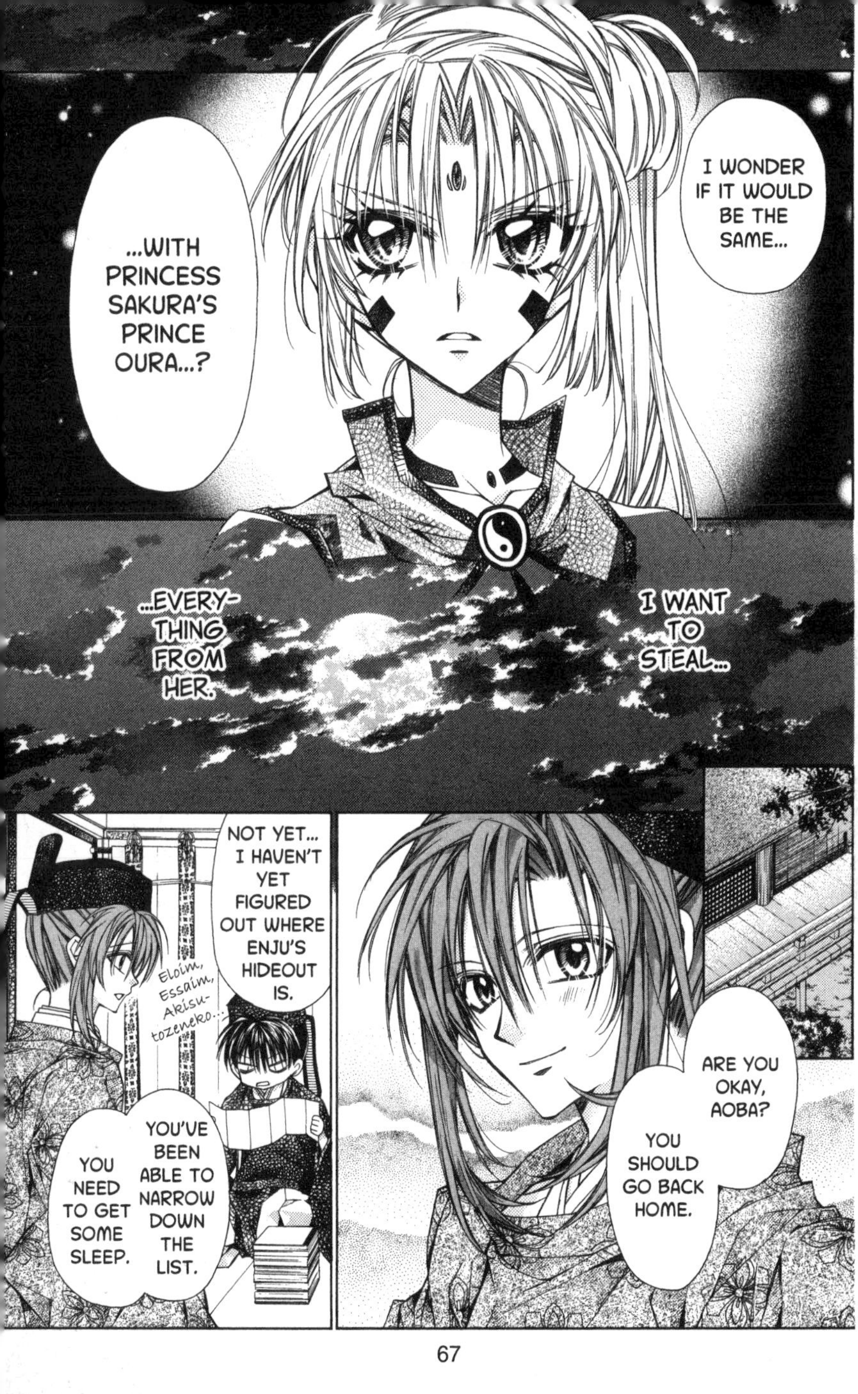
I WONDER IF IT WOULD BE THE SAME...
...WITH PRINCESS SAKURA'S PRINCE OURA...?
I WANT TO STEAL...
...EVERY-THING FROM HER.
ARE YOU OKAY, AOBA?
YOU SHOULD GO BACK HOME.
NOT YET... I HAVEN'T YET FIGURED OUT WHERE ENJU'S HIDEOUT IS.
Eloím, Essaim, Akisu-tozeneko...
YOU'VE BEEN ABLE TO NARROW DOWN THE LIST.
YOU NEED TO GET SOME SLEEP.

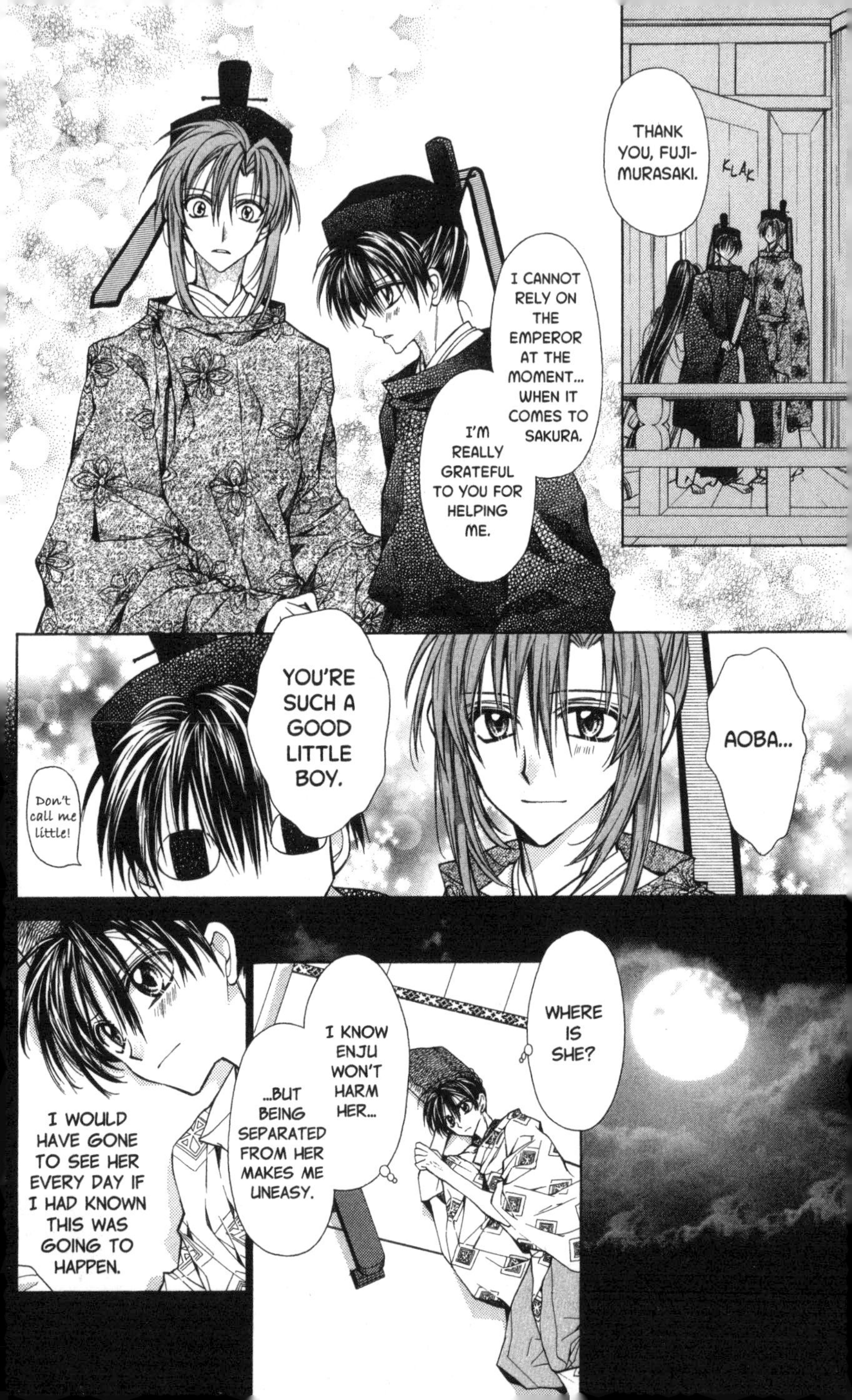
THANK YOU, FUJI-MURASAKI.
KLAK
I CANNOT RELY ON THE EMPEROR AT THE MOMENT... WHEN IT COMES TO SAKURA.
I'M REALLY GRATEFUL TO YOU FOR HELPING ME.
AOBA...
YOU'RE SUCH A GOOD LITTLE BOY.
Don't call me little!
WHERE IS SHE?
I KNOW ENJU WON'T HARM HER...
...BUT BEING SEPARATED FROM HER MAKES ME UNEASY.
I WOULD HAVE GONE TO SEE HER EVERY DAY IF I HAD KNOWN THIS WAS GOING TO HAPPEN.

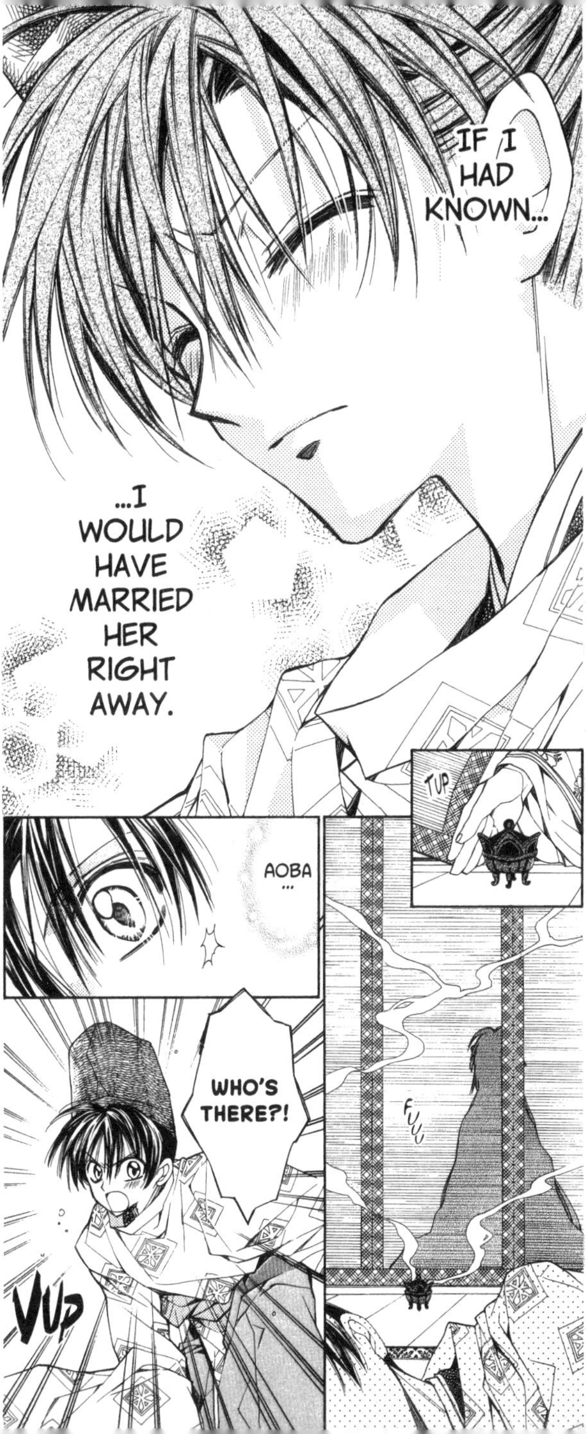
IF I HAD KNOWN...
...I WOULD HAVE MARRIED HER RIGHT AWAY.
TUP
FUUU
AOBA...
WHO'S THERE?!
VUP

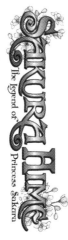

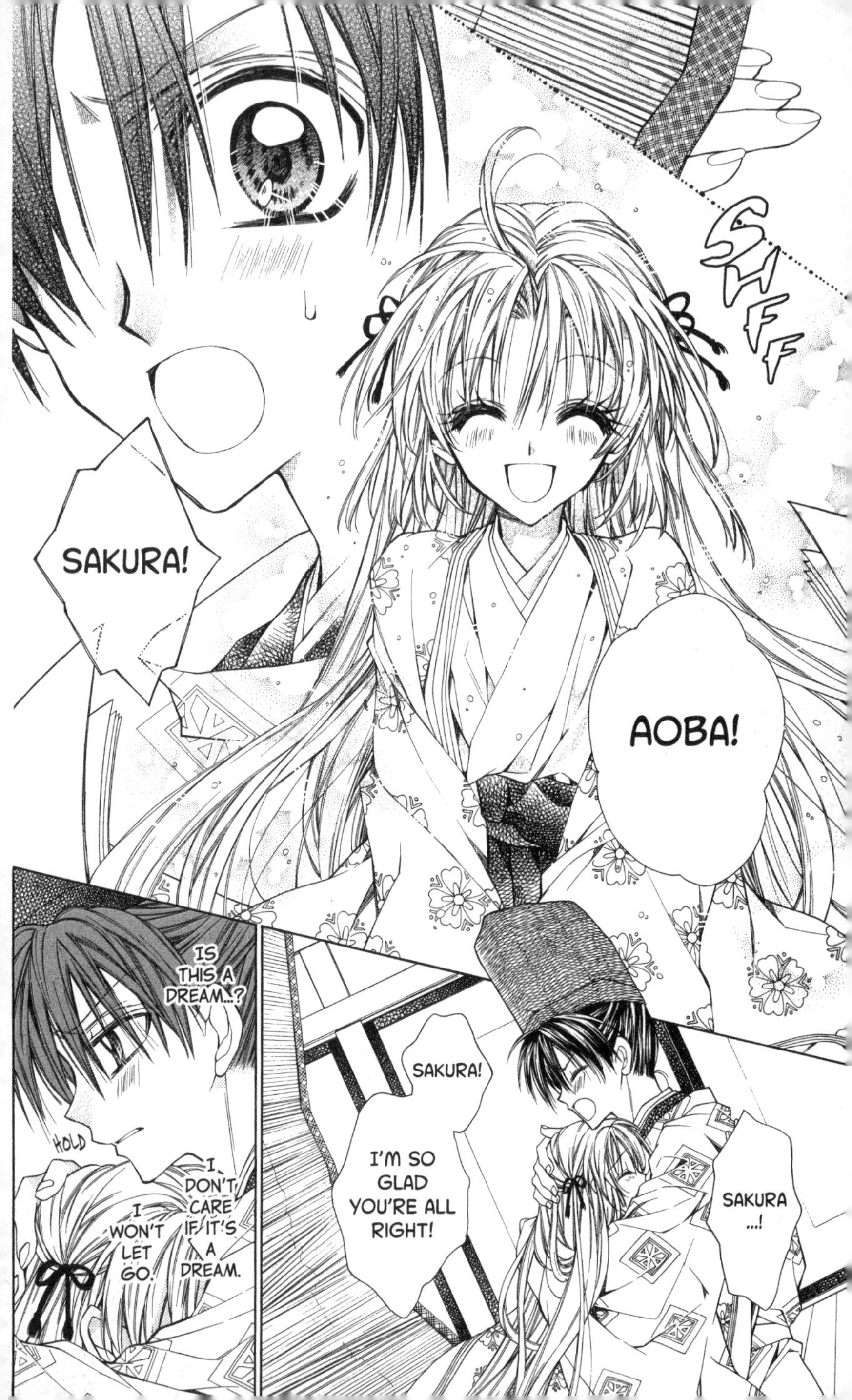
SHFF
AOBA!
SAKURA!
SAKURA!
I'M SO GLAD YOU'RE ALL RIGHT!
SAKURA ...!
IS THIS A DREAM...?
HOLD
I DON'T CARE IF IT'S A DREAM.
I WON'T LET GO.

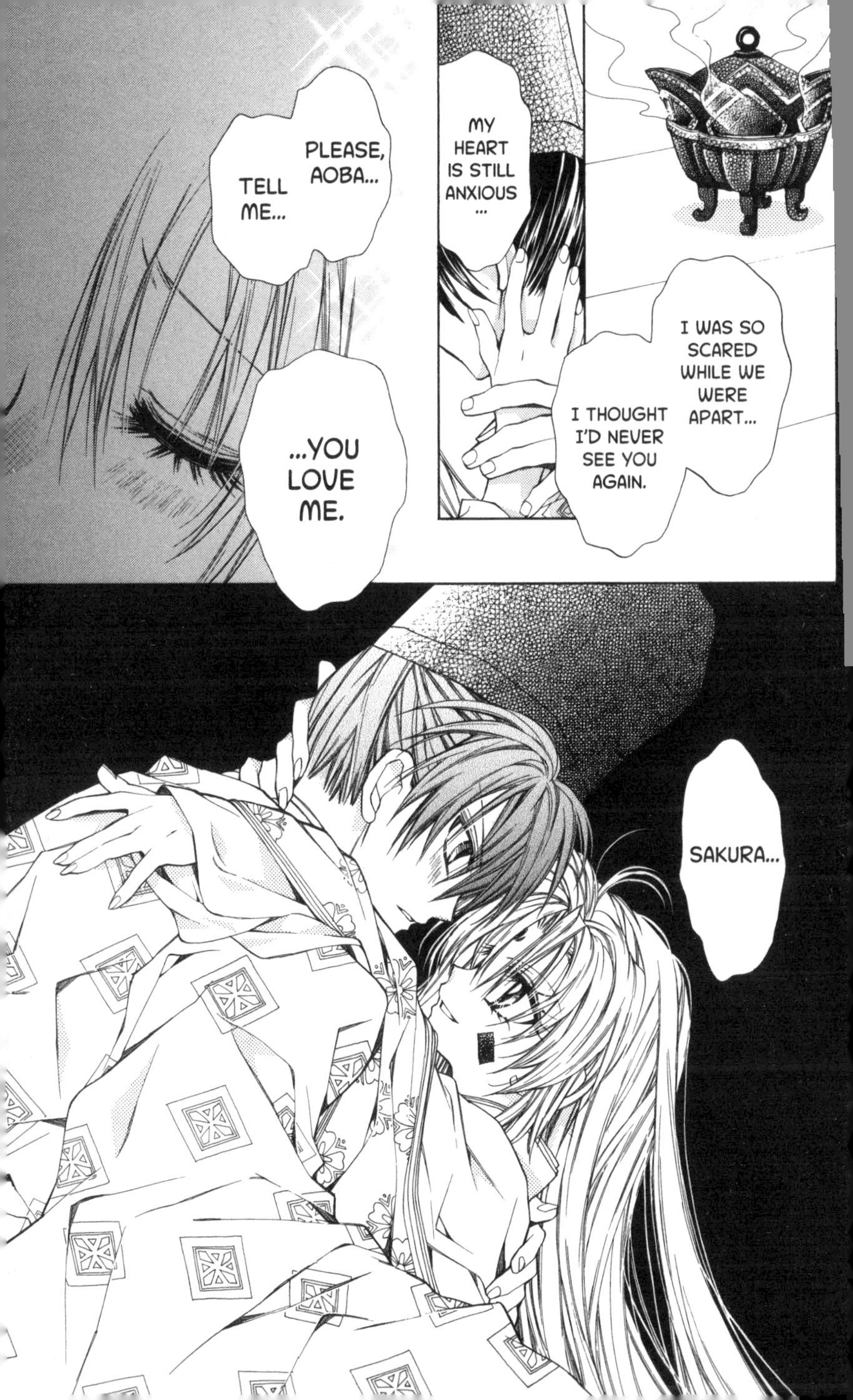
I WAS SO SCARED WHILE WE WERE APART...
I THOUGHT I'D NEVER SEE YOU AGAIN.
MY HEART IS STILL ANXIOUS...
PLEASE, AOBA...
TELL ME...
...YOU LOVE ME.
SAKURA...

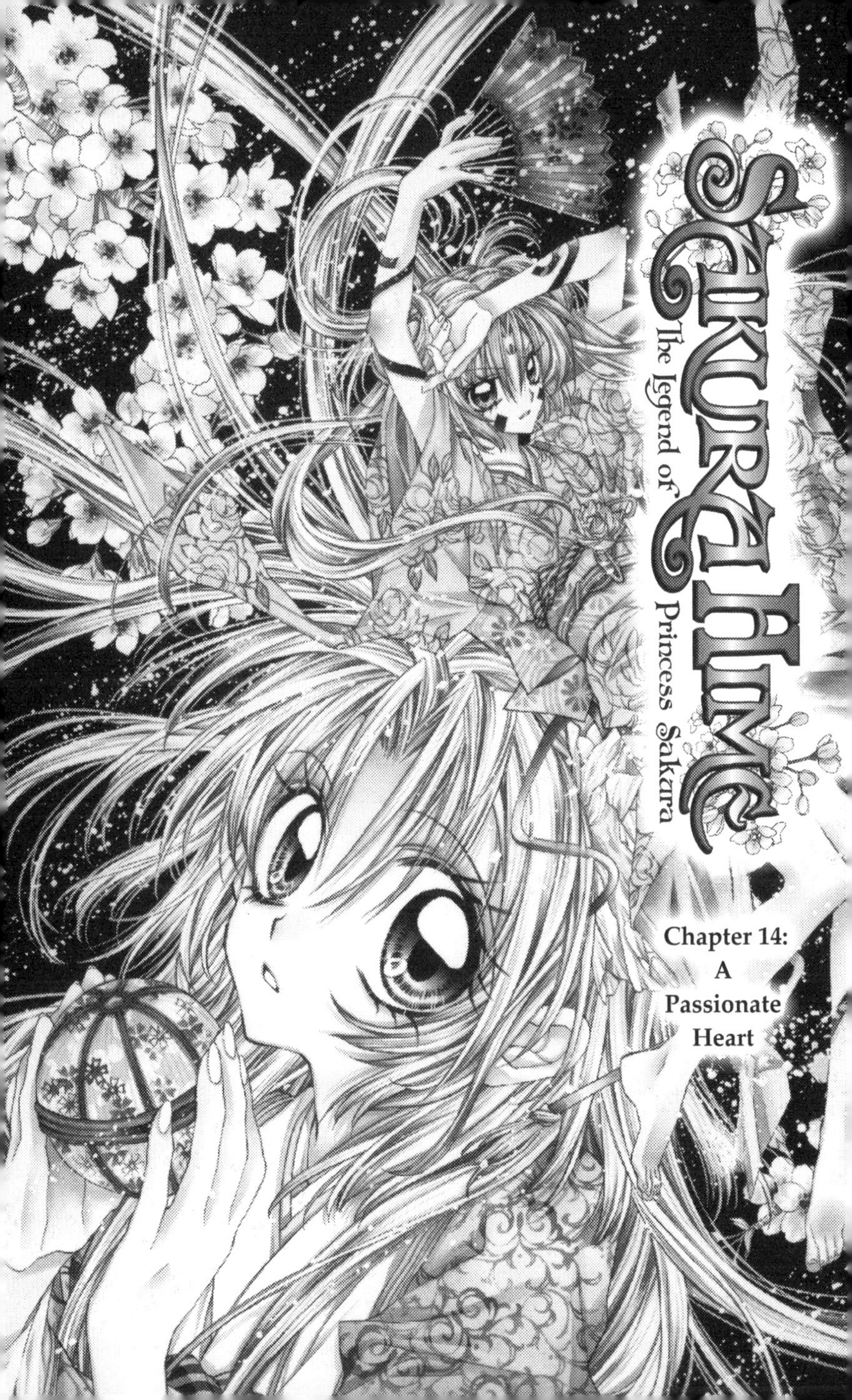
Sakura Hime
The Legend of Princess Sakura
Chapter 14:
A
Passionate
Heart

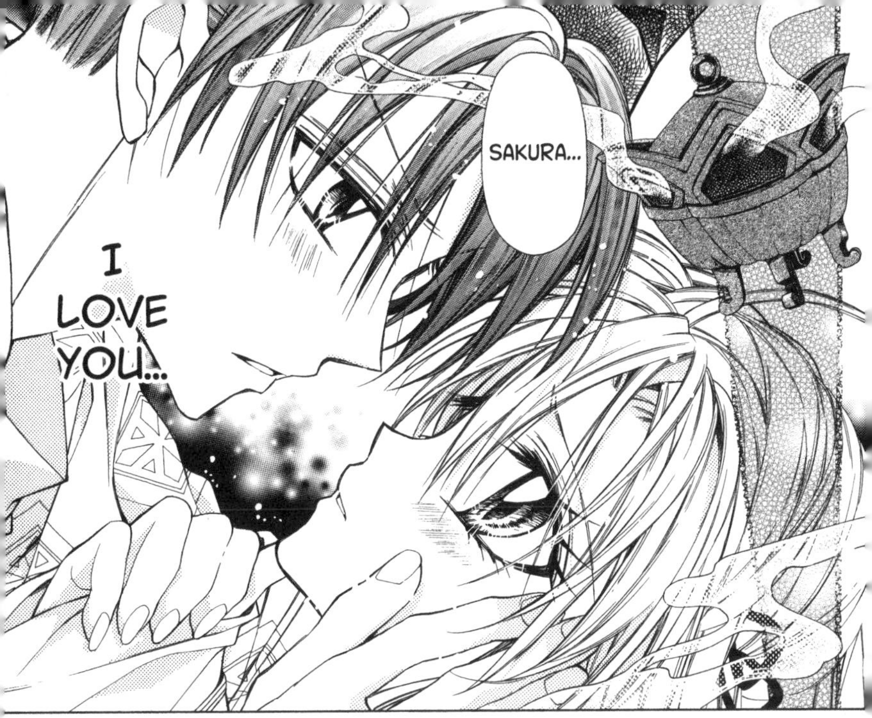
SAKURA...
I LOVE YOU...

Chapter 14: A Passionate Heart

※ I'm giving away the story.

Some people may think Rurijo is somewhat hard to understand, but, how can I put it... She has a different kind of common sense(?). She acts on instinct and is animal-like, so she's basically exactly as you see her. (She reverts into leaves in the story. Those leaves will scatter if she doesn't have the marks drawn on her body.)

Enju has already left me and is moving completely on his own... Before working on the storyboard, I often daydream and hold a meeting inside my head, but he won't even talk to me anymore... It seems he doesn't like idiots...

I'm sorry. ; We've just entered this arc (the battle against the members of the moon), so there are so many things I can't tell you yet. That's why I'm being so hesitant. ;

The battles begin in the last half of this chapter. The others all have a reason to fight because of the past except Byakuya and Maimai. I was worried that Maimai may not stand out among the other characters, so that's why I made him a boy. (I was really wondering whether I should do that or not until the very end.) ← And if Maimai was a girl, she'd be slightly similar to Kohaku...

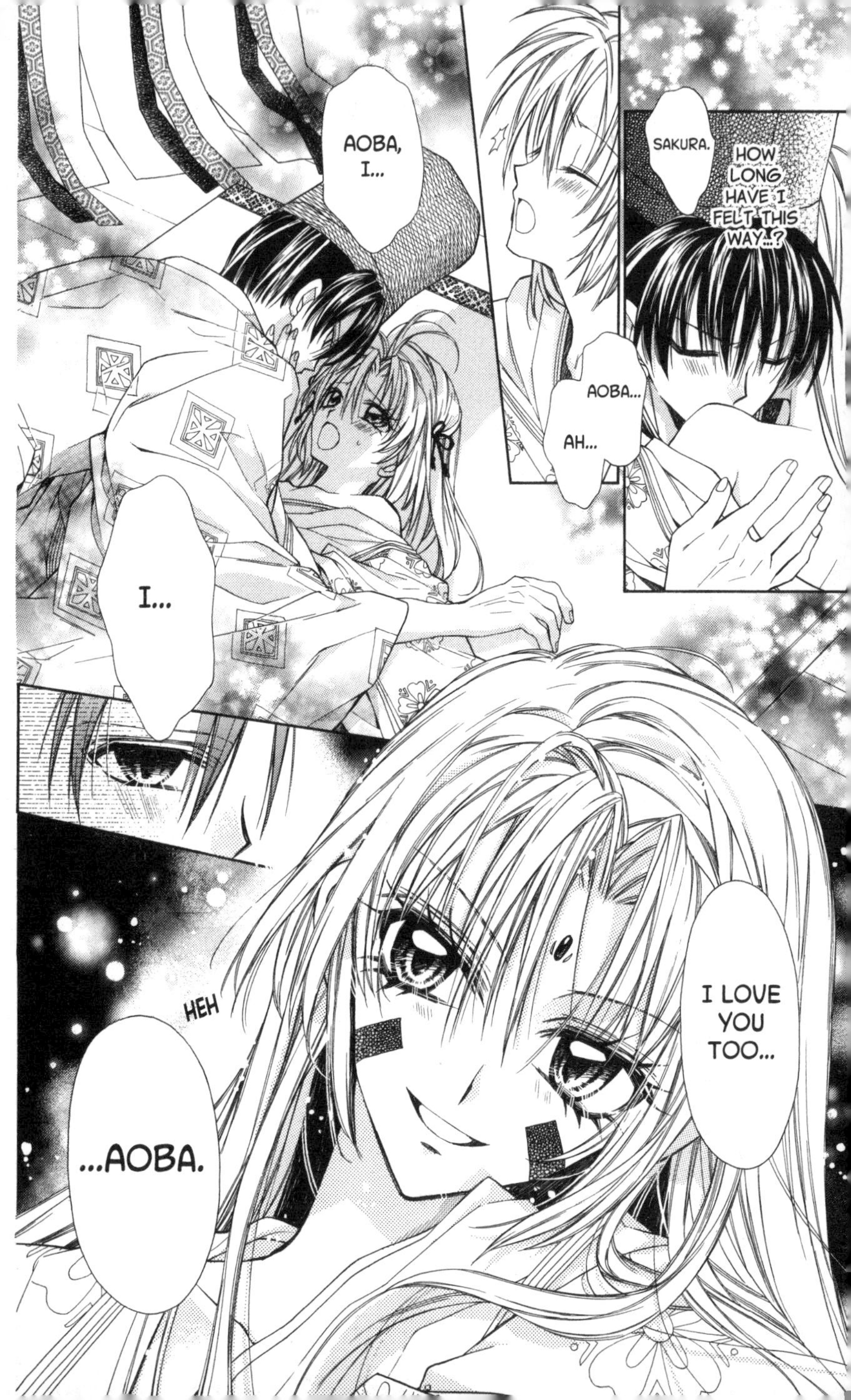
SAKURA.
HOW LONG HAVE I FELT THIS WAY...?
AOBA...
AH...
AOBA, I...
I...
I LOVE YOU TOO...
HEH
...AOBA.

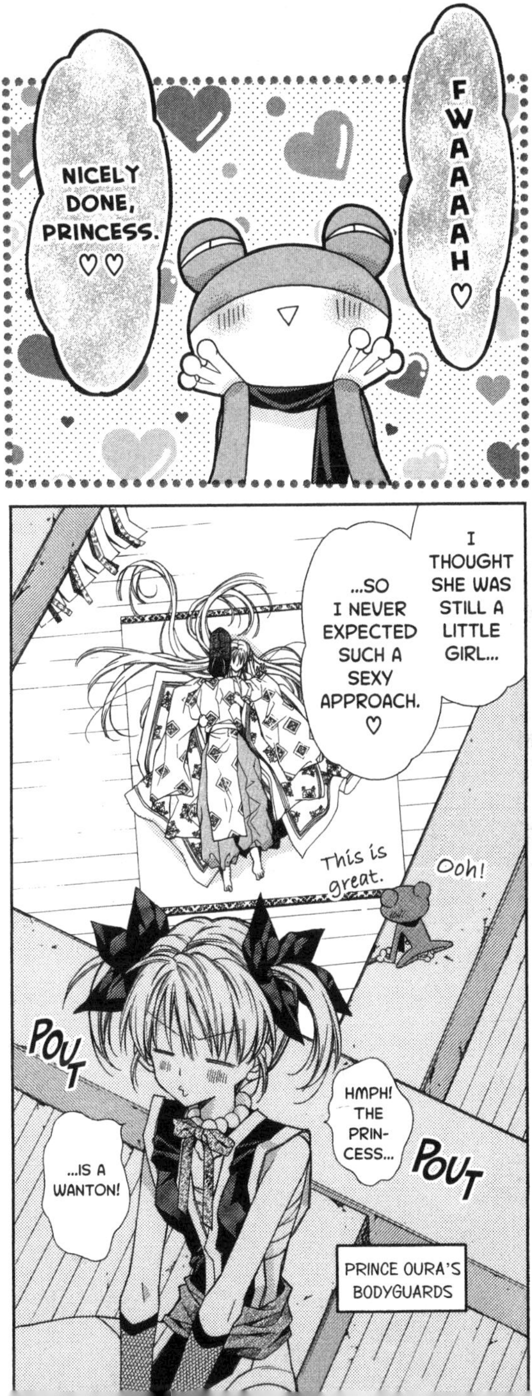
FWAAAAH ♡
NICELY DONE, PRINCESS. ♡♡
I THOUGHT SHE WAS STILL A LITTLE GIRL...
...SO I NEVER EXPECTED SUCH A SEXY APPROACH. ♡
Ooh!
This is great.
POUT
HMPH! THE PRIN-CESS...
POUT
...IS A WANTON!
PRINCE OURA'S BODYGUARDS

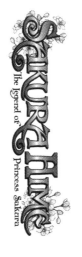

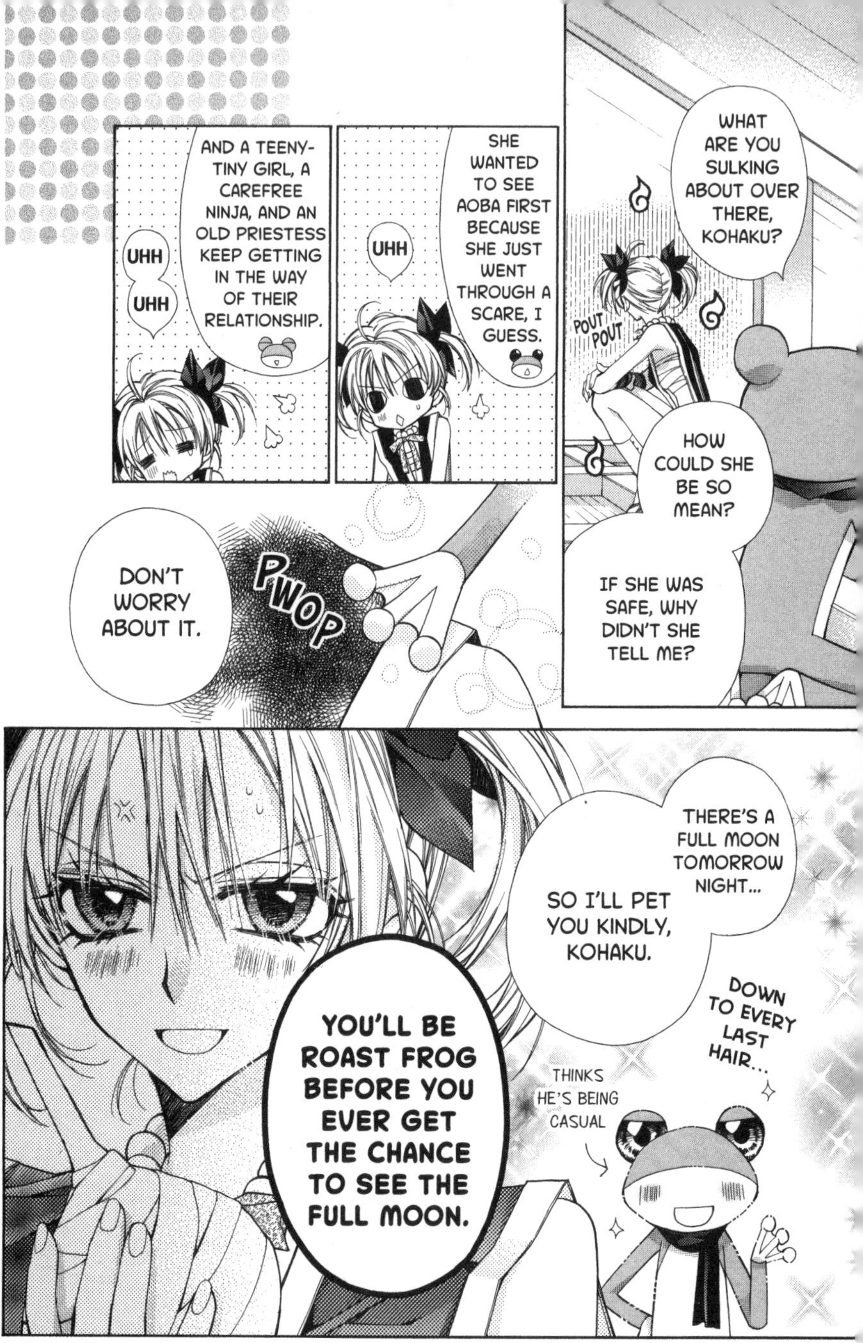
WHAT ARE YOU SULKING ABOUT OVER THERE, KOHAKU?
POUT POUT
HOW COULD SHE BE SO MEAN?
IF SHE WAS SAFE, WHY DIDN'T SHE TELL ME?
SHE WANTED TO SEE AOBA FIRST BECAUSE SHE JUST WENT THROUGH A SCARE, I GUESS.
UHH
AND A TEENY-TINY GIRL, A CAREFREE NINJA, AND AN OLD PRIESTESS KEEP GETTING IN THE WAY OF THEIR RELATIONSHIP.
UHH
UHH
PWOP
DON'T WORRY ABOUT IT.
THERE'S A FULL MOON TOMORROW NIGHT...
SO I'LL PET YOU KINDLY, KOHAKU.
DOWN TO EVERY LAST HAIR...
THINKS HE'S BEING CASUAL
YOU'LL BE ROAST FROG BEFORE YOU EVER GET THE CHANCE TO SEE THE FULL MOON.

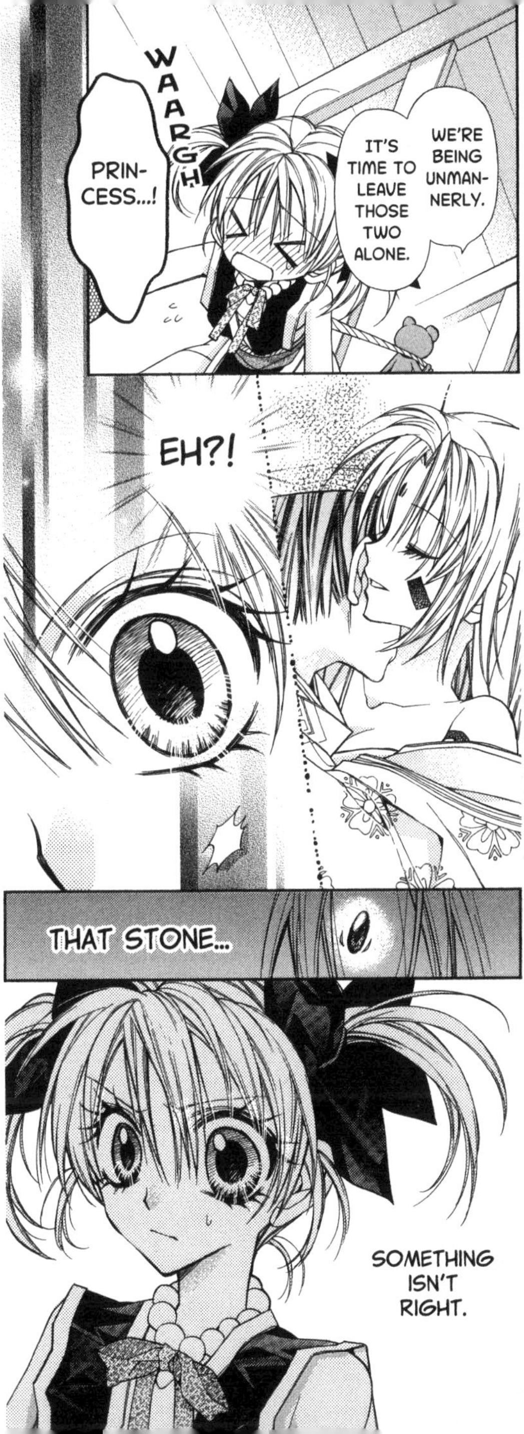
WE'RE BEING UNMANNERLY.
IT'S TIME TO LEAVE THOSE TWO ALONE.
WAARGH
PRIN-CESS...!
EH?!
THAT STONE...
SOMETHING ISN'T RIGHT.

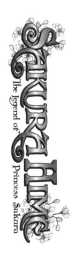

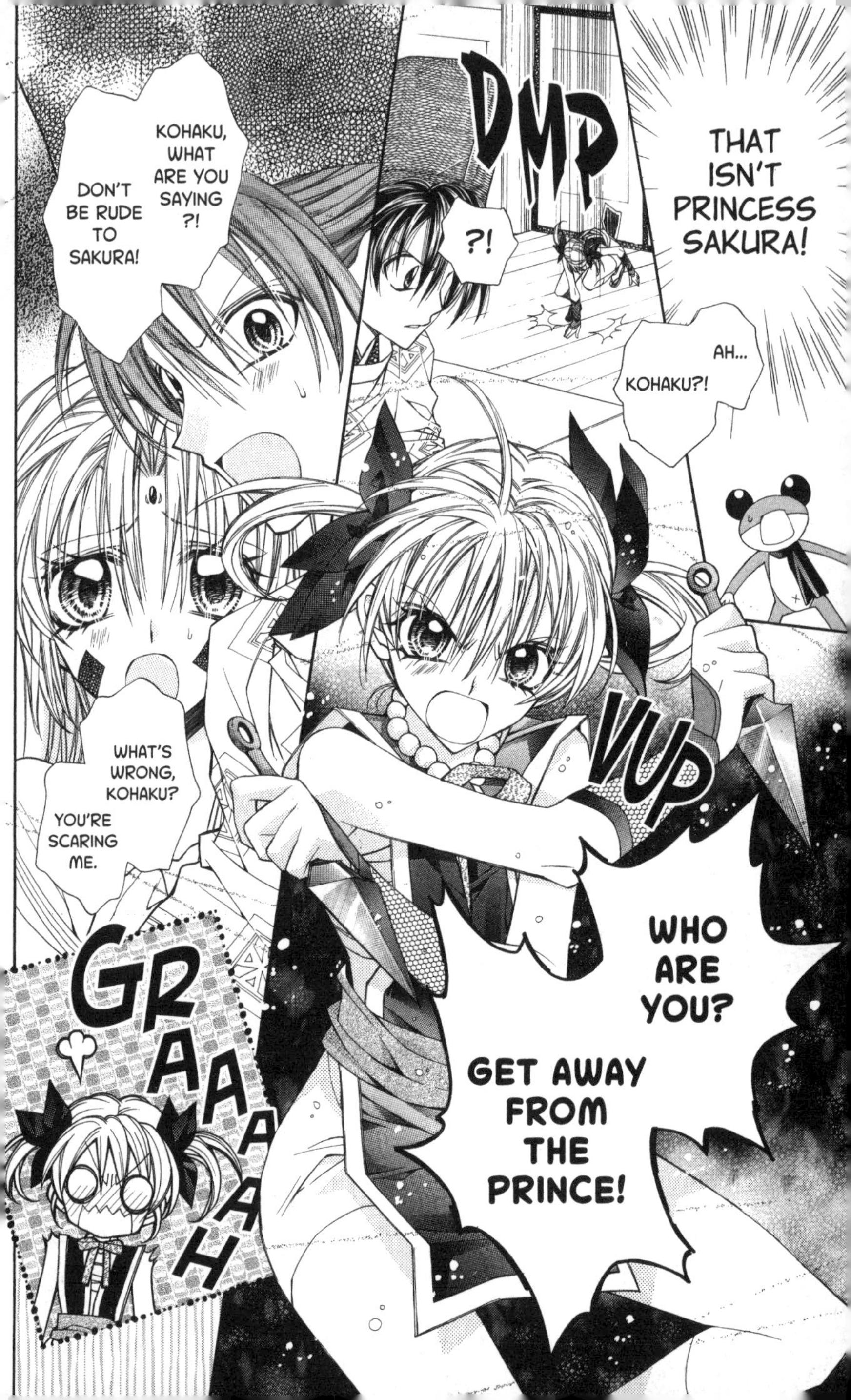
THAT ISN'T PRINCESS SAKURA!
DMP
?!
AH... KOHAKU?!
KOHAKU, WHAT ARE YOU SAYING?!
DON'T BE RUDE TO SAKURA!
VUP
WHO ARE YOU?
GET AWAY FROM THE PRINCE!
WHAT'S WRONG, KOHAKU?
YOU'RE SCARING ME.
GRAAAAAH

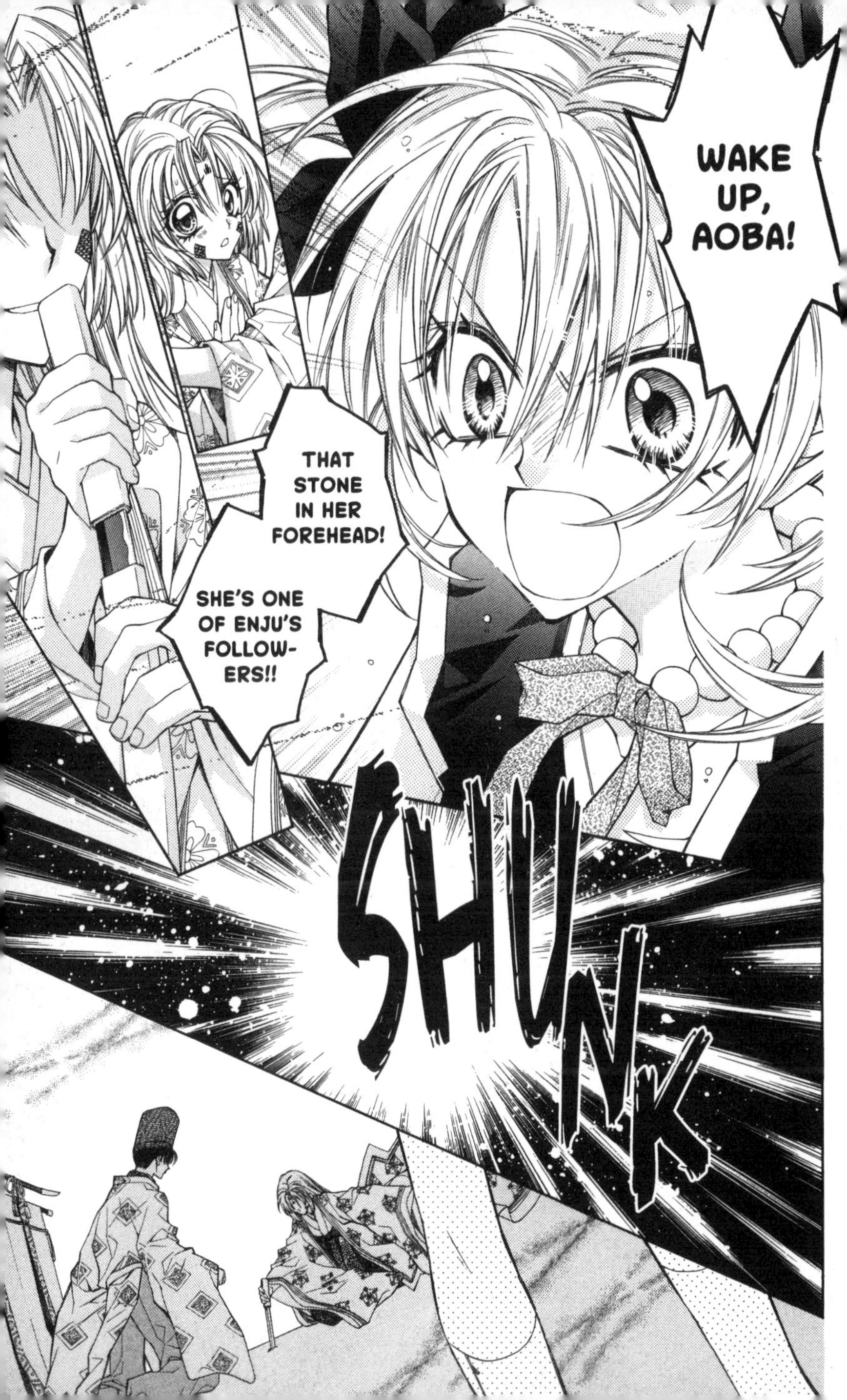
WAKE UP, AOBA!
THAT STONE IN HER FOREHEAD!
SHE'S ONE OF ENJU'S FOLLOW-ERS!!
SHUNK

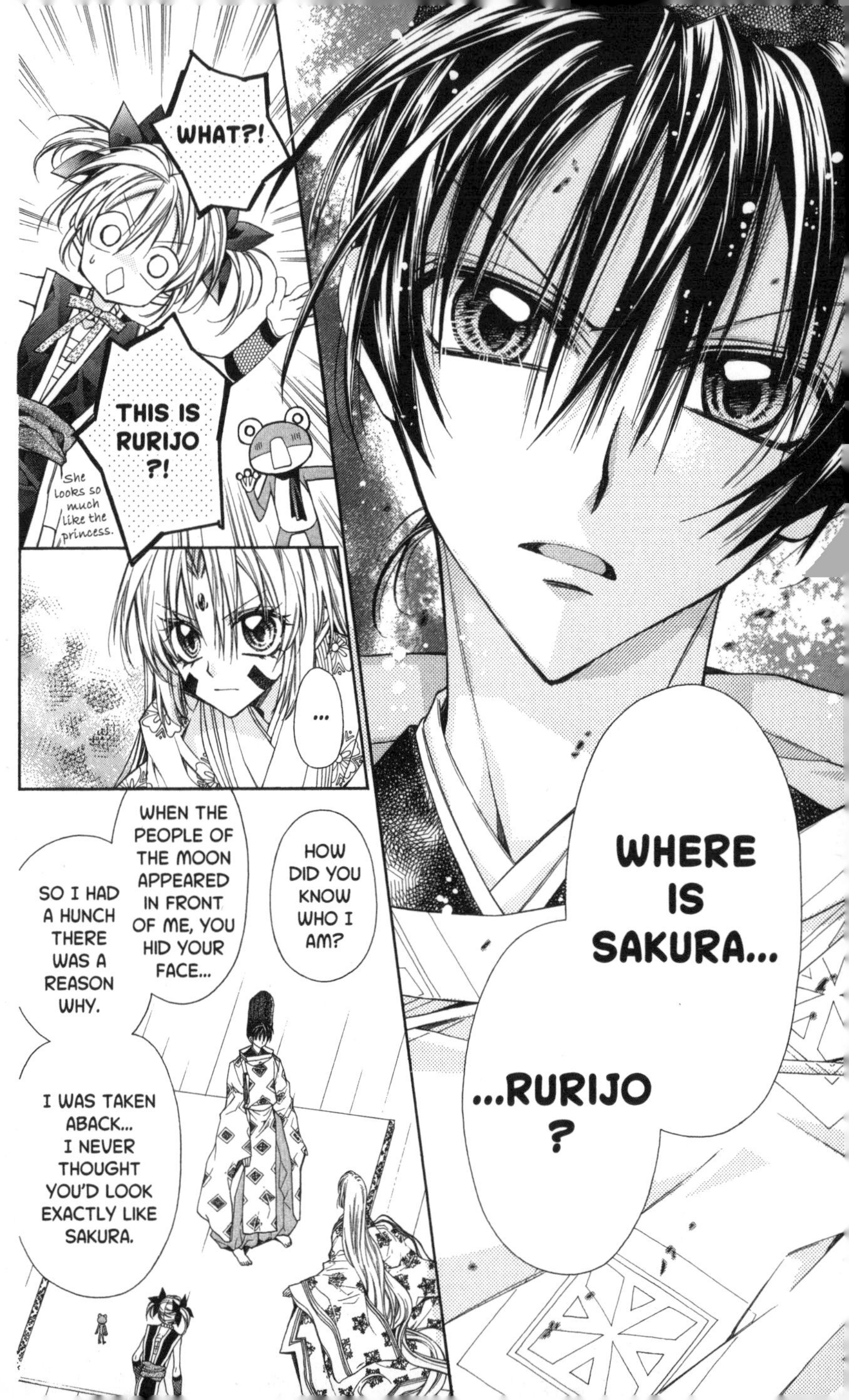
WHERE IS SAKURA...
...RURIJO ?
WHAT?!
THIS IS RURIJO ?!
She looks so much like the princess.
...
HOW DID YOU KNOW WHO I AM?
WHEN THE PEOPLE OF THE MOON APPEARED IN FRONT OF ME, YOU HID YOUR FACE...
SO I HAD A HUNCH THERE WAS A REASON WHY.
I WAS TAKEN ABACK... I NEVER THOUGHT YOU'D LOOK EXACTLY LIKE SAKURA.

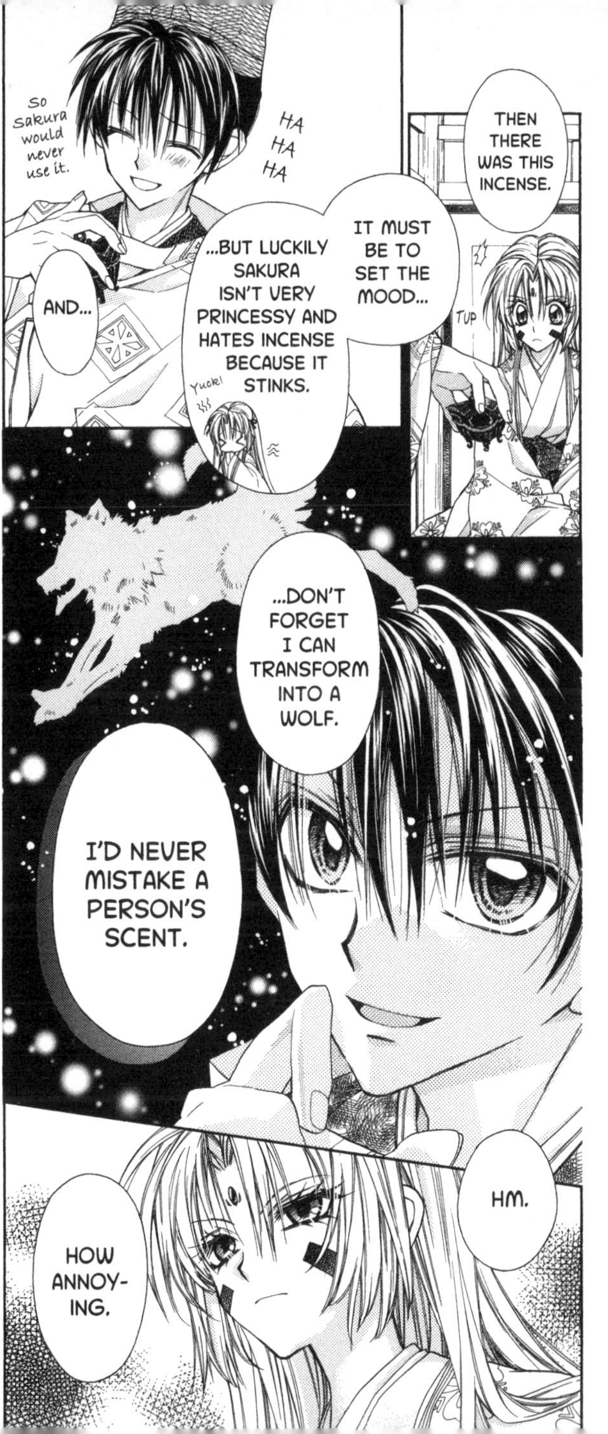
THEN THERE WAS THIS INCENSE.
TUP
IT MUST BE TO SET THE MOOD...
...BUT LUCKILY SAKURA ISN'T VERY PRINCESSY AND HATES INCENSE BECAUSE IT STINKS.
Yuck!
HA HA HA
So sakura would never use it.
AND...
...DON'T FORGET I CAN TRANSFORM INTO A WOLF.
I'D NEVER MISTAKE A PERSON'S SCENT.
HM.
HOW ANNOY-ING.

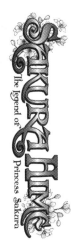

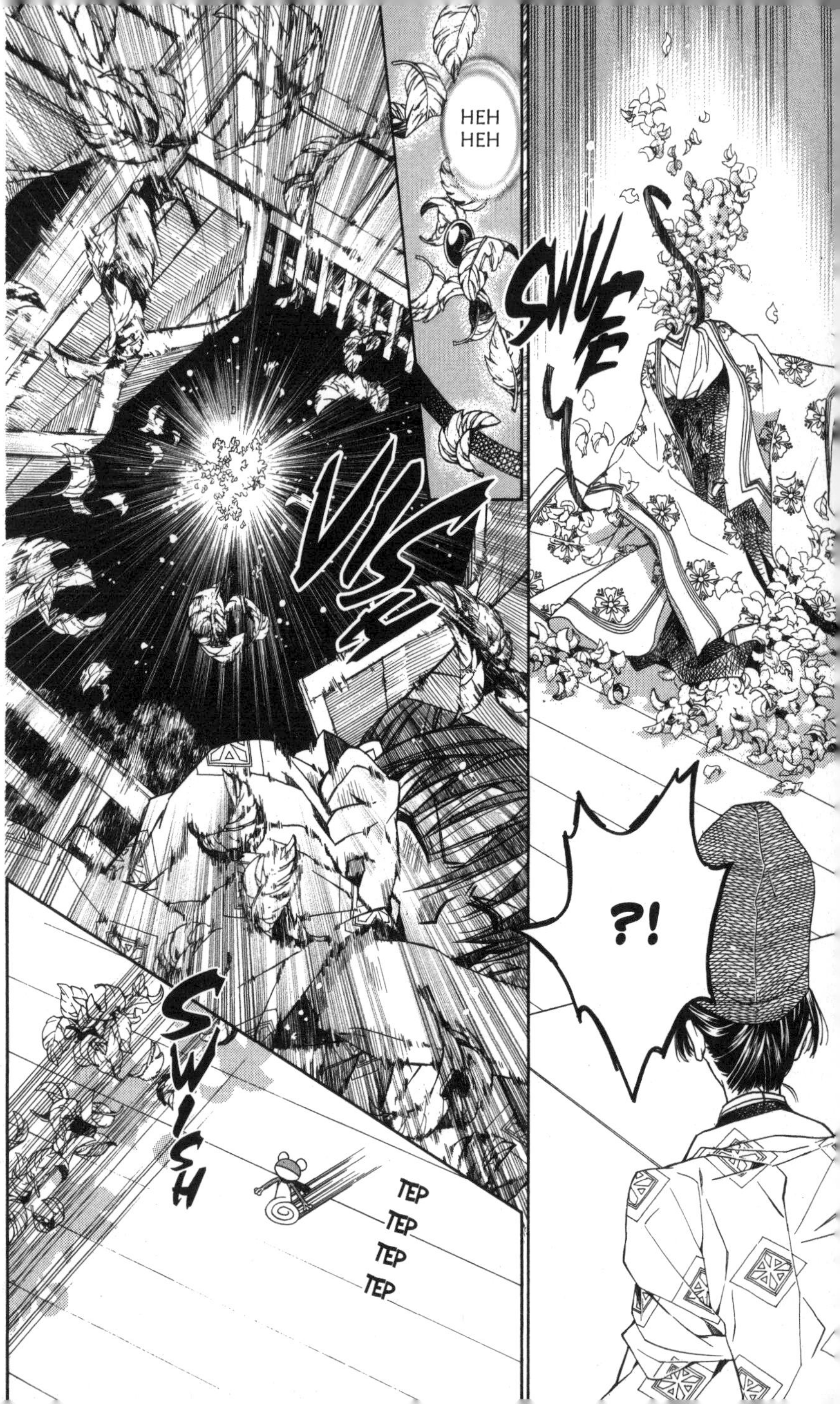
SWUFF
?!
HEH HEH
VISH
SWISH
TEP
TEP
TEP
TEP

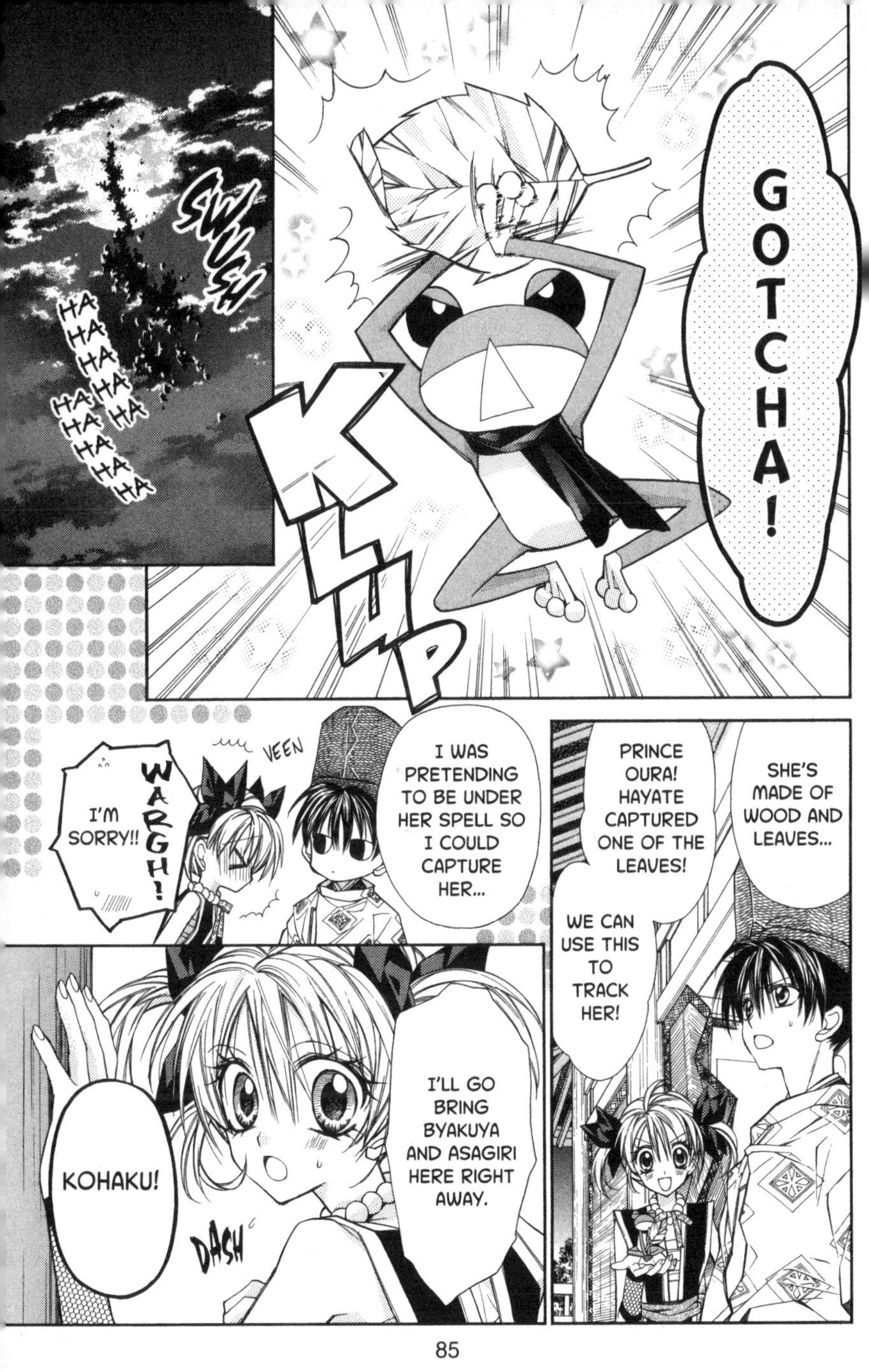
GOTCHA!
KLUP
SWUSH
HA HA HA HA HA HA HA HA HA HA HA
SHE'S MADE OF WOOD AND LEAVES...
PRINCE OURA! HAYATE CAPTURED ONE OF THE LEAVES!
WE CAN USE THIS TO TRACK HER!
I WAS PRETENDING TO BE UNDER HER SPELL SO I COULD CAPTURE HER...
VEEN
WARGH!
I'M SORRY!!
I'LL GO BRING BYAKUYA AND ASAGIRI HERE RIGHT AWAY.
KOHAKU!
DASH

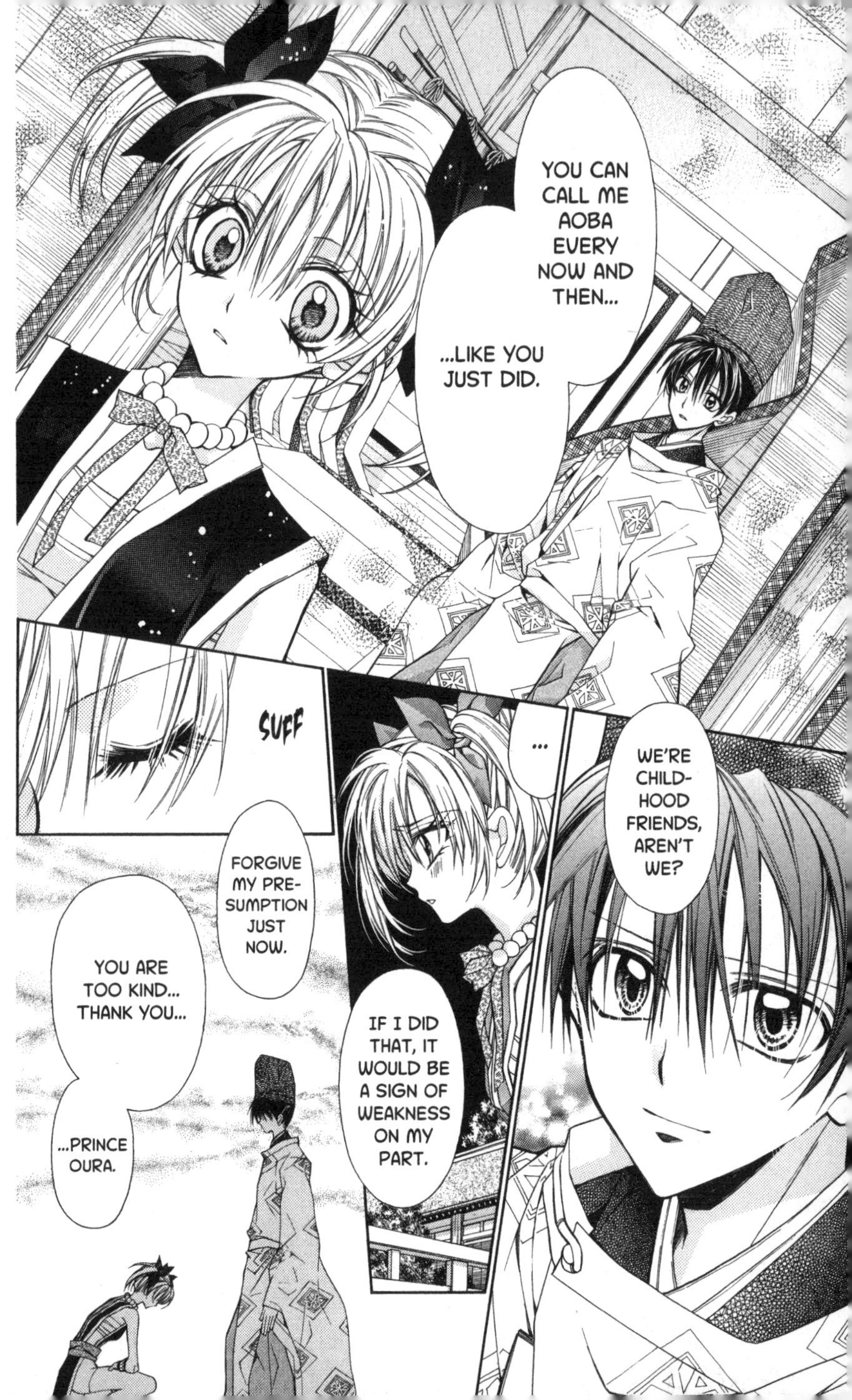
YOU CAN CALL ME AOBA EVERY NOW AND THEN...
...LIKE YOU JUST DID.
WE'RE CHILD-HOOD FRIENDS, AREN'T WE?
...
IF I DID THAT, IT WOULD BE A SIGN OF WEAKNESS ON MY PART.
SUFF
FORGIVE MY PRE-SUMPTION JUST NOW.
YOU ARE TOO KIND... THANK YOU...
...PRINCE OURA.

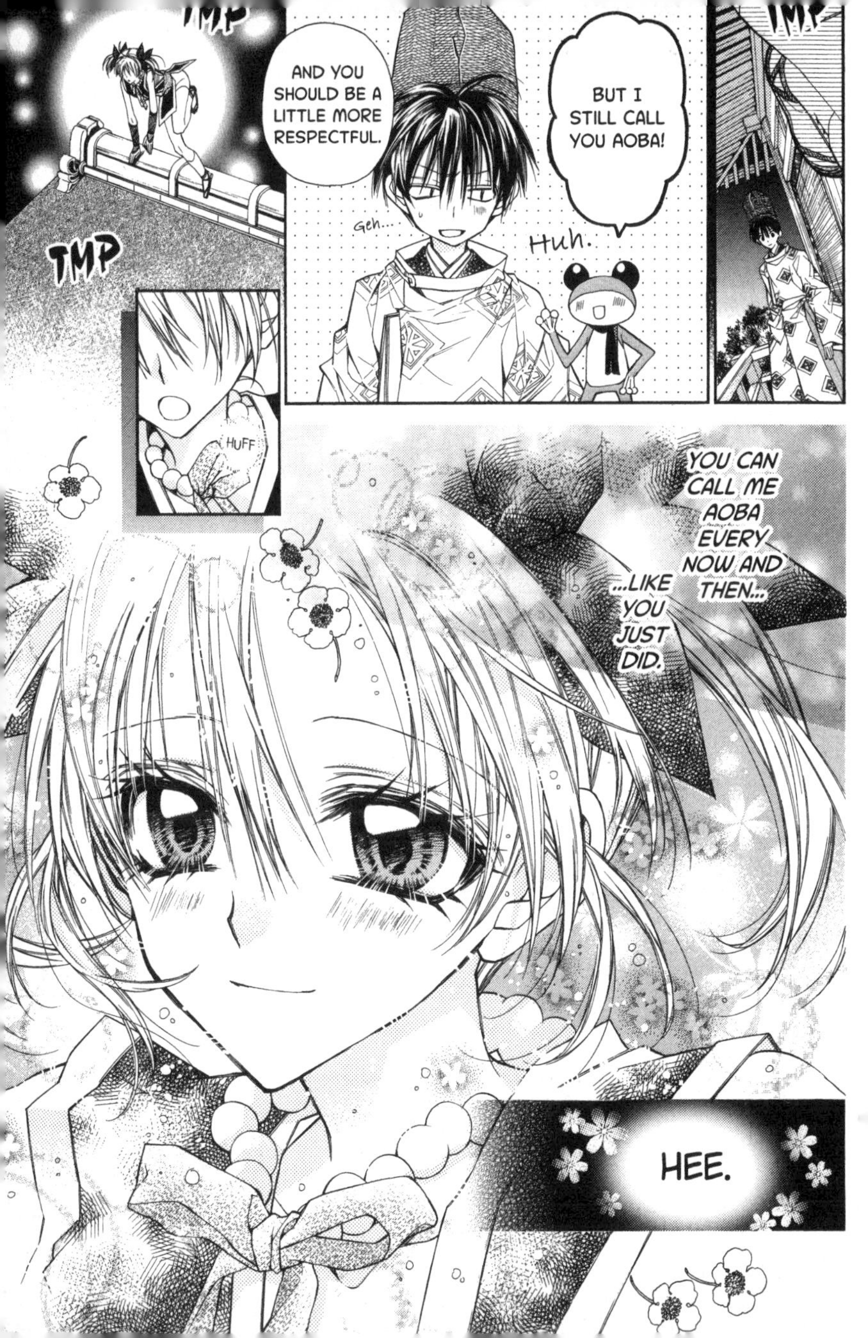
TMP
BUT I STILL CALL YOU AOBA!
Huh.
AND YOU SHOULD BE A LITTLE MORE RESPECTFUL.
Geh...
TMP
TMP
HUFF
YOU CAN CALL ME AOBA EVERY NOW AND THEN...
...LIKE YOU JUST DID.
HEE.

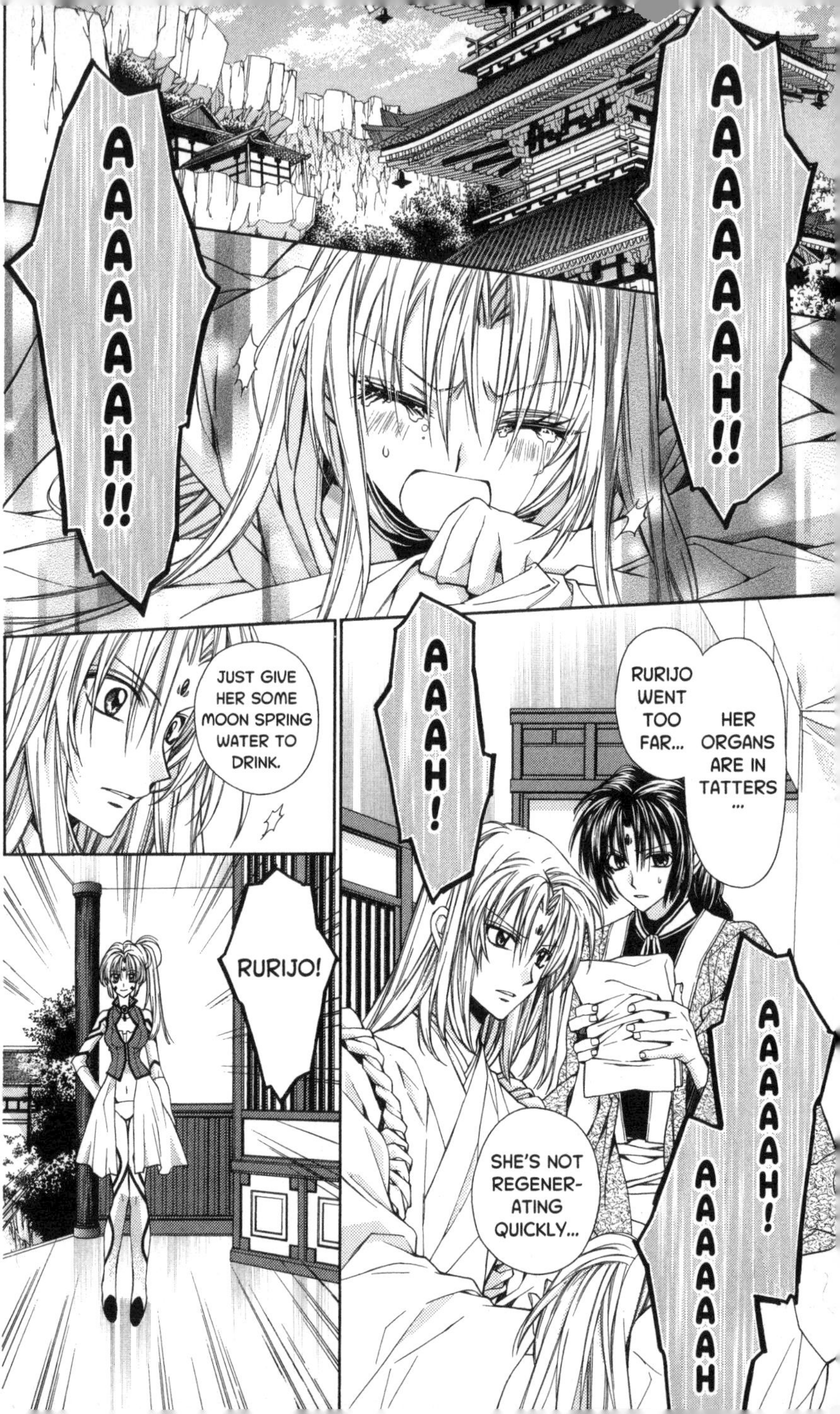

AAAAAAH!!
AAAAAAH!!
AAAH!
RURIJO WENT TOO FAR...
HER ORGANS ARE IN TATTERS...
SHE'S NOT REGENER-ATING QUICKLY...
AAAAAH!
AAAAAAH
JUST GIVE HER SOME MOON SPRING WATER TO DRINK.
RURIJO!

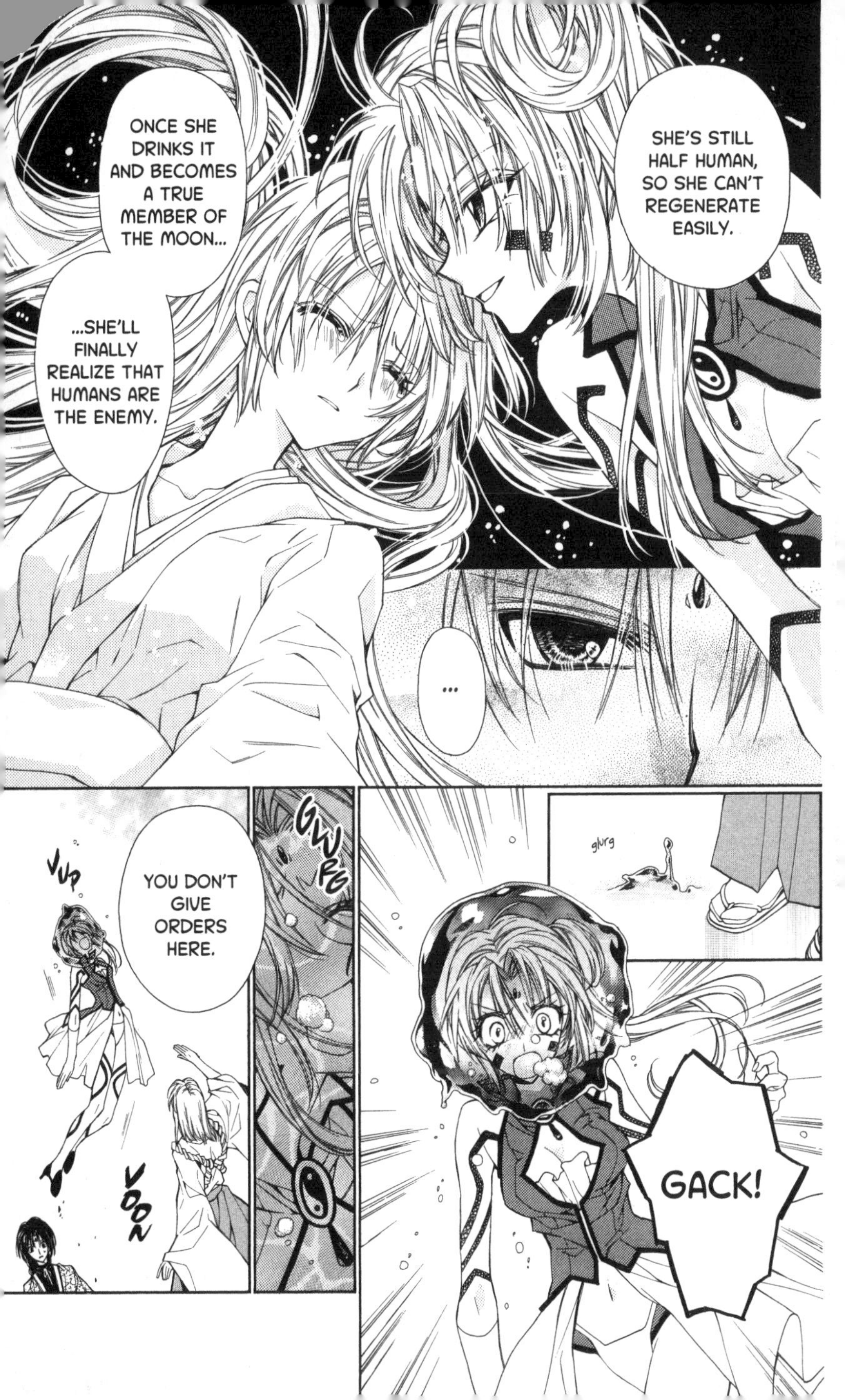

SHE'S STILL HALF HUMAN, SO SHE CAN'T REGENERATE EASILY.
ONCE SHE DRINKS IT AND BECOMES A TRUE MEMBER OF THE MOON...
...SHE'LL FINALLY REALIZE THAT HUMANS ARE THE ENEMY.
...
glurg
GACK!
GWURG
YOU DON'T GIVE ORDERS HERE.
VUP
VOON

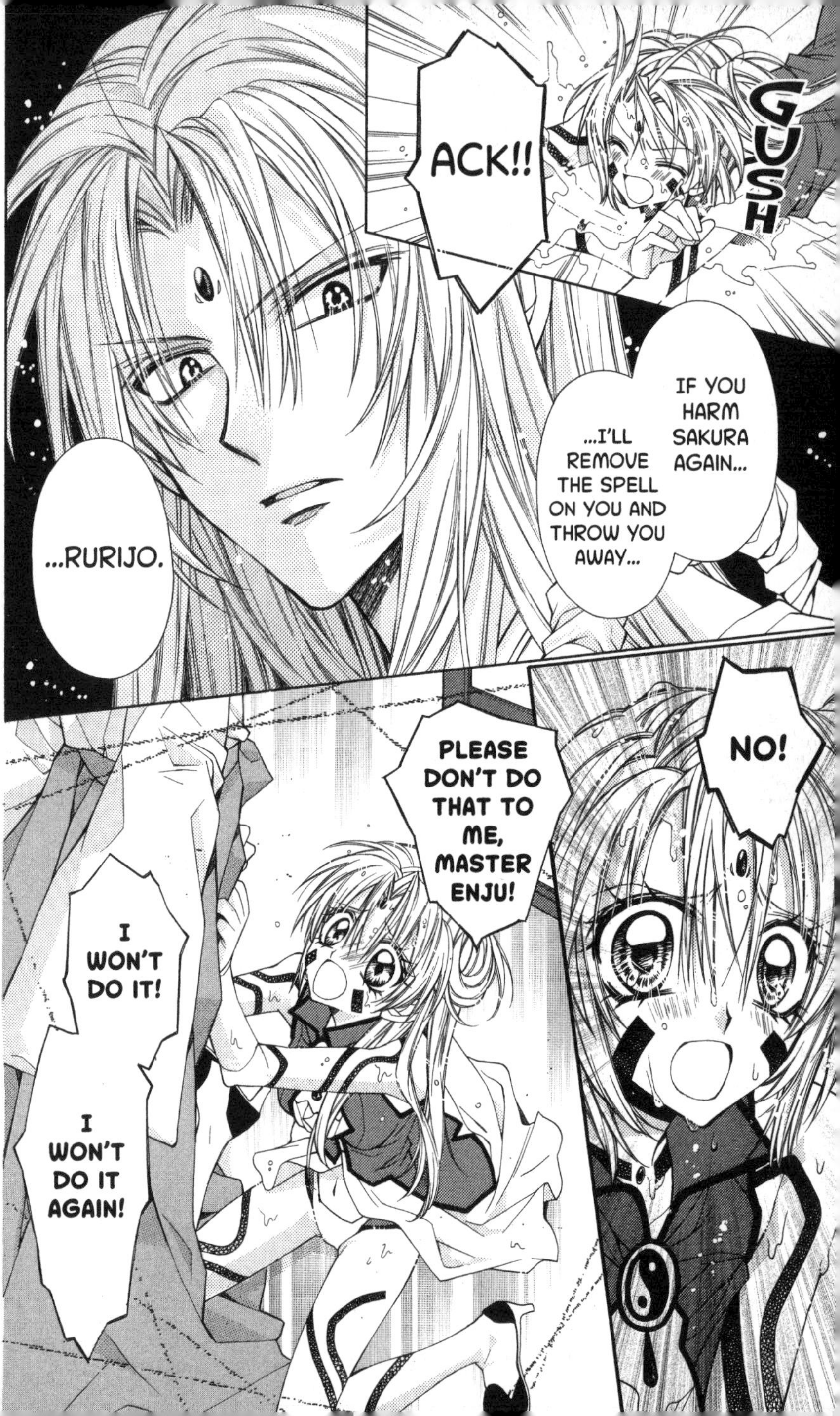
GUSH
ACK!!
IF YOU HARM SAKURA AGAIN...
...I'LL REMOVE THE SPELL ON YOU AND THROW YOU AWAY...
...RURIJO.
NO!
PLEASE DON'T DO THAT TO ME, MASTER ENJU!
I WON'T DO IT!
I WON'T DO IT AGAIN!

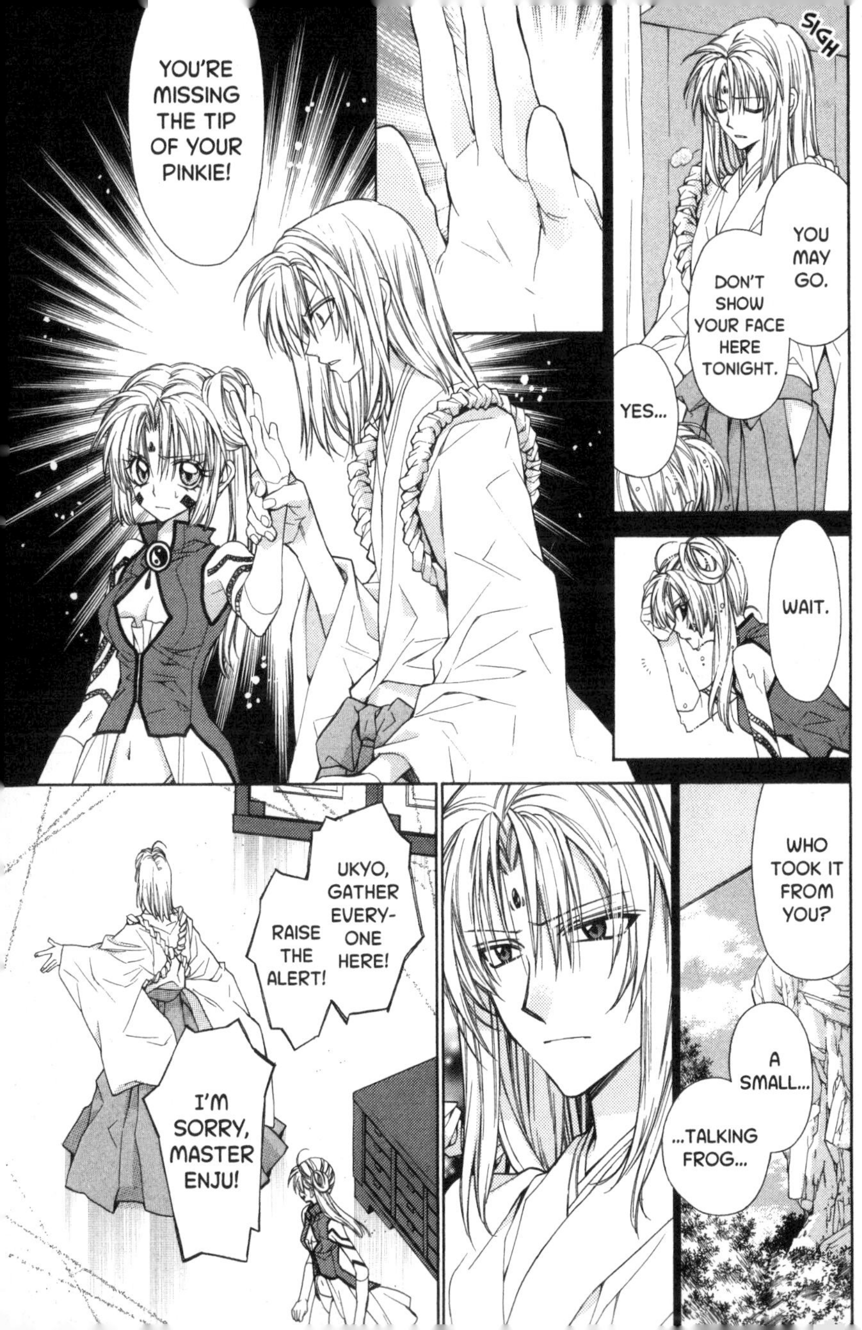
SIGH
YOU MAY GO.
DON'T SHOW YOUR FACE HERE TONIGHT.
YES...
WAIT.
YOU'RE MISSING THE TIP OF YOUR PINKIE!
WHO TOOK IT FROM YOU?
A SMALL...
...TALKING FROG...
UKYO, GATHER EVERY-ONE HERE!
RAISE THE ALERT!
I'M SORRY, MASTER ENJU!

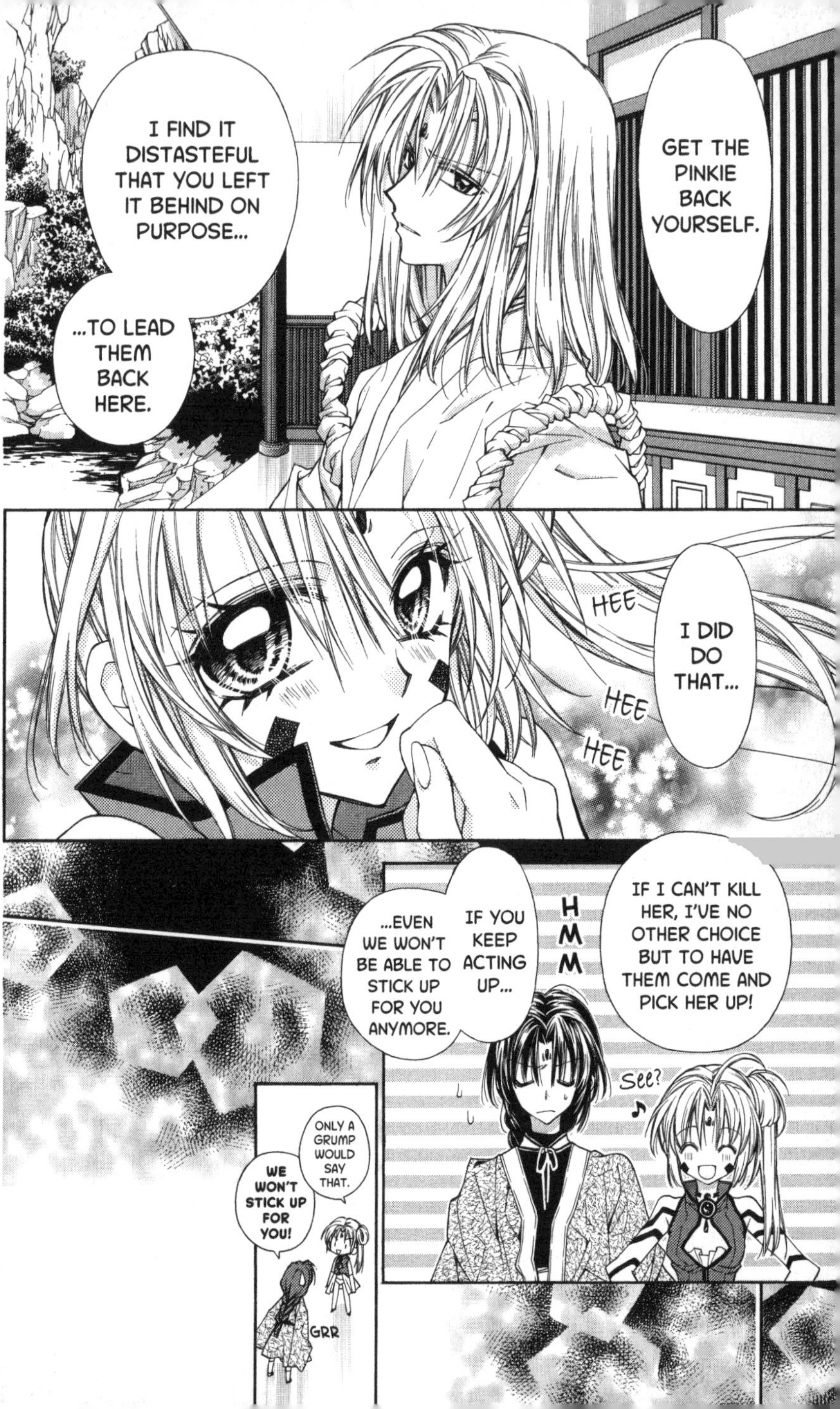
GET THE PINKIE BACK YOURSELF.
I FIND IT DISTASTEFUL THAT YOU LEFT IT BEHIND ON PURPOSE...
...TO LEAD THEM BACK HERE.
I DID DO THAT...
HEE
HEE
HEE
IF I CAN'T KILL HER, I'VE NO OTHER CHOICE BUT TO HAVE THEM COME AND PICK HER UP!
HMM
IF YOU KEEP ACTING UP...
...EVEN WE WON'T BE ABLE TO STICK UP FOR YOU ANYMORE.
See? ♪
ONLY A GRUMP WOULD SAY THAT.
WE WON'T STICK UP FOR YOU!
GRR

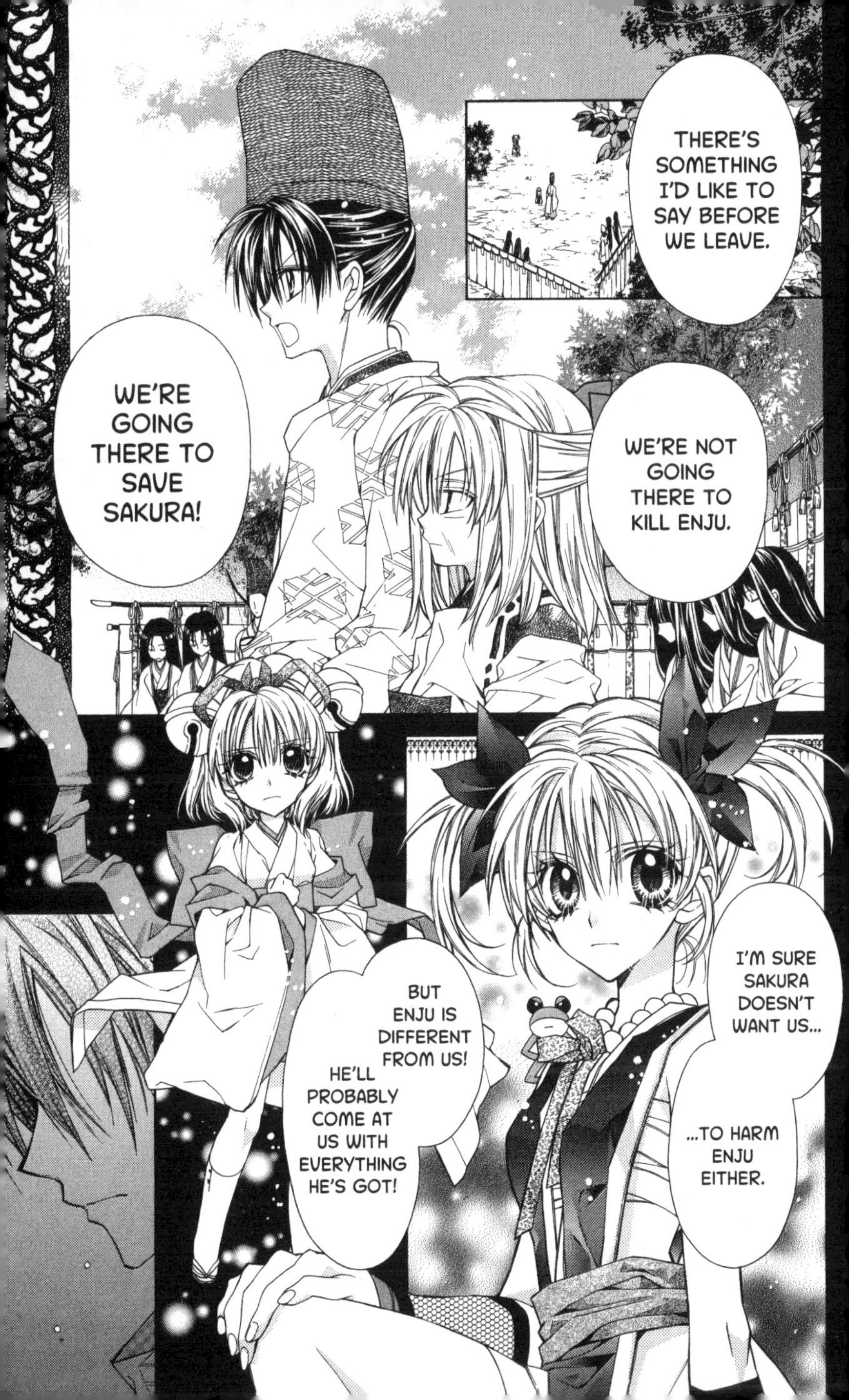
THERE'S SOMETHING I'D LIKE TO SAY BEFORE WE LEAVE.
WE'RE NOT GOING THERE TO KILL ENJU.
WE'RE GOING THERE TO SAVE SAKURA!
I'M SURE SAKURA DOESN'T WANT US...
...TO HARM ENJU EITHER.
BUT ENJU IS DIFFERENT FROM US!
HE'LL PROBABLY COME AT US WITH EVERYTHING HE'S GOT!

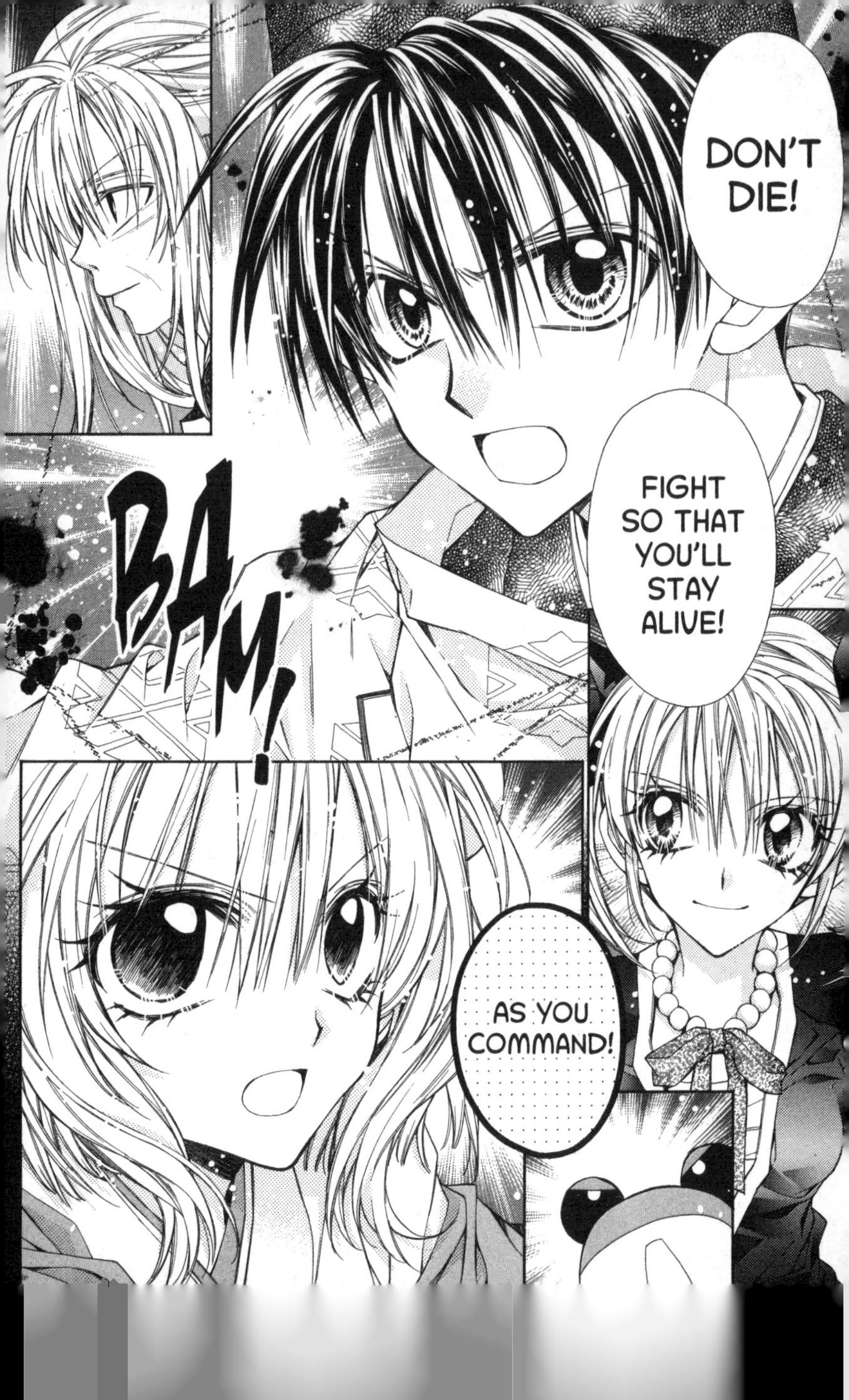
DON'T DIE!
FIGHT SO THAT YOU'LL STAY ALIVE!
BAM!
AS YOU COMMAND!

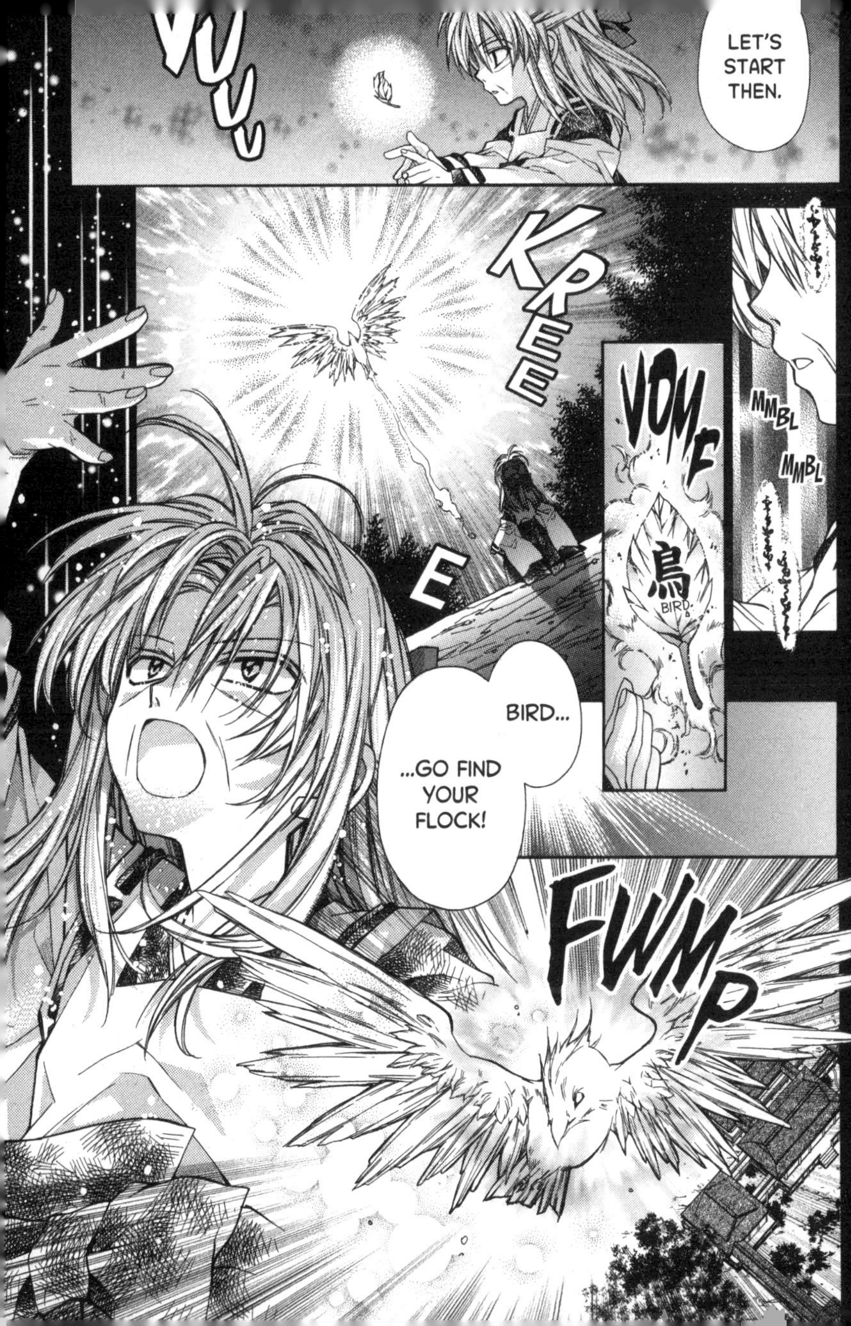
LET'S START THEN.
VUUU
MMBL
MMBL
VOMF
鳥
BIRD
KREEE
E
BIRD...
...GO FIND YOUR FLOCK!
FWMP

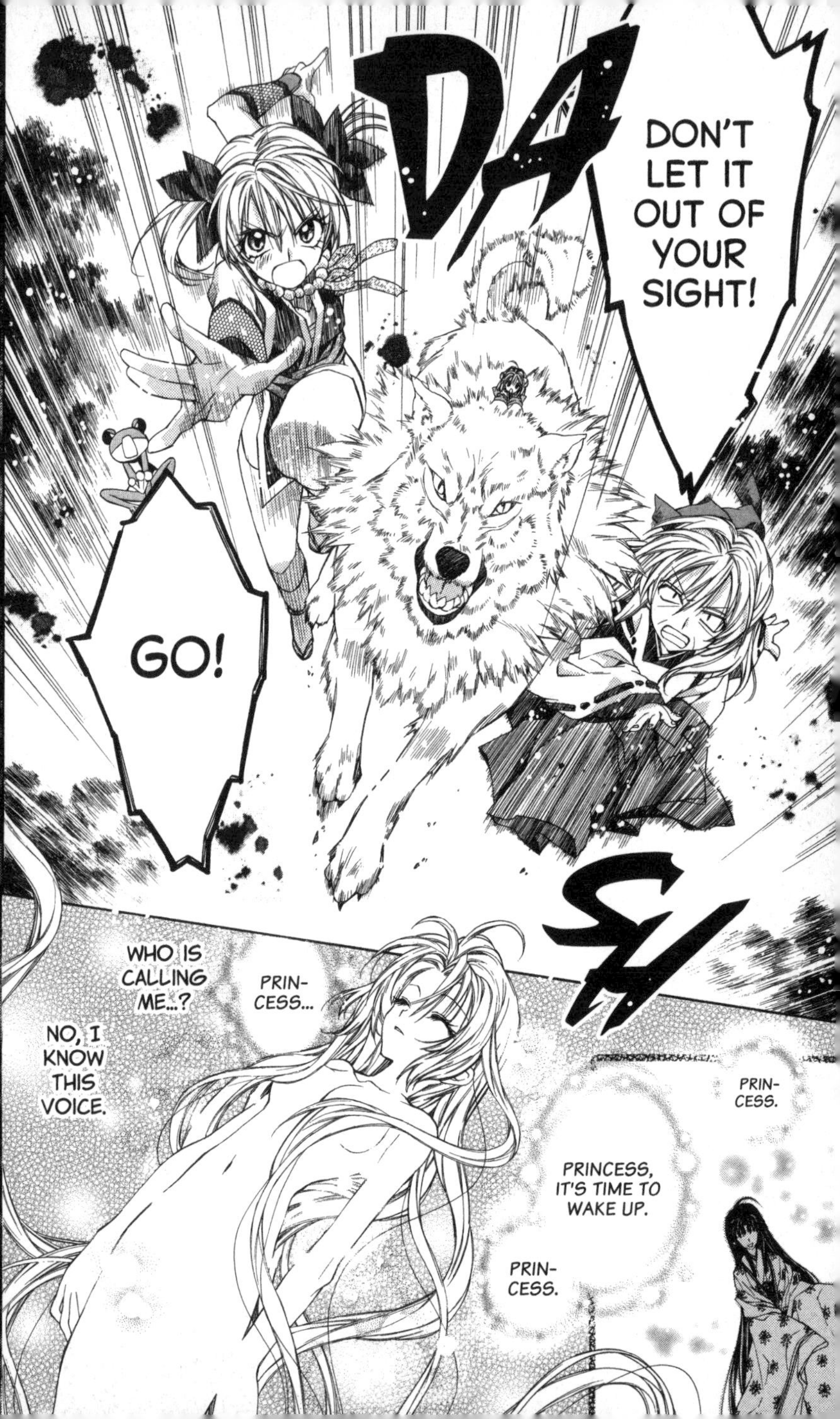
DA
DON'T LET IT OUT OF YOUR SIGHT!
GO!
SH
PRIN-CESS.
PRINCESS, IT'S TIME TO WAKE UP.
PRIN-CESS.
PRIN-CESS...
WHO IS CALLING ME...?
NO, I KNOW THIS VOICE.

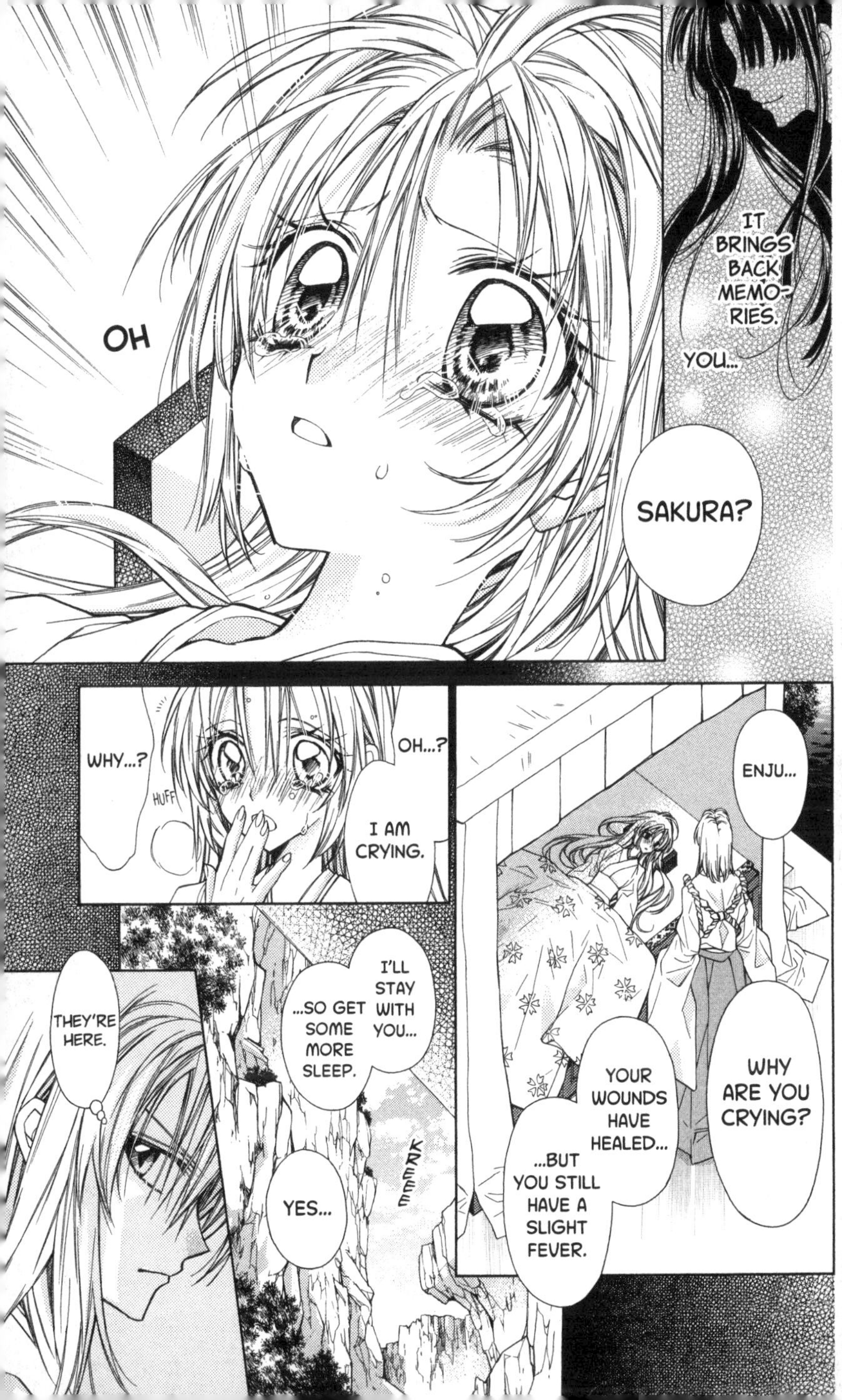
IT BRINGS BACK MEMORIES.
YOU...
SAKURA?
OH
ENJU...
WHY ARE YOU CRYING?
YOUR WOUNDS HAVE HEALED...
...BUT YOU STILL HAVE A SLIGHT FEVER.
OH...?
I AM CRYING.
WHY...?
HUFF
I'LL STAY WITH YOU...
...SO GET SOME MORE SLEEP.
KREEE
YES...
THEY'RE HERE.

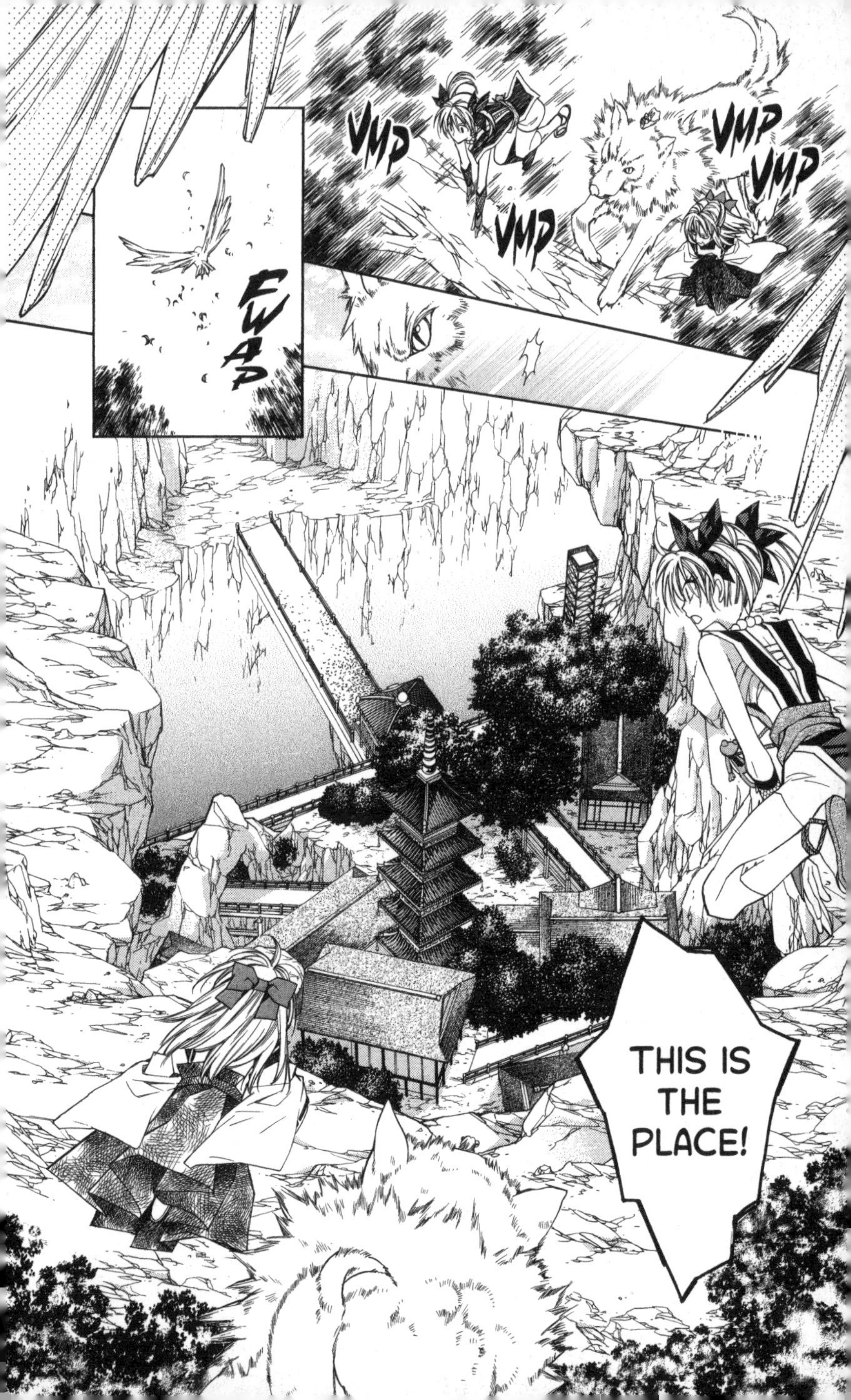
VMP
VMP
VMP
VMP
FWAP
THIS IS THE PLACE!

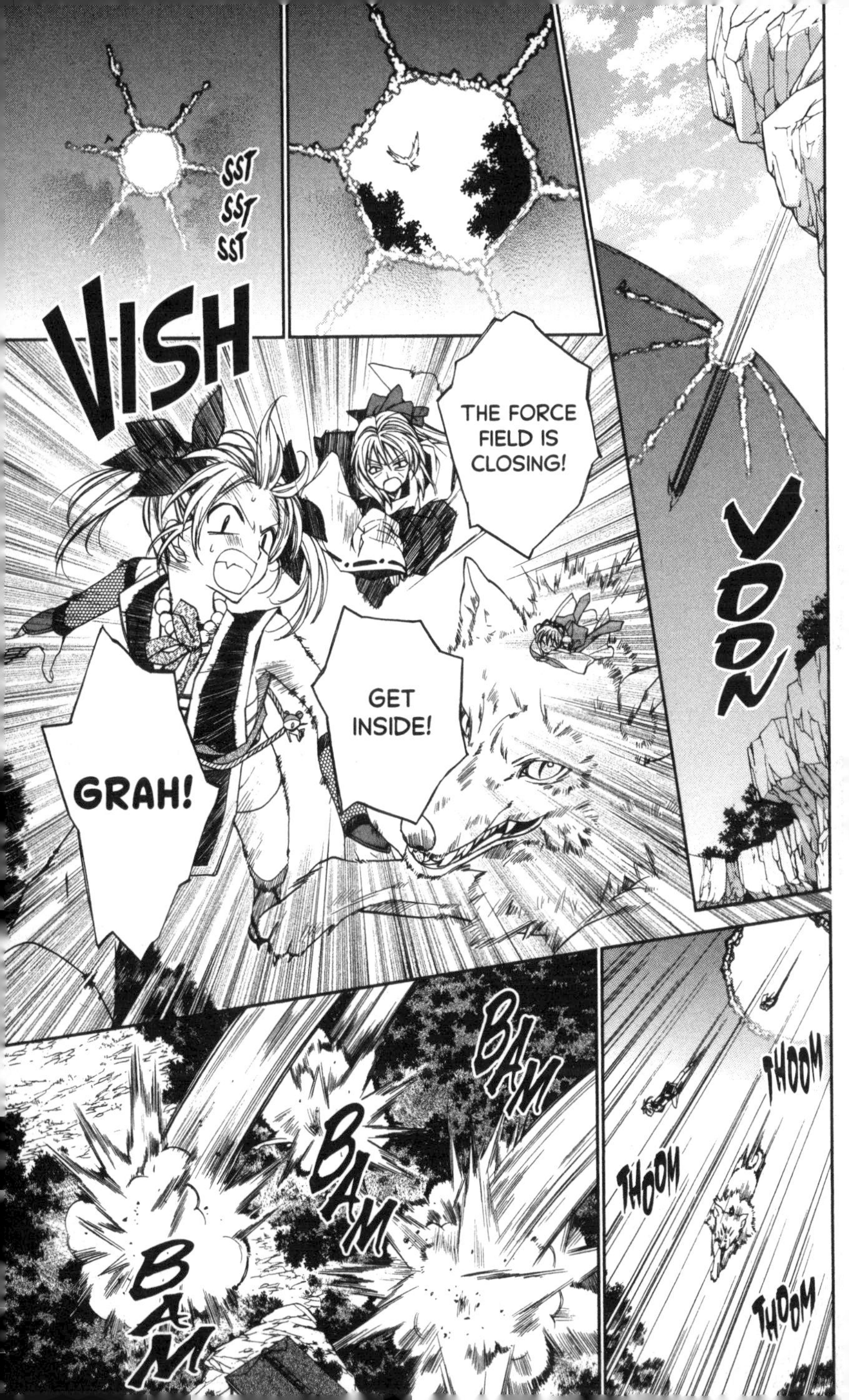
VDOON
SST
SST
SST
VISH
THE FORCE FIELD IS CLOSING!
GET INSIDE!
GRAH!
THOOM
THOOM
THOOM
BAM
BAM
BAM

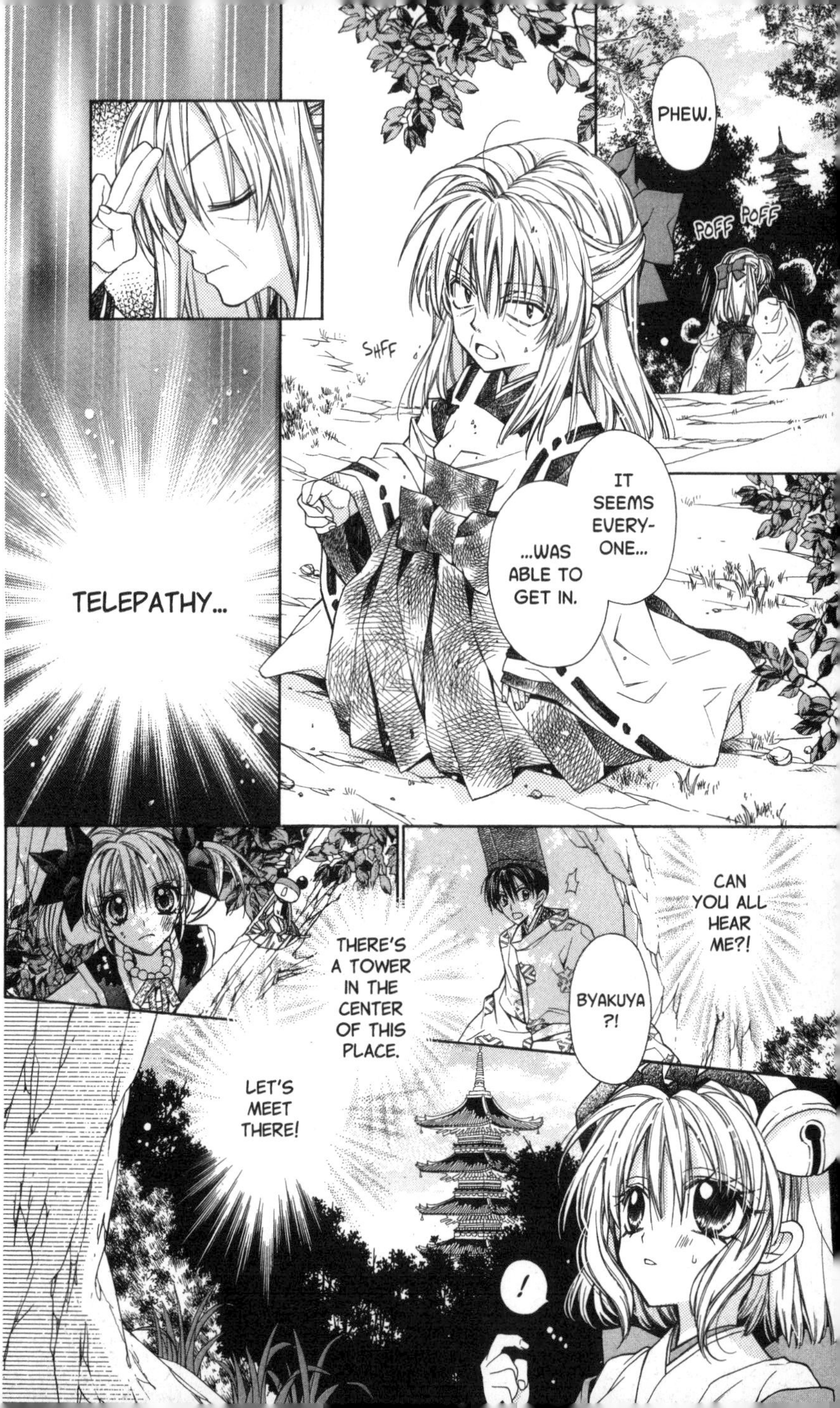
PHEW.
POFF POFF
SHFF
IT SEEMS EVERY-ONE...
...WAS ABLE TO GET IN.
TELEPATHY...
CAN YOU ALL HEAR ME?!
BYAKUYA?!
THERE'S A TOWER IN THE CENTER OF THIS PLACE.
LET'S MEET THERE!
!

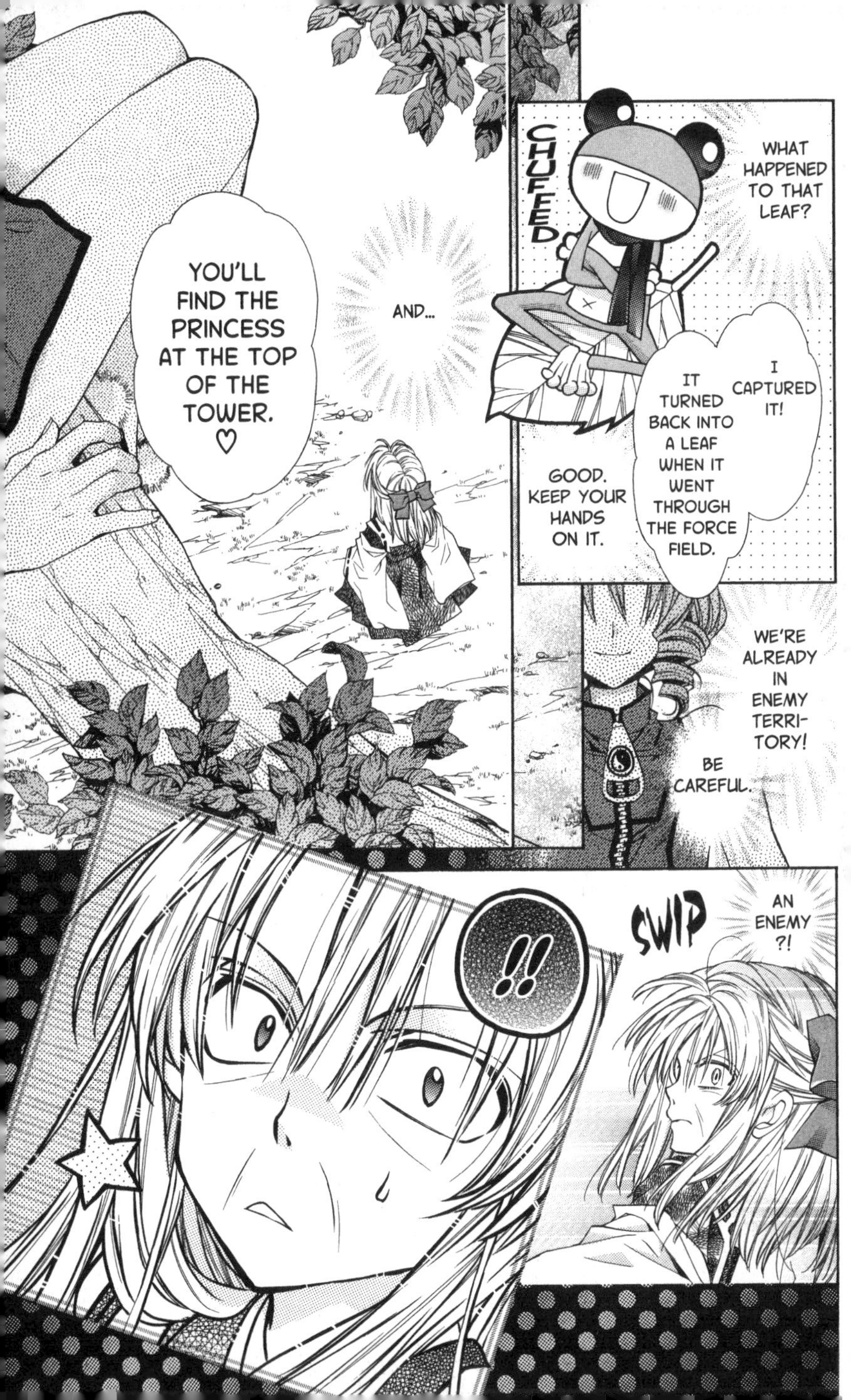
CHUFFED
WHAT HAPPENED TO THAT LEAF?
I CAPTURED IT!
IT TURNED BACK INTO A LEAF WHEN IT WENT THROUGH THE FORCE FIELD.
GOOD. KEEP YOUR HANDS ON IT.
WE'RE ALREADY IN ENEMY TERRITORY!
BE CAREFUL.
AND...
YOU'LL FIND THE PRINCESS AT THE TOP OF THE TOWER. ♡
SWIP
AN ENEMY ?!
!!

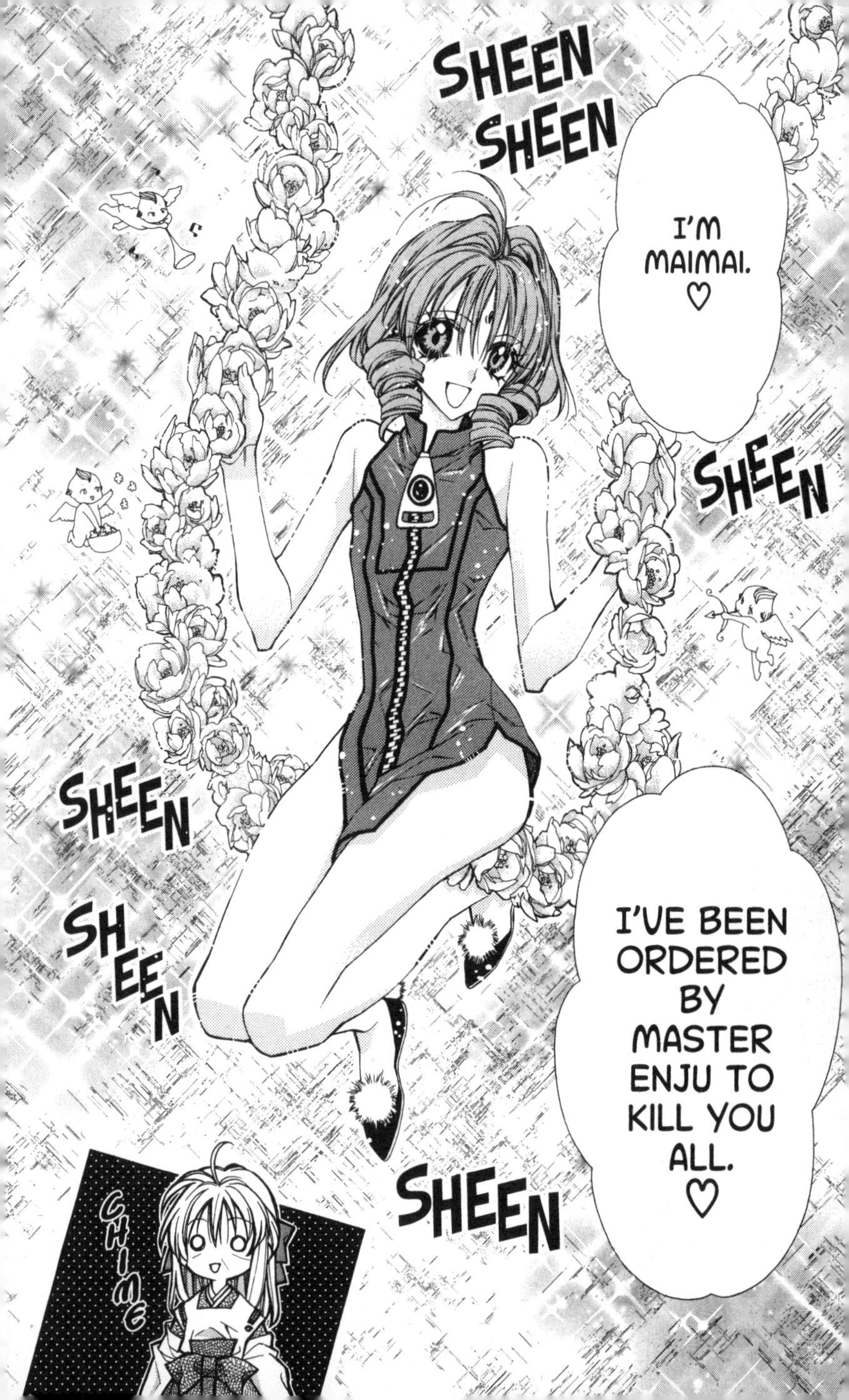
I'M MAIMAI. ♡
SHEEN SHEEN
SHEEN
I'VE BEEN ORDERED BY MASTER ENJU TO KILL YOU ALL. ♡
SHEEN
SHEEN
SHEEN
SHEEN
CHIME

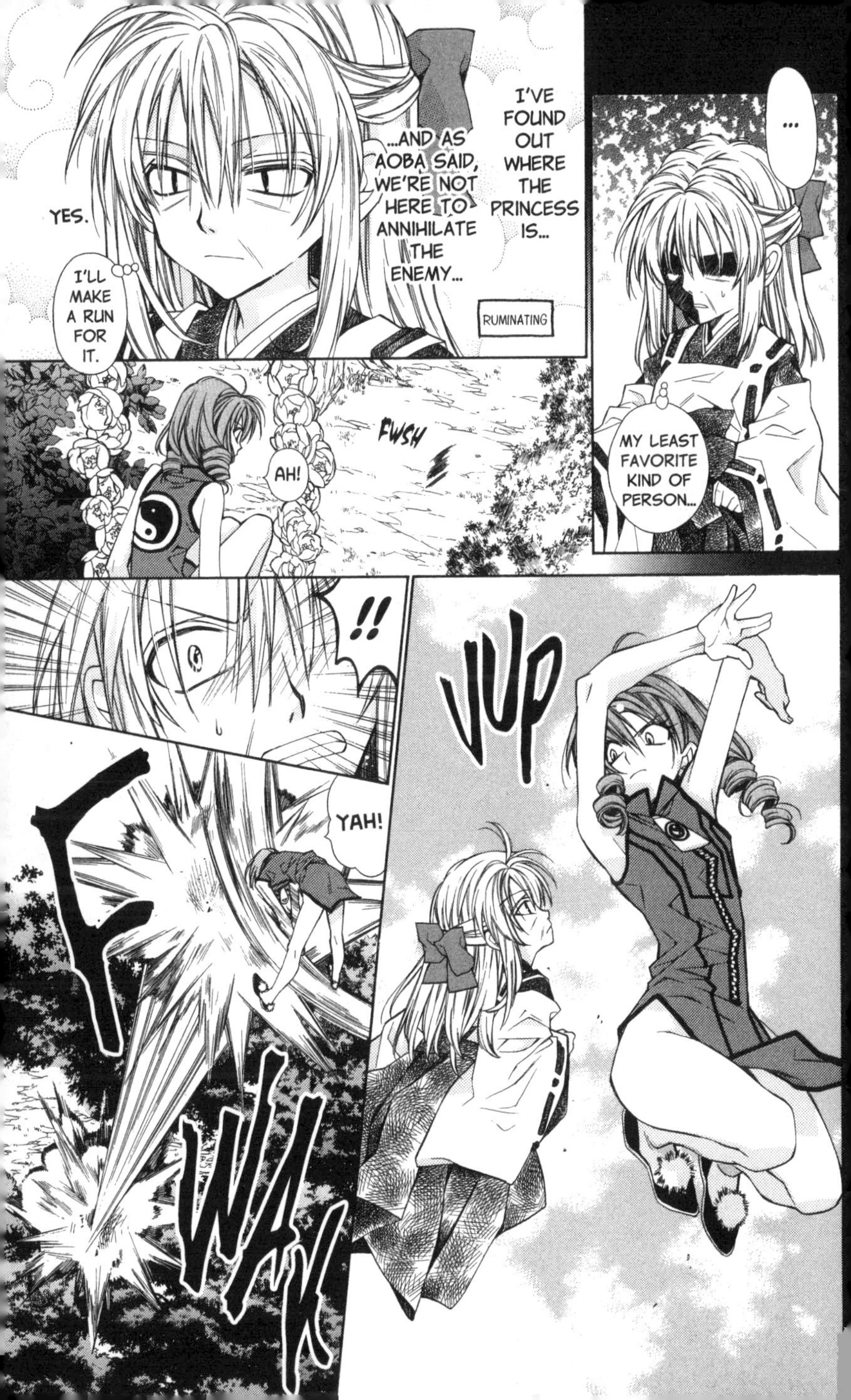
...
MY LEAST FAVORITE KIND OF PERSON...
I'VE FOUND OUT WHERE THE PRINCESS IS...
...AND AS AOBA SAID, WE'RE NOT HERE TO ANNIHILATE THE ENEMY...
RUMINATING
YES.
I'LL MAKE A RUN FOR IT.
FWSH
AH!
JUP
!!
YAH!
WAK

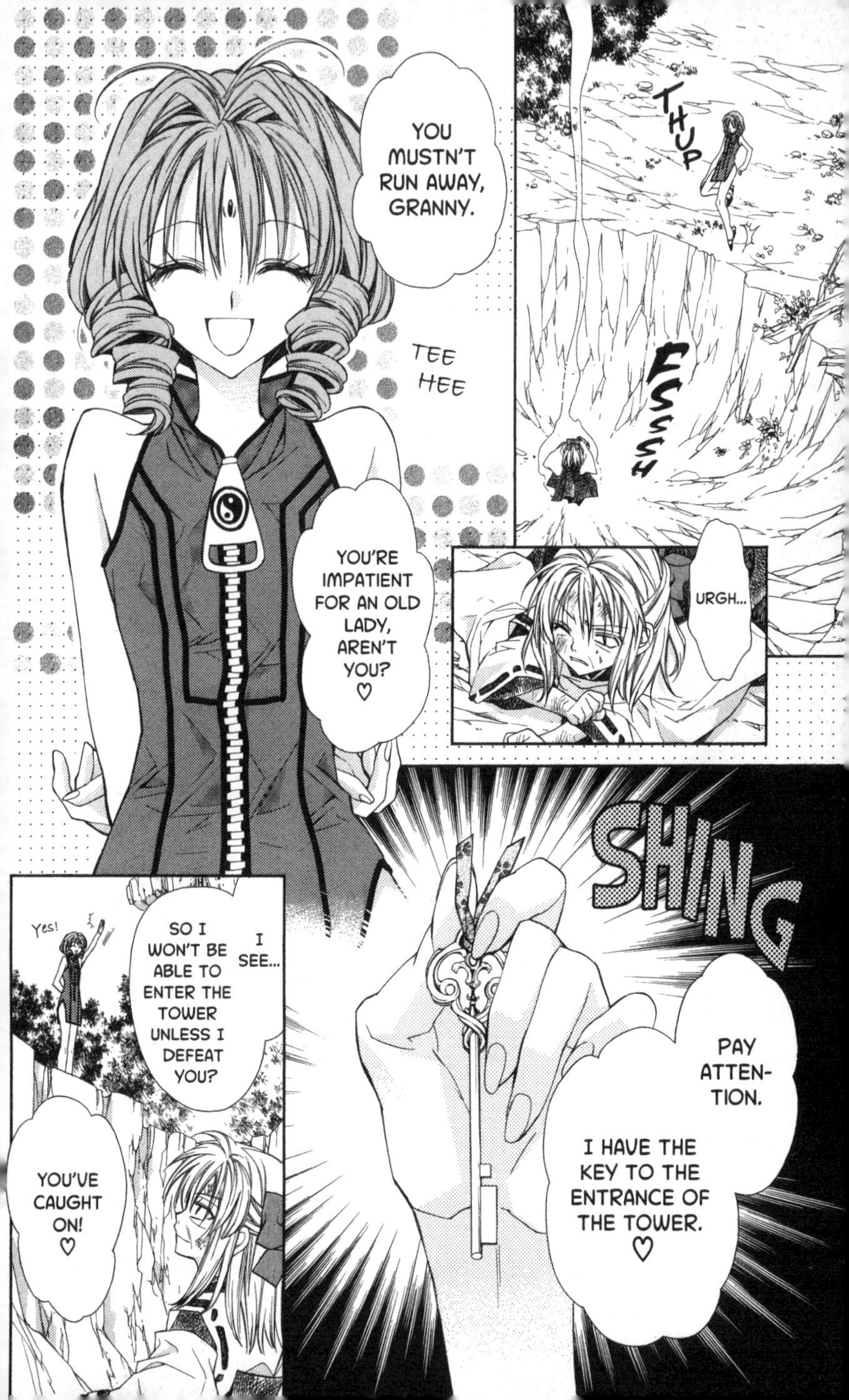
THUP
FSSSH
URGH...
YOU MUSTN'T RUN AWAY, GRANNY.
TEE HEE
YOU'RE IMPATIENT FOR AN OLD LADY, AREN'T YOU? ♡
SHING
PAY ATTEN-TION.
I HAVE THE KEY TO THE ENTRANCE OF THE TOWER. ♡
I SEE...
SO I WON'T BE ABLE TO ENTER THE TOWER UNLESS I DEFEAT YOU?
Yes!
YOU'VE CAUGHT ON! ♡

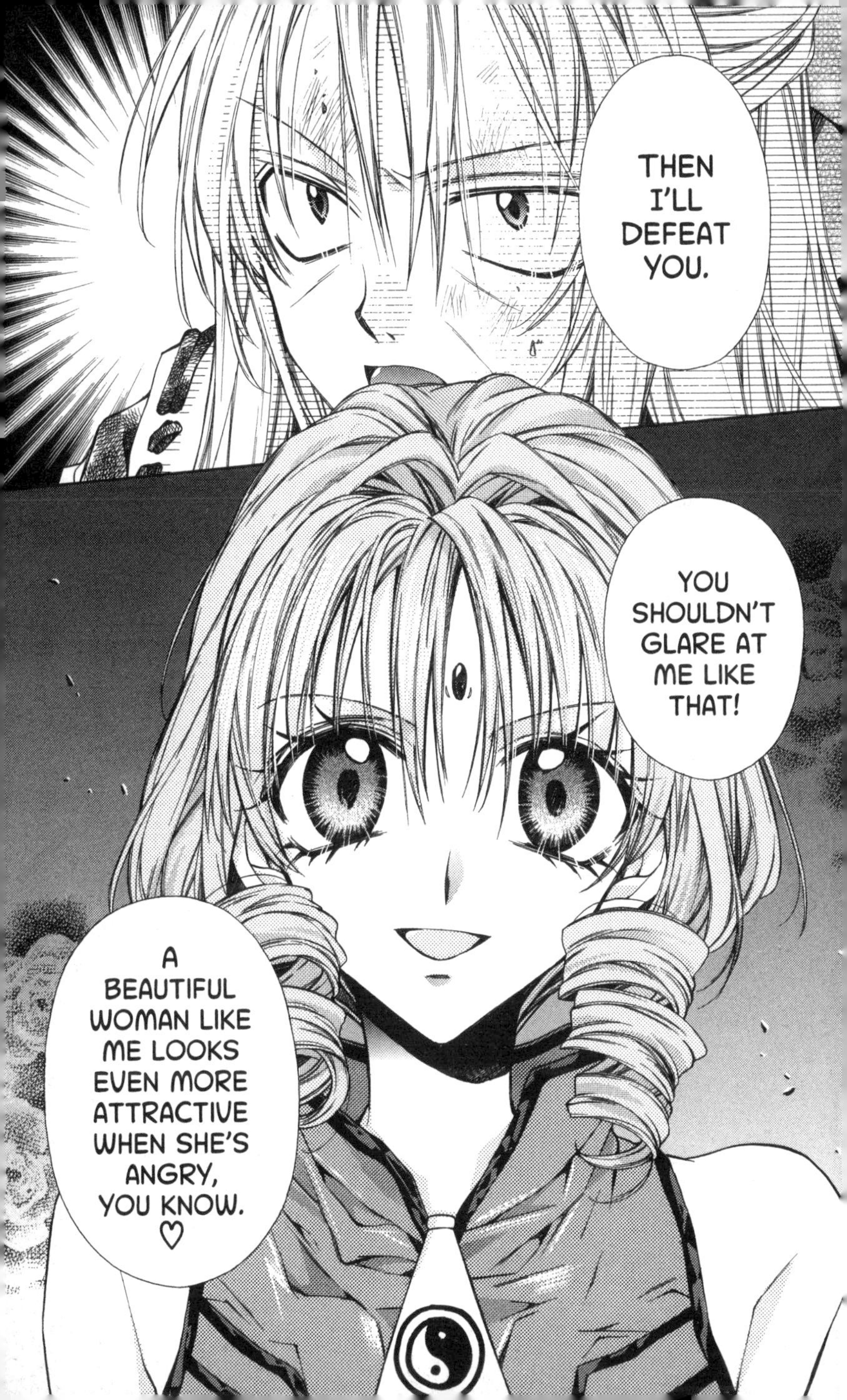
THEN I'LL DEFEAT YOU.
YOU SHOULDN'T GLARE AT ME LIKE THAT!
A BEAUTIFUL WOMAN LIKE ME LOOKS EVEN MORE ATTRACTIVE WHEN SHE'S ANGRY, YOU KNOW. ♡

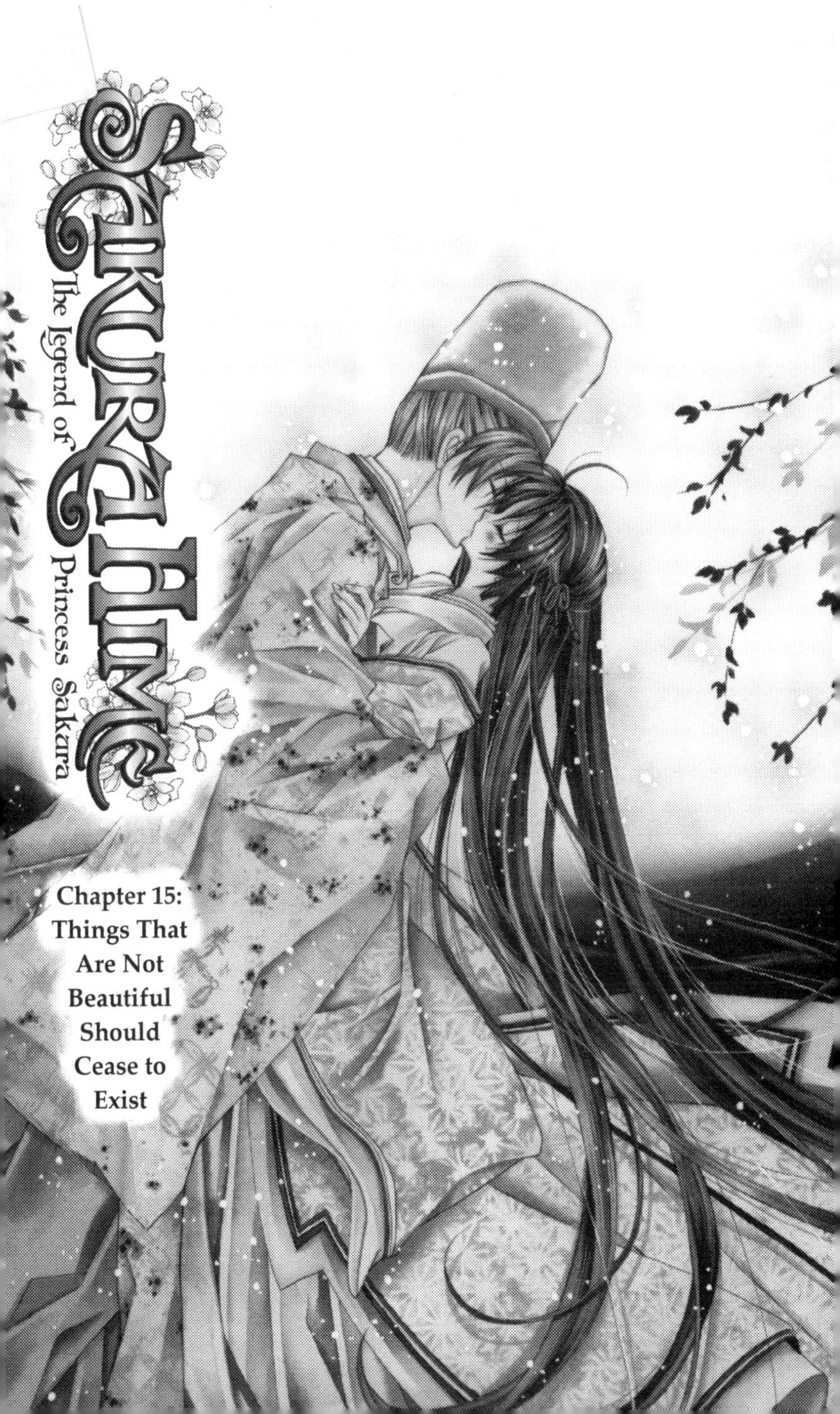
Sakura Hime
The Legend of Princess Sakura
Chapter 15: Things That Are Not Beautiful Should Cease to Exist

WHAT'S SO IMPORTANT ABOUT BEAUTY?

Chapter 15: Things That Are Not Beautiful Should Cease to Exist

☀ I'm giving away the story.

I think Enju's followers are quite similar to Aoba and his friends. I talk about that with my editor sometimes. The reason the moon followers took a different path from Aoba and his friends is because of a minor difference in their lives... One slight change and the situation could have been reversed.

Thoughts when I was trying to come up with Maimai's previous name:
↙ Arina's thoughts.
"'Mai' sounds like a girl's name, so he must have taken it from his first love. Then it should be a totally different name... Something that sounds old, something that sounds old... I wonder how 'Den' would sound?" Then I started to look at the dictionary on my cell to find the origin of the word. ↙ There were 45 pages for it. "Hmm... Like I suspected, it comes from 田 for rice paddy... Maybe it doesn't sound that nice. ↵ Hmm, it doesn't click... Oh, but there's a *dendenmushi* (snail). That's it! Okay, *dendenmushi* it is, then." That's how I decided on his name, and I told my friend (Ai Mizuse) on the other side of the kotatsu table, "I'm going to have Den's name taken from *dendenmushi*, to which she replied, "A Maimai, huh. I see." !!!!!! ↙ (A *dendenmushi* (snail) is also known as a Maimai.) (An alias?)

This was a complete coincidence, but things like this often happen in my manga...

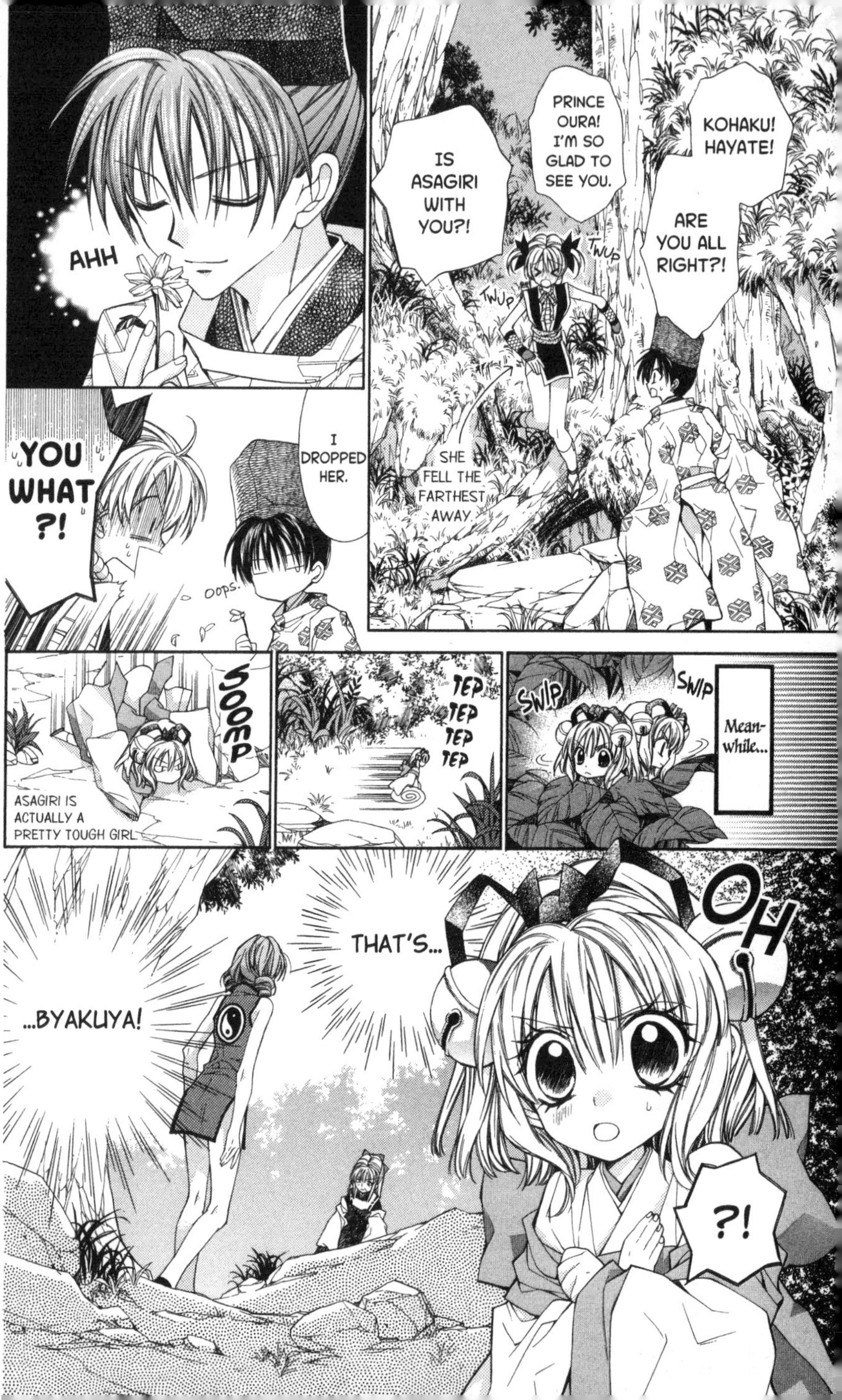
KOHAKU! HAYATE!
ARE YOU ALL RIGHT?!
PRINCE OURA! I'M SO GLAD TO SEE YOU.
TWUP
IS ASAGIRI WITH YOU?!
TWUP
SHE FELL THE FARTHEST AWAY.
AHH
I DROPPED HER.
YOU WHAT?!
OOPS.
Mean-while...
SWIP
SWIP
TEP TEP TEP TEP
SOOMP
ASAGIRI IS ACTUALLY A PRETTY TOUGH GIRL.
OH
THAT'S...
...BYAKUYA!
?!

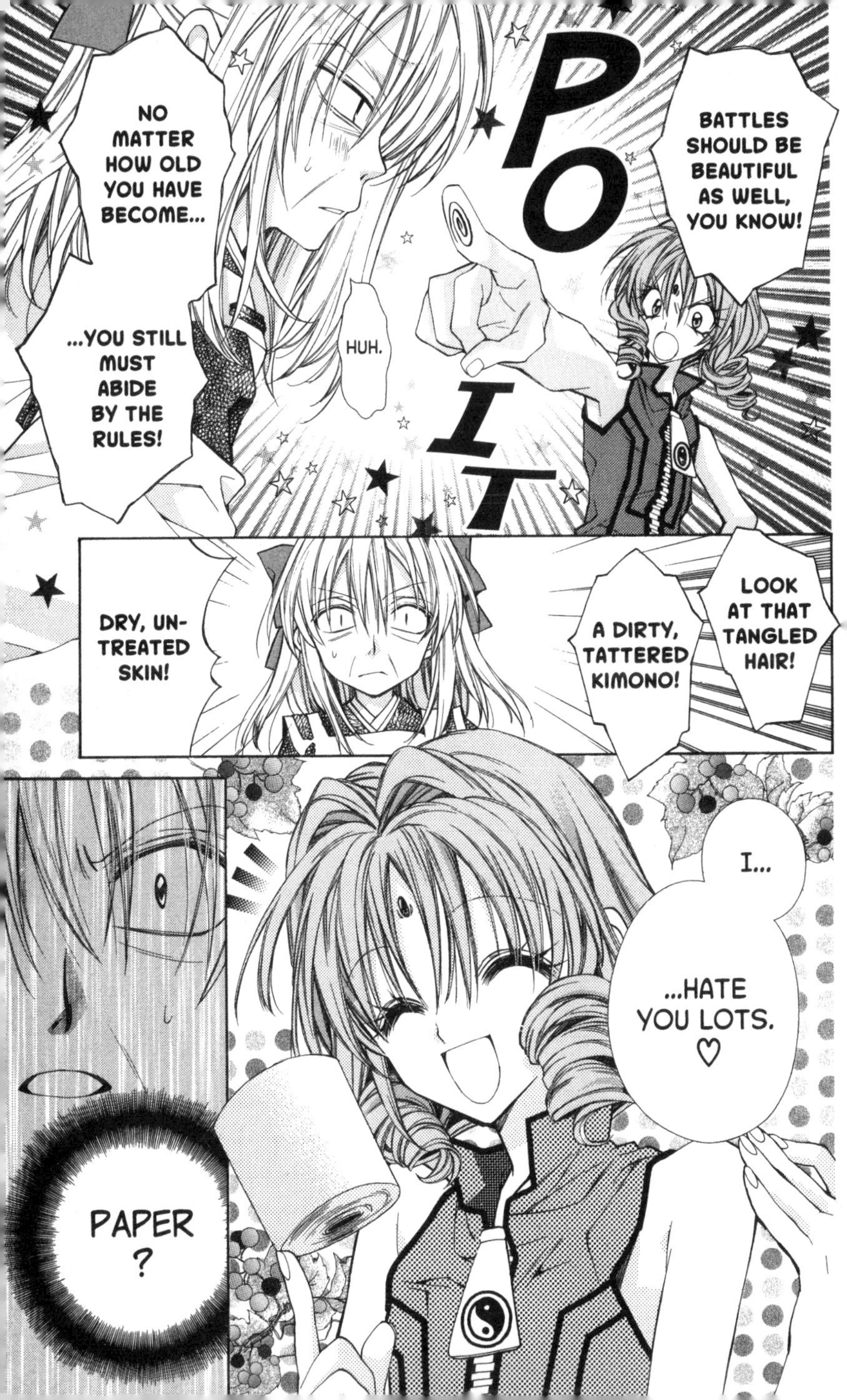
BATTLES SHOULD BE BEAUTIFUL AS WELL, YOU KNOW!
POIT
NO MATTER HOW OLD YOU HAVE BECOME...
HUH.
...YOU STILL MUST ABIDE BY THE RULES!
LOOK AT THAT TANGLED HAIR!
A DIRTY, TATTERED KIMONO!
DRY, UN-TREATED SKIN!
I...
...HATE YOU LOTS. ♡
PAPER?

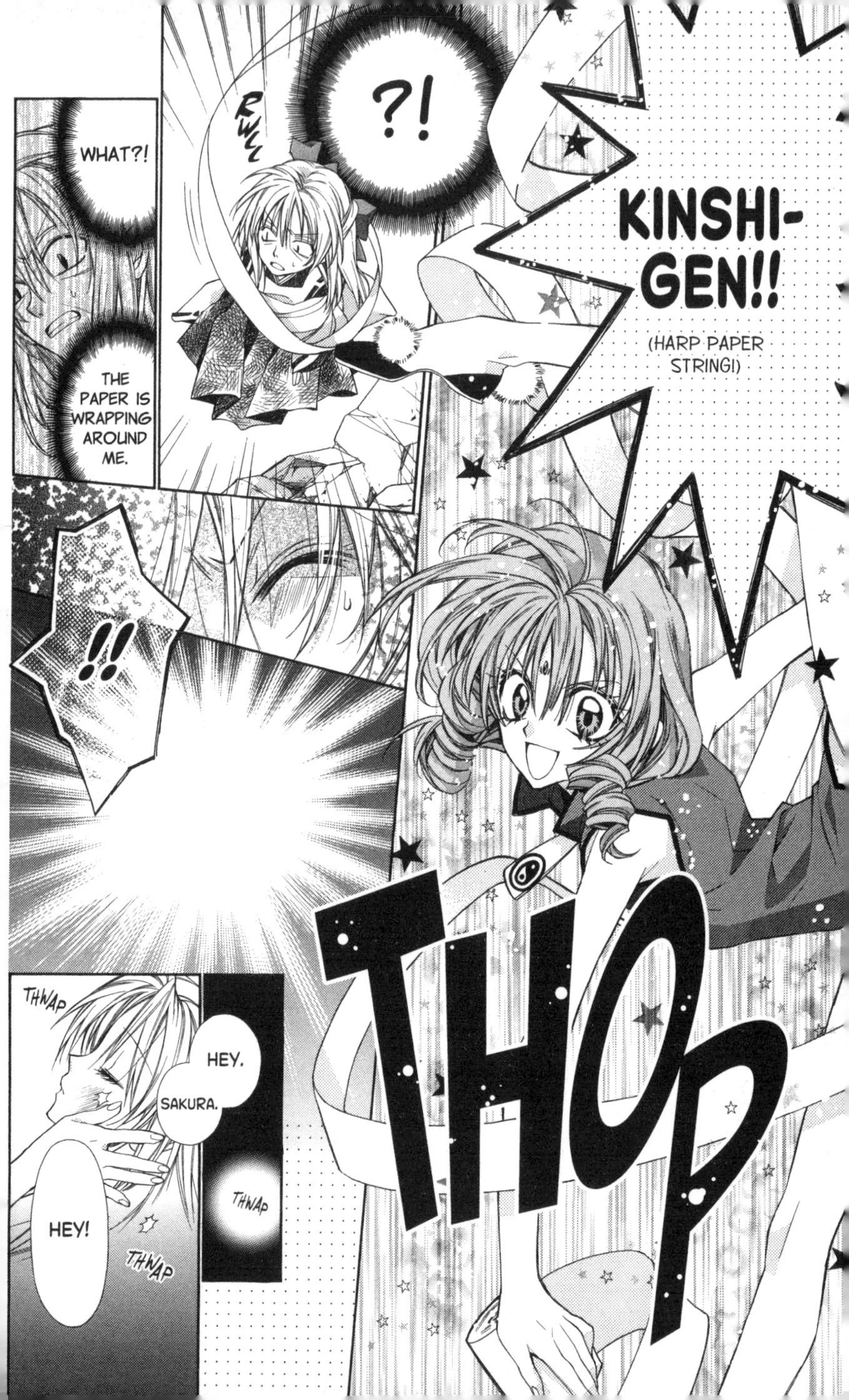
KINSHI-GEN!!
(HARP PAPER STRING!)
?!
RWLL
WHAT?!
THE PAPER IS WRAPPING AROUND ME.
!!
THOP
HEY.
SAKURA.
THWAP
THWAP
HEY!
THWAP

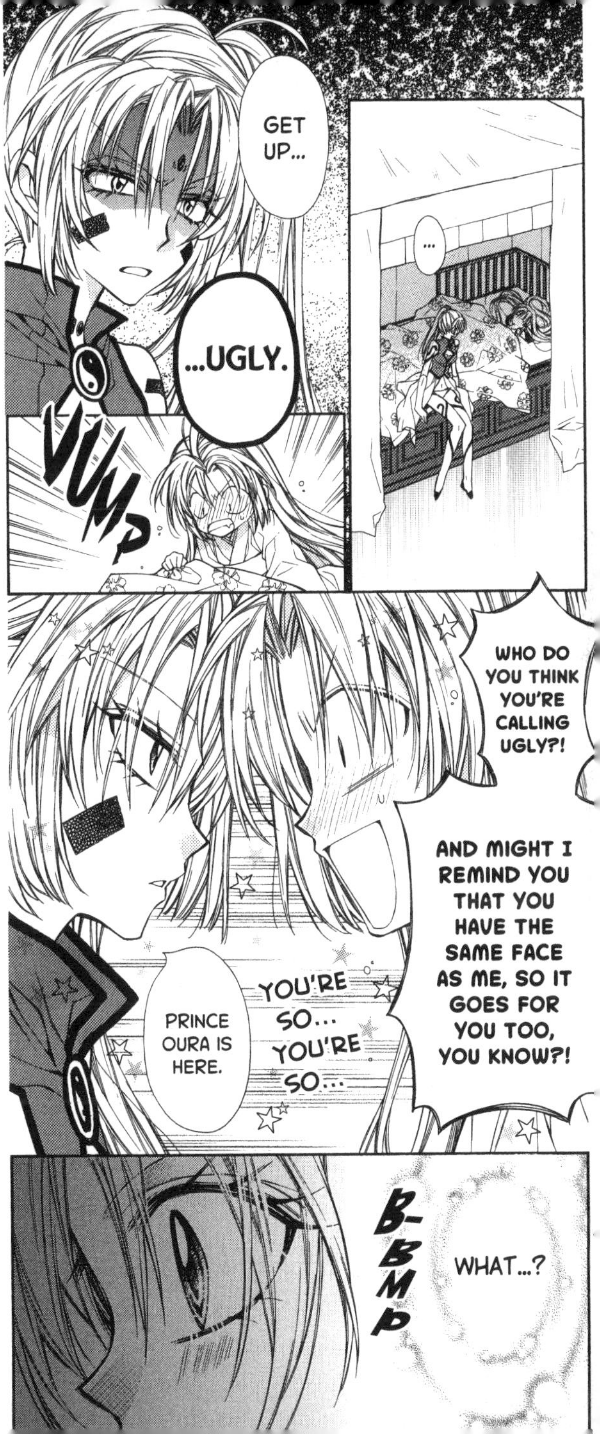
...
GET UP...
...UGLY.
VUMP
WHO DO YOU THINK YOU'RE CALLING UGLY?!
AND MIGHT I REMIND YOU THAT YOU HAVE THE SAME FACE AS ME, SO IT GOES FOR YOU TOO, YOU KNOW?!
YOU'RE SO... YOU'RE SO...
PRINCE OURA IS HERE.
WHAT...?
B-BMP

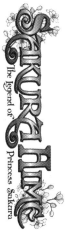

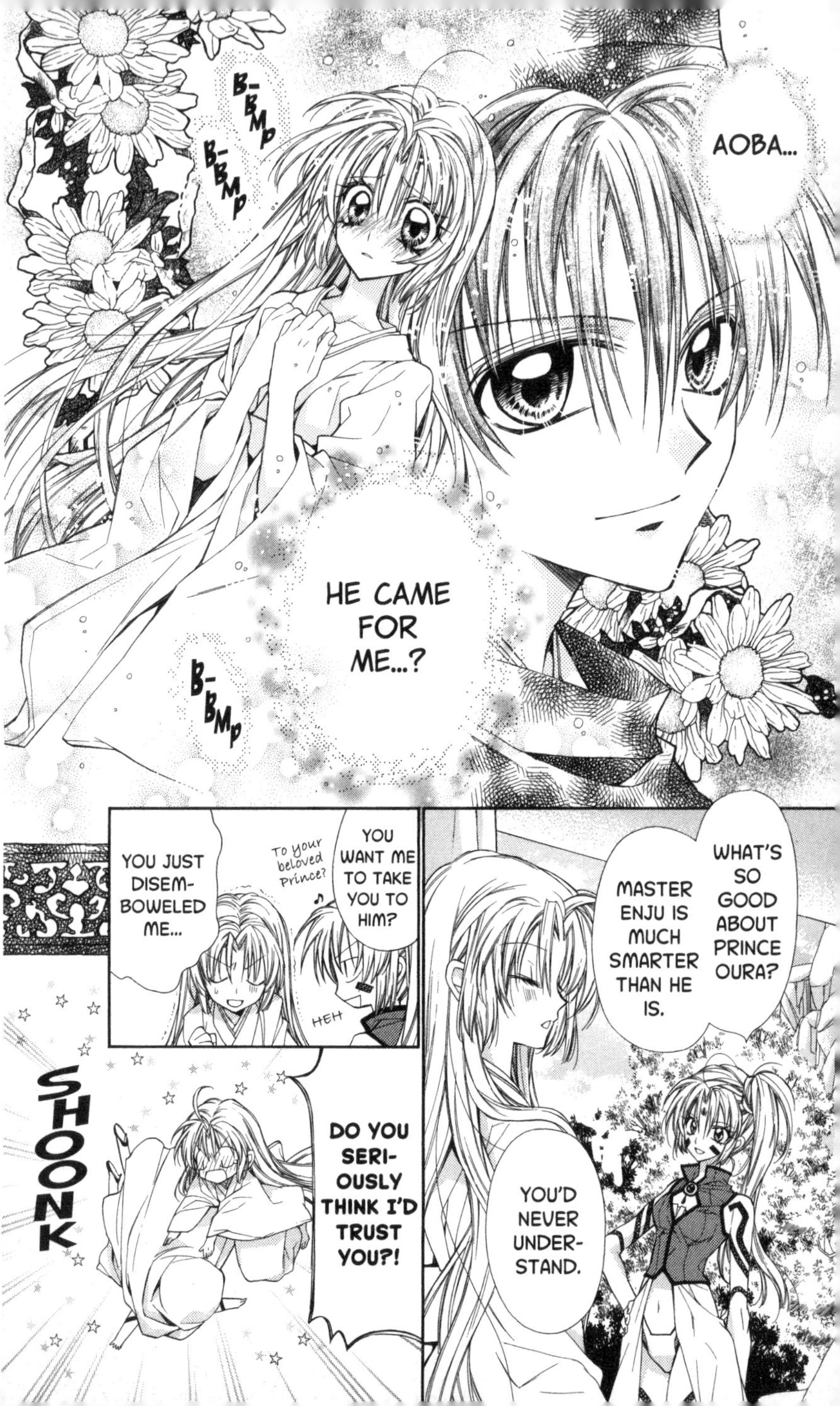
AOBA...
B-BMP
B-BMP
HE CAME FOR ME...?
B-BMP
WHAT'S SO GOOD ABOUT PRINCE OURA?
MASTER ENJU IS MUCH SMARTER THAN HE IS.
YOU'D NEVER UNDERSTAND.
YOU WANT ME TO TAKE YOU TO HIM?
To your beloved Prince? ♪
HEH
YOU JUST DISEMBOWELED ME...
DO YOU SERIOUSLY THINK I'D TRUST YOU?!
SHOONK

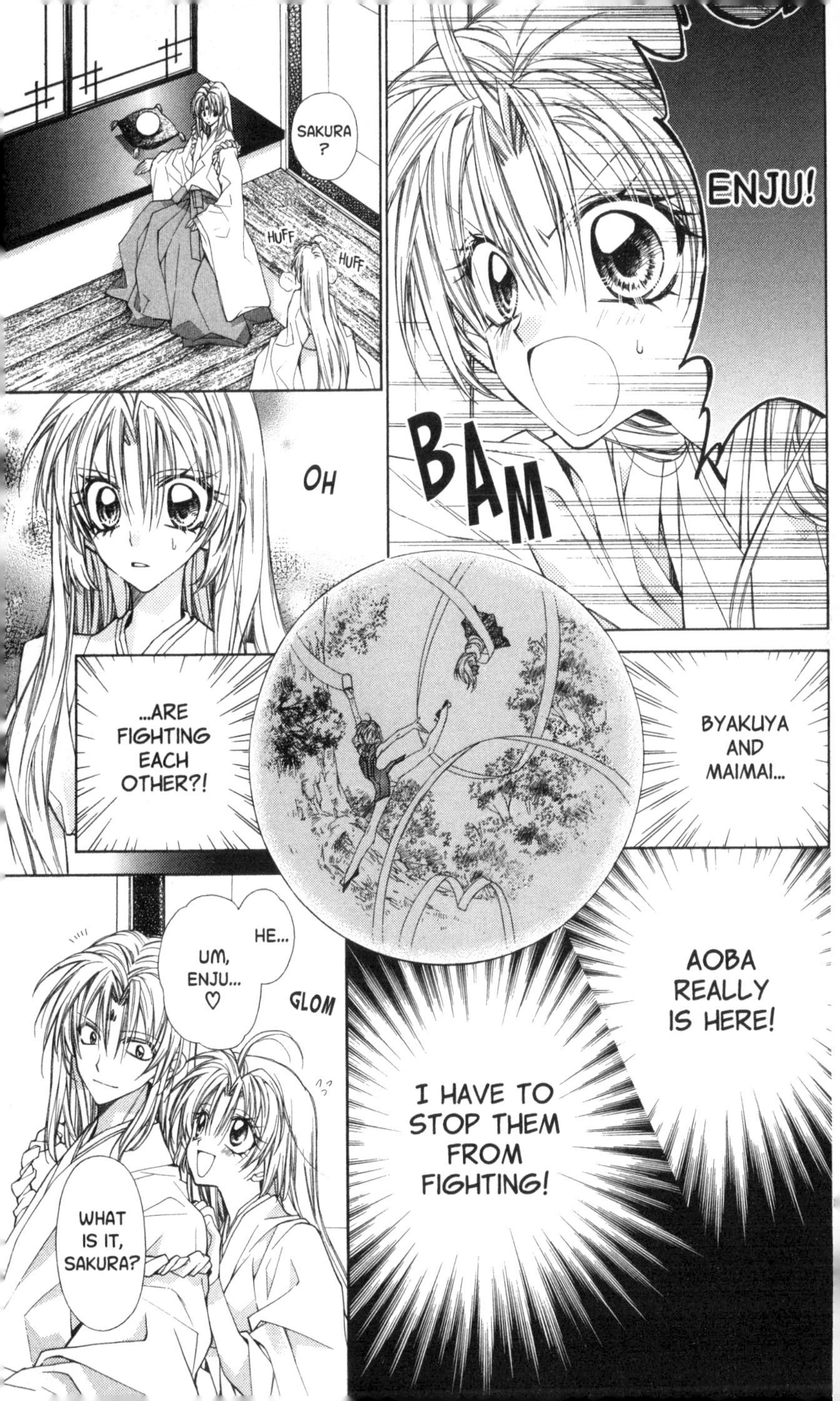
ENJU!
BAM
SAKURA?
HUFF
HUFF
BYAKUYA AND MAIMAI...
...ARE FIGHTING EACH OTHER?!
OH
AOBA REALLY IS HERE!
I HAVE TO STOP THEM FROM FIGHTING!
HE...
UM, ENJU... ♡
GLOM
WHAT IS IT, SAKURA?

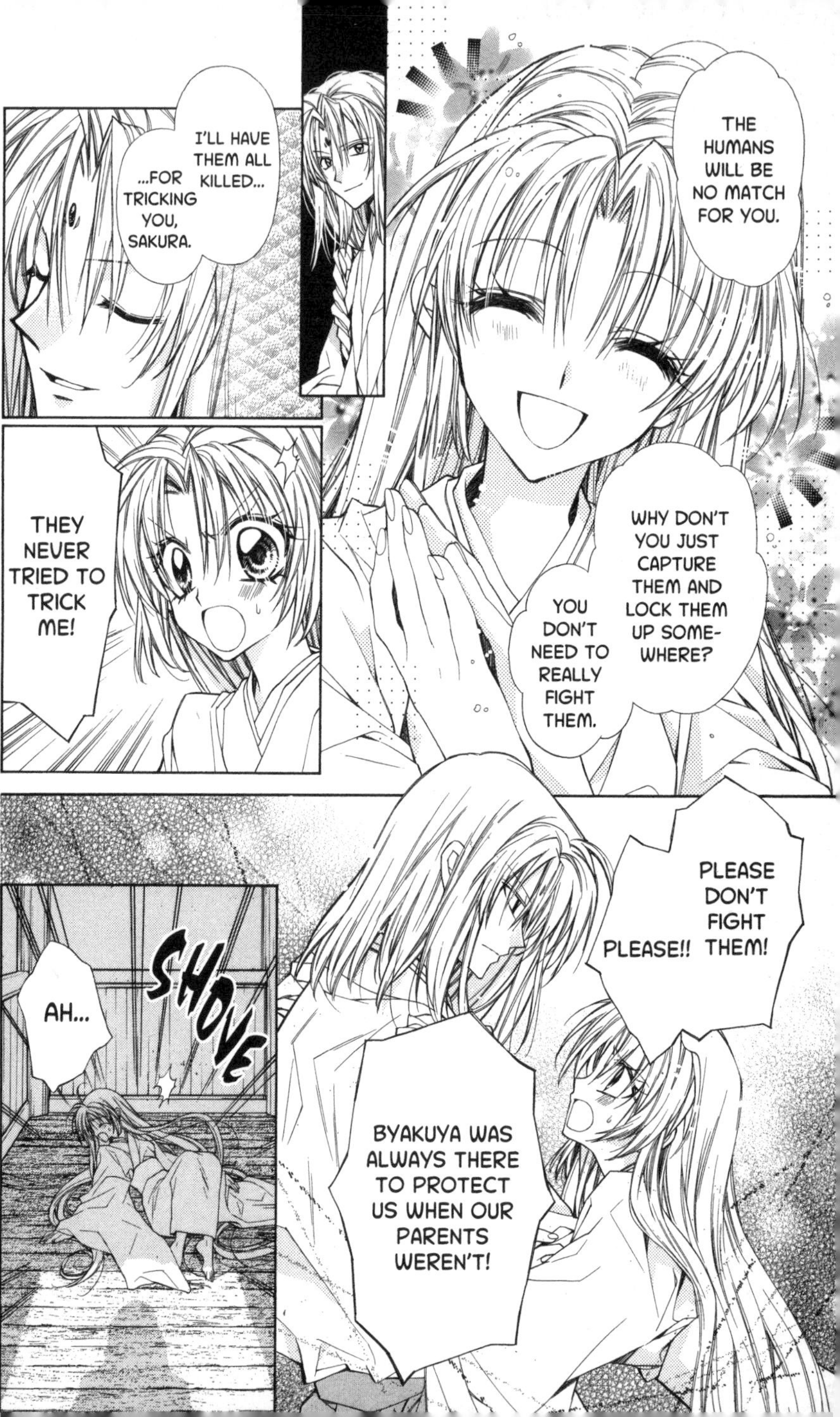
THE HUMANS WILL BE NO MATCH FOR YOU.
WHY DON'T YOU JUST CAPTURE THEM AND LOCK THEM UP SOME-WHERE?
YOU DON'T NEED TO REALLY FIGHT THEM.
I'LL HAVE THEM ALL KILLED...
...FOR TRICKING YOU, SAKURA.
THEY NEVER TRIED TO TRICK ME!
PLEASE DON'T FIGHT THEM!
PLEASE!!
BYAKUYA WAS ALWAYS THERE TO PROTECT US WHEN OUR PARENTS WEREN'T!
SHOVE
AH...

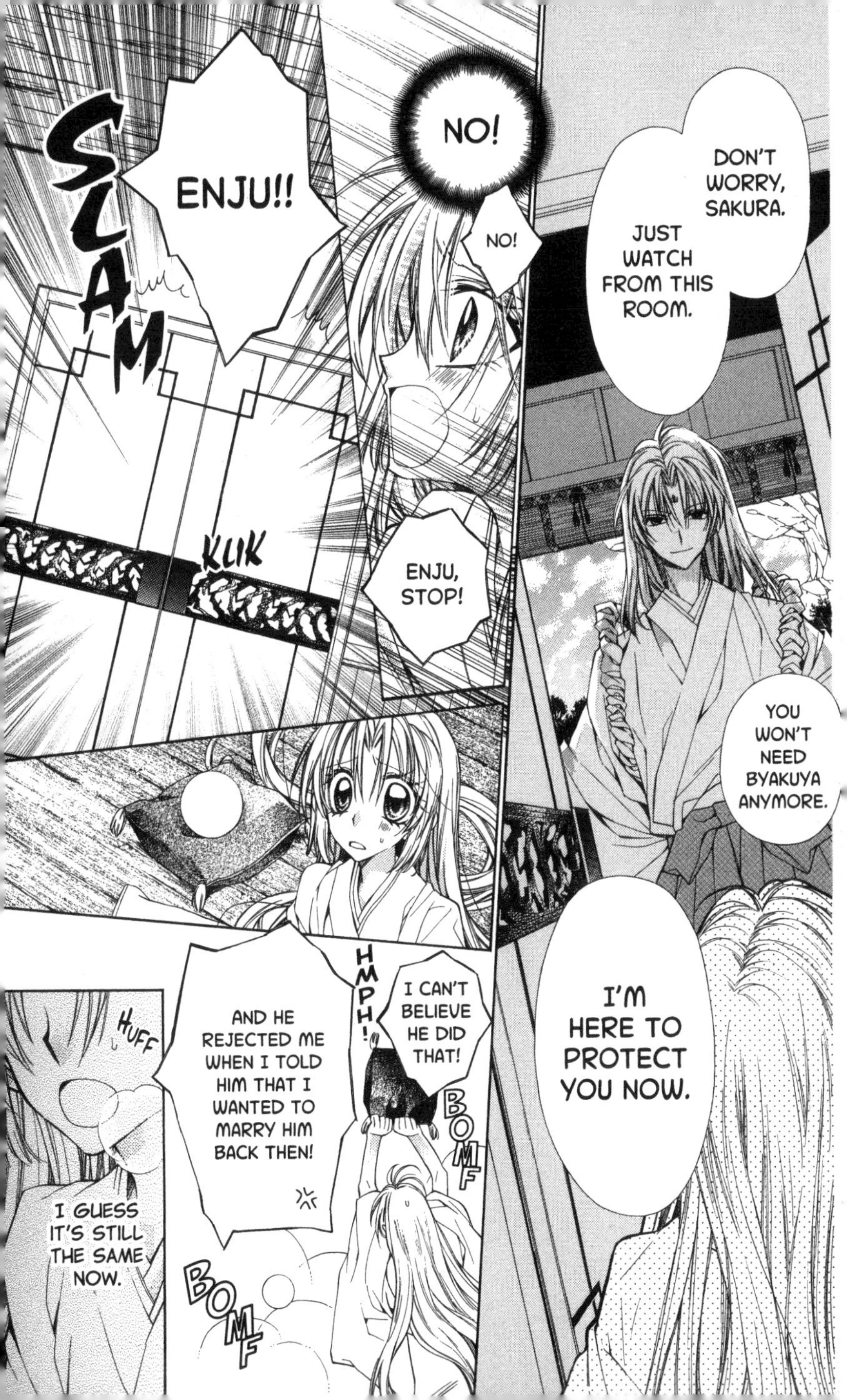
DON'T WORRY, SAKURA.
JUST WATCH FROM THIS ROOM.
YOU WON'T NEED BYAKUYA ANYMORE.
I'M HERE TO PROTECT YOU NOW.
NO!
NO!
ENJU, STOP!
ENJU!!
SLAM
KLIK
HMPH!
I CAN'T BELIEVE HE DID THAT!
AND HE REJECTED ME WHEN I TOLD HIM THAT I WANTED TO MARRY HIM BACK THEN!
BOMF
BOMF
HUFF
I GUESS IT'S STILL THE SAME NOW.

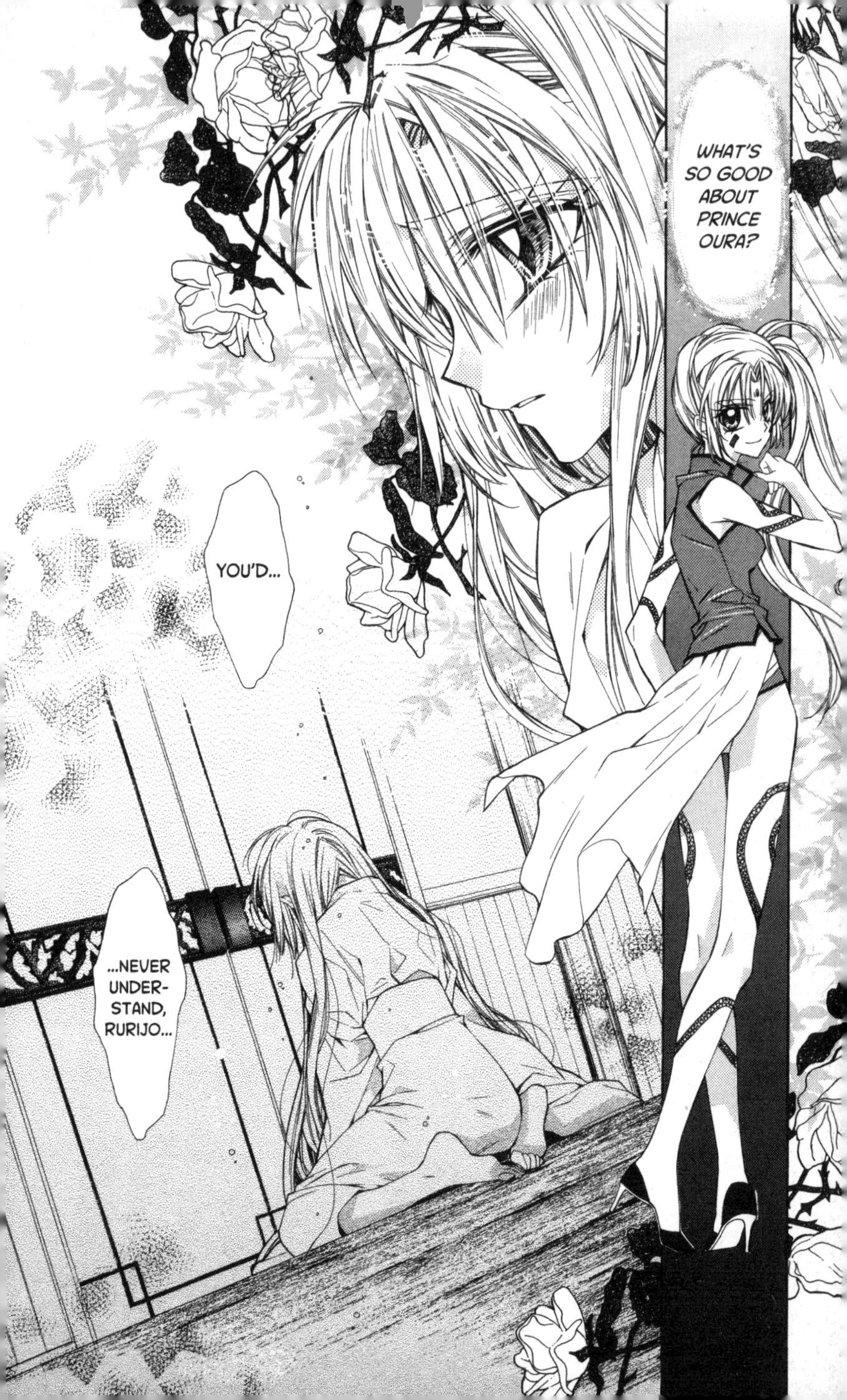
WHAT'S SO GOOD ABOUT PRINCE OURA?
YOU'D...
...NEVER UNDER-STAND, RURIJO...

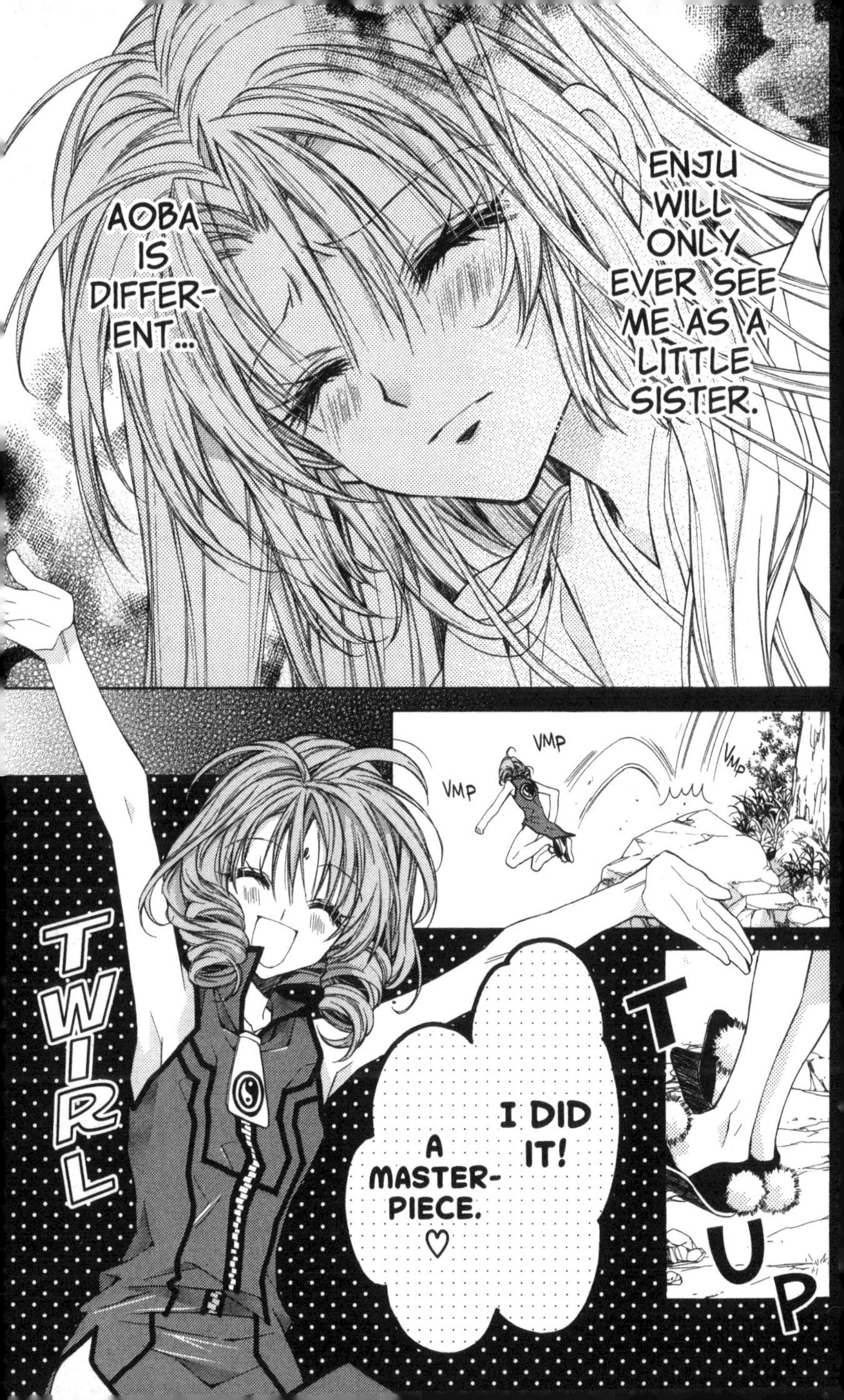
ENJU WILL ONLY EVER SEE ME AS A LITTLE SISTER.
AOBA IS DIFFER-ENT...
VMP
VMP
VMP
TUP
I DID IT!
A MASTER-PIECE. ♡
TWIRL

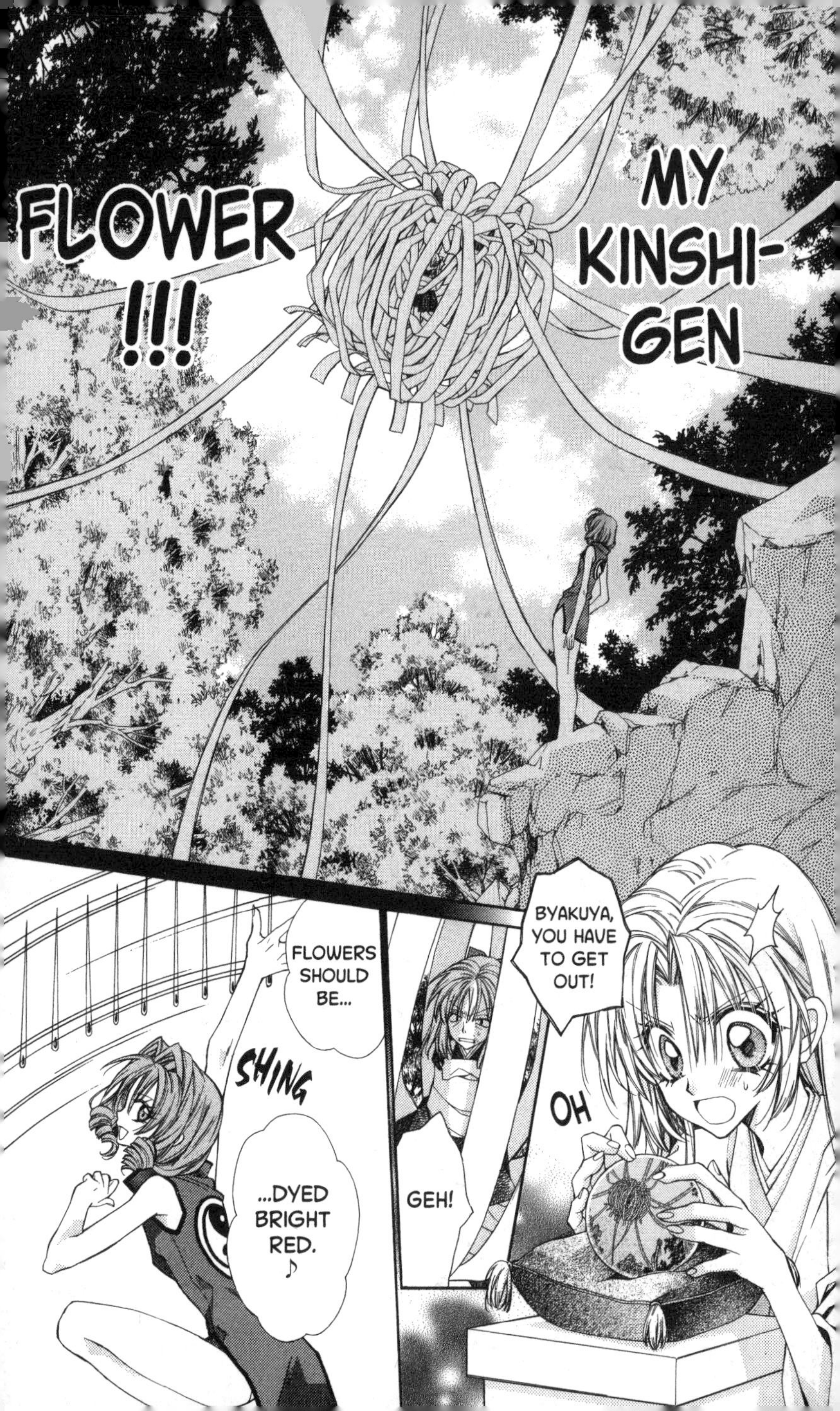
MY KINSHI-GEN
FLOWER !!!
BYAKUYA, YOU HAVE TO GET OUT!
OH
GEH!
FLOWERS SHOULD BE...
SHING
...DYED BRIGHT RED. ♪

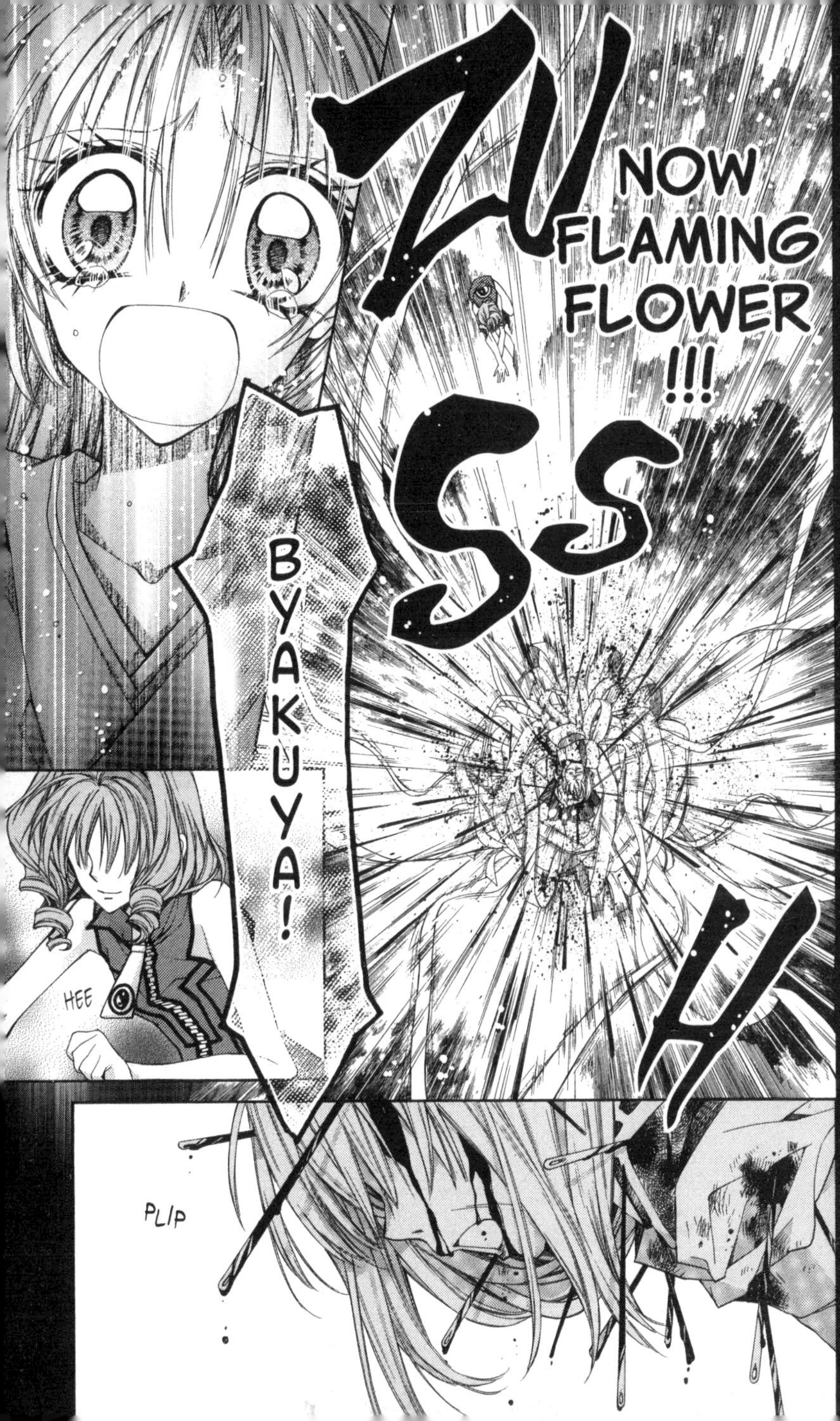
ZUSSH
NOW FLAMING FLOWER!!!
BYAKUYA!
HEE
PLIP

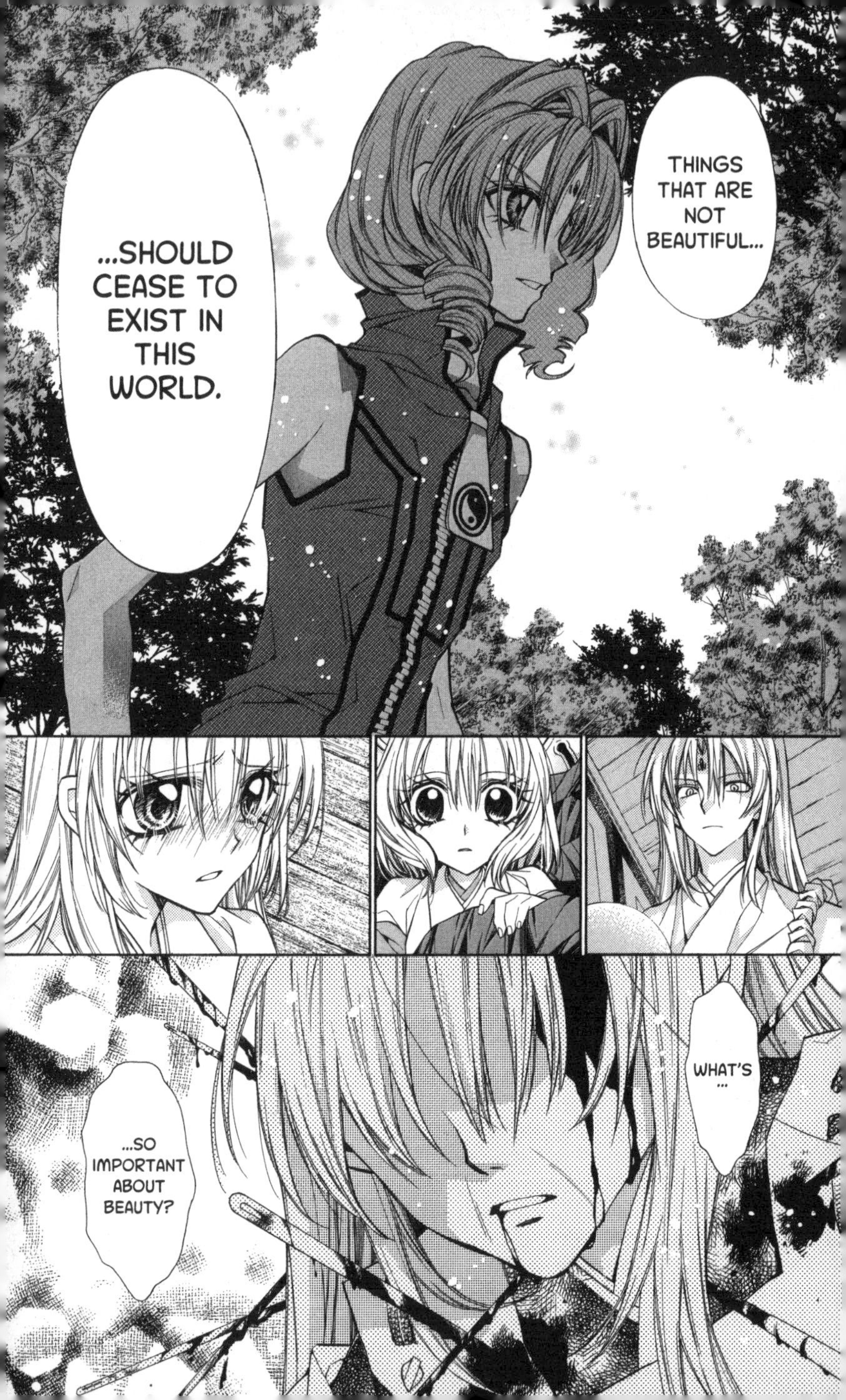
THINGS THAT ARE NOT BEAUTIFUL...
...SHOULD CEASE TO EXIST IN THIS WORLD.
WHAT'S ...
...SO IMPORTANT ABOUT BEAUTY?

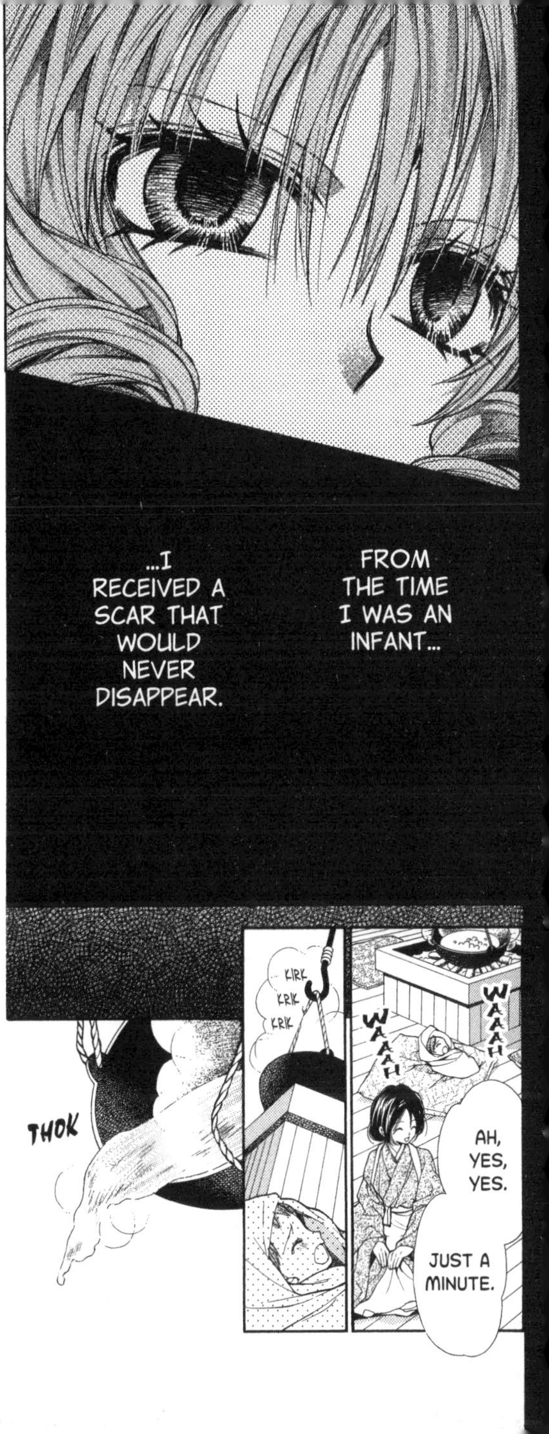
FROM THE TIME I WAS AN INFANT...
...I RECEIVED A SCAR THAT WOULD NEVER DISAPPEAR.
WAAAH
WAAAH
AH, YES, YES.
JUST A MINUTE.
KIRK KRIK KRIK
THOK

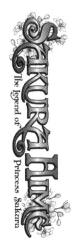

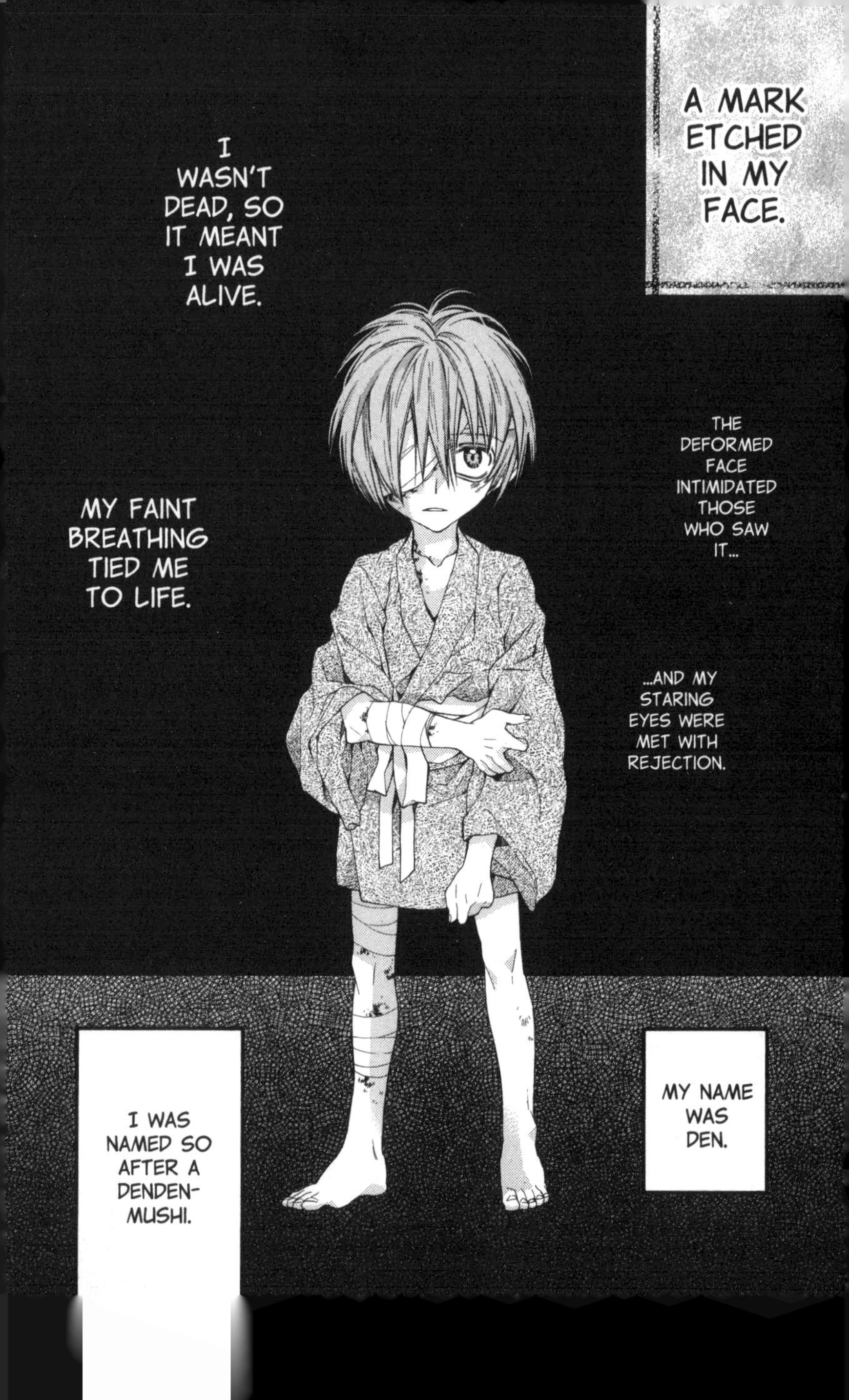
A MARK ETCHED IN MY FACE.
THE DEFORMED FACE INTIMIDATED THOSE WHO SAW IT...
...AND MY STARING EYES WERE MET WITH REJECTION.
I WASN'T DEAD, SO IT MEANT I WAS ALIVE.
MY FAINT BREATHING TIED ME TO LIFE.
MY NAME WAS DEN.
I WAS NAMED SO AFTER A DENDEN-MUSHI.

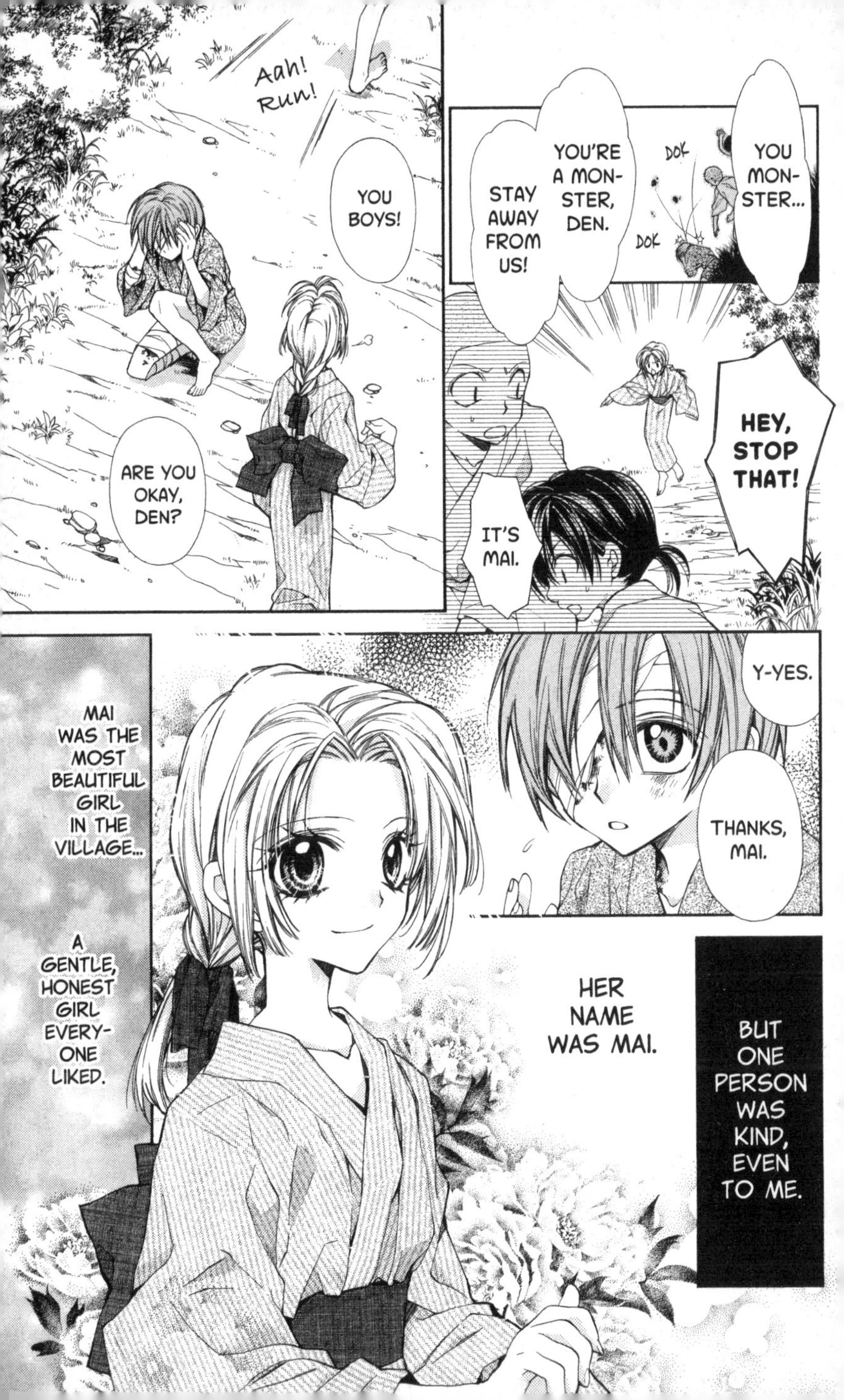
YOU MONSTER...
DOK
YOU'RE A MONSTER, DEN.
DOK
STAY AWAY FROM US!
HEY, STOP THAT!
IT'S MAI.
Aah! Run!
YOU BOYS!
ARE YOU OKAY, DEN?
Y-YES.
THANKS, MAI.
BUT ONE PERSON WAS KIND, EVEN TO ME.
HER NAME WAS MAI.
MAI WAS THE MOST BEAUTIFUL GIRL IN THE VILLAGE...
A GENTLE, HONEST GIRL EVERYONE LIKED.

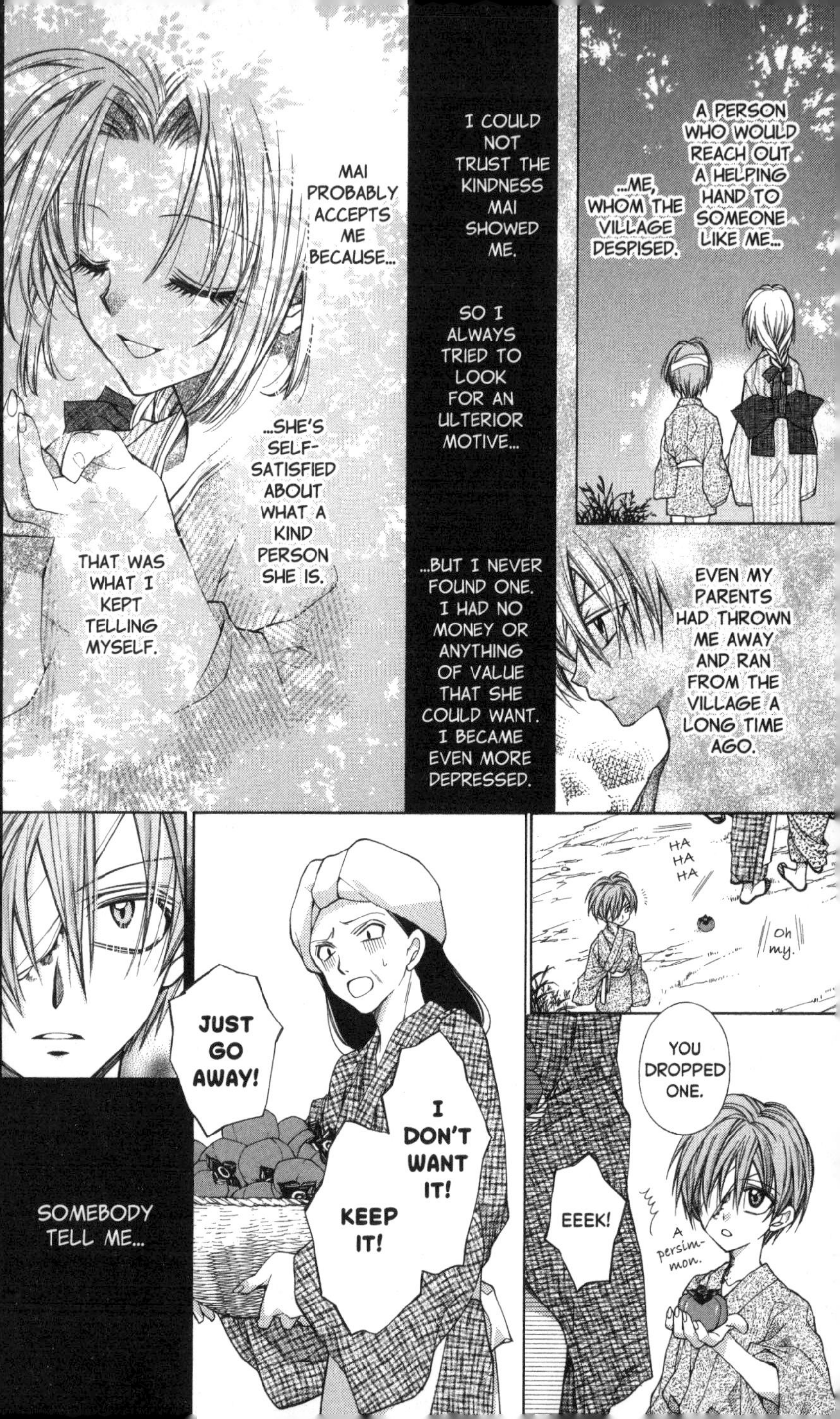
A PERSON WHO WOULD REACH OUT A HELPING HAND TO SOMEONE LIKE ME...
...ME, WHOM THE VILLAGE DESPISED.
EVEN MY PARENTS HAD THROWN ME AWAY AND RAN FROM THE VILLAGE A LONG TIME AGO.
I COULD NOT TRUST THE KINDNESS MAI SHOWED ME.
SO I ALWAYS TRIED TO LOOK FOR AN ULTERIOR MOTIVE...
...BUT I NEVER FOUND ONE. I HAD NO MONEY OR ANYTHING OF VALUE THAT SHE COULD WANT. I BECAME EVEN MORE DEPRESSED.
MAI PROBABLY ACCEPTS ME BECAUSE...
...SHE'S SELF-SATISFIED ABOUT WHAT A KIND PERSON SHE IS.
THAT WAS WHAT I KEPT TELLING MYSELF.
HA HA HA
Oh my.
YOU DROPPED ONE.
A persimmon.
EEEK!
I DON'T WANT IT!
KEEP IT!
JUST GO AWAY!
SOMEBODY TELL ME...

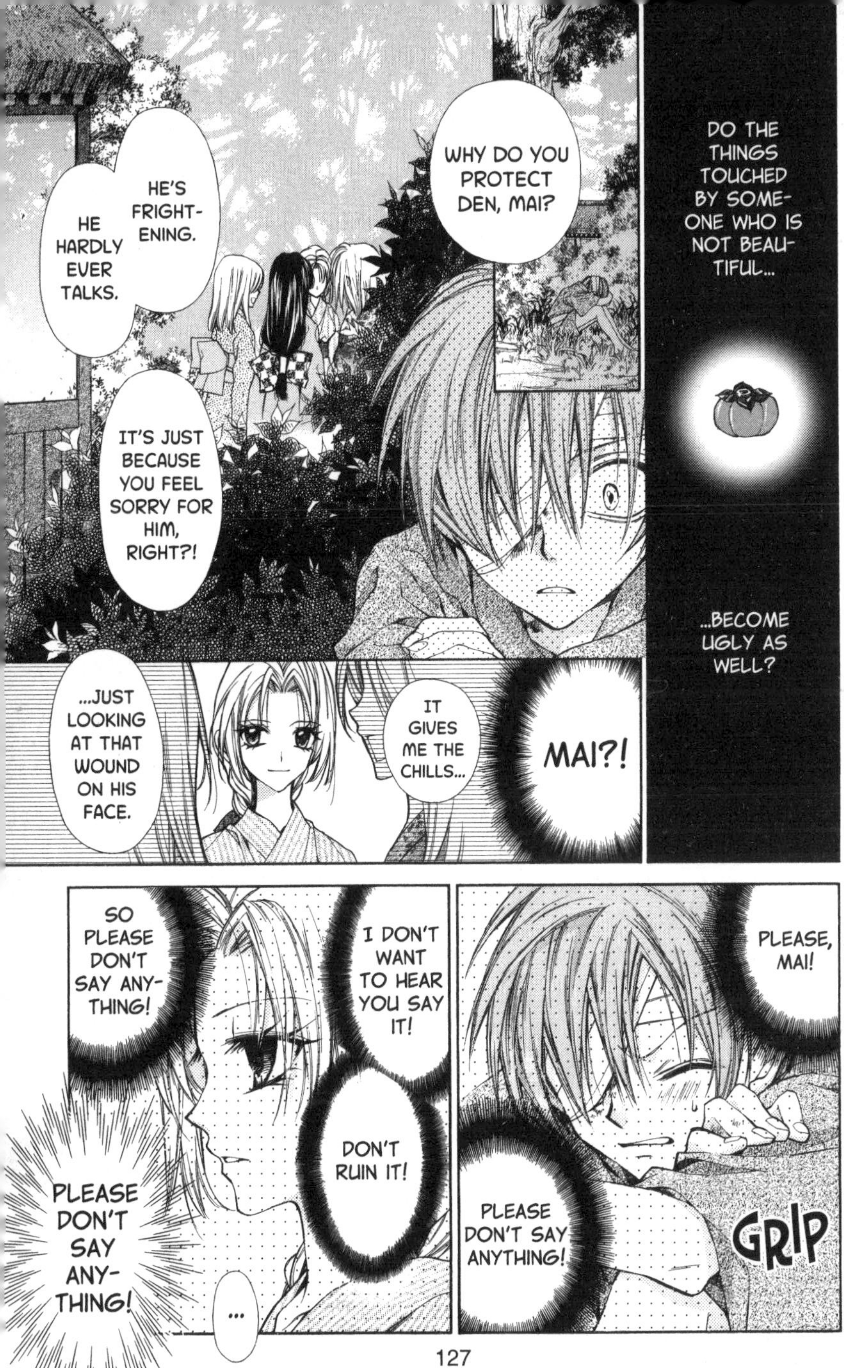
DO THE THINGS TOUCHED BY SOME-ONE WHO IS NOT BEAU-TIFUL...
...BECOME UGLY AS WELL?
WHY DO YOU PROTECT DEN, MAI?
HE'S FRIGHT-ENING.
HE HARDLY EVER TALKS.
IT'S JUST BECAUSE YOU FEEL SORRY FOR HIM, RIGHT?!
MAI?!
IT GIVES ME THE CHILLS...
...JUST LOOKING AT THAT WOUND ON HIS FACE.
PLEASE, MAI!
PLEASE DON'T SAY ANYTHING!
GRIP
I DON'T WANT TO HEAR YOU SAY IT!
SO PLEASE DON'T SAY ANY-THING!
DON'T RUIN IT!
PLEASE DON'T SAY ANY-THING!
...

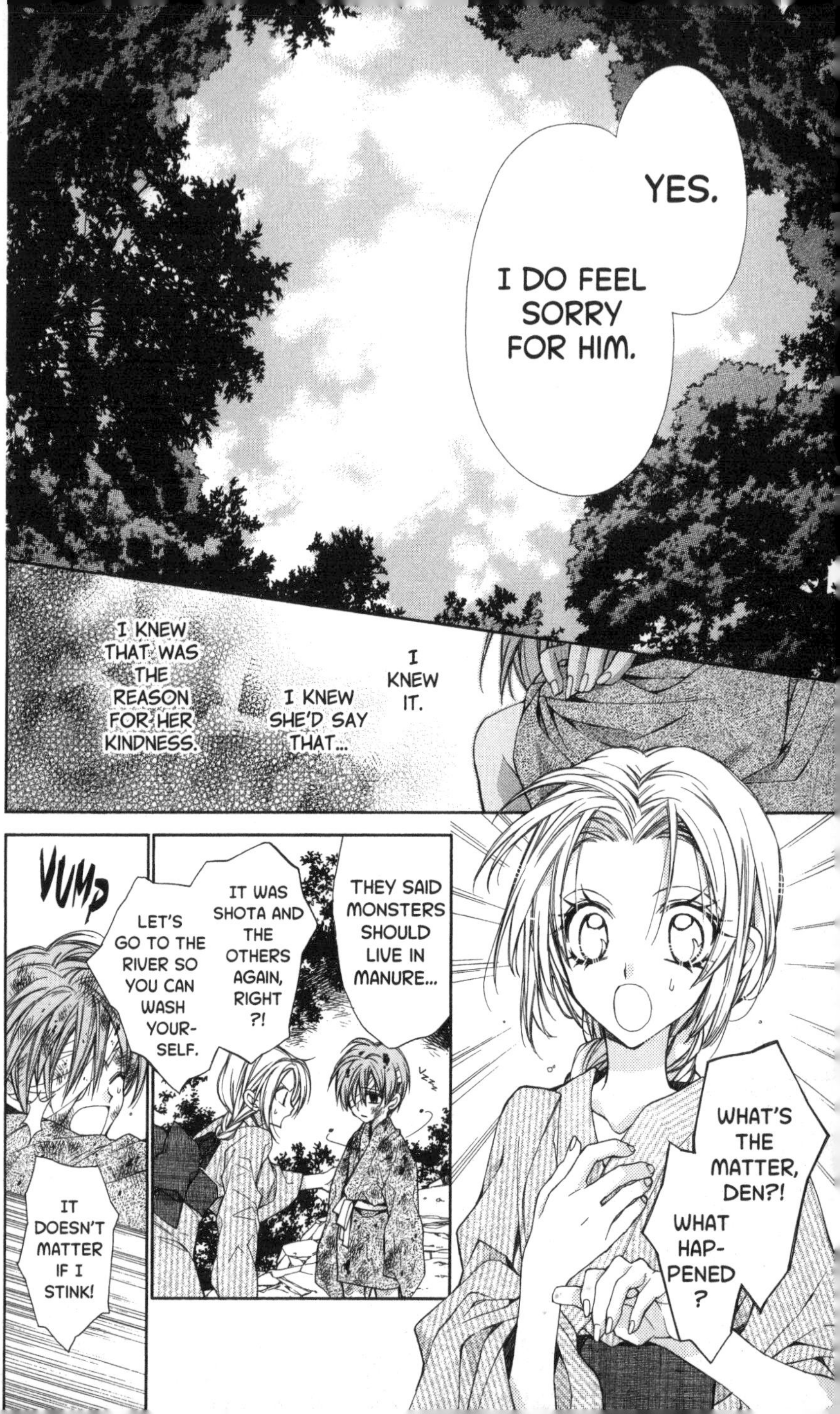
YES.
I DO FEEL SORRY FOR HIM.
I KNEW IT.
I KNEW SHE'D SAY THAT...
I KNEW THAT WAS THE REASON FOR HER KINDNESS.
WHAT'S THE MATTER, DEN?!
WHAT HAP-PENED?
THEY SAID MONSTERS SHOULD LIVE IN MANURE...
IT WAS SHOTA AND THE OTHERS AGAIN, RIGHT?!
LET'S GO TO THE RIVER SO YOU CAN WASH YOUR-SELF.
VUMP
IT DOESN'T MATTER IF I STINK!

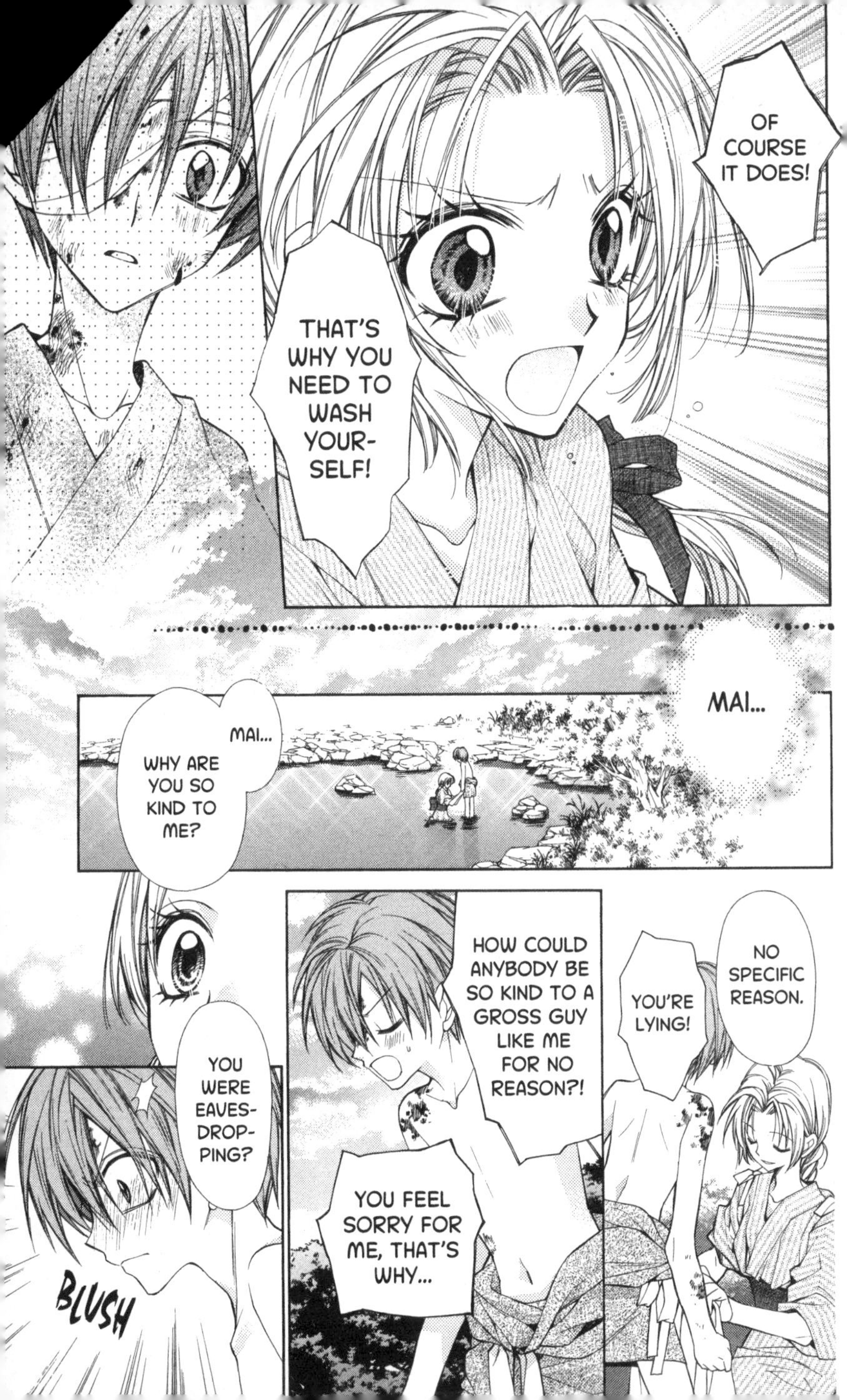
OF COURSE IT DOES!
THAT'S WHY YOU NEED TO WASH YOUR-SELF!
MAI...
MAI...
WHY ARE YOU SO KIND TO ME?
NO SPECIFIC REASON.
YOU'RE LYING!
HOW COULD ANYBODY BE SO KIND TO A GROSS GUY LIKE ME FOR NO REASON?!
YOU FEEL SORRY FOR ME, THAT'S WHY...
YOU WERE EAVES-DROP-PING?
BLUSH

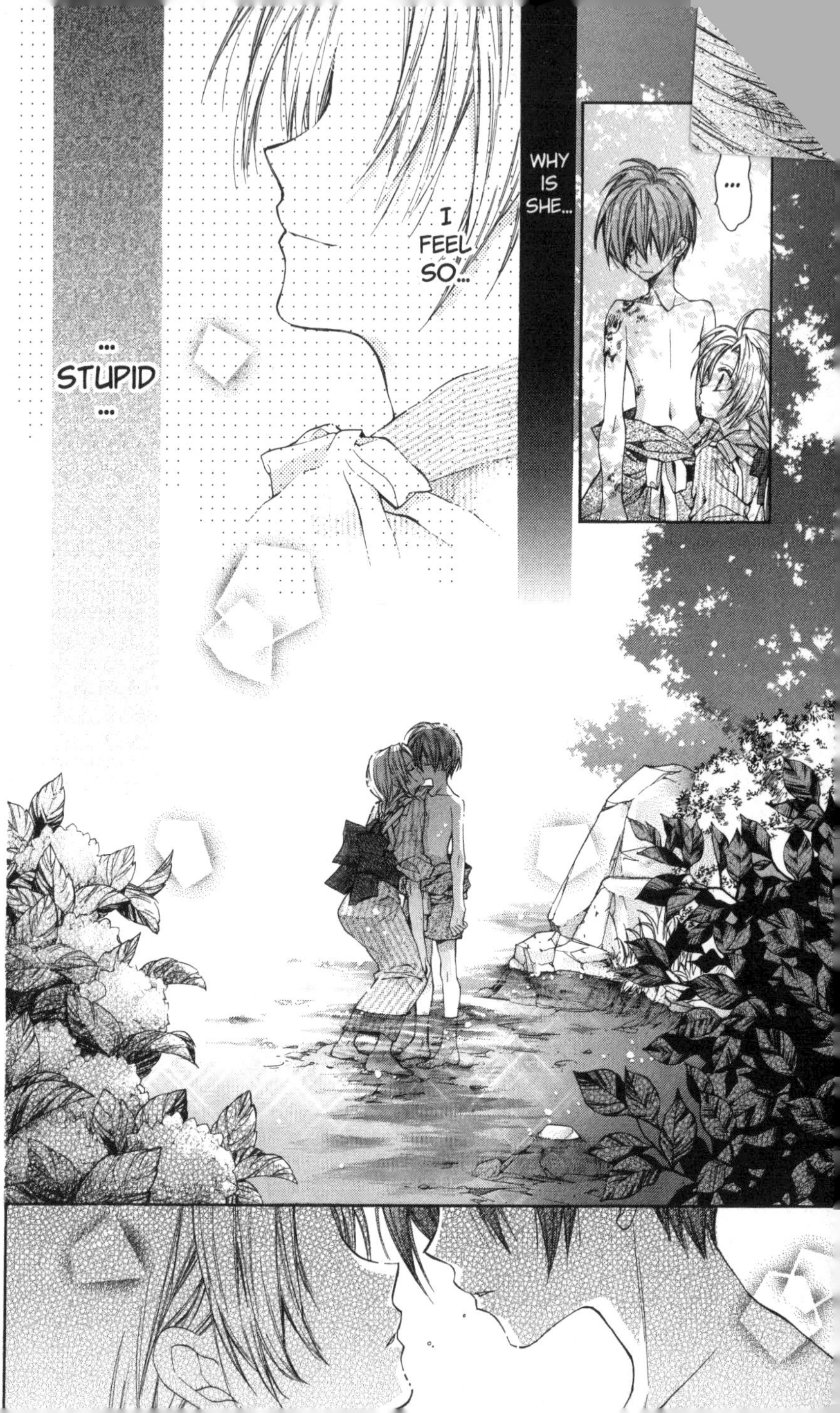
...
WHY IS SHE...
I FEEL SO...
... STUPID ...

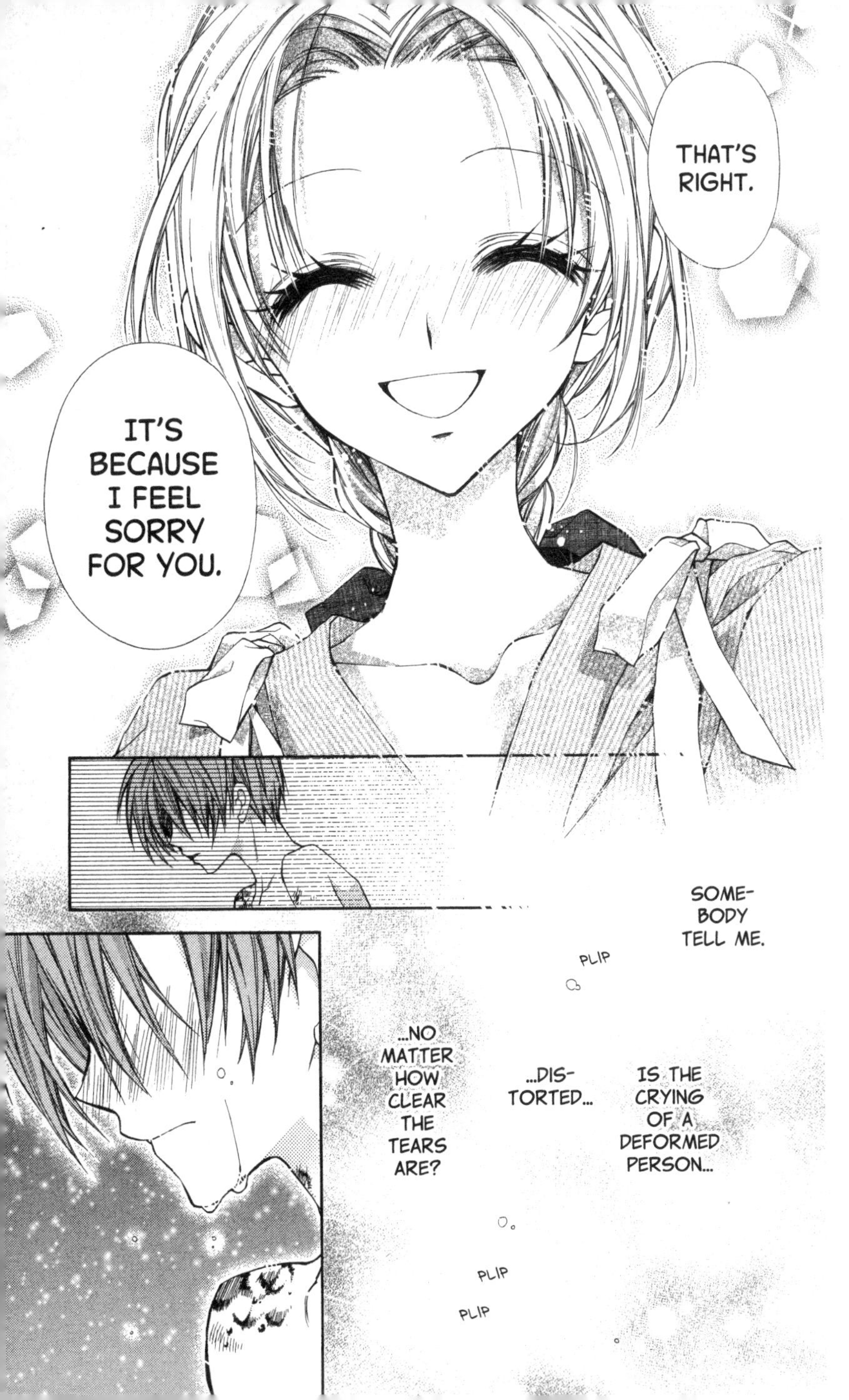
THAT'S RIGHT.
IT'S BECAUSE I FEEL SORRY FOR YOU.
SOME-BODY TELL ME.
PLIP
IS THE CRYING OF A DEFORMED PERSON...
...DIS-TORTED...
...NO MATTER HOW CLEAR THE TEARS ARE?
PLIP
PLIP

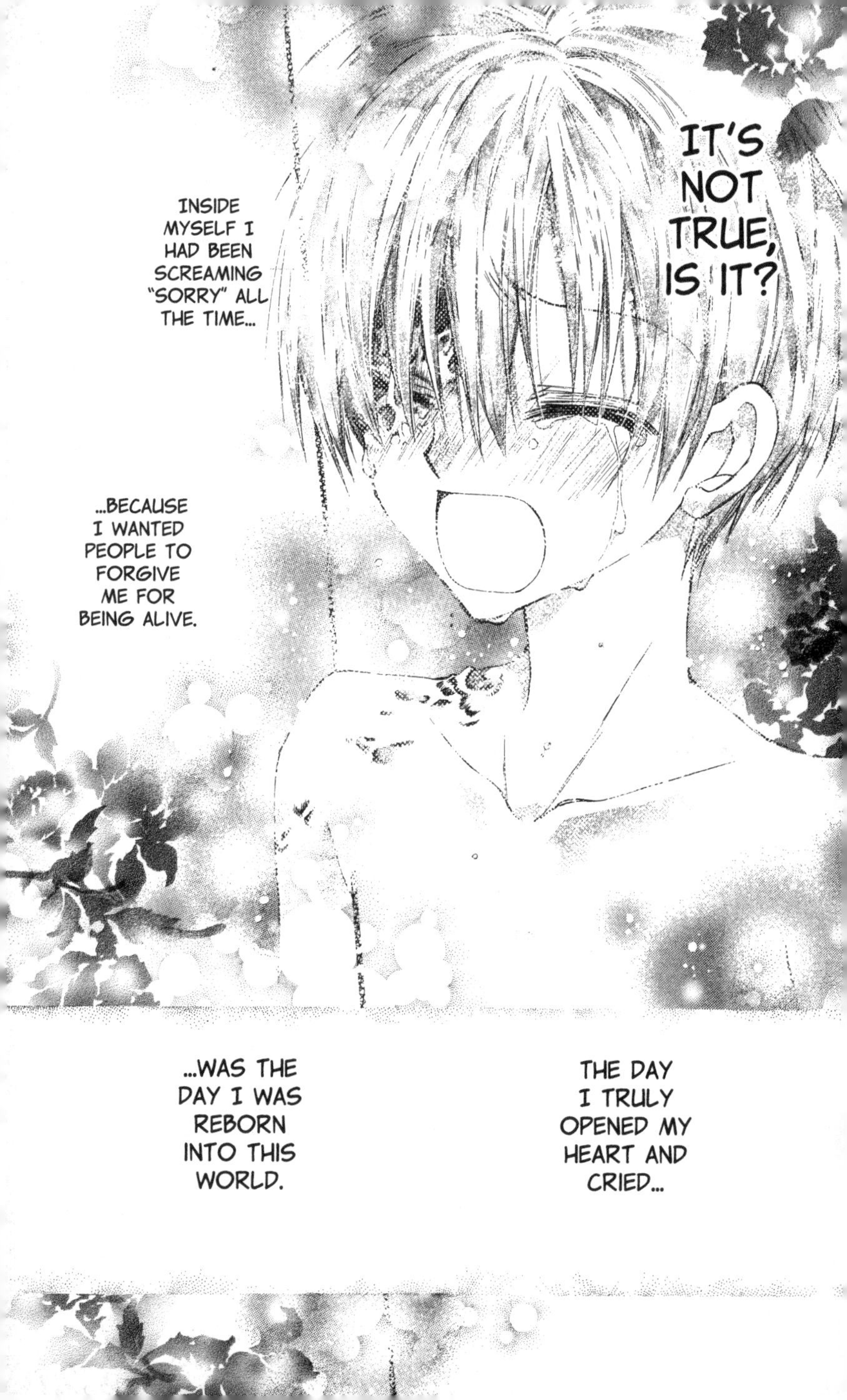
IT'S NOT TRUE, IS IT?
INSIDE MYSELF I HAD BEEN SCREAMING "SORRY" ALL THE TIME...
...BECAUSE I WANTED PEOPLE TO FORGIVE ME FOR BEING ALIVE.
THE DAY I TRULY OPENED MY HEART AND CRIED...
...WAS THE DAY I WAS REBORN INTO THIS WORLD.

Special Thanks

Nakame

Miichi
Ikurun
Konako
Kawanishi-san
Yoshizawa-san
Yuki-san
Hina-chan
Yamada-san
Kyomoto-san
Sakakura-san

Shueisha,
Ribon Editorial Department

Editor T-sama
Editor in Chief S-sama

Aguri Hiramatsu-sama

Thank you very much!

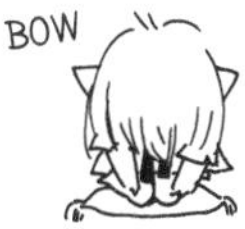
BOW

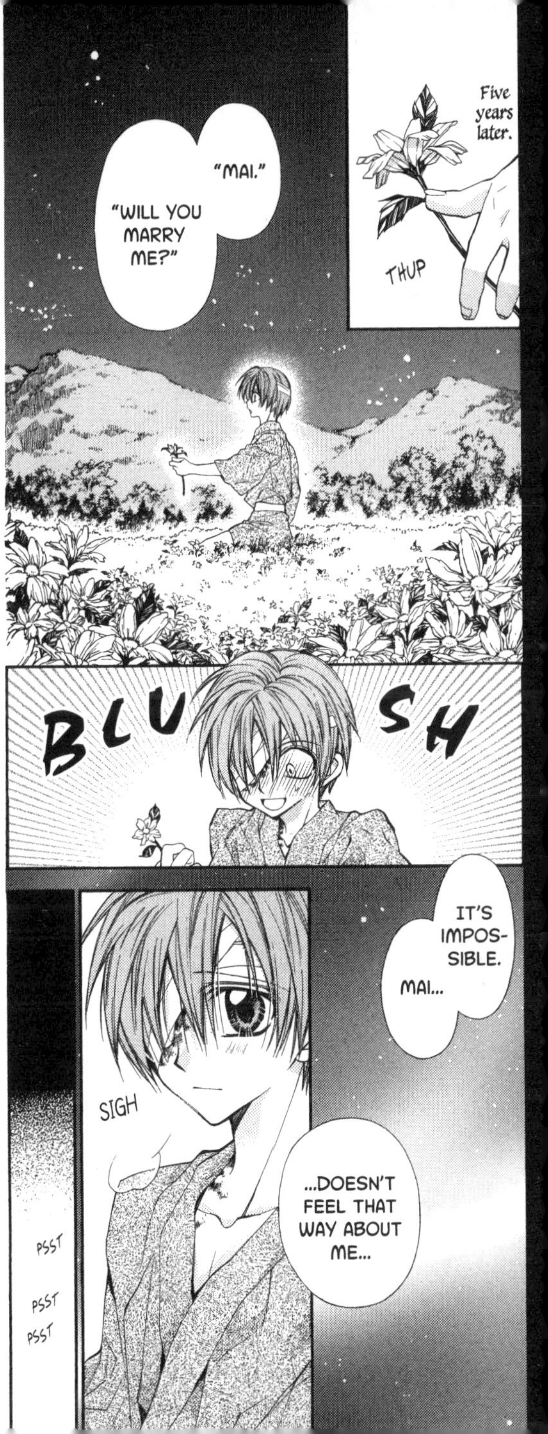
Five years later.
THUP
"MAI."
"WILL YOU MARRY ME?"
BLUSH
IT'S IMPOSSIBLE.
MAI...
SIGH
...DOESN'T FEEL THAT WAY ABOUT ME...
PSST
PSST
PSST

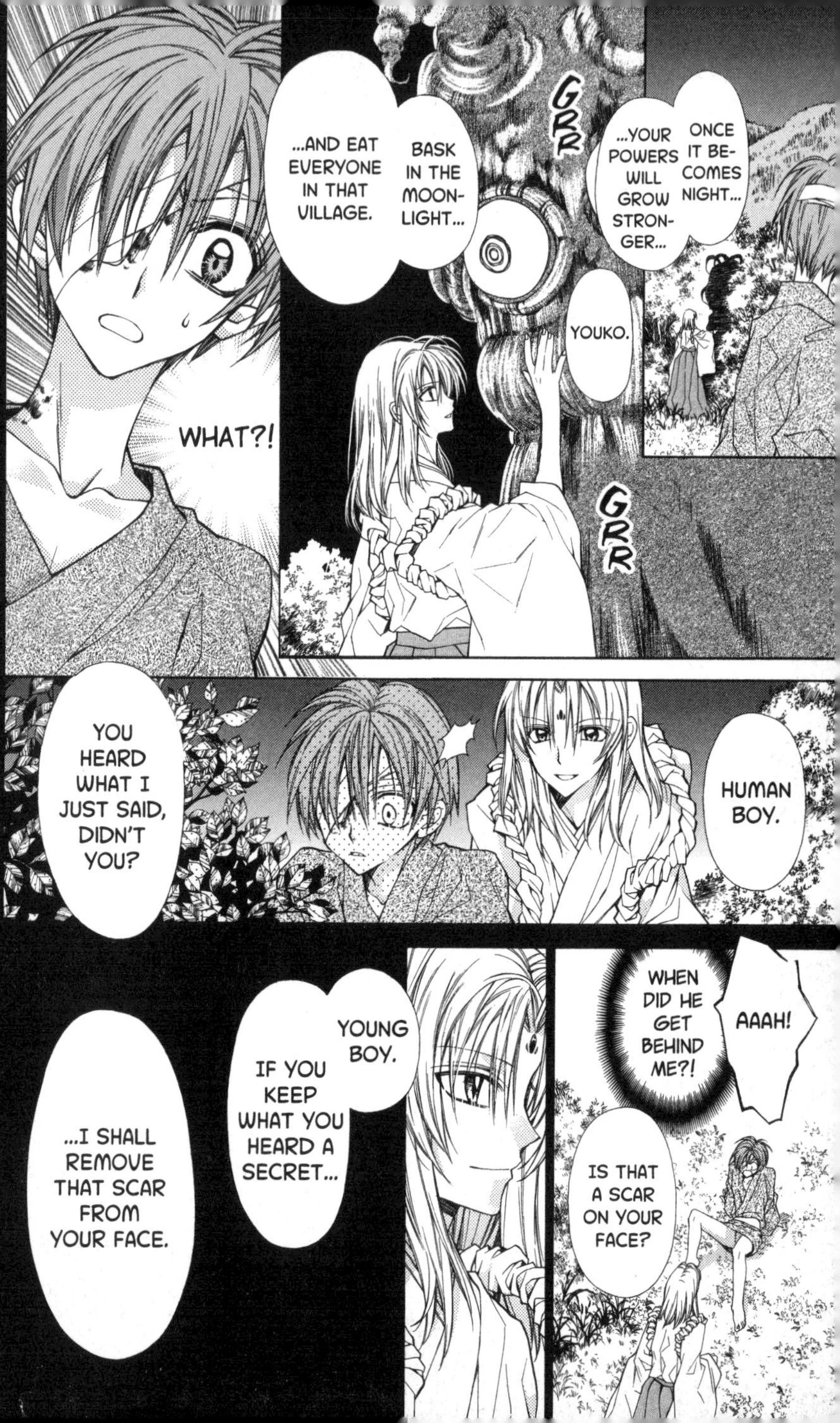
ONCE IT BECOMES NIGHT...
...YOUR POWERS WILL GROW STRONGER...
YOUKO.
GRR
BASK IN THE MOONLIGHT...
...AND EAT EVERYONE IN THAT VILLAGE.
GRR
WHAT?!
HUMAN BOY.
YOU HEARD WHAT I JUST SAID, DIDN'T YOU?
AAAH!
WHEN DID HE GET BEHIND ME?!
IS THAT A SCAR ON YOUR FACE?
YOUNG BOY.
IF YOU KEEP WHAT YOU HEARD A SECRET...
...I SHALL REMOVE THAT SCAR FROM YOUR FACE.

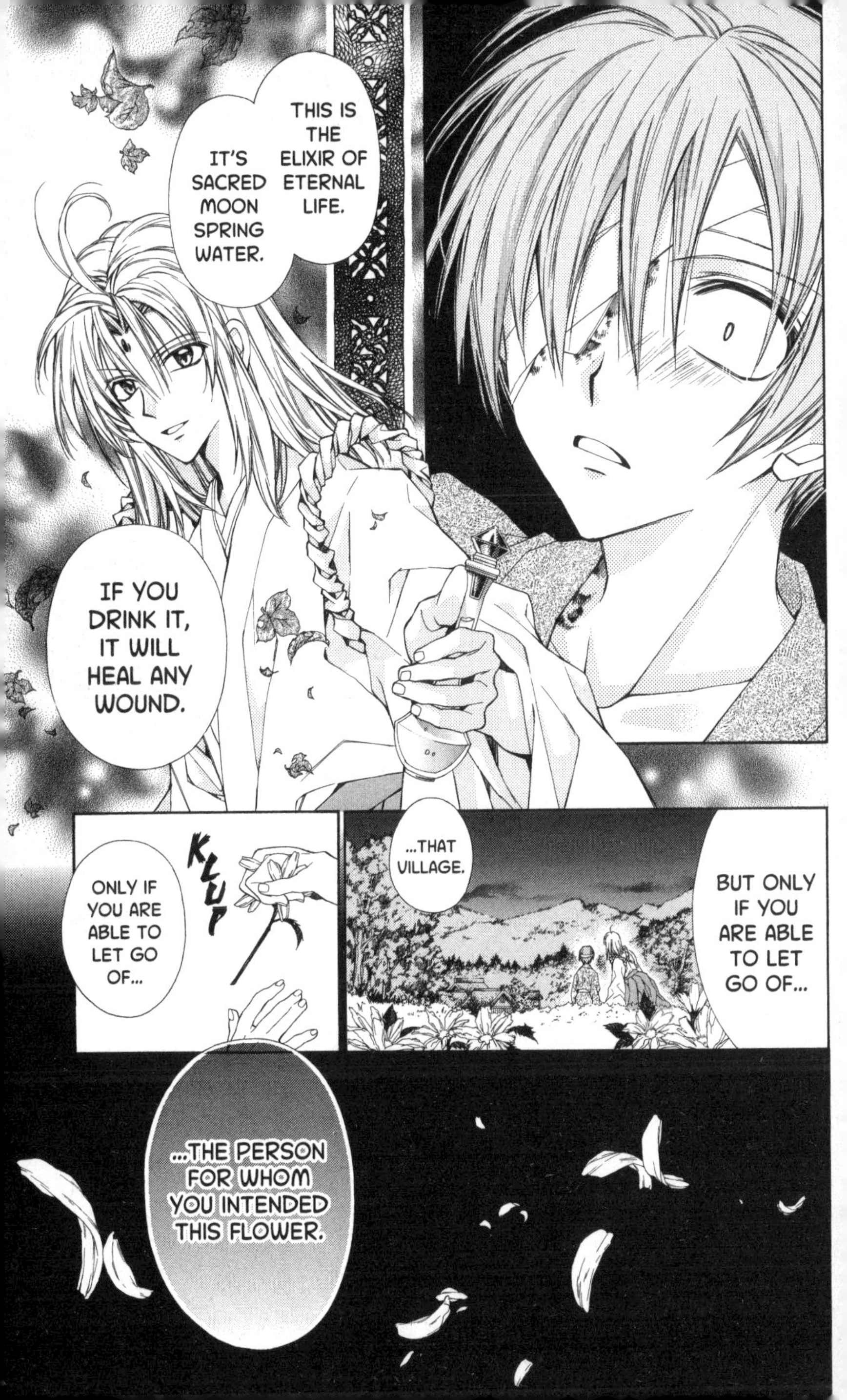
THIS IS THE ELIXIR OF ETERNAL LIFE.
IT'S SACRED MOON SPRING WATER.
IF YOU DRINK IT, IT WILL HEAL ANY WOUND.
BUT ONLY IF YOU ARE ABLE TO LET GO OF...
...THAT VILLAGE.
KLUP
ONLY IF YOU ARE ABLE TO LET GO OF...
...THE PERSON FOR WHOM YOU INTENDED THIS FLOWER.

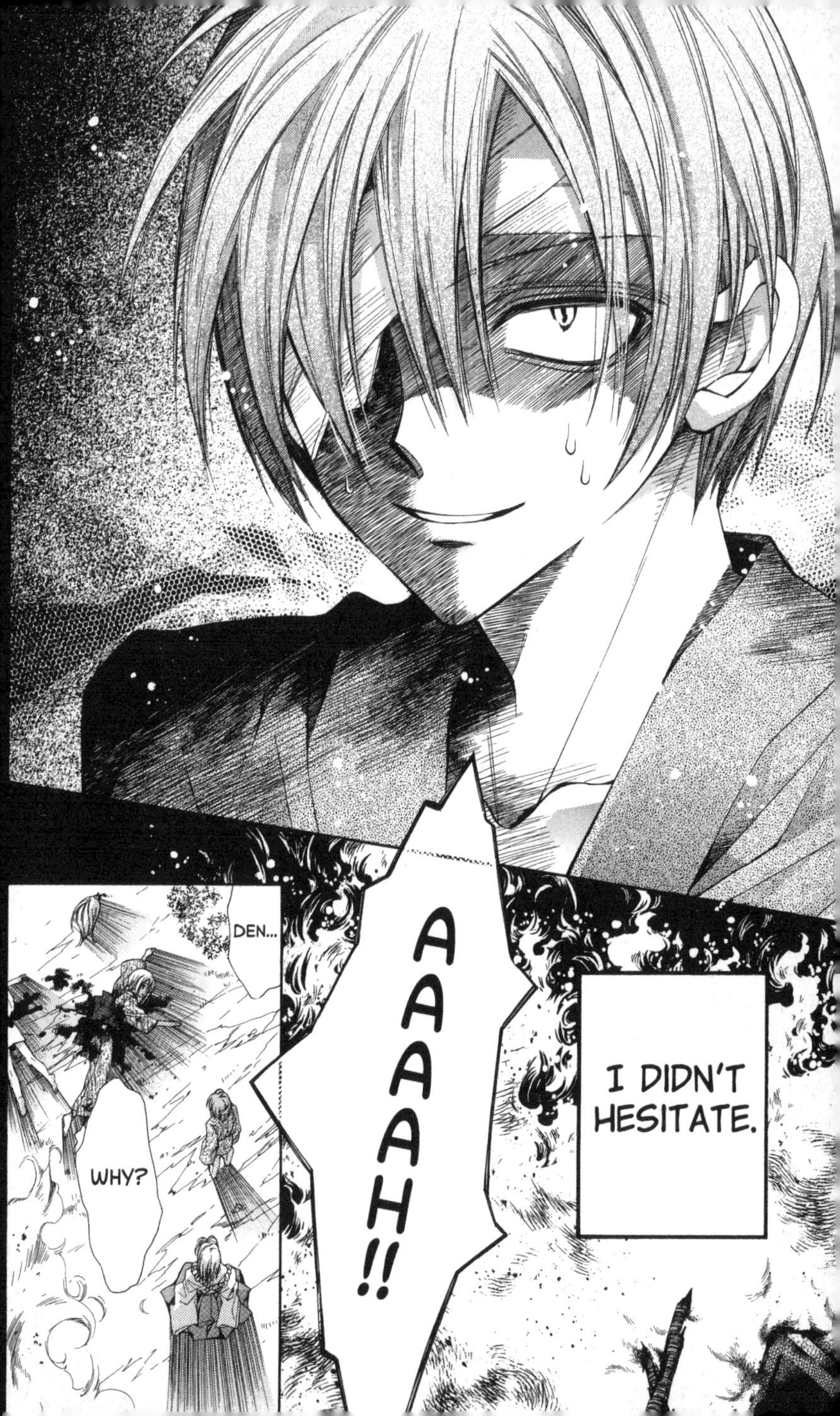
I DIDN'T HESITATE.
AAAAH!!
DEN...
WHY?

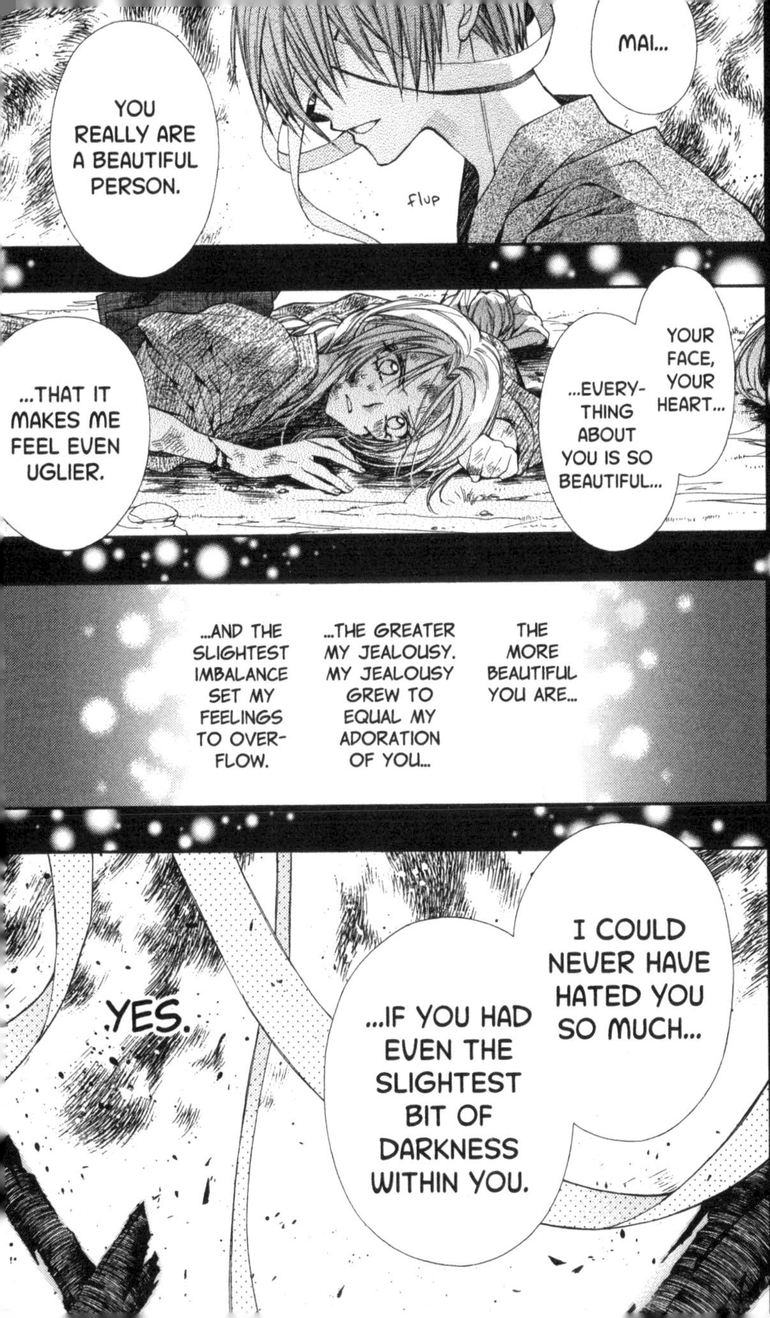
MAI...
YOU REALLY ARE A BEAUTIFUL PERSON.
flup
YOUR FACE, YOUR HEART...
...EVERY-THING ABOUT YOU IS SO BEAUTIFUL...
...THAT IT MAKES ME FEEL EVEN UGLIER.
THE MORE BEAUTIFUL YOU ARE...
...THE GREATER MY JEALOUSY. MY JEALOUSY GREW TO EQUAL MY ADORATION OF YOU...
...AND THE SLIGHTEST IMBALANCE SET MY FEELINGS TO OVER-FLOW.
I COULD NEVER HAVE HATED YOU SO MUCH...
...IF YOU HAD EVEN THE SLIGHTEST BIT OF DARKNESS WITHIN YOU.
YES.

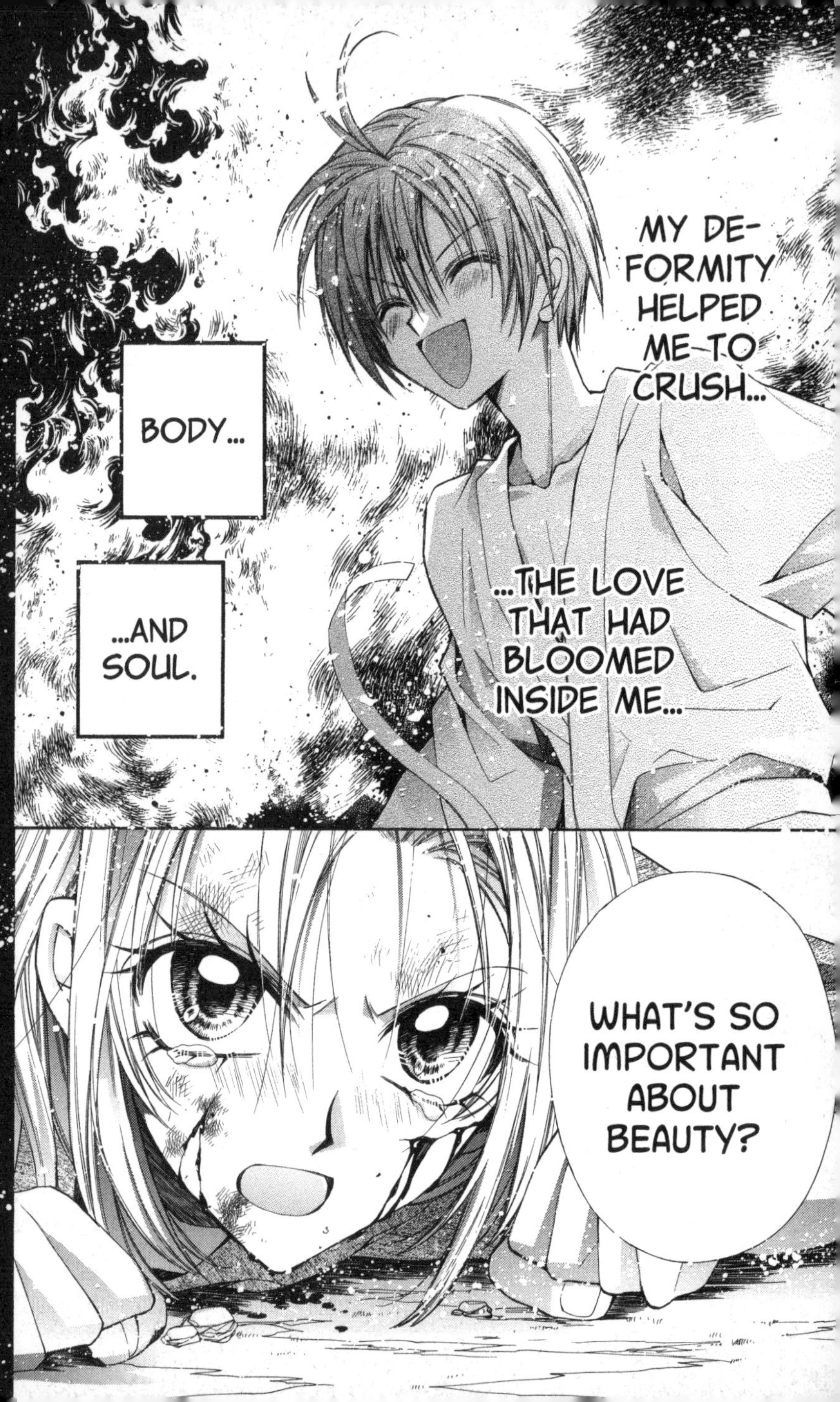
MY DE-FORMITY HELPED ME TO CRUSH...
...THE LOVE THAT HAD BLOOMED INSIDE ME...
BODY...
...AND SOUL.
WHAT'S SO IMPORTANT ABOUT BEAUTY?

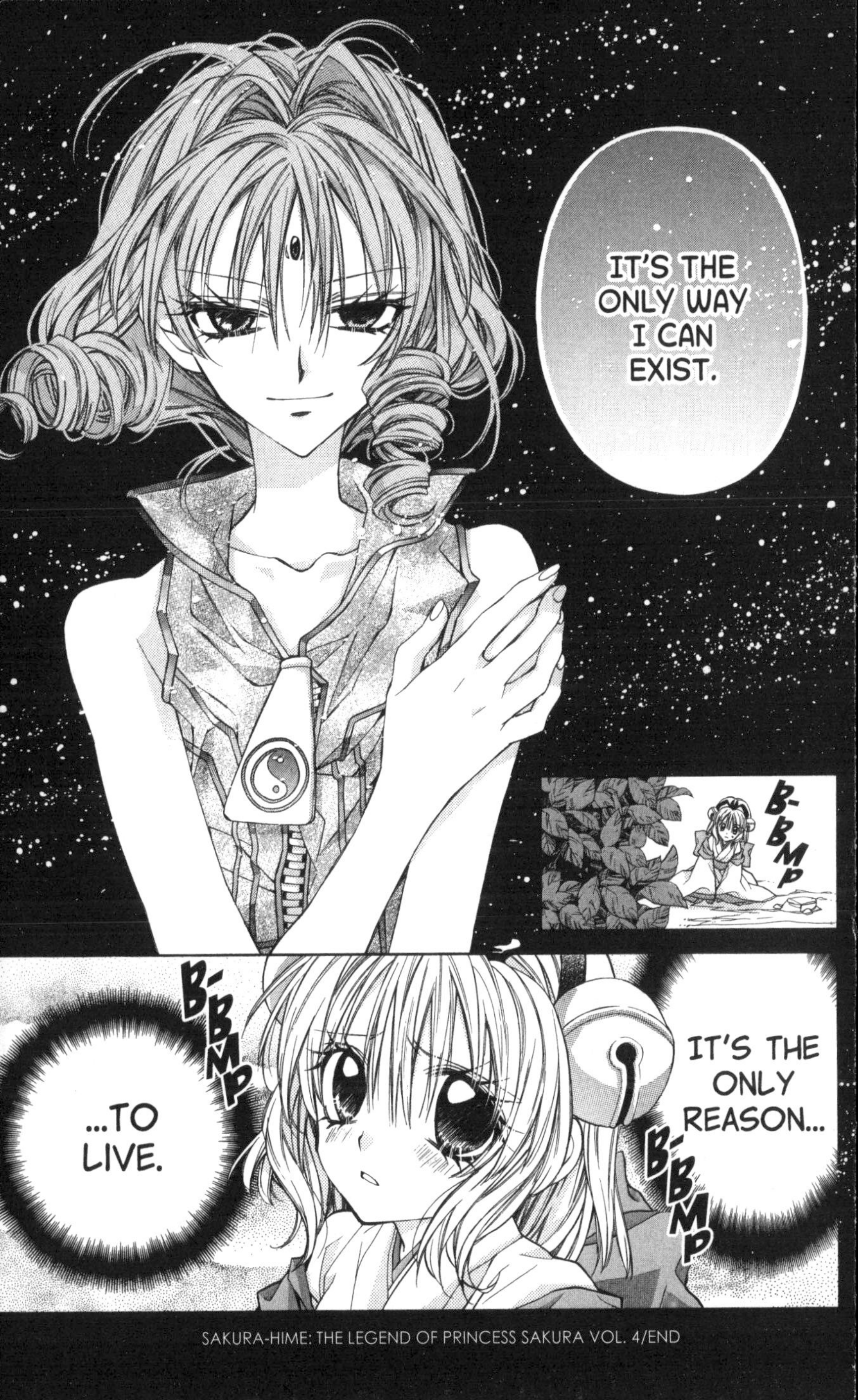
IT'S THE ONLY WAY I CAN EXIST.
B-BMP
IT'S THE ONLY REASON...
B-BMP
B-BMP
...TO LIVE.

SAKURA-HIME: THE LEGEND OF PRINCESS SAKURA VOL. 4/END

Asagiri Snow Legend Bonus Story

This is the bonus story that ran in the extra issue of *Ribon* and received a strong response from the readers. Thank you very much. ♪

Before this series started, Asagiri was an ordinary human-sized girl around 17 years old. ← I actually drew her on the bonus calendar around the time the series started with those looks. ♪ But she looked a lot like Ushio from *The Gentlemen's Alliance †* that I worked on two series ago, and I didn't know what to do. But I was watching the DVD of *This Is No Task for Kids* when Mat-chan was talking about how the partner in *Space Sheriff* was small enough to stand on the palm of a hand. I thought, "That's it!" (laugh) And that was how the current Asagiri was created.

I couldn't find a suitable place for this in the earlier volumes, so I kind of squeezed it into this volume. I really want you to read this before Asagiri's arc starts in the main story. Please understand. ♪

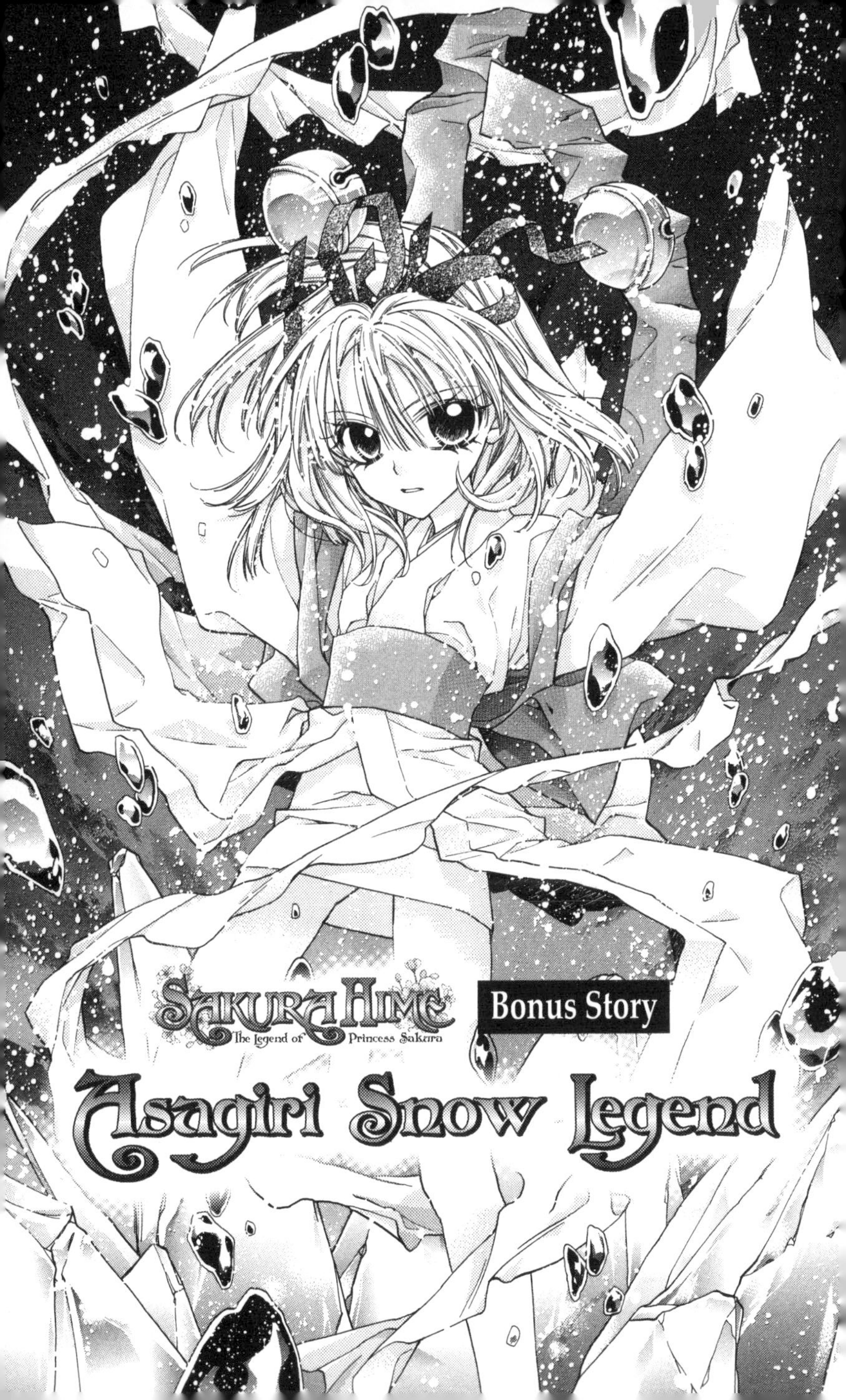
SAKURA HIME
The Legend of Princess Sakura
Bonus Story
Asagiri Snow Legend

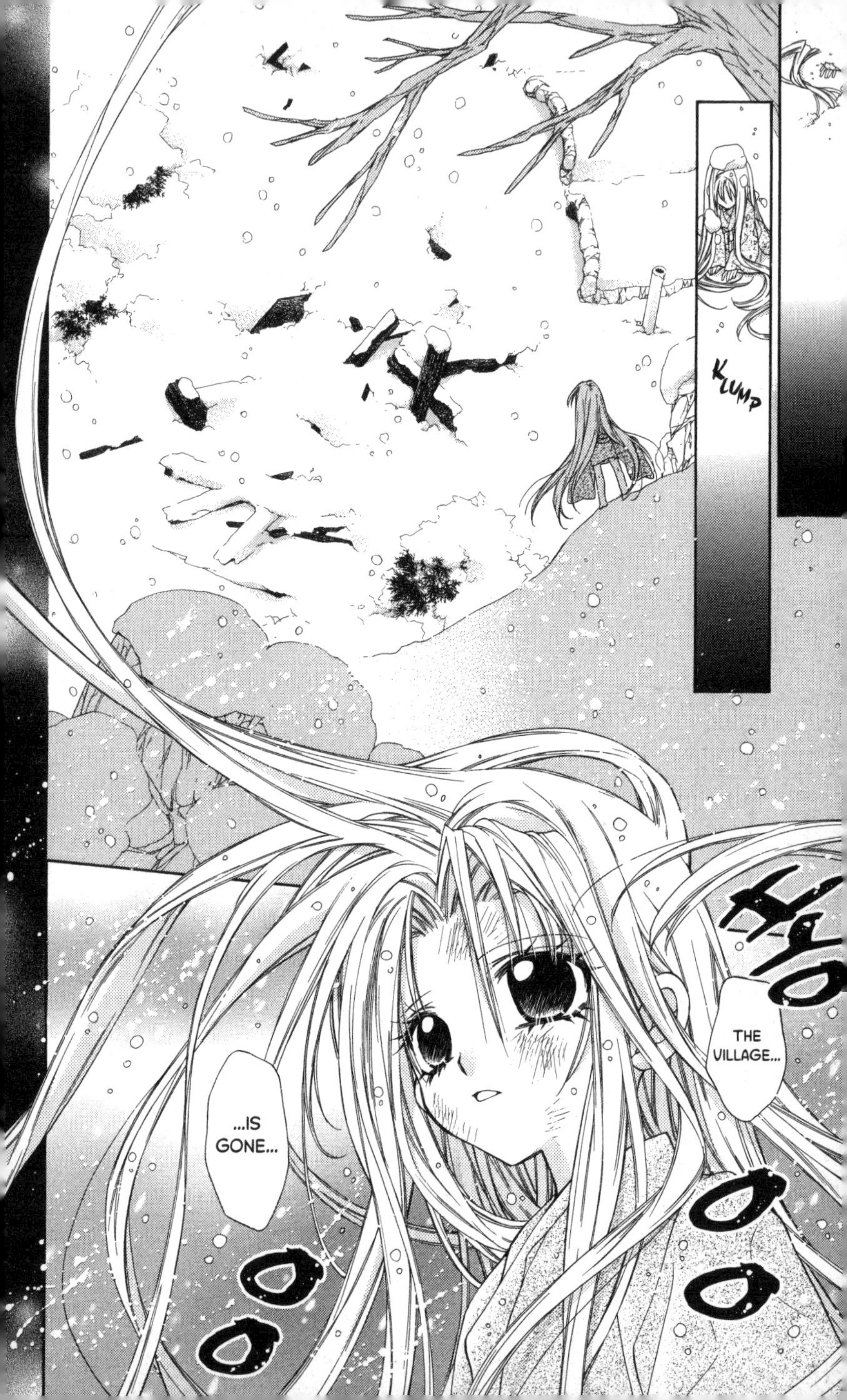
KLUMP
HYOOOO
THE VILLAGE...
...IS GONE...
OOO

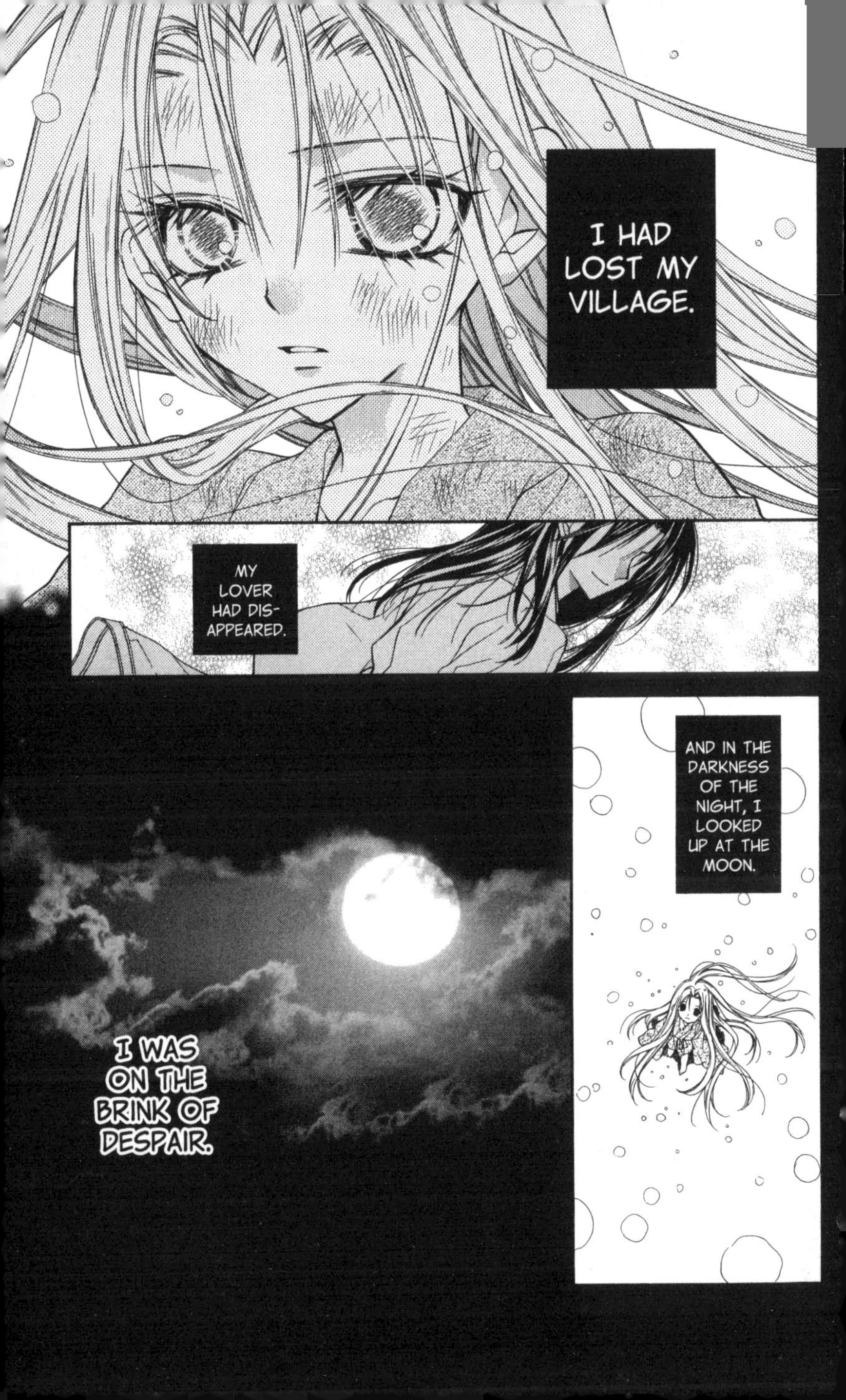
I HAD LOST MY VILLAGE.
MY LOVER HAD DIS-APPEARED.
AND IN THE DARKNESS OF THE NIGHT, I LOOKED UP AT THE MOON.
I WAS ON THE BRINK OF DESPAIR.

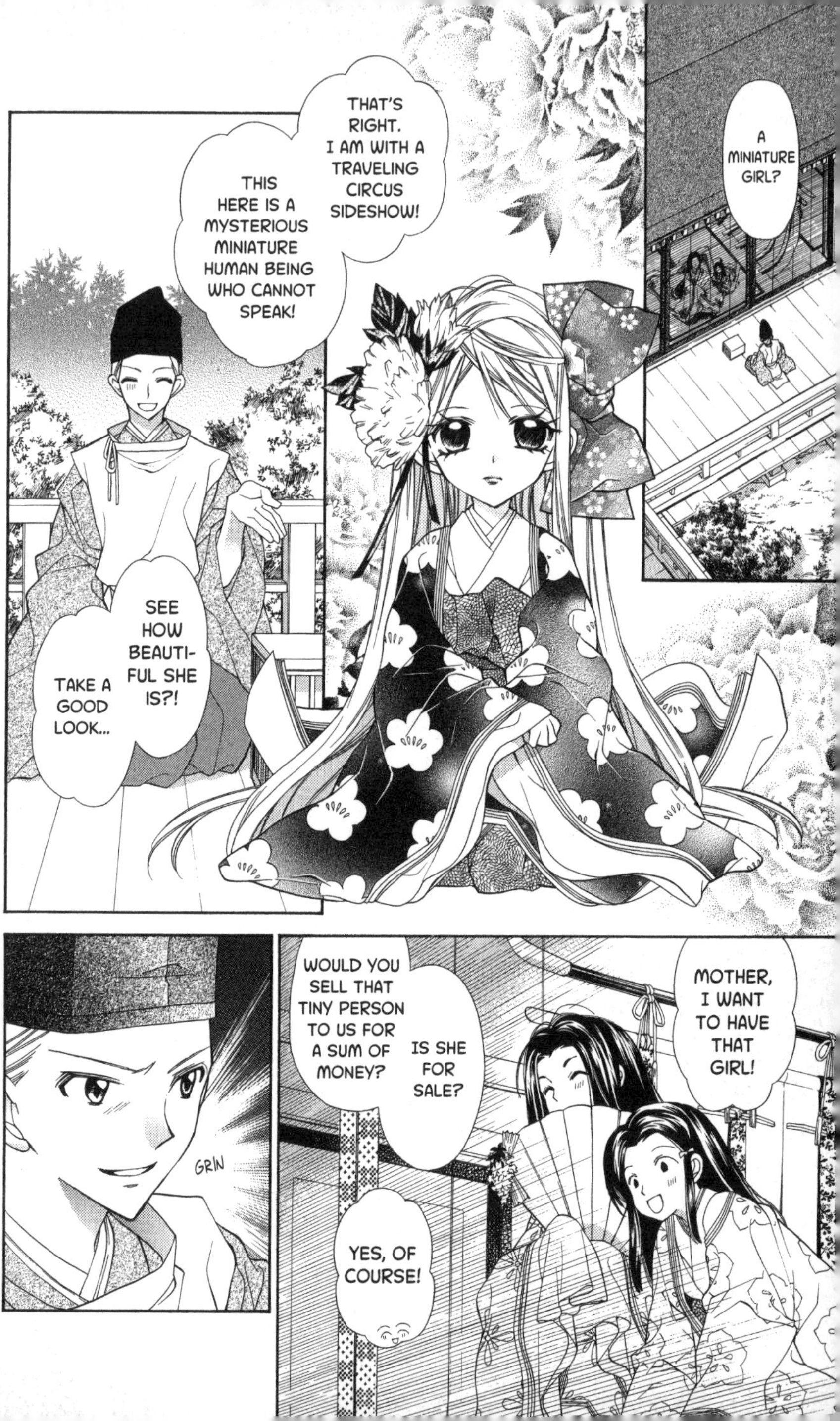
A MINIATURE GIRL?
THAT'S RIGHT. I AM WITH A TRAVELING CIRCUS SIDESHOW!
THIS HERE IS A MYSTERIOUS MINIATURE HUMAN BEING WHO CANNOT SPEAK!
SEE HOW BEAUTI-FUL SHE IS?!
TAKE A GOOD LOOK...
MOTHER, I WANT TO HAVE THAT GIRL!
IS SHE FOR SALE?
WOULD YOU SELL THAT TINY PERSON TO US FOR A SUM OF MONEY?
YES, OF COURSE!
GRIN

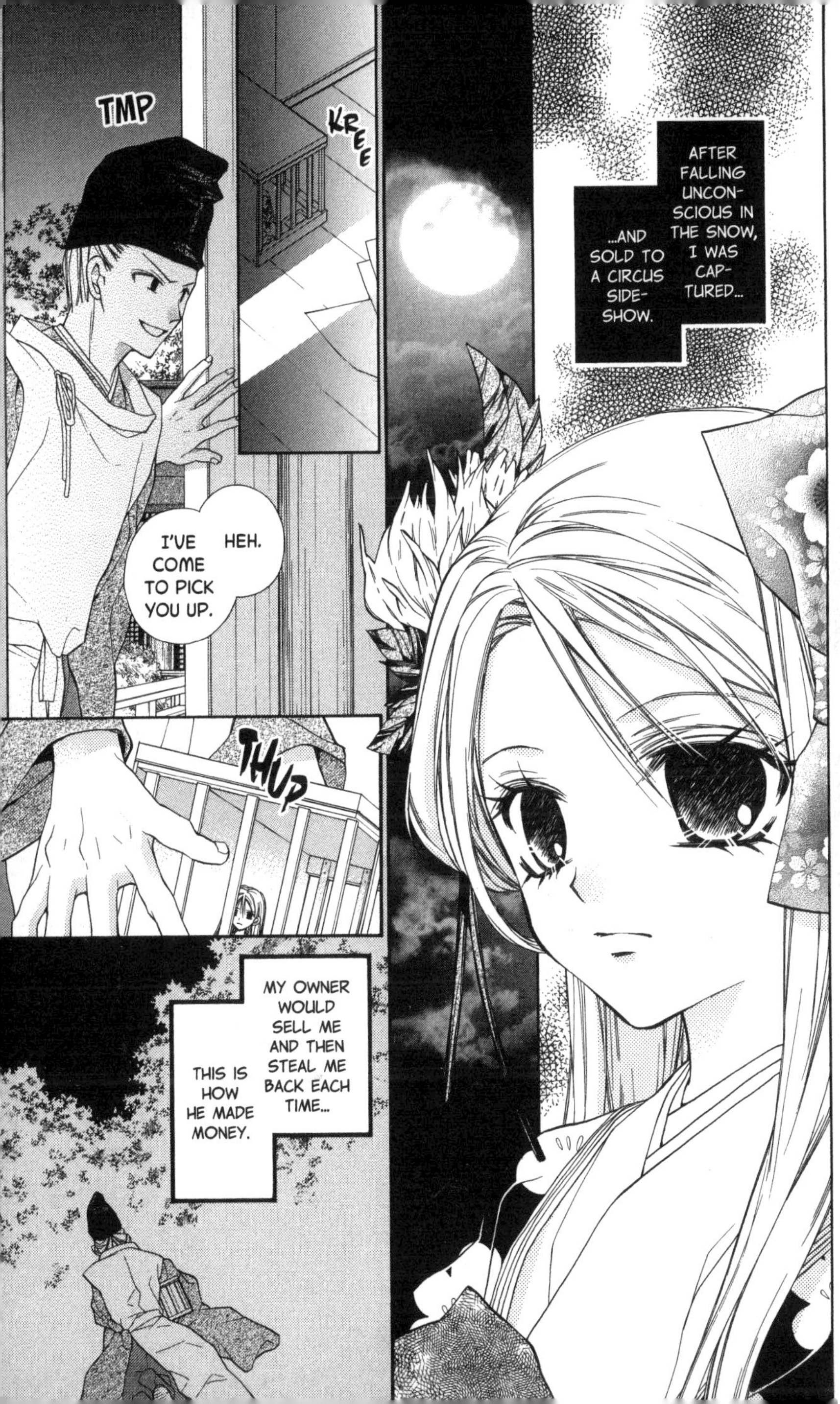
AFTER FALLING UNCON-SCIOUS IN THE SNOW, I WAS CAP-TURED...
...AND SOLD TO A CIRCUS SIDE-SHOW.
KREE
TMP
HEH.
I'VE COME TO PICK YOU UP.
THUD
MY OWNER WOULD SELL ME AND THEN STEAL ME BACK EACH TIME...
THIS IS HOW HE MADE MONEY.

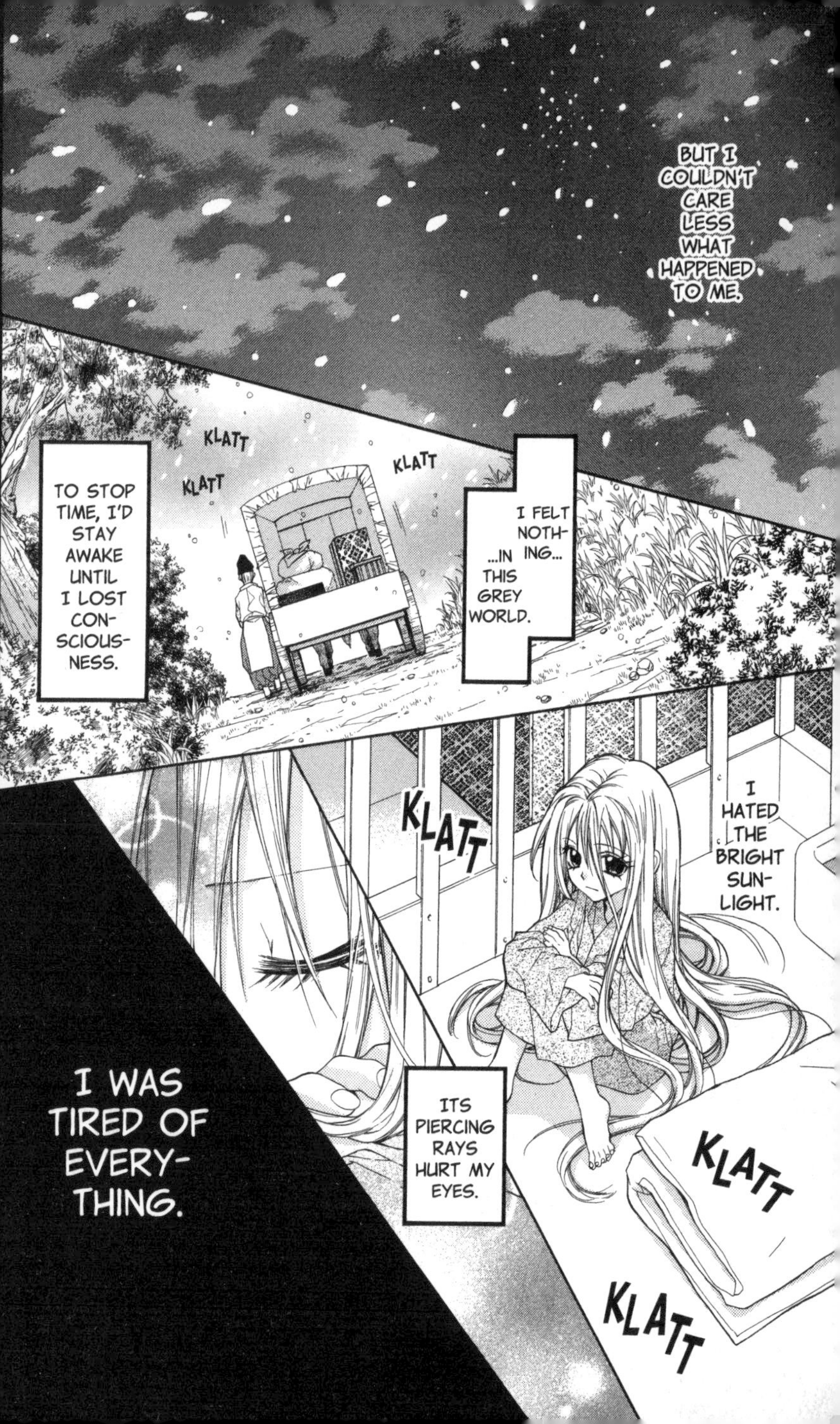
BUT I COULDN'T CARE LESS WHAT HAPPENED TO ME.
I FELT NOTHING...
...IN THIS GREY WORLD.
KLATT
KLATT
KLATT
TO STOP TIME, I'D STAY AWAKE UNTIL I LOST CONSCIOUSNESS.
I HATED THE BRIGHT SUNLIGHT.
KLATT
KLATT
ITS PIERCING RAYS HURT MY EYES.
KLATT
I WAS TIRED OF EVERYTHING.

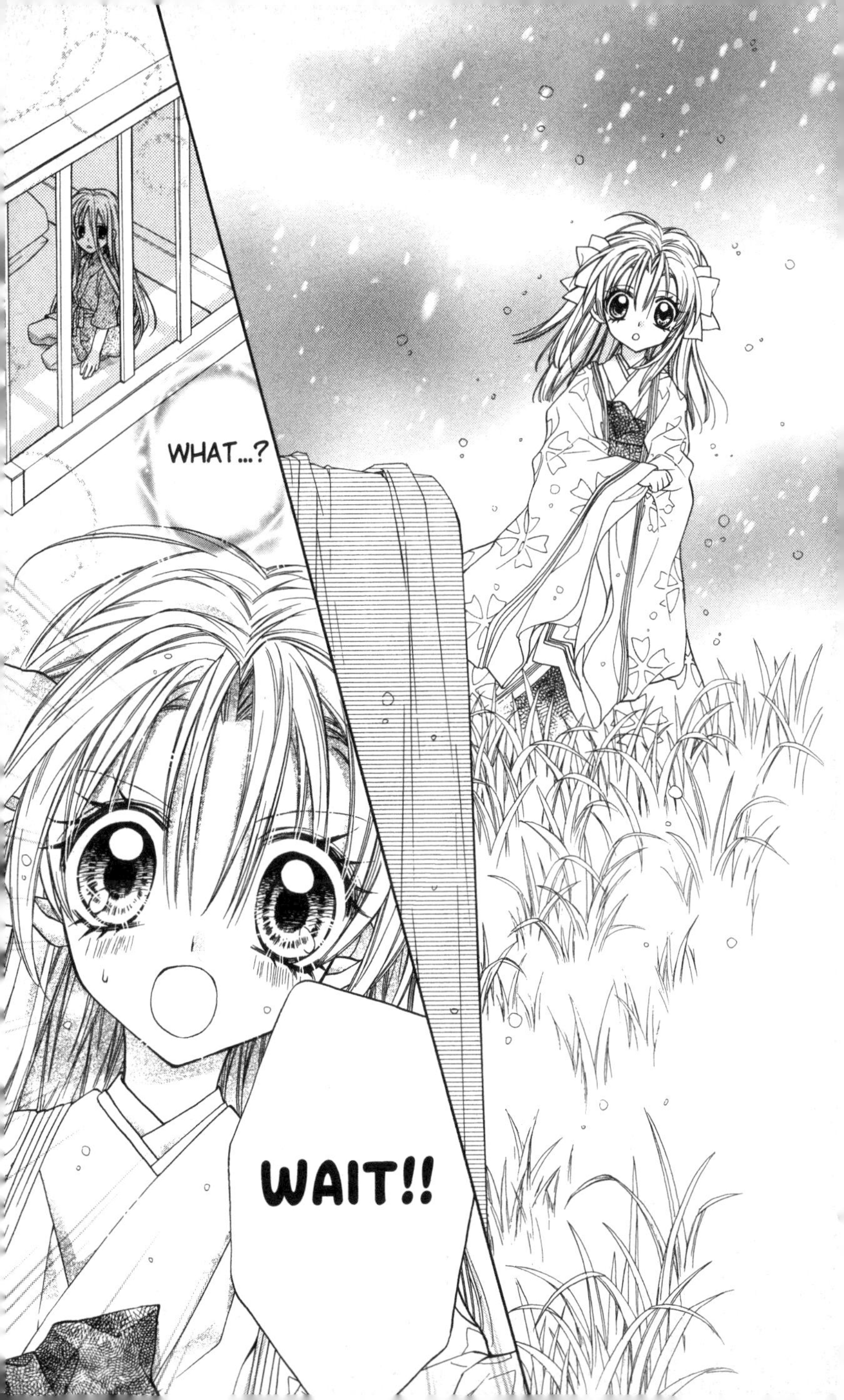
WHAT...?
WAIT!!

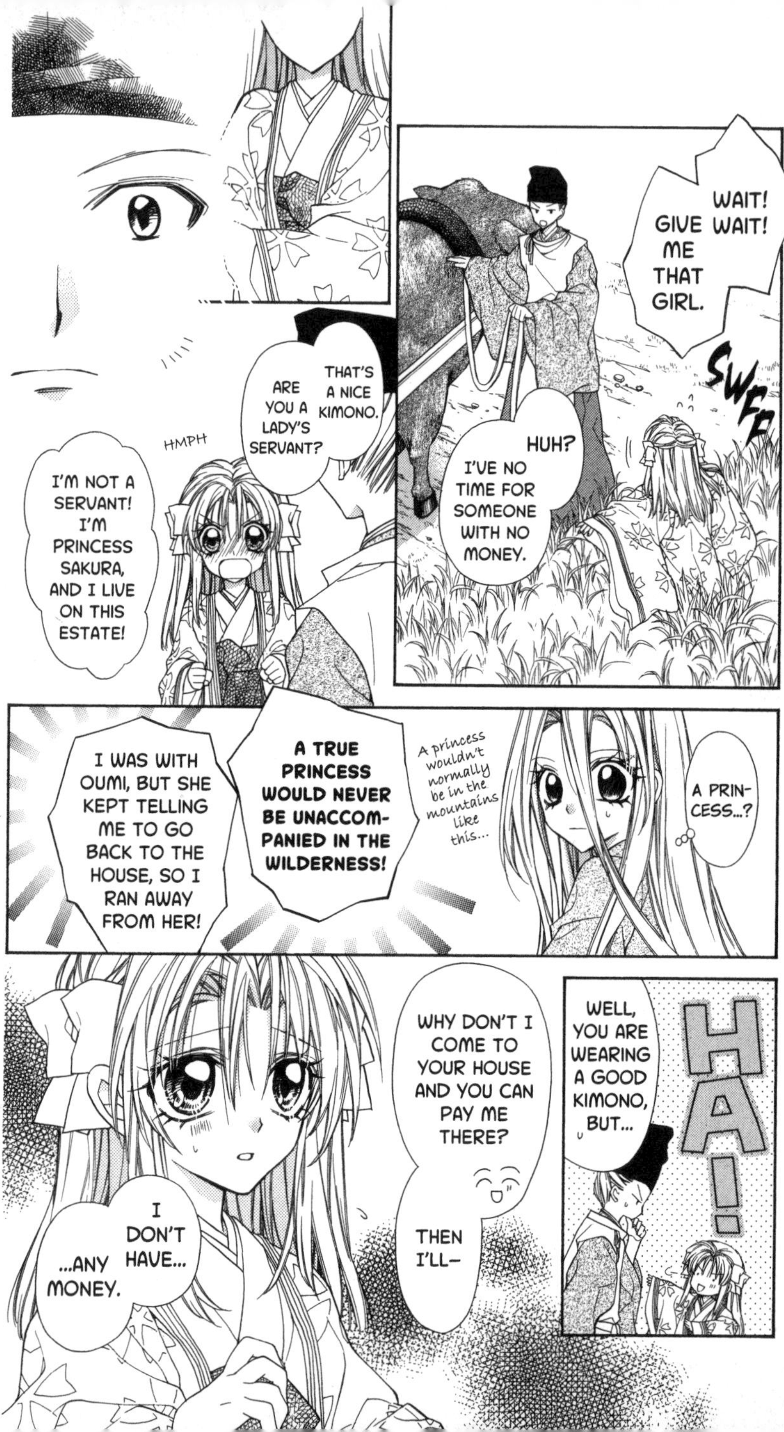
WAIT! WAIT! GIVE ME THAT GIRL.
SWFF
HUH?
I'VE NO TIME FOR SOMEONE WITH NO MONEY.
THAT'S A NICE KIMONO.
ARE YOU A LADY'S SERVANT?
HMPH
I'M NOT A SERVANT! I'M PRINCESS SAKURA, AND I LIVE ON THIS ESTATE!
A PRIN-CESS...?
A princess wouldn't normally be in the mountains like this...
A TRUE PRINCESS WOULD NEVER BE UNACCOM-PANIED IN THE WILDERNESS!
I WAS WITH OUMI, BUT SHE KEPT TELLING ME TO GO BACK TO THE HOUSE, SO I RAN AWAY FROM HER!
HA!
WELL, YOU ARE WEARING A GOOD KIMONO, BUT...
WHY DON'T I COME TO YOUR HOUSE AND YOU CAN PAY ME THERE?
THEN I'LL–
I DON'T HAVE...
...ANY MONEY.

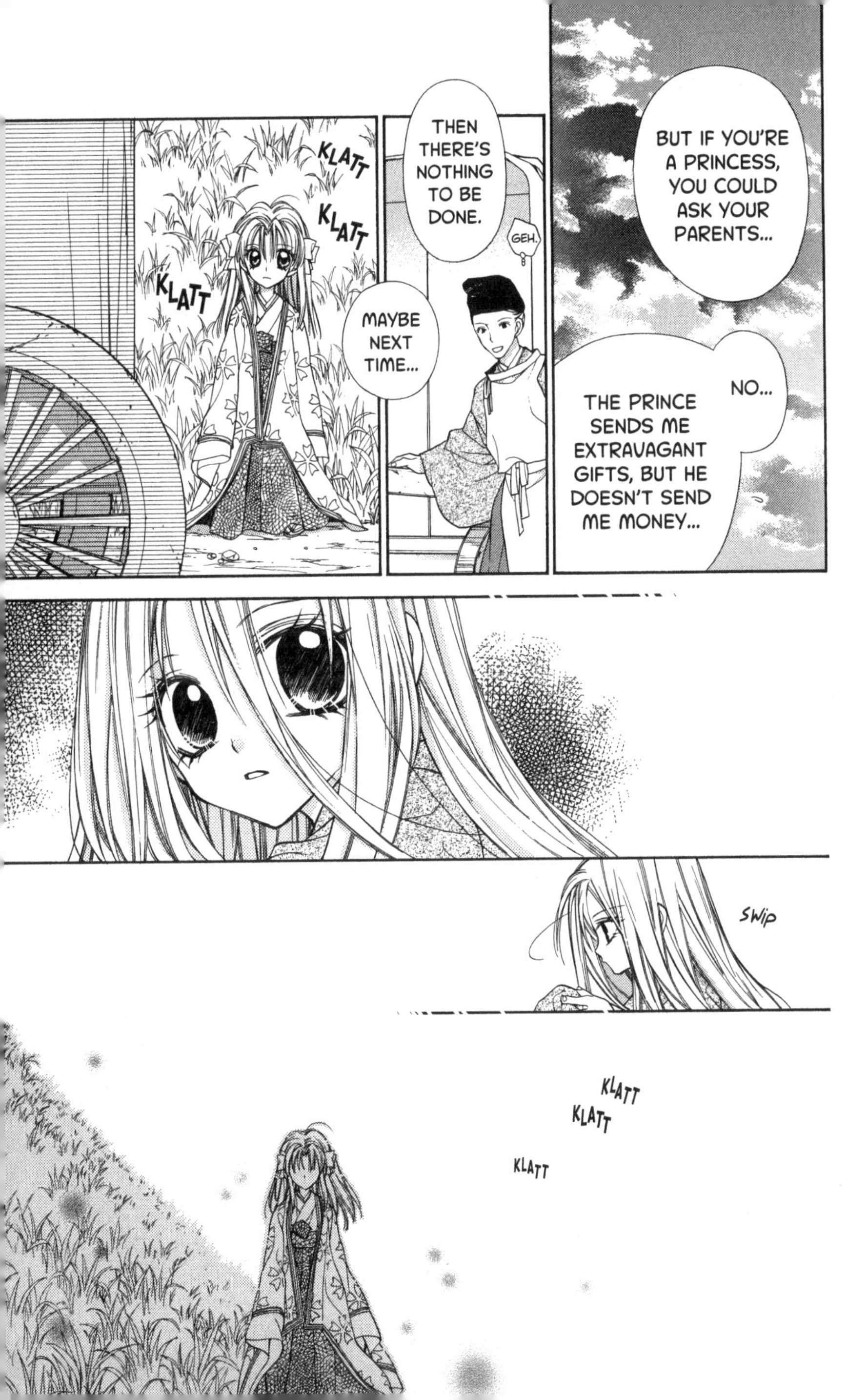
BUT IF YOU'RE A PRINCESS, YOU COULD ASK YOUR PARENTS...
NO...
THE PRINCE SENDS ME EXTRAVAGANT GIFTS, BUT HE DOESN'T SEND ME MONEY...
THEN THERE'S NOTHING TO BE DONE.
GEH.
MAYBE NEXT TIME...
KLATT
KLATT
KLATT
SWIP
KLATT
KLATT
KLATT

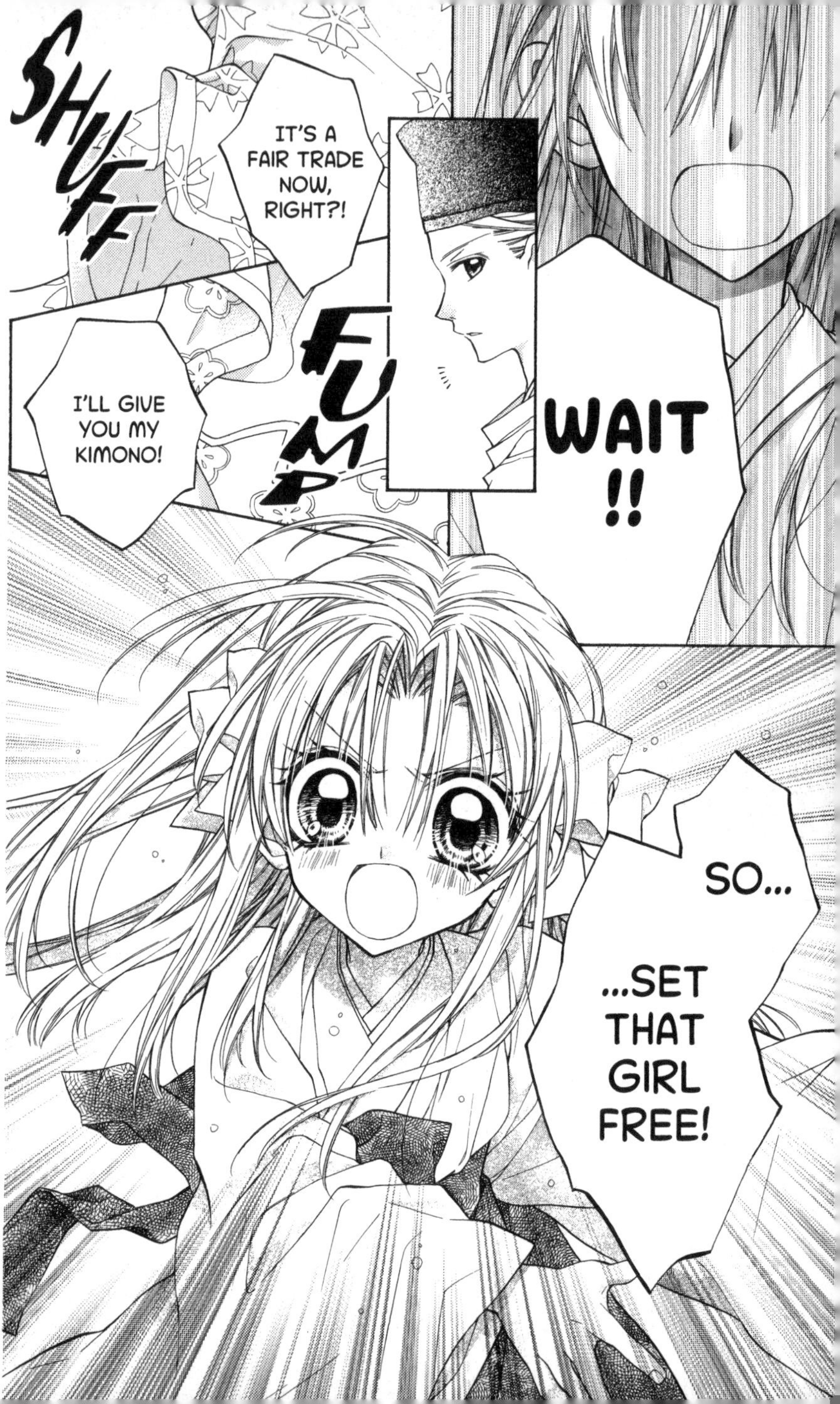
WAIT!!
SHUFF
IT'S A FAIR TRADE NOW, RIGHT?!
I'LL GIVE YOU MY KIMONO!
FUMP
SO...
...SET THAT GIRL FREE!

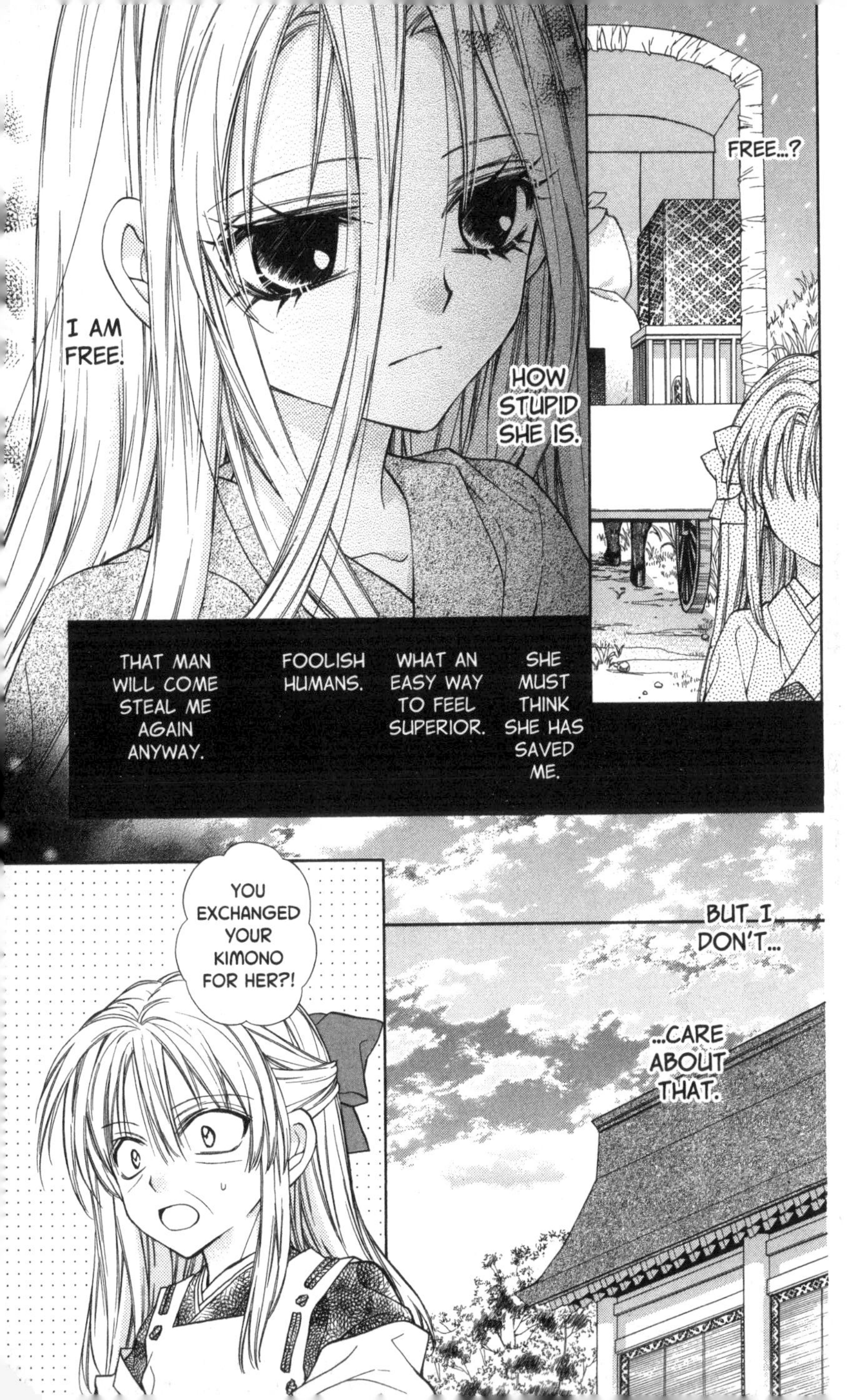
FREE...?
I AM FREE.
HOW STUPID SHE IS.
SHE MUST THINK SHE HAS SAVED ME.
WHAT AN EASY WAY TO FEEL SUPERIOR.
FOOLISH HUMANS.
THAT MAN WILL COME STEAL ME AGAIN ANYWAY.
BUT...I DON'T...
...CARE ABOUT THAT.
YOU EXCHANGED YOUR KIMONO FOR HER?!

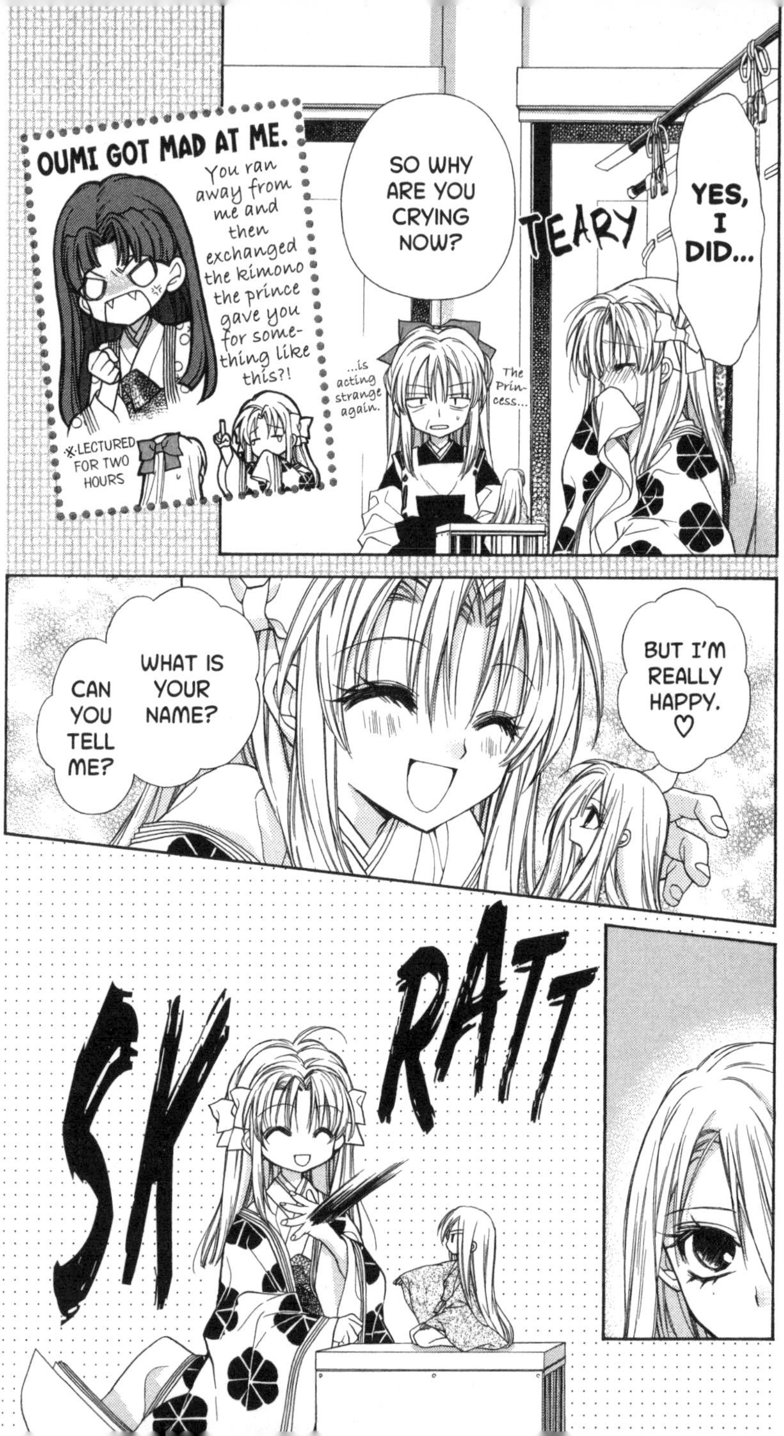
YES, I DID...
TEARY
SO WHY ARE YOU CRYING NOW?
The Princess...
...is acting strange again.
OUMI GOT MAD AT ME.
You ran away from me and then exchanged the kimono the prince gave you for something like this?!
※·LECTURED FOR TWO HOURS
BUT I'M REALLY HAPPY. ♡
WHAT IS YOUR NAME?
CAN YOU TELL ME?
SK
RATT

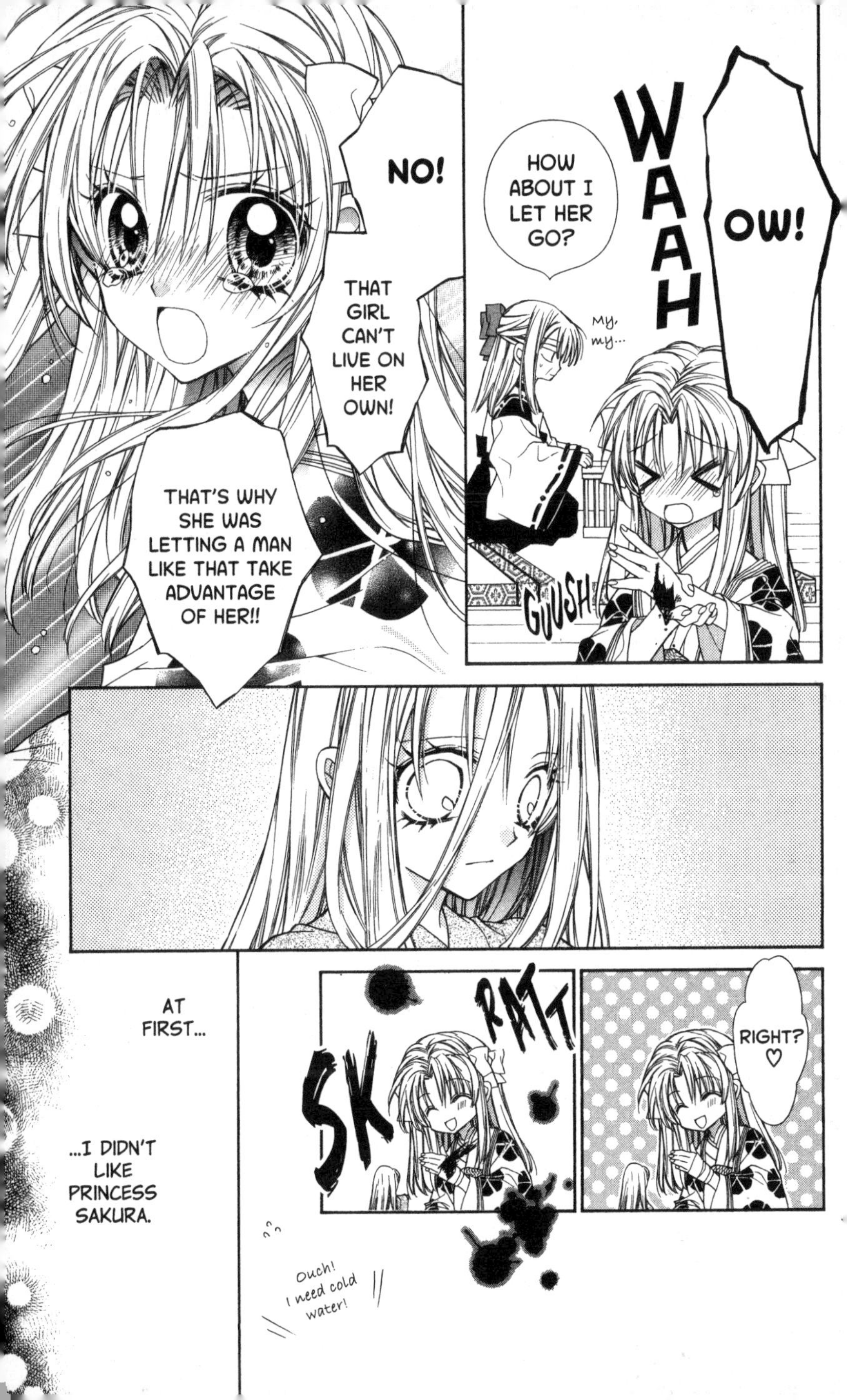
OW!
WAAH
HOW ABOUT I LET HER GO?
My, my...
GUUSH
NO!
THAT GIRL CAN'T LIVE ON HER OWN!
THAT'S WHY SHE WAS LETTING A MAN LIKE THAT TAKE ADVANTAGE OF HER!!
RIGHT? ♡
SKRATT
AT FIRST...
...I DIDN'T LIKE PRINCESS SAKURA.
Ouch! I need cold water!

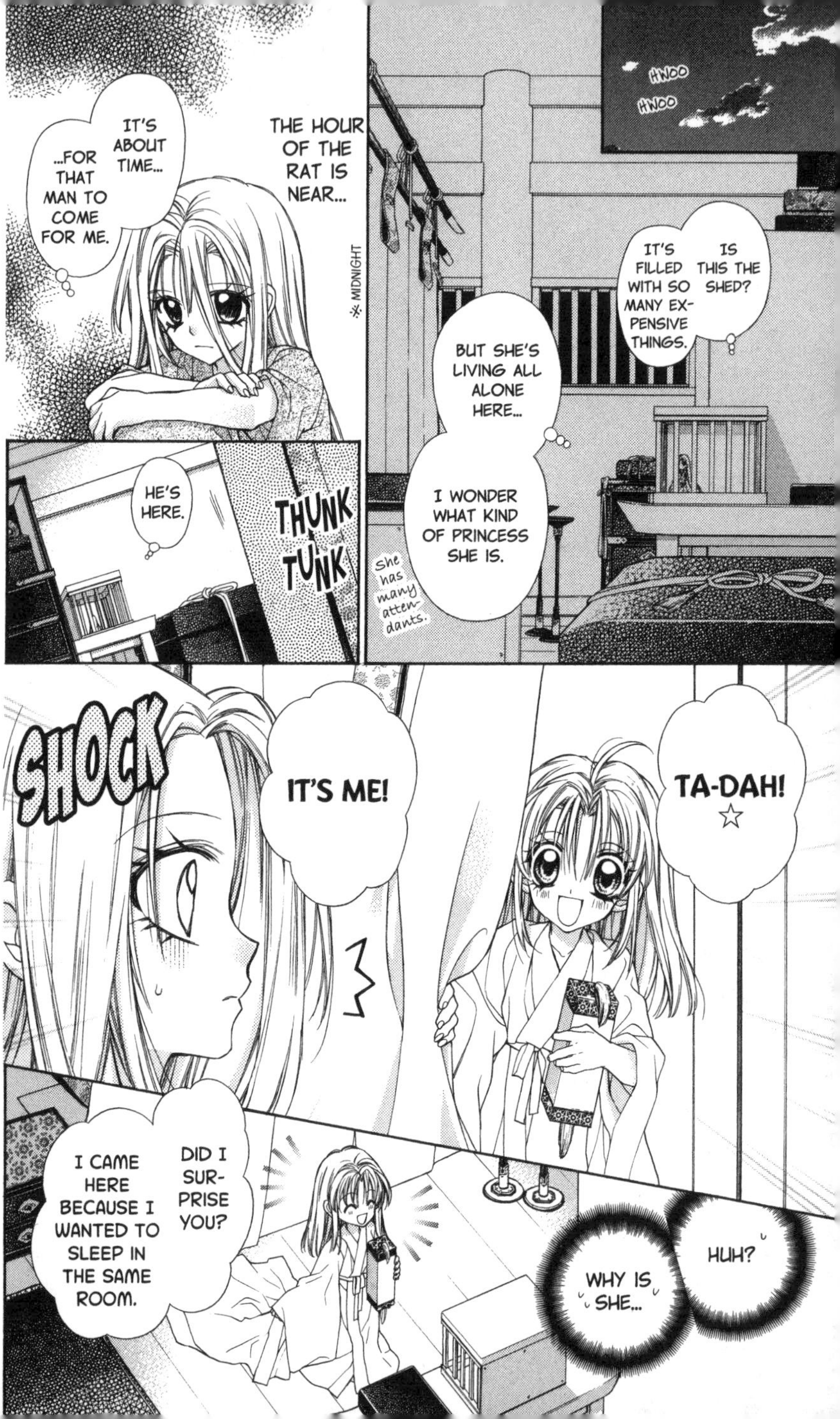
HWOO
HWOO
IS THIS THE SHED?
IT'S FILLED WITH SO MANY EXPENSIVE THINGS.
BUT SHE'S LIVING ALL ALONE HERE...
I WONDER WHAT KIND OF PRINCESS SHE IS.
she has many attendants.
THE HOUR OF THE RAT IS NEAR...
※MIDNIGHT
IT'S ABOUT TIME...
...FOR THAT MAN TO COME FOR ME.
HE'S HERE.
THUNK
TUNK
TA-DAH! ☆
IT'S ME!
SHOCK
HUH?
WHY IS SHE...
DID I SURPRISE YOU?
I CAME HERE BECAUSE I WANTED TO SLEEP IN THE SAME ROOM.

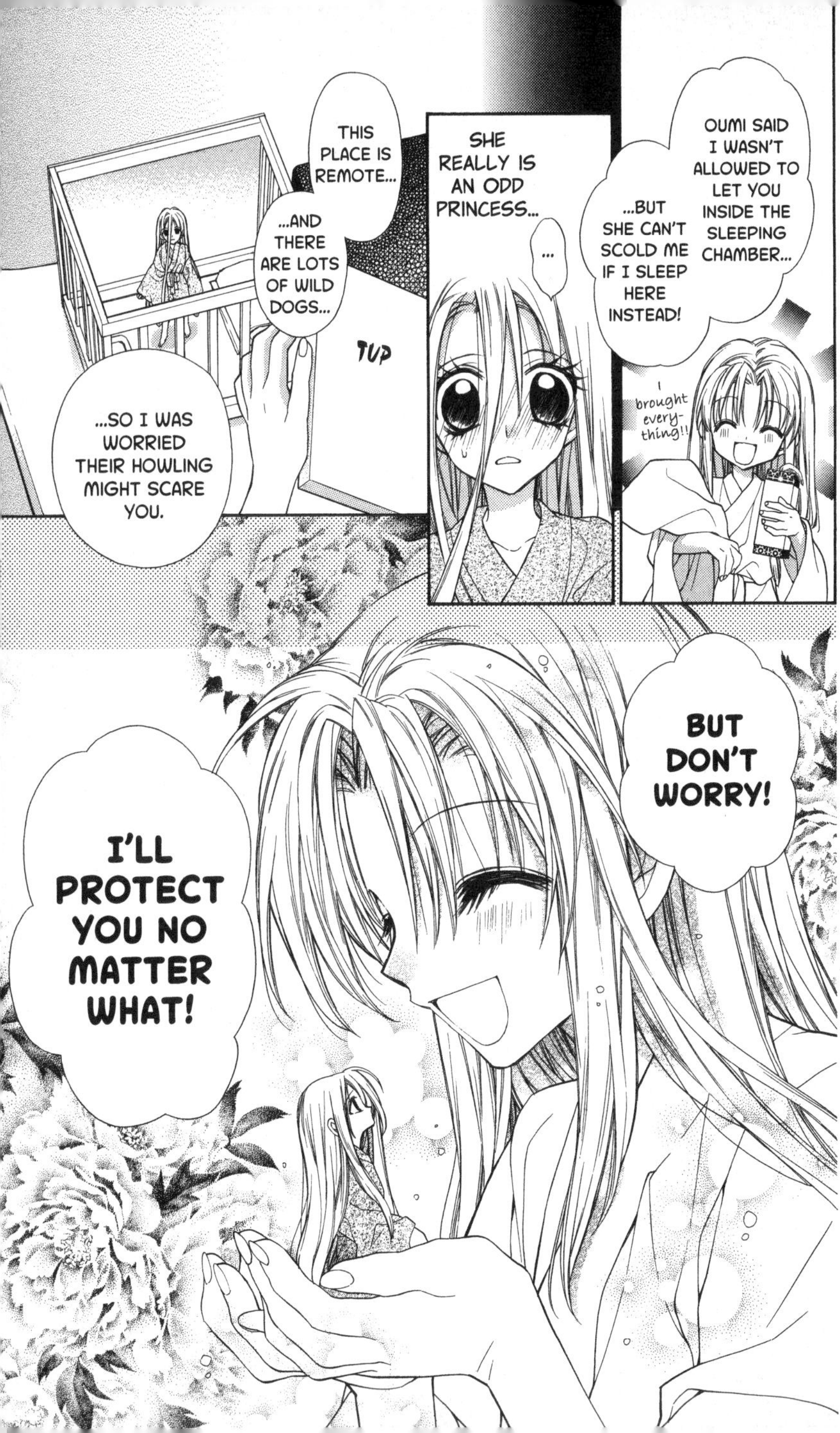
OUMI SAID I WASN'T ALLOWED TO LET YOU INSIDE THE SLEEPING CHAMBER...
...BUT SHE CAN'T SCOLD ME IF I SLEEP HERE INSTEAD!
I brought every-thing!!
SHE REALLY IS AN ODD PRINCESS...
...
THIS PLACE IS REMOTE...
...AND THERE ARE LOTS OF WILD DOGS...
TUP
...SO I WAS WORRIED THEIR HOWLING MIGHT SCARE YOU.
BUT DON'T WORRY!
I'LL PROTECT YOU NO MATTER WHAT!

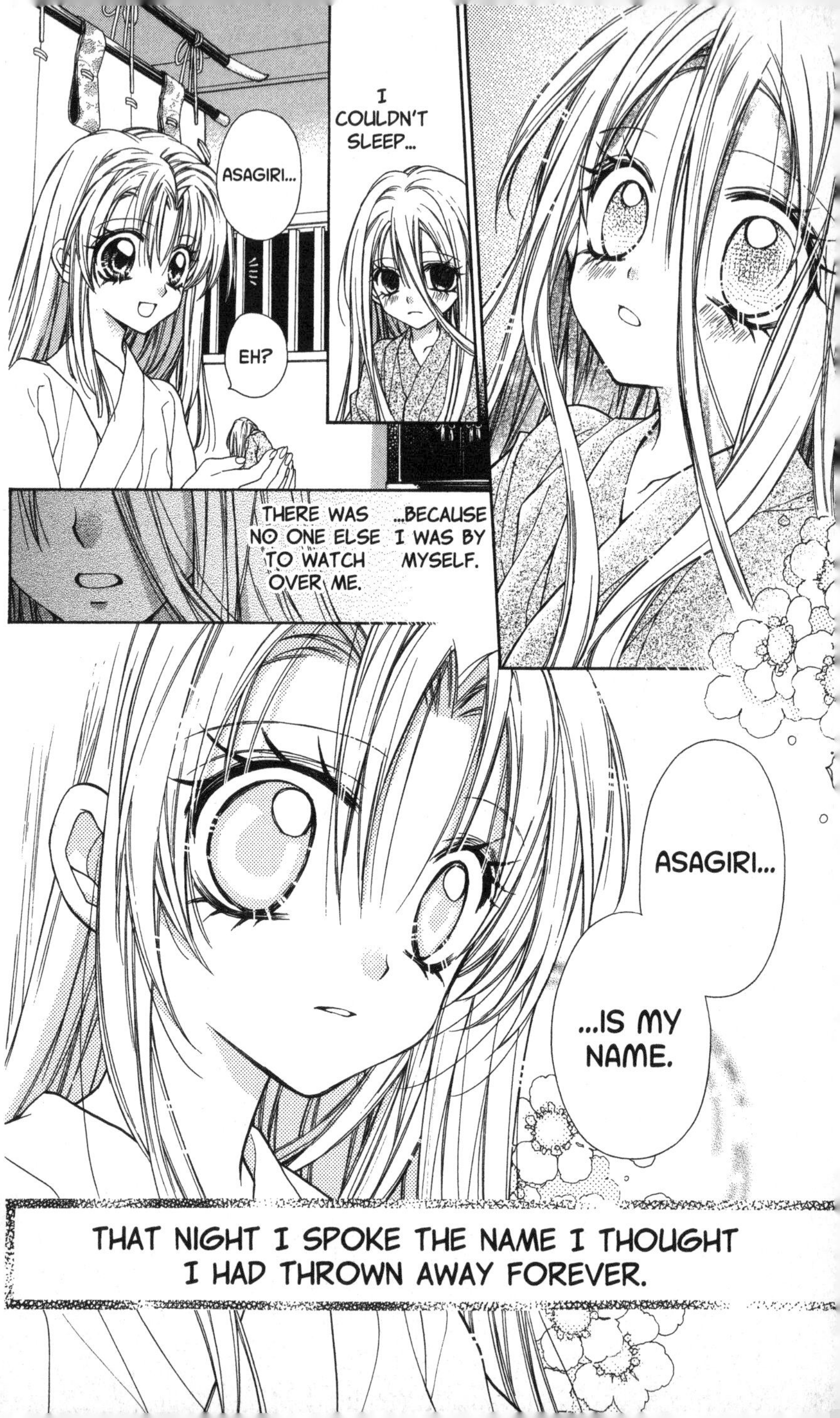
I COULDN'T SLEEP...
ASAGIRI...
EH?
...BECAUSE I WAS BY MYSELF.
THERE WAS NO ONE ELSE TO WATCH OVER ME.
ASAGIRI...
...IS MY NAME.
THAT NIGHT I SPOKE THE NAME I THOUGHT I HAD THROWN AWAY FOREVER.

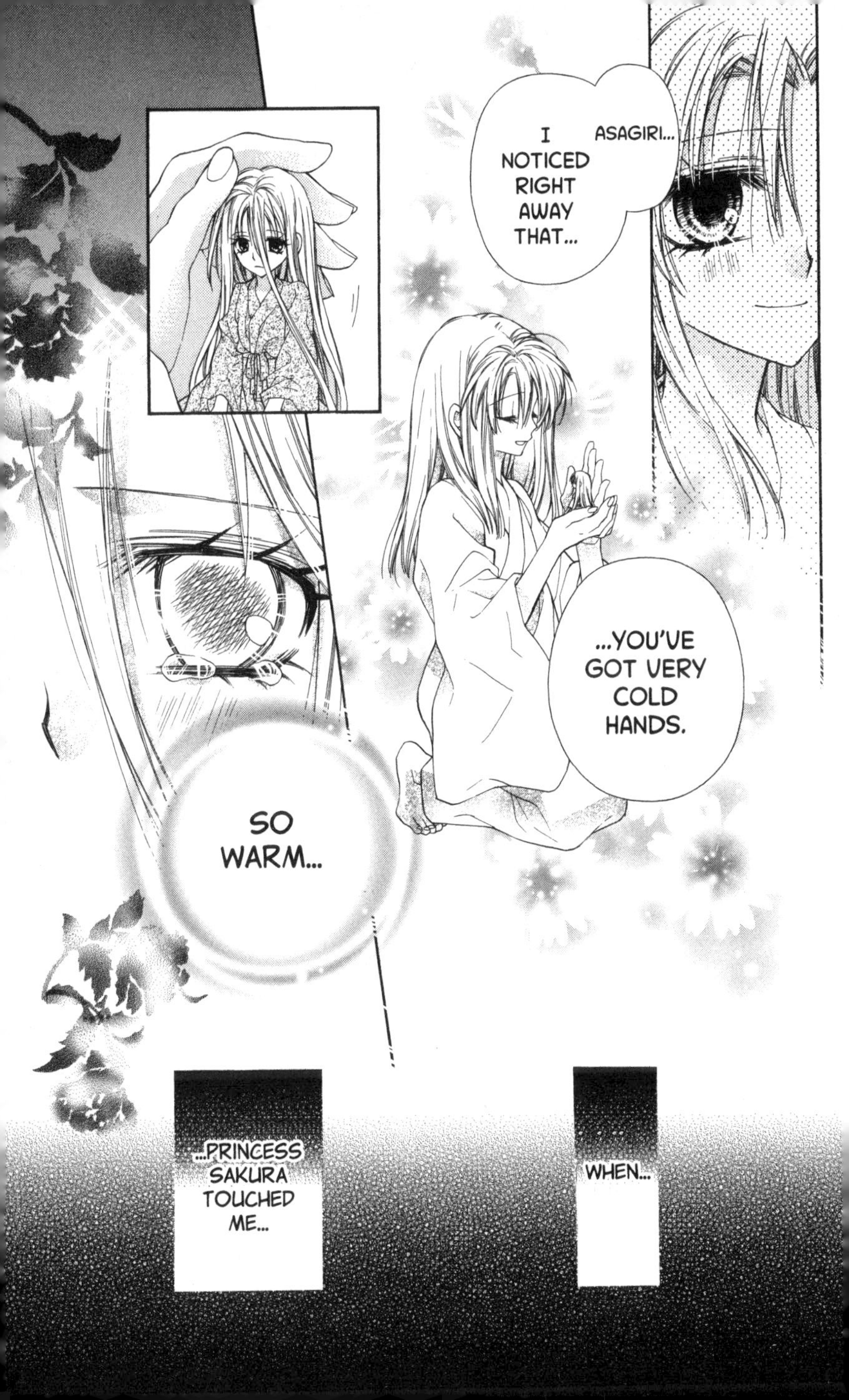
ASAGIRI...
I NOTICED RIGHT AWAY THAT...
...YOU'VE GOT VERY COLD HANDS.
SO WARM...
WHEN...
...PRINCESS SAKURA TOUCHED ME...

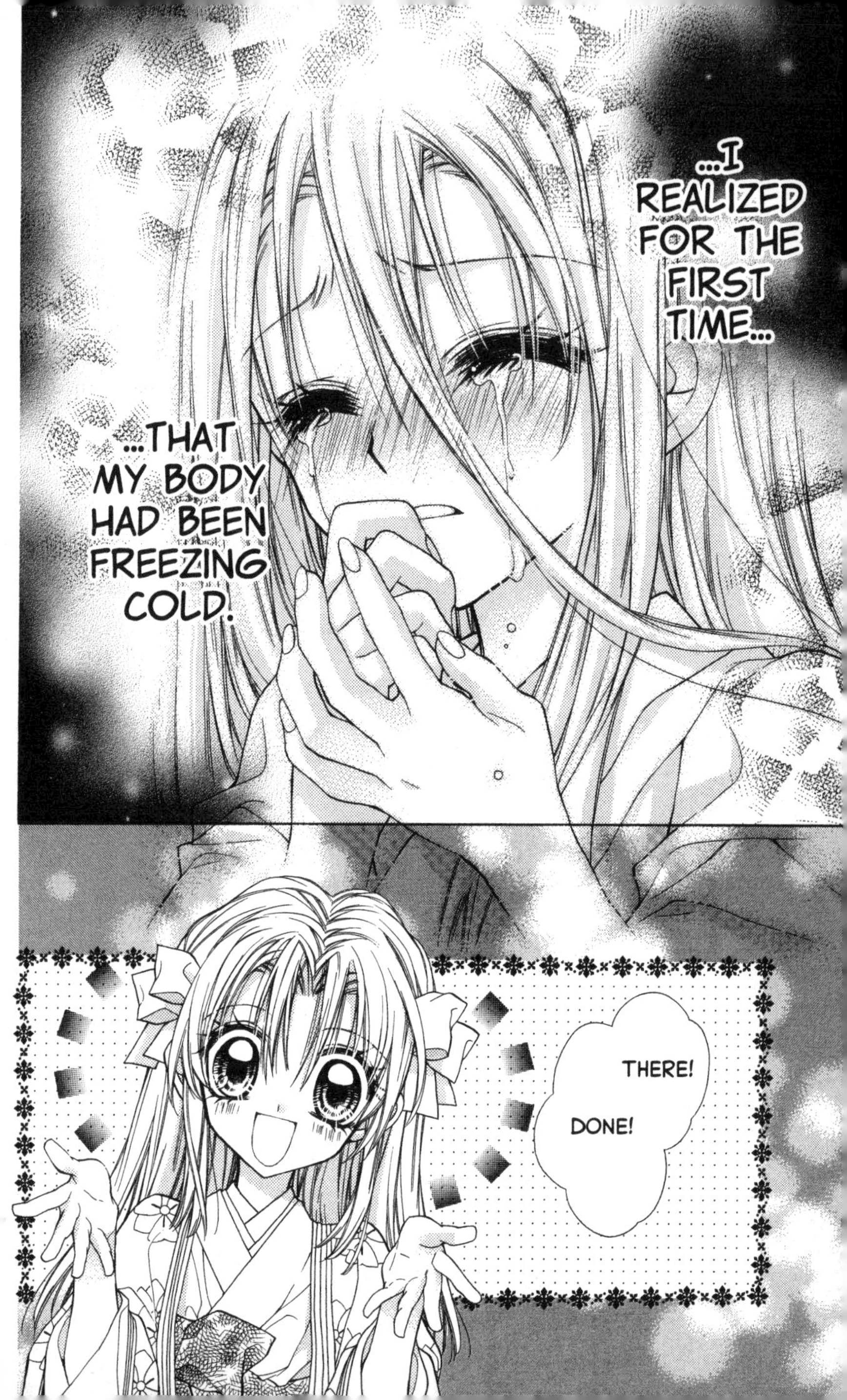
...I REALIZED FOR THE FIRST TIME...
...THAT MY BODY HAD BEEN FREEZING COLD.
THERE! DONE!

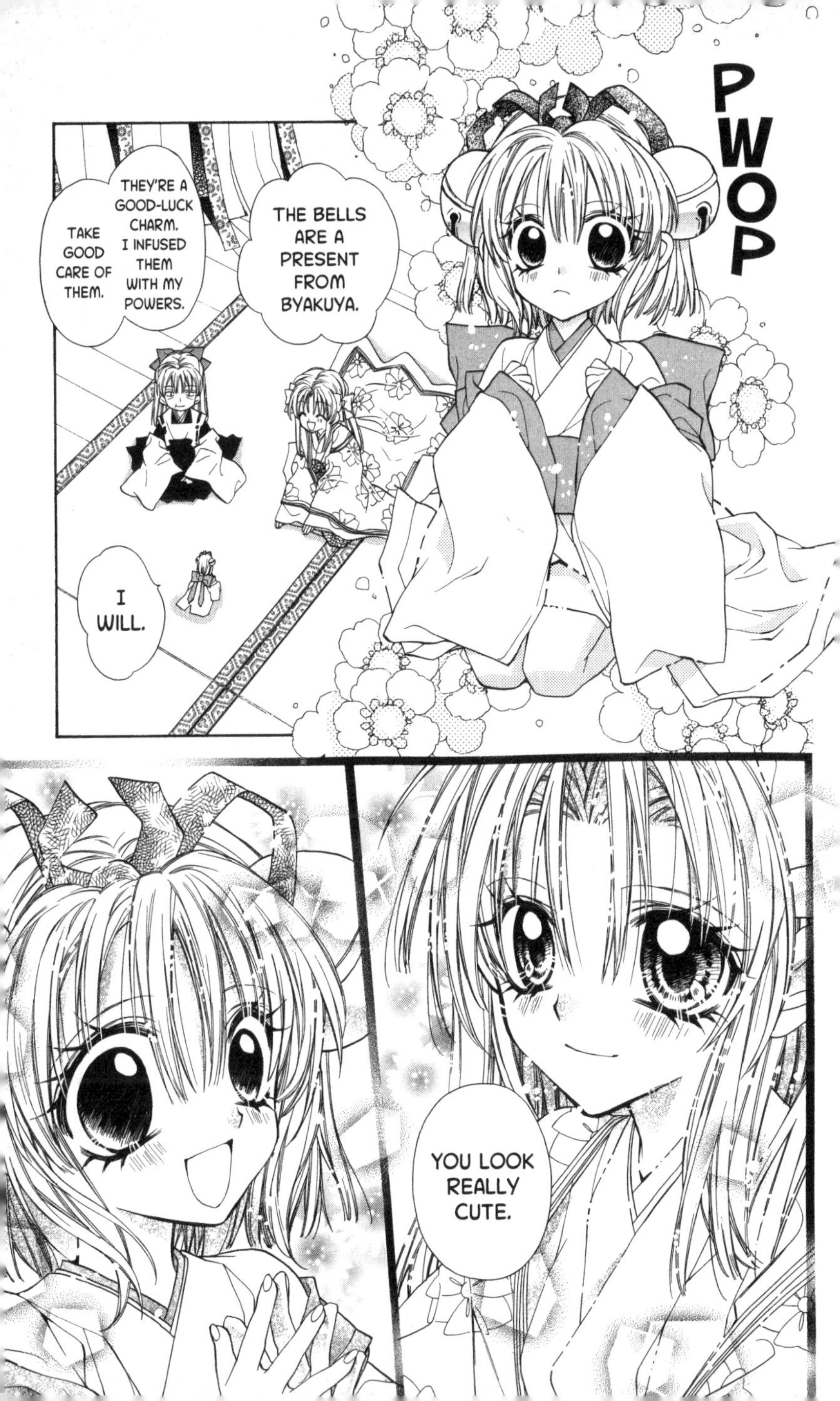
PWOP
THE BELLS ARE A PRESENT FROM BYAKUYA.
THEY'RE A GOOD-LUCK CHARM. I INFUSED THEM WITH MY POWERS.
TAKE GOOD CARE OF THEM.
I WILL.
YOU LOOK REALLY CUTE.

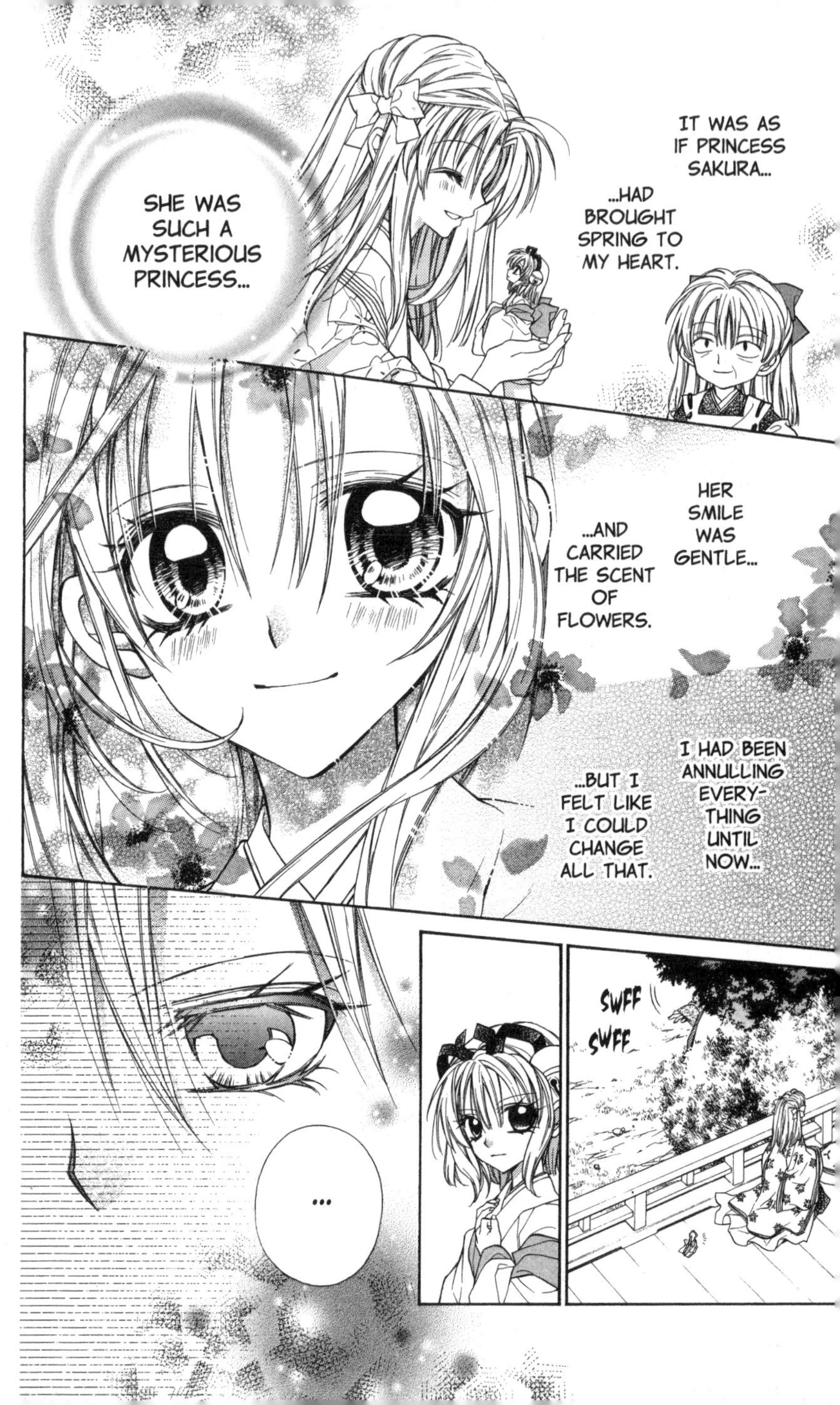
IT WAS AS IF PRINCESS SAKURA...
...HAD BROUGHT SPRING TO MY HEART.
SHE WAS SUCH A MYSTERIOUS PRINCESS...
HER SMILE WAS GENTLE...
...AND CARRIED THE SCENT OF FLOWERS.
I HAD BEEN ANNULLING EVERY-THING UNTIL NOW...
...BUT I FELT LIKE I COULD CHANGE ALL THAT.
SWFF
SWFF
...

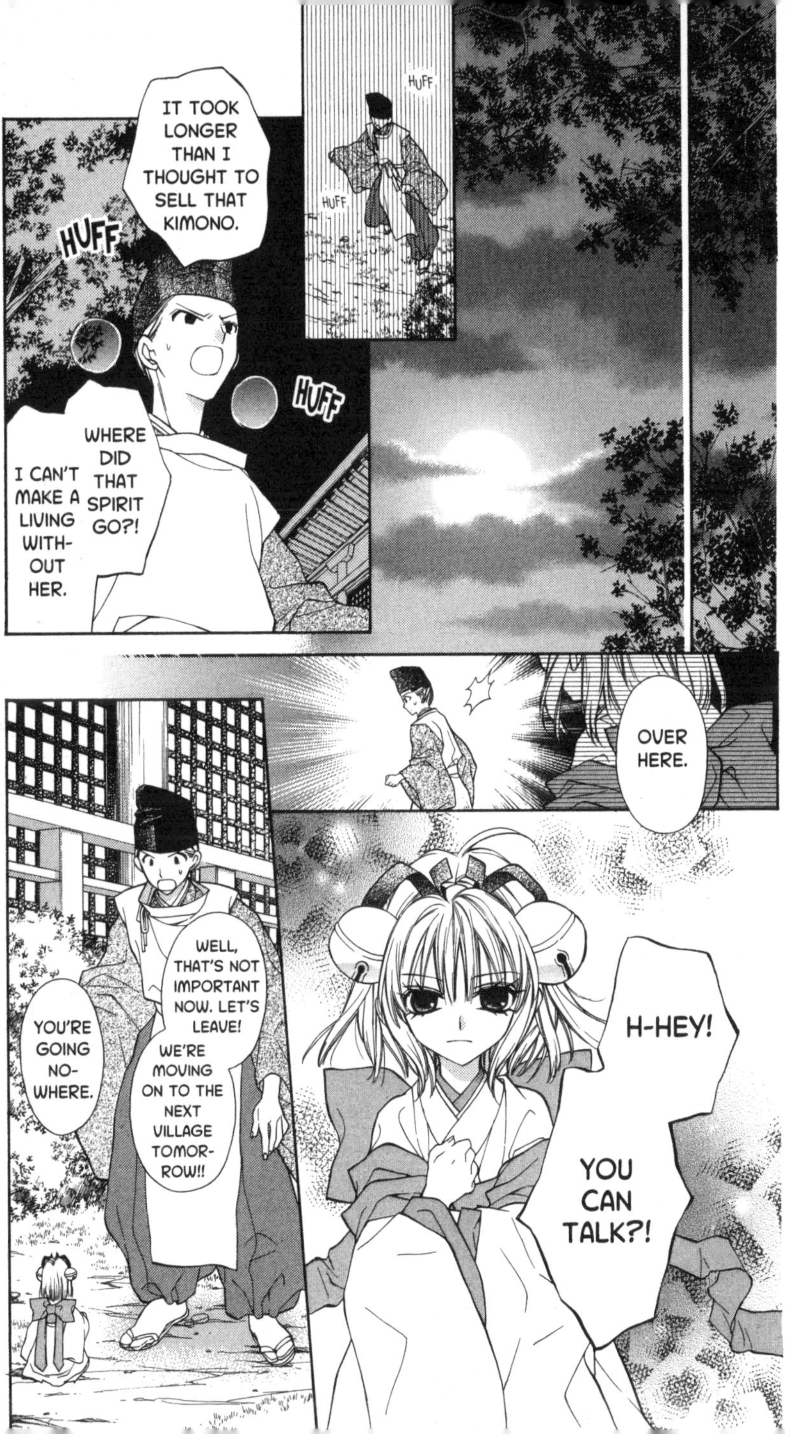
HUFF
HUFF
IT TOOK LONGER THAN I THOUGHT TO SELL THAT KIMONO.
HUFF
HUFF
WHERE DID THAT SPIRIT GO?!
I CAN'T MAKE A LIVING WITHOUT HER.
OVER HERE.
H-HEY!
YOU CAN TALK?!
WELL, THAT'S NOT IMPORTANT NOW. LET'S LEAVE!
WE'RE MOVING ON TO THE NEXT VILLAGE TOMORROW!!
YOU'RE GOING NOWHERE.

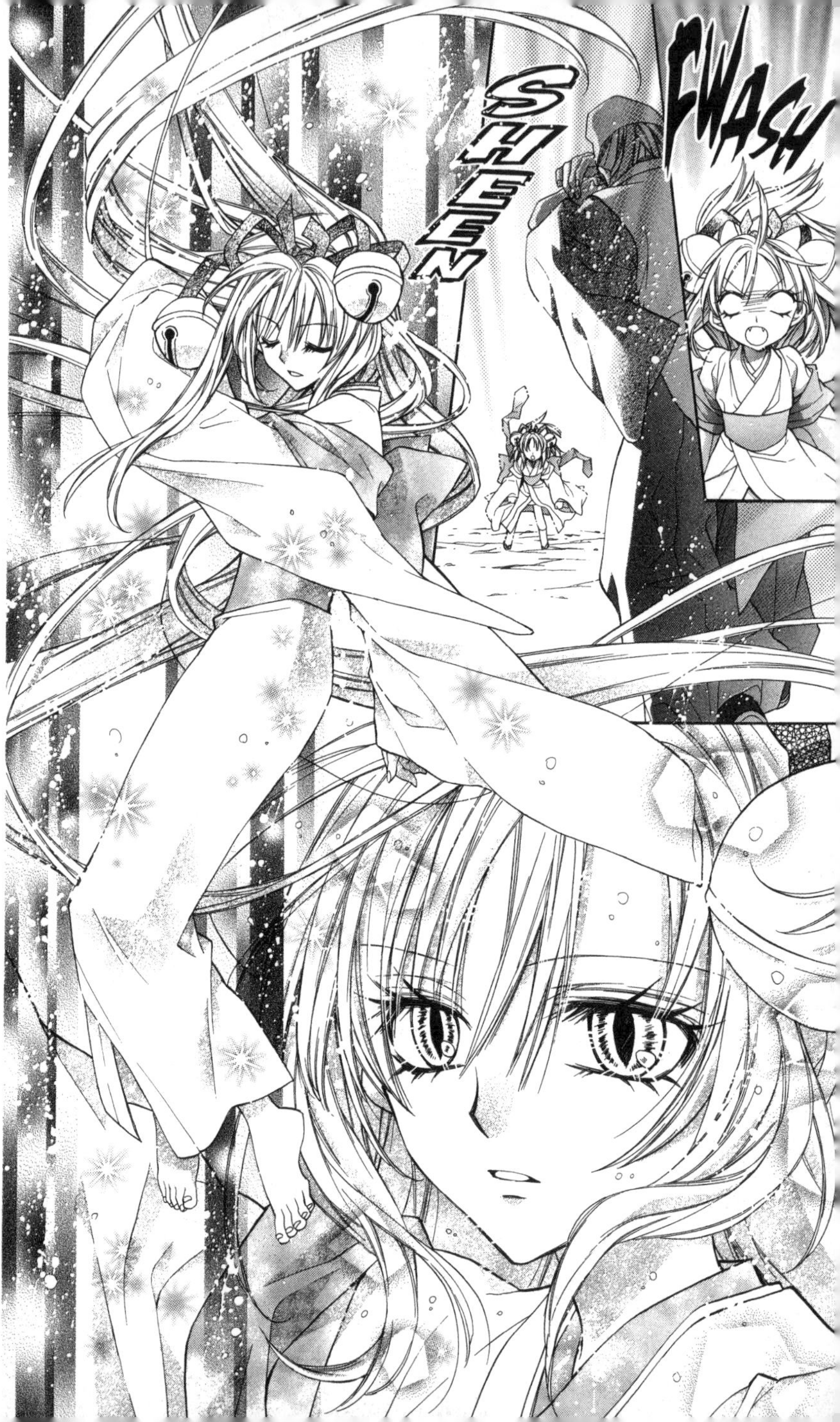
FWASH
SHEEN

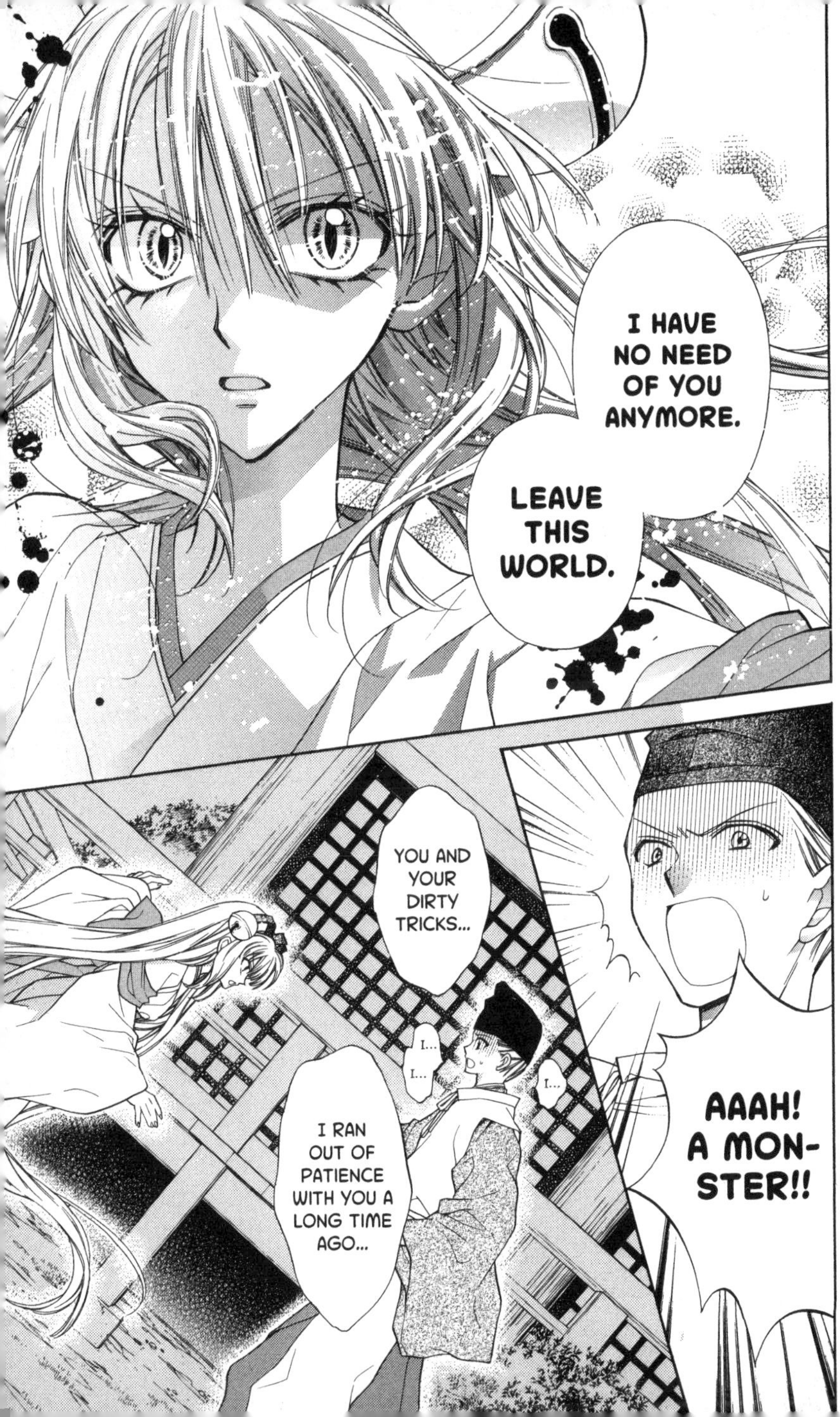
I HAVE NO NEED OF YOU ANYMORE.
LEAVE THIS WORLD.
AAAH! A MON-STER!!
YOU AND YOUR DIRTY TRICKS...
I...
I... I...
I RAN OUT OF PATIENCE WITH YOU A LONG TIME AGO...

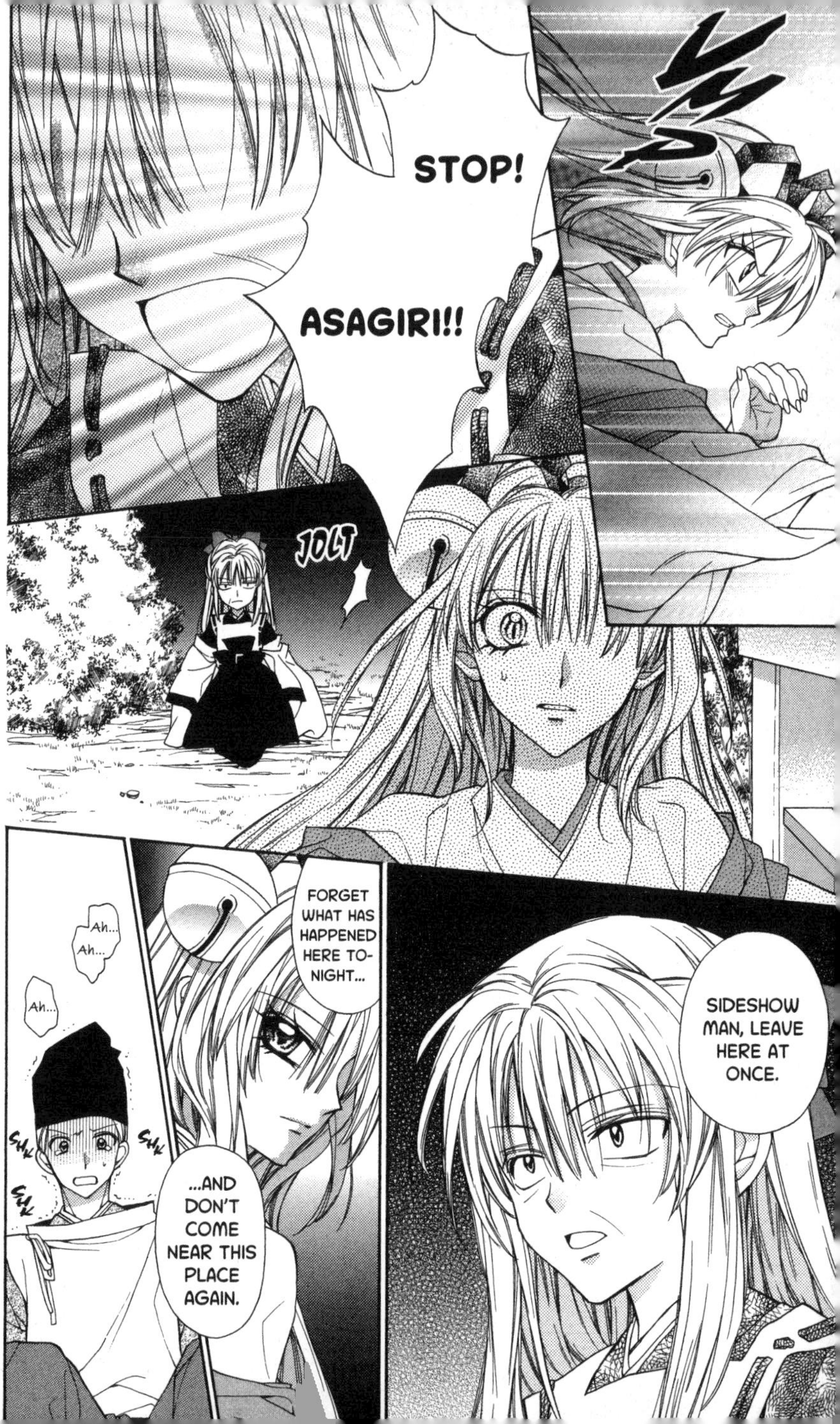
STOP!
ASAGIRI!!
JOLT
SIDESHOW MAN, LEAVE HERE AT ONCE.
FORGET WHAT HAS HAPPENED HERE TO-NIGHT...
...AND DON'T COME NEAR THIS PLACE AGAIN.
Ah... Ah...
Ah...
SHK
SHK
SHK

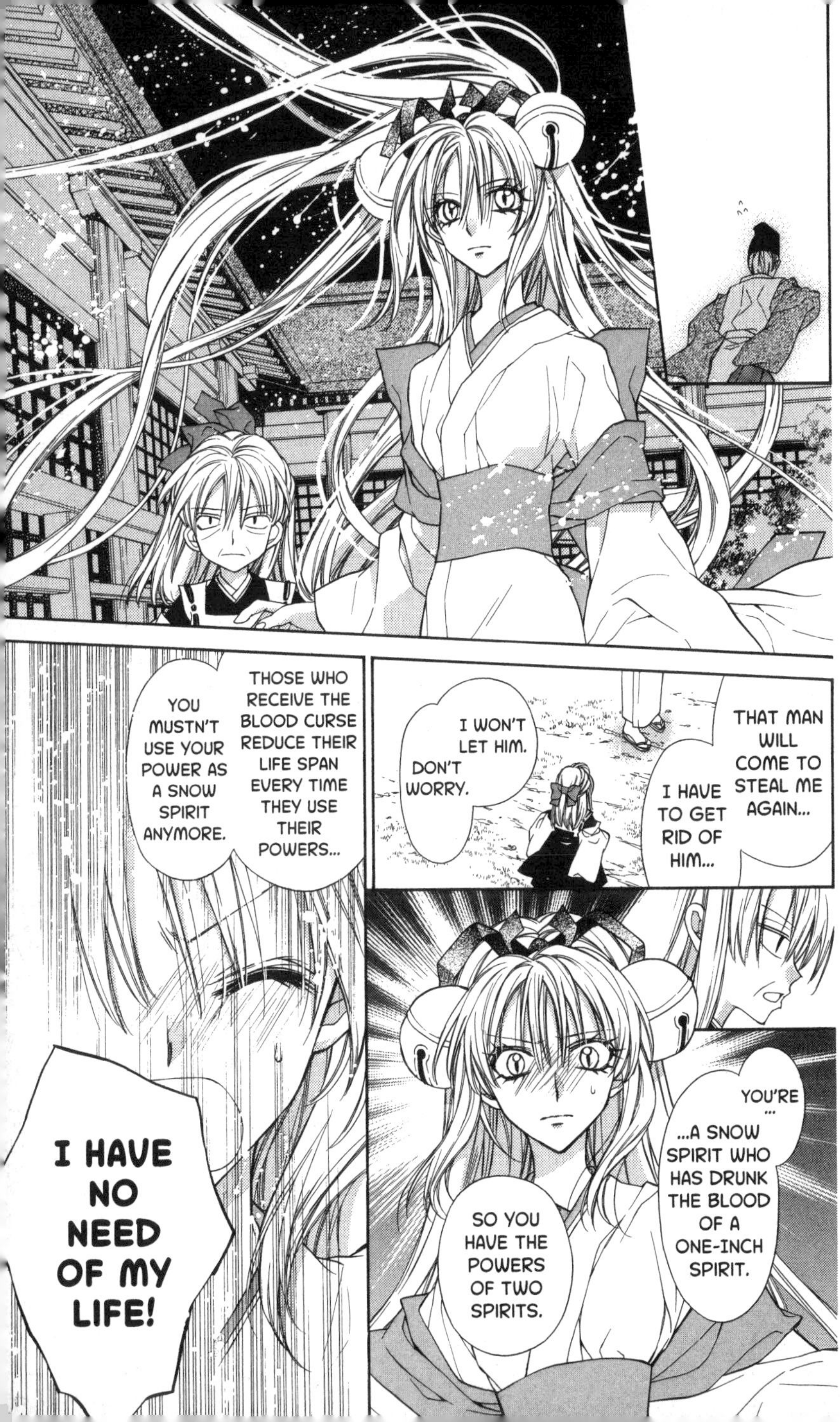
THAT MAN WILL COME TO STEAL ME AGAIN...
I HAVE TO GET RID OF HIM...
I WON'T LET HIM. DON'T WORRY.
YOU'RE ...
...A SNOW SPIRIT WHO HAS DRUNK THE BLOOD OF A ONE-INCH SPIRIT.
SO YOU HAVE THE POWERS OF TWO SPIRITS.
THOSE WHO RECEIVE THE BLOOD CURSE REDUCE THEIR LIFE SPAN EVERY TIME THEY USE THEIR POWERS...
YOU MUSTN'T USE YOUR POWER AS A SNOW SPIRIT ANYMORE.
I HAVE NO NEED OF MY LIFE!

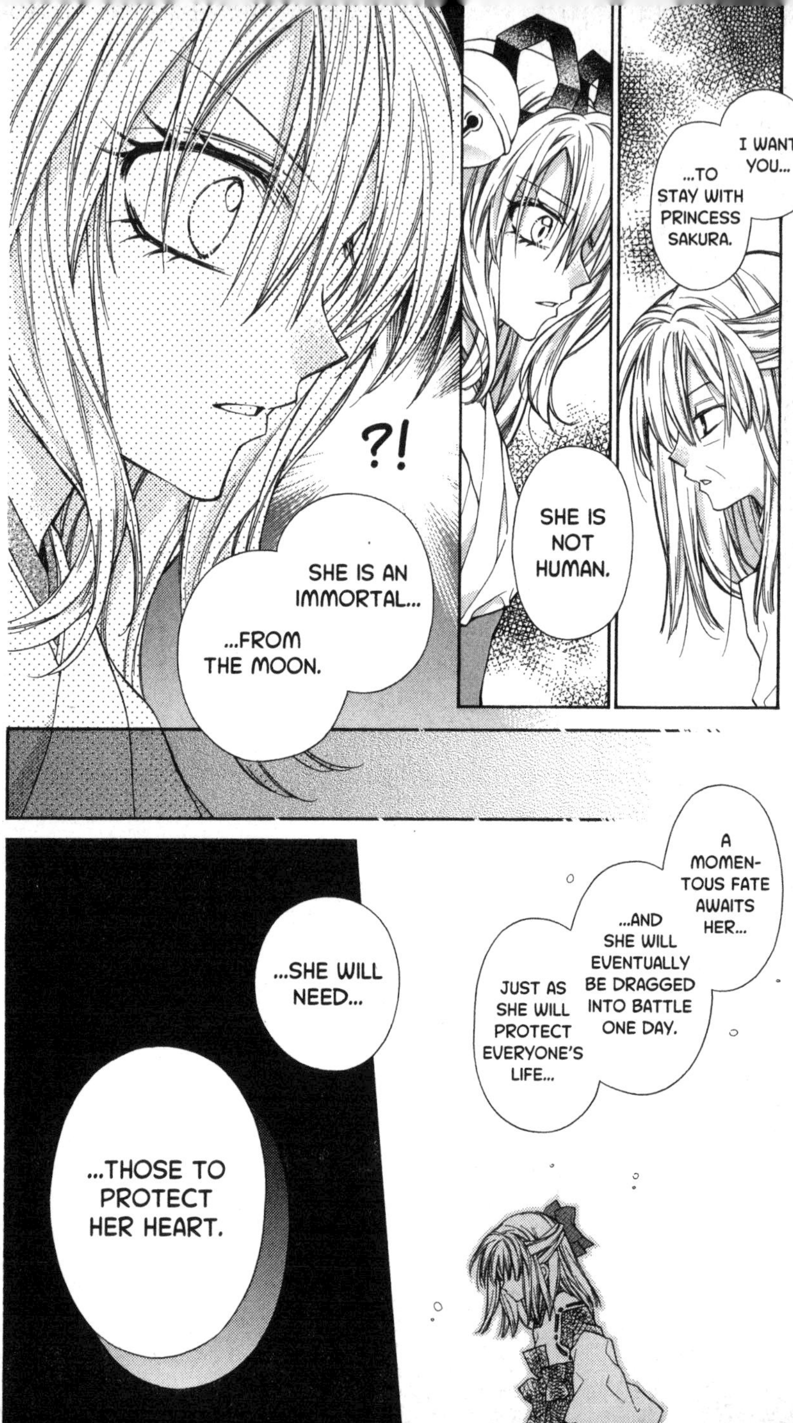
I WANT YOU...
...TO STAY WITH PRINCESS SAKURA.
SHE IS NOT HUMAN.
?!
SHE IS AN IMMORTAL...
...FROM THE MOON.
A MOMEN-TOUS FATE AWAITS HER...
...AND SHE WILL EVENTUALLY BE DRAGGED INTO BATTLE ONE DAY.
JUST AS SHE WILL PROTECT EVERYONE'S LIFE...
...SHE WILL NEED...
...THOSE TO PROTECT HER HEART.

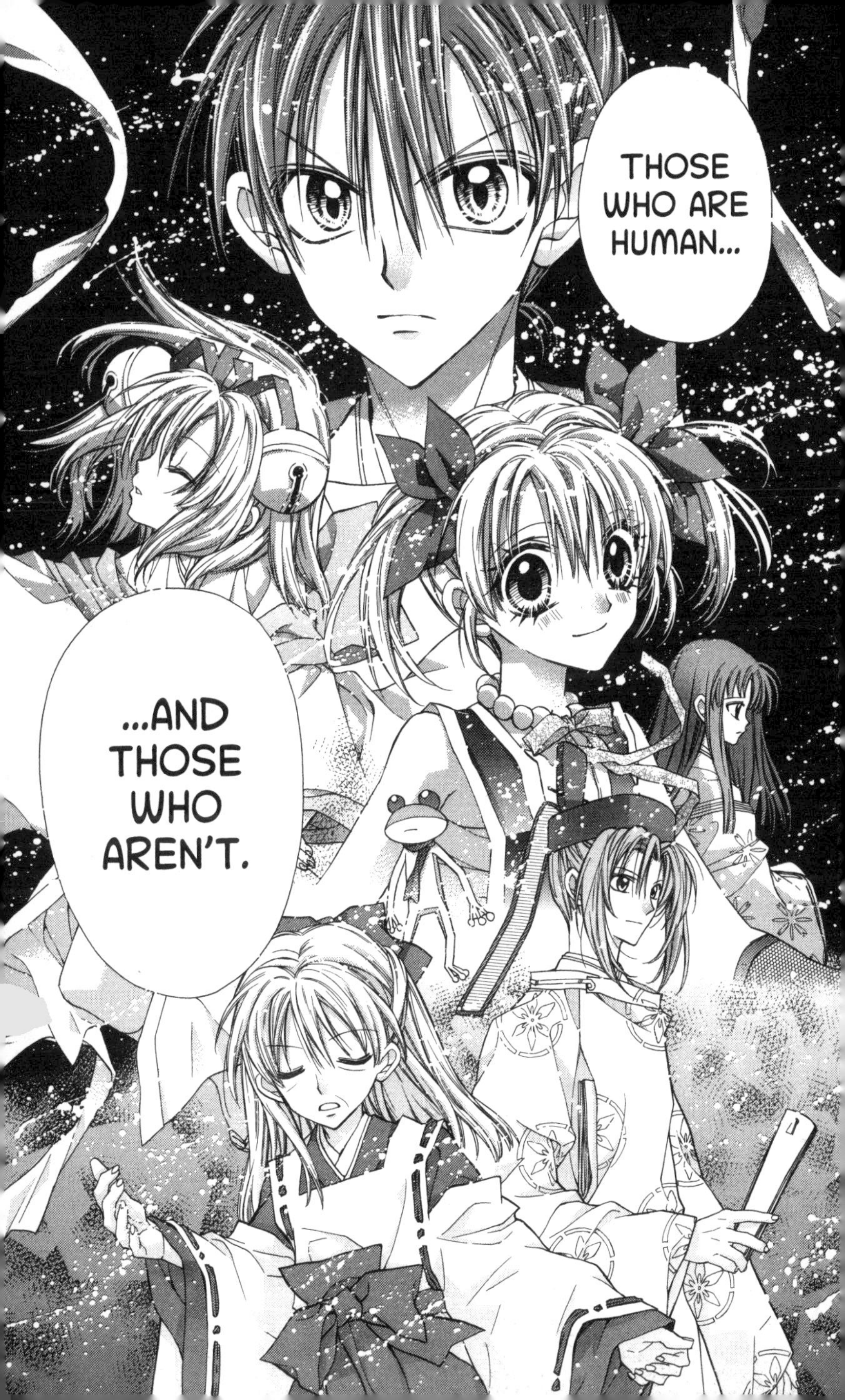
THOSE WHO ARE HUMAN...
...AND THOSE WHO AREN'T.

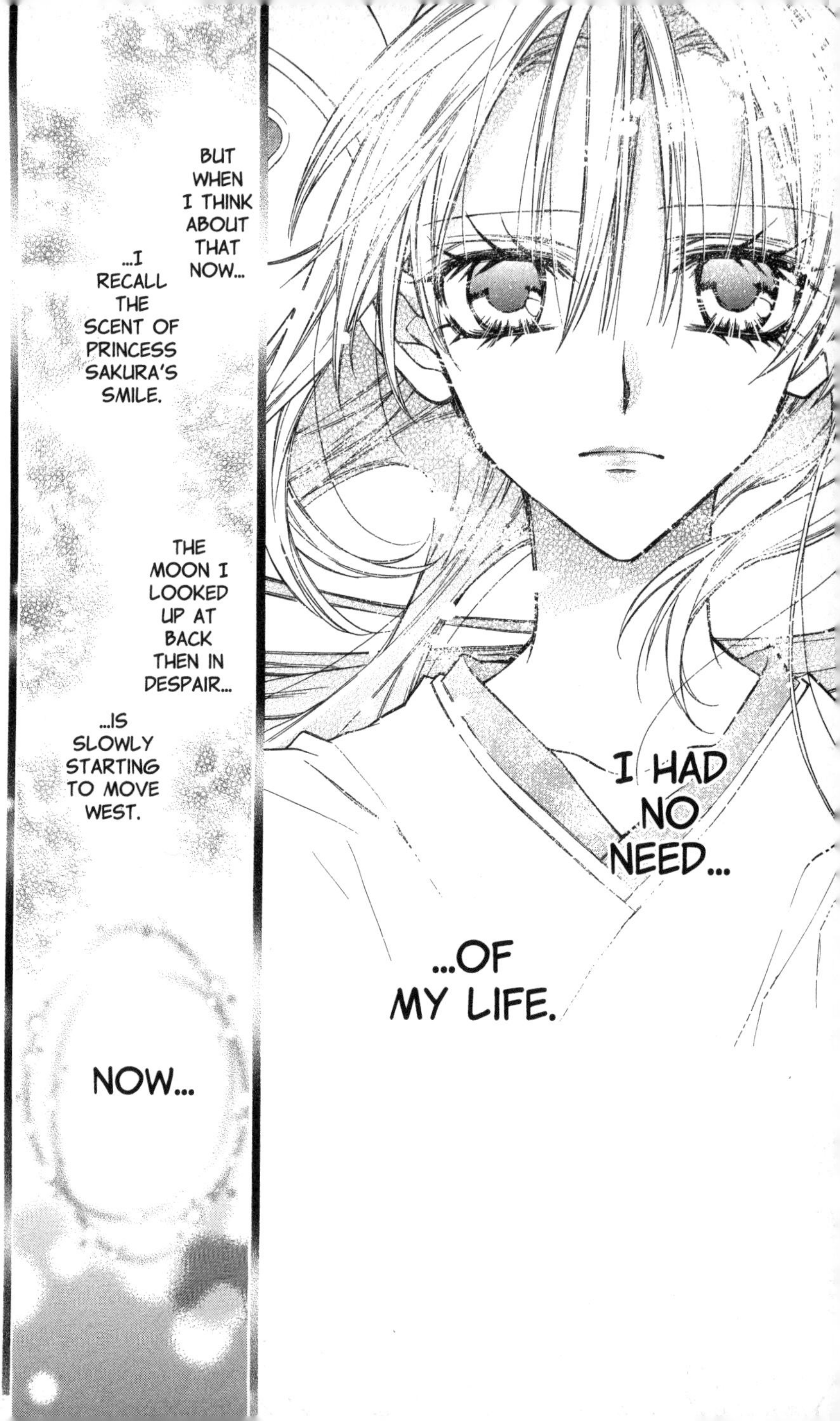
I HAD NO NEED...
...OF MY LIFE.
BUT WHEN I THINK ABOUT THAT NOW...
...I RECALL THE SCENT OF PRINCESS SAKURA'S SMILE.
THE MOON I LOOKED UP AT BACK THEN IN DESPAIR...
...IS SLOWLY STARTING TO MOVE WEST.
NOW...

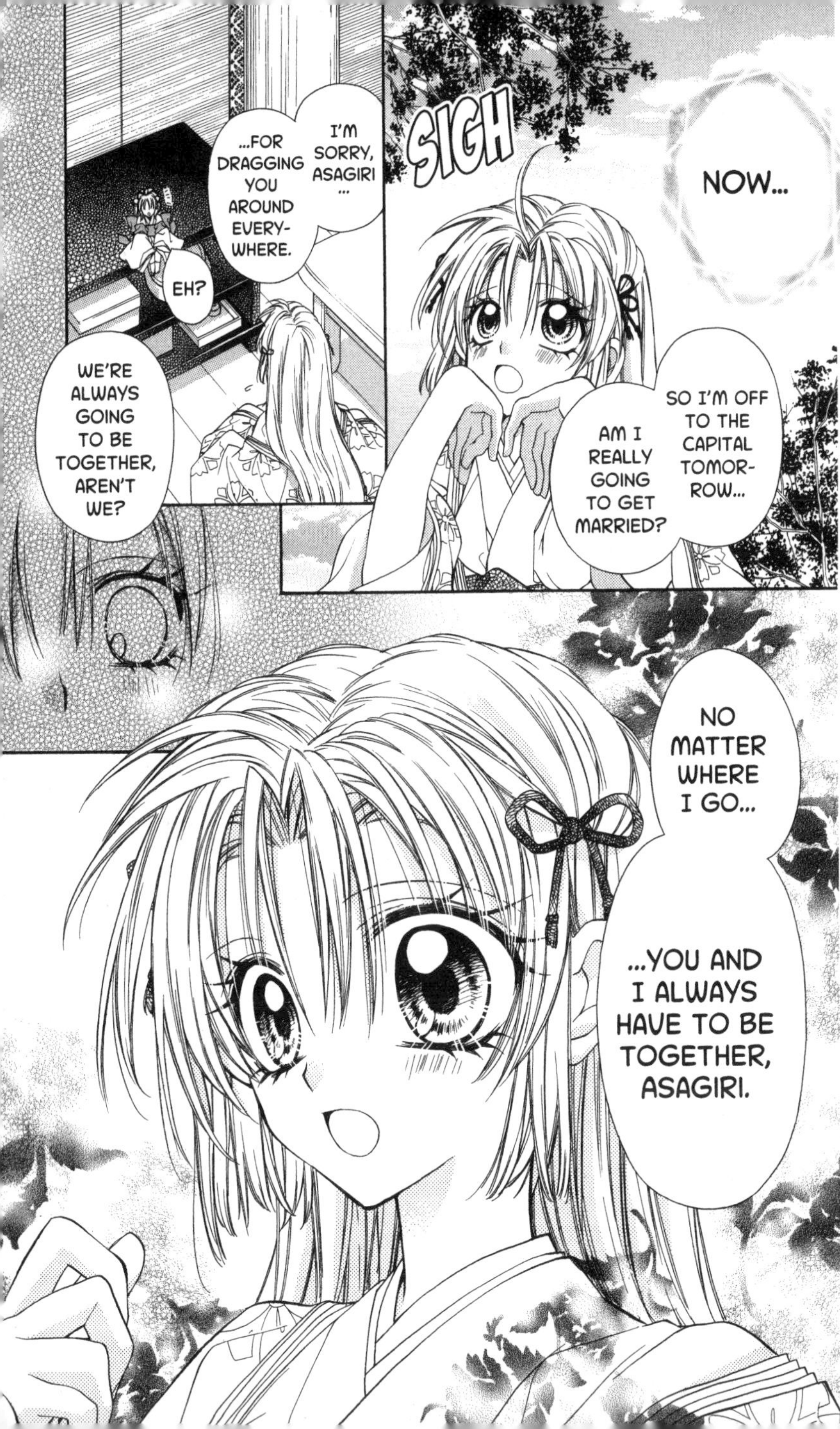
NOW...
SIGH
SO I'M OFF TO THE CAPITAL TOMORROW...
AM I REALLY GOING TO GET MARRIED?
I'M SORRY, ASAGIRI...
...FOR DRAGGING YOU AROUND EVERYWHERE.
EH?
WE'RE ALWAYS GOING TO BE TOGETHER, AREN'T WE?
NO MATTER WHERE I GO...
...YOU AND I ALWAYS HAVE TO BE TOGETHER, ASAGIRI.

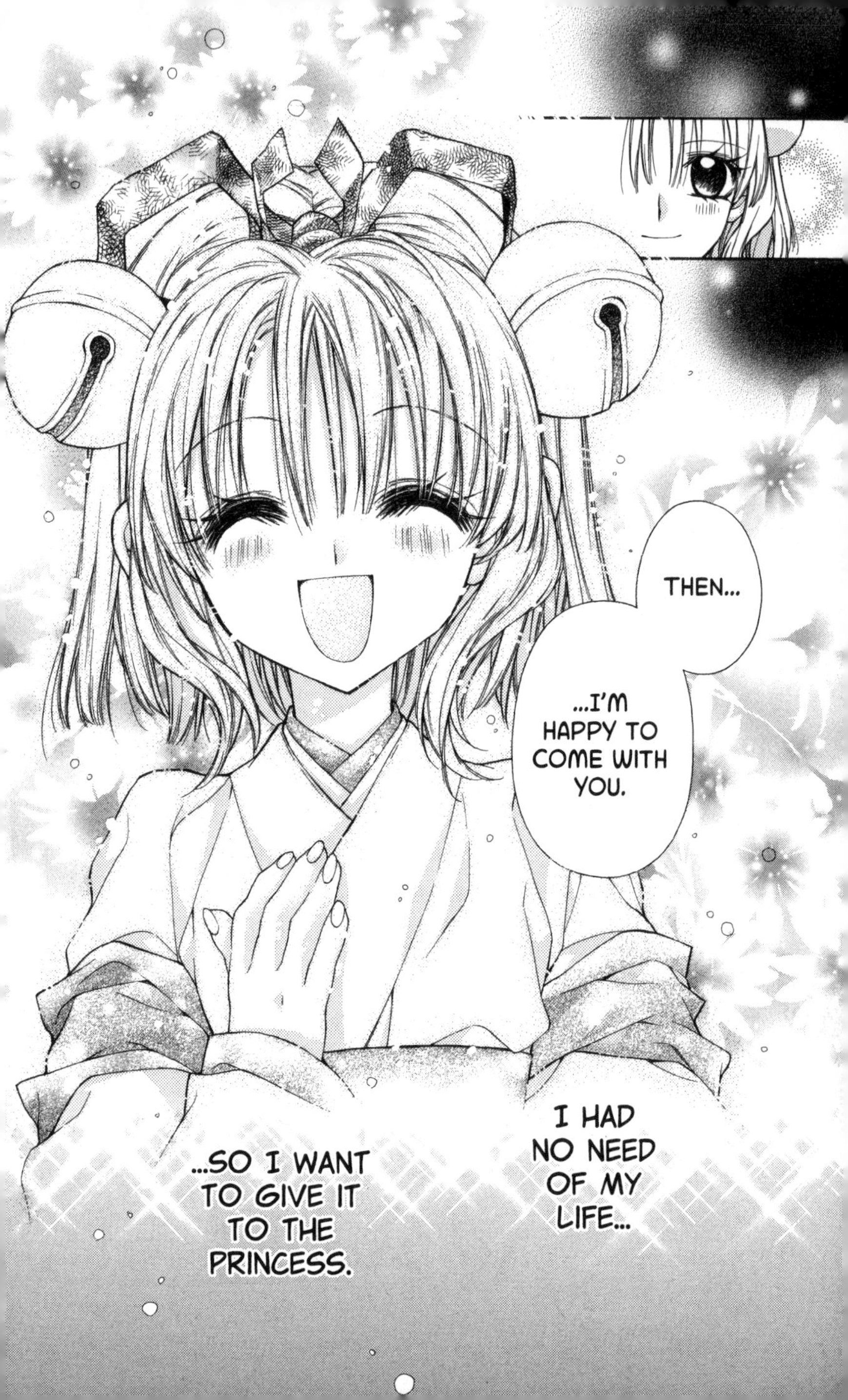
THEN...
...I'M HAPPY TO COME WITH YOU.
I HAD NO NEED OF MY LIFE...
...SO I WANT TO GIVE IT TO THE PRINCESS.

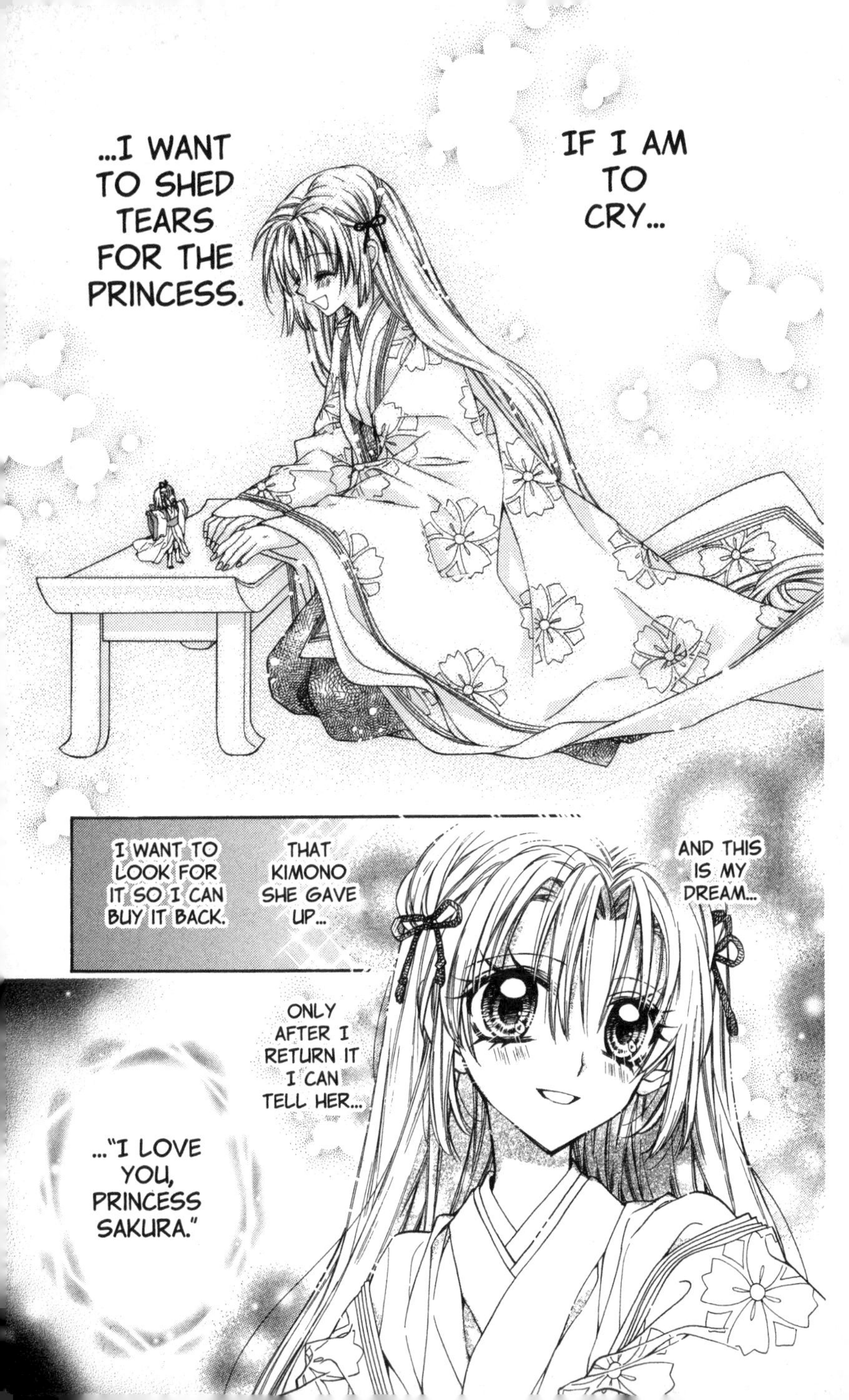
IF I AM TO CRY...
...I WANT TO SHED TEARS FOR THE PRINCESS.
AND THIS IS MY DREAM...
THAT KIMONO SHE GAVE UP...
I WANT TO LOOK FOR IT SO I CAN BUY IT BACK.
ONLY AFTER I RETURN IT I CAN TELL HER...
..."I LOVE YOU, PRINCESS SAKURA."

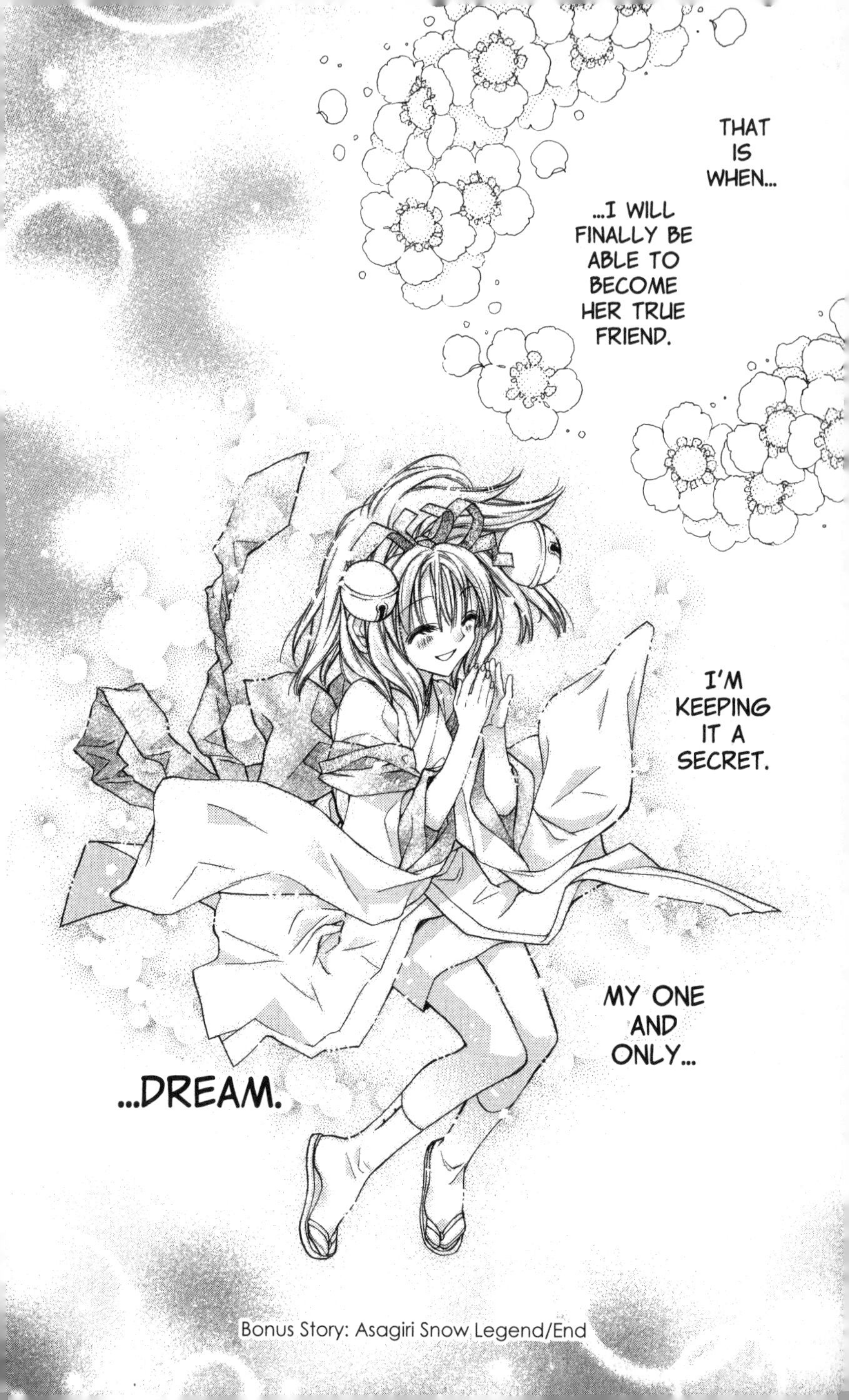
THAT IS WHEN...
...I WILL FINALLY BE ABLE TO BECOME HER TRUE FRIEND.
I'M KEEPING IT A SECRET.
MY ONE AND ONLY...
...DREAM.

Bonus Story: Asagiri Snow Legend/End

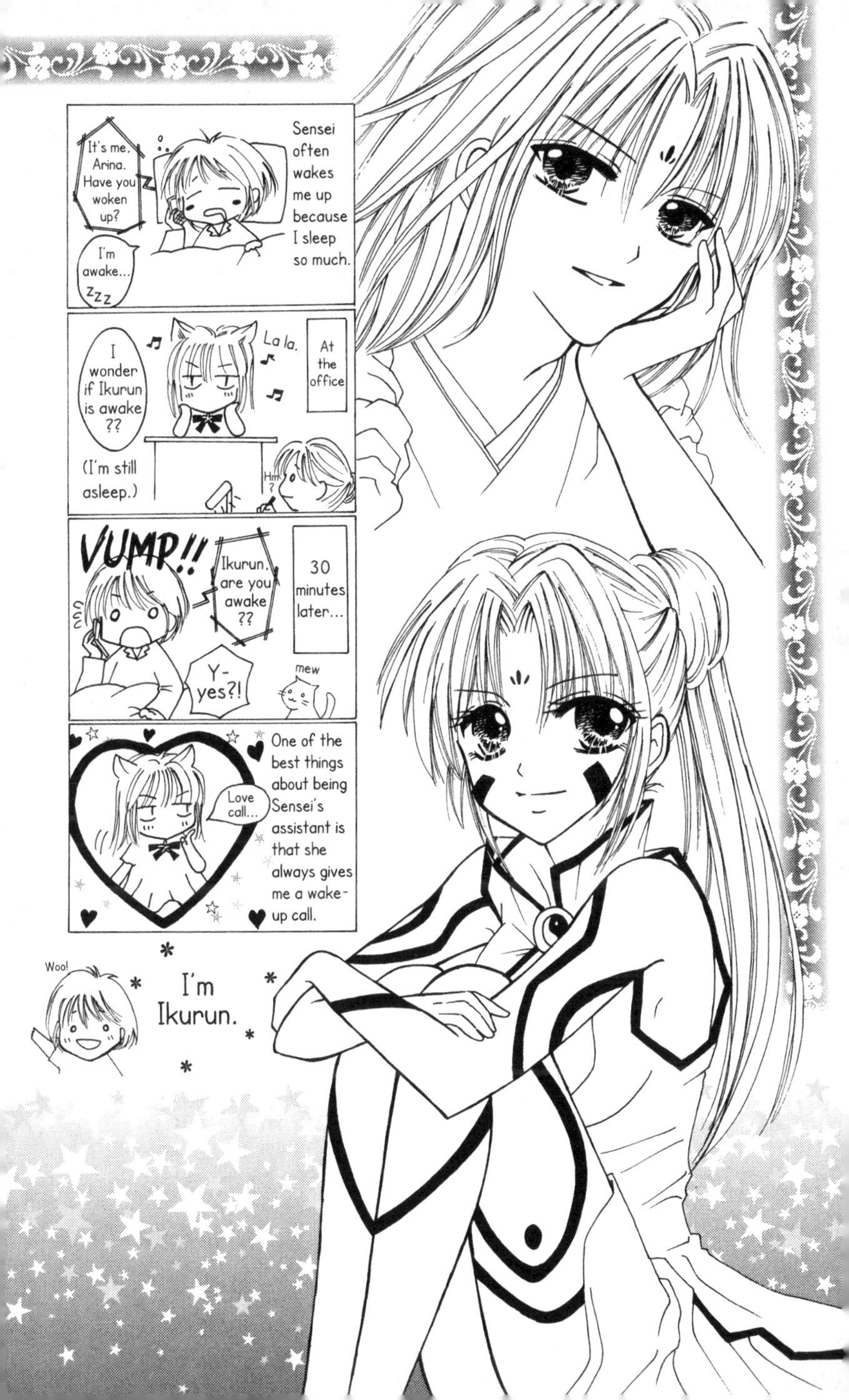
Sensei often wakes me up because I sleep so much.
It's me, Arina. Have you woken up?
I'm awake... zzz
At the office
La la.
I wonder if Ikurun is awake ??
Hm ?
(I'm still asleep.)
30 minutes later...
Ikurun, are you awake ??
VUMP!!
mew
Y-yes?!
One of the best things about being Sensei's assistant is that she always gives me a wake-up call.
Love call...
I'm Ikurun.
Woo!

HINACHI GA SHAKIN☆

~ The Truth Is Revealed!! Assistant Diary ~

Maybe you'll catch a glimpse...?!*

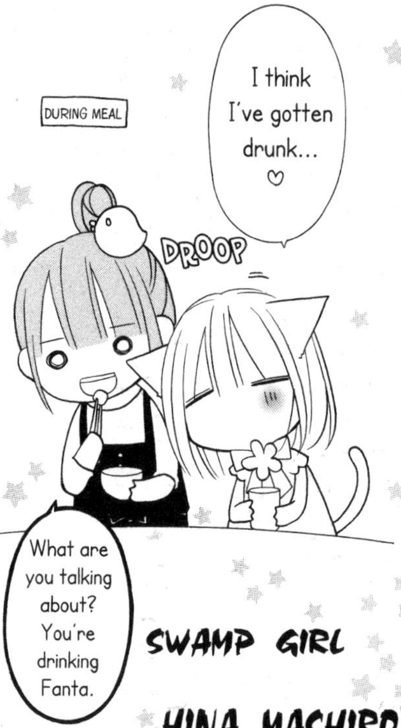
DURING MEAL
I think I've gotten drunk... ♡
DROOP
What are you talking about? You're drinking Fanta.

SWAMP GIRL

HINA MASHIRO

RMC *Yaya Puri* volume 1 on sale now in Japan!!

Her Kindness: Priceless

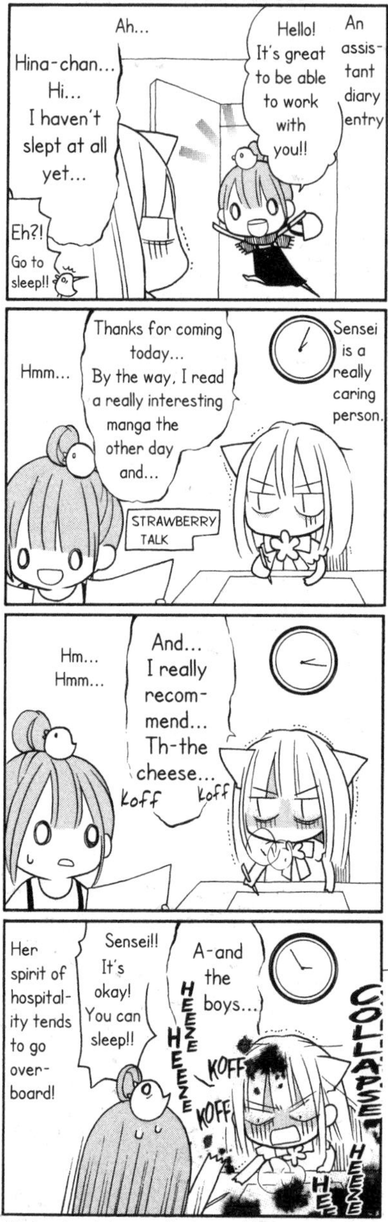
An assistant diary entry
Hello! It's great to be able to work with you!!
Ah...
Hina-chan... Hi... I haven't slept at all yet...
Eh?!
Go to sleep!!
Sensei is a really caring person.
Thanks for coming today... By the way, I read a really interesting manga the other day and...
Hmm...
STRAWBERRY TALK
And... I really recommend... Th-the cheese...
Hm... Hmm...
Koff
Koff
COLLAPSE
A-and the boys...
Sensei!! It's okay! You can sleep!!
Her spirit of hospitality tends to go overboard!
HEEZE
HEEZE
KOFF
KOFF
HEEZE
HEE

*A stereotypical phrase used in Japanese TV programs that show girls in swimsuits.

Synchronization

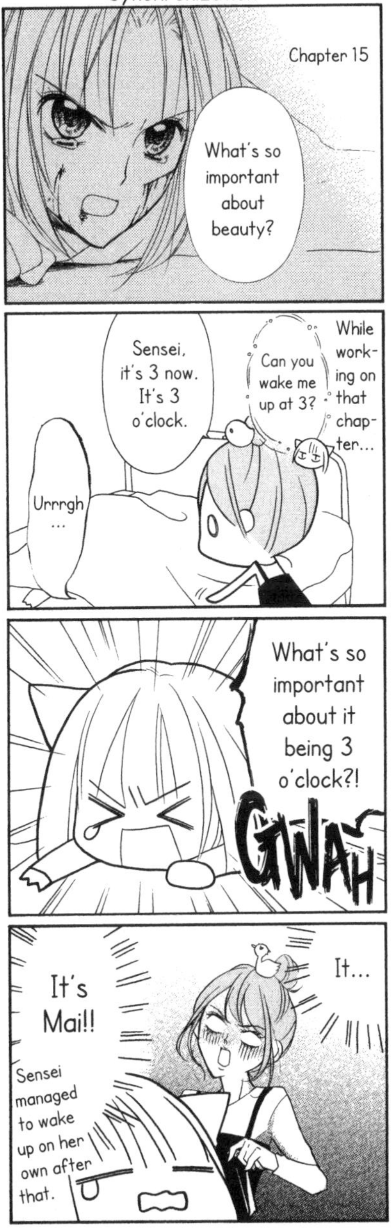
Chapter 15
What's so important about beauty?
While work-ing on that chap-ter...
Can you wake me up at 3?
Sensei, it's 3 now. It's 3 o'clock.
Urrrgh...
What's so important about it being 3 o'clock?!
GWAH
It...
It's Mai!!
Sensei managed to wake up on her own after that.

Waiting for Mummy

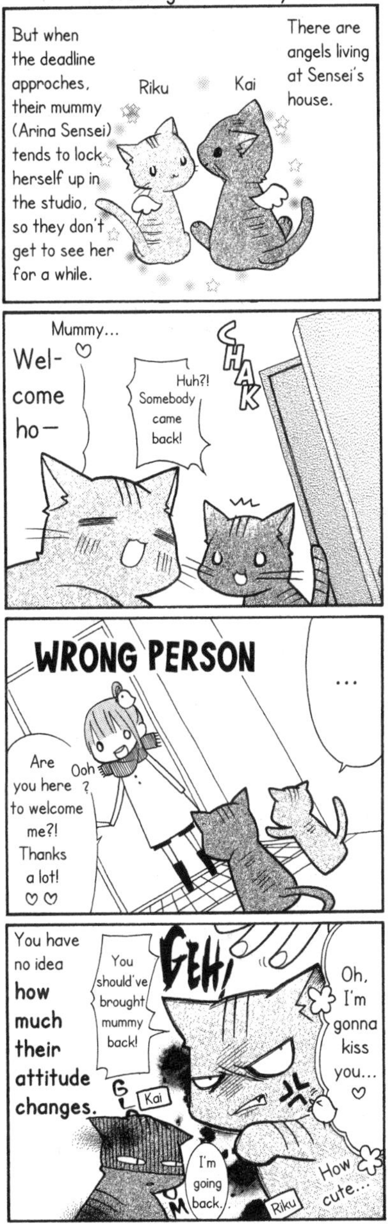
There are angels living at Sensei's house.
Kai
Riku
But when the deadline approches, their mummy (Arina Sensei) tends to lock herself up in the studio, so they don't get to see her for a while.
CHAK
Huh?! Somebody came back!
Mummy...
Wel-come ho—
...
WRONG PERSON
Ooh?
Are you here to welcome me?! Thanks a lot!
Oh, I'm gonna kiss you...
GEH
You should've brought mummy back!
You have no idea how much their attitude changes.
Kai
How cute...
I'm going back.
Riku

A Hunter Among Us!

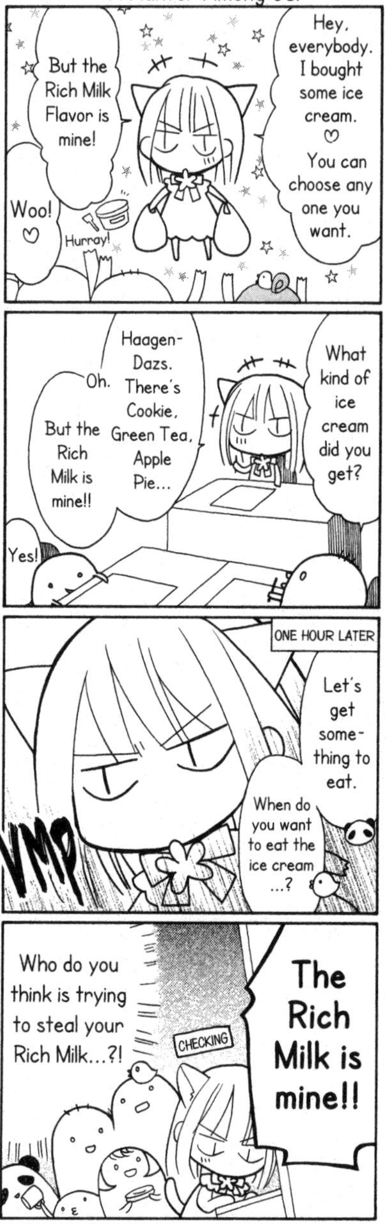
Hey, everybody. I bought some ice cream. ♡ You can choose any one you want.
But the Rich Milk Flavor is mine!
Woo! ♡
Hurray!
What kind of ice cream did you get?
Haagen-Dazs. There's Cookie, Green Tea, Apple Pie...
Oh.
But the Rich Milk is mine!!
Yes!
ONE HOUR LATER
Let's get some-thing to eat.
When do you want to eat the ice cream ...?
VMP
The Rich Milk is mine!!
CHECKING
Who do you think is trying to steal your Rich Milk...?!

Assistant's Mind

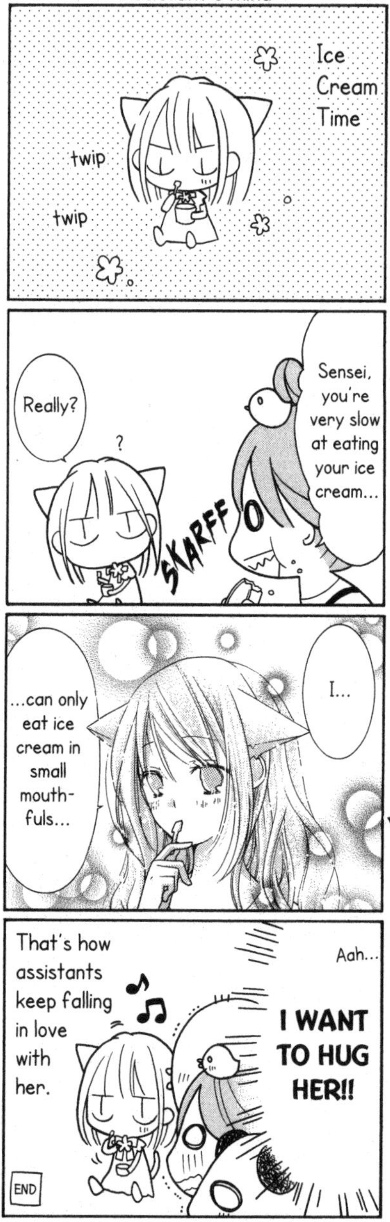
Ice Cream Time
twip
twip
Sensei, you're very slow at eating your ice cream...
SKARFF
Really?
?
I...
...can only eat ice cream in small mouth-fuls...
Aah...
I WANT TO HUG HER!!
That's how assistants keep falling in love with her.
END

Volume 4 Special Bonus

HINA MASHIRO & ARINA TANEMURA SPECIAL INTERVIEW

(Arina, "Ari" from below) Hello, everybody! I'm Arina Tanemura!!

(Hina, "H" from below) Hello, I'm Hina Mashiro, a *Ribon* mangaka and Arina Sensei's assistant!!

(Ari) Not only did Hina-chan create the funnies in this volume, but she also has come to sleep over at my house to interview me.

(H) She even held a crepe party for me and included **that** in this volume too. (laugh) Thank you very much.

(Ari) I asked you over the phone, "Can I include an interview of us in volume 4?" Then you suddenly said, "I also drew some funnies too!" and handed them to me when we went to eat Korean barbecue in Shibuya. I know I'm the butt of the jokes, but I thought they were really funny!!!

(H) Ha ha ha! You are too kind!! Speaking of which, you took me to a Korean barbecue restaurant just because I said that I wanted to eat meat. Even though you were on a diet, and you ate only three slices of meat. (laugh)

(Ari) That's okay... Barbecued vegetables are good to eat too. And I like the atmosphere of a barbecue restaurant... I'm satisfied with just being in the restaurant...

(H) And you kept drinking water too. (laugh) How cute. By the way, who is your favorite character in *Sakura Hime*?

(Ari) I'm actually pretty fond of everybody. My favorite is Sakura, Asagiri, and Rurijo, though... I guess these three are special to me. What about you, Hina-chan?

(H) Oooh, that's a nice choice. Girls are invincible!! Fujimurasaki and Enju are special to me. They're my favorites. For sure!

(Ari) My favorites are girls, and your favorites are guys... (laugh) I want Fujimurasaki to appear more, but I can't do that because of his status... Then which character would you choose as your boyfriend?

(H) I'd definitely choose his highness Fujimurasaki for my boyfriend...!! I want him to play the flute for me every day. I'll sit beside him and play the castanets. Enju is more of a one-night stand relationship. (laugh) Who would you choose to marry?

(Ari) I'd choose Fujimurasaki as my boyfriend, but I'd choose to marry Aoba. Fujimurasaki will probably take good care of his girlfriends. But when it comes to marriage, he's the Togu so he'll ignore personal feelings... Aoba is actually a very cooperative guy, so he'll do well in a marriage... Or am I thinking about this too realistically? (laugh) Enju isn't a choice for me because he's too androgynous for my taste.

(H) That's deep... But Sensei, we haven't said anything about you-know-who, who received ninth place in the popularity vote. (laugh)

(Ari) You mean Hayate? He's more of a pet to me. (How mean.) But he's my editor's favorite character. My editor keeps making good remarks about his scenes when reviewing the storyboard. (laugh) Please pay close attention to the serious scenes too, Dear Editor. Which character would you like to become?

(H) A pet! (laugh) I agree. \(´▽`)/ I like his bellybutton when he's a frog. The character I'd like to become...is probably Asagiri. She's always with Sakura.

(Ari) I...guess I want to become Sakura because she can use Chizakura... I want to fight. I want you, youko! Now, now...

(H) I want youuu!! (laugh) Sensei, you mustn't forget to protect your right hand. (laugh) But Sakura's battle scenes are cool, aren't they? Do you have any favorite scenes?

(Ari) My favorite scenes are when Sakura is told about her soul symbol in chapter 1, and the first time Sakura and Rurijo come face to face and fight in this volume. The way I judge my "favorite" scenes is whether they've turned out better than I had imagined them in my mind when I was drawing them. Wh-what about you, Hina-chan? B-BMP B-BMP

(H) Right! I really like that scene too!! I especially like the scenes with the Rurijo monologue... I started to feel so sad when I thought about how Rurijo must have felt. You hand over the final draft of the manga for me to work on as an assistant, and this was a chapter that had a lot of memorable scenes.

(Ari) Th-thank you. I think I got into that scene a little too much. I tend to be cool towards my work, but there are times when I concentrate so much that I forget to breathe when I'm working on *Sakura Hime*. The scene with Rurijo and Sakura was a very important part of this series, so I really put a lot of effort into it.

(H) I can't wait to see how the relationship between those two will turn out!!! The works you create are very delicate—like a glass sculpture—but you'll break out into song when we're working and try to make the assistants laugh... I don't know what to make of it. (laugh) The gap is too...

(Ari) Sure, I sing. But to be honest, I start to sing without being conscious of it... I'm sorry I'm so noisy. But it's a lot of fun. (laugh) By the way, we invited our fans and held a Christmas party last year, didn't we?

(H) We did. I participated in it too, and we had singing, bingo, and hugs. (laugh) It was so much fun... I hope we can do it again.

(Continues)

↓ (Continued from previous page)

(An) I wasn't used to doing things like that, so I was in a panic. But I hope we can invite the fans over and do something again. Enjoying something together is so nice.

(H) It was fun to watch you tease your fans. (laugh) It'll probably be fun to go somewhere together too! ♡

(An) Good idea. We could do a bus tour for a certain price! We could go on an excursion, or a short trip. I'll be the bus guide with my strawberry talk. (laugh)
Attention please! (Wrong.)

(H) I want to go to Hakone!! (laugh) And... And at night we'll all have a pillow fight, and you'll burst into the room saying, "What do you think you're doing?! Go to sleep!!"（´ʖ`） I bet a lot of the fans will stay up on purpose just because they want you to scold them. (laugh)

(An) I see, I am a "Sensei" after all! (laugh) I want to shout "Roll call!" I like Hakone, so I would like to go there...
Kamogawa Sea World would be fun too. It's a large place so we could probably take a lot of people there. Should we really give it some thought?

(H) That'd be great! I'll ask my friend who works at a tour company about it. ♡ Kamogawa Sea World sounds great too...! I want to see the dolphin show! ✝

(An) But the participants will have to be 20 years old or older, I guess. I want to challenge a lot of things this year so, I intend to do many new things!!

(H) As a fan of yours, I can't wait to see the various worlds of Arinacchi. ♪ I'll be looking forward to it... ♡ Are you planning anything new at the moment?

(An) I'm thinking about creating a music CD with my assistant, Miwa-chan... ///
We'll have somebody create the music, and I'll write the lyrics. ///

(H) Oooh!! Wow!!! ♡ Then it's going to be an independent music CD?! What kind of music will it be?!

(An) ?? Is it an indie? Maybe it is? Eh, I'm currently thinking about creating songs that are like the theme songs for all my works so far... This is embarrassing. ///

(H) That sounds like a dream!! Then you're going to do theme songs for your earlier works too?

(An) For the moment, I'm thinking about starting with I.O.N. I want to become good at writing lyrics, so I thought the only way to do that would be to get some practice by actually writing a song. I'm a total amateur at music though... ♩

(H) Writing lyrics must be hard... ♧ But it'll be so fun to hear your lovely words in a song!! I love Kyoko— will you create something for that as well?

(An) Uh-huh, Kyoko will be in it too. What? ♪ Hina-chan, you like Kyoko?! I never knew that... ♪ I'm looking forward to working on the lyrics for it because I think I'll be able to create something that suits fantasy. I've already completed the lyrics for Sakura Hime, you know. ♥

(H) What?‼ You didn't know about how much I like Kyoko? (laugh) Hmm? But I've been expressing my love for Kyoko with my whole body all the time... (What?) I was still in middle school when the series was in the magazine, so it had a huge effect on me! I bet Kyoko's song will be cool. ♡ What kind of song does Sakura-Hime have?!

(An) It's in a cool, fast-paced Japanese style that reminds you of Sakura fighting from start to finish! I cannot thank the composer enough for it. ♥ I'd also like people who are interested in it to be able to get ahold of the CD. I'm such a lucky person to have so many people helping me with it... ♥ ♪

(H) That's so nice... ♡ That's so nice... ♡ Then...could it be... No, it's got to be. The vocalist is you, isn't it, Arina Sensei?! Your fans will love it!! I hope you do a live performance somewhere! ♡ I want to listen to you sing at some large hall.

(An) Me? The vocalist?? What are you talking about? ♪ Sakura will sing the theme song for Sakura Hime, and Kyoko-chan will be singing the theme song for Kyoko. ♪ The other staff members are very motivated, so I would like to do a live performance. I'm going to enjoy my hobbies this year too!!! Would you please help me, Hina-chan? ♥ With many things...

(H) Aaah...! (laugh) Yes... You're right! Sorry about that. I'm looking forward to hearing all the heroines sing. ♥ You're starting a lot of things aren't you? I'd love you help you as much as I can, Sensei. ♪ So please have his highness Fujimurasaki appear more often.

(An) Uh... ♪ Right, I'm sure there'll be a Fujimurasaki chapter someday... Is there anything you'd like to try this year, Hina-chan?

(H) I actually want him to appear in every issue of the magazine. (Impossible.) As for this year... I'd like to try to create a story manga!!

(An) Ah!! That's something worth striving for! On the other hand, I'm going to try to create something short! A story I've wanted to do so much may finally take shape. ♥ I hope we can enjoy this year together!

(H) I've hardly ever drawn things like that, so I'm already feeling nervous, but I'll do my best!! I'm looking forward to your short manga too. ♡ I can't wait to read all your puns and jokes. ♡♥ I hope we watch over each other this year too. ♧ Thank you very much for today!!

2/24/2010 At the Tanemura residence

↗

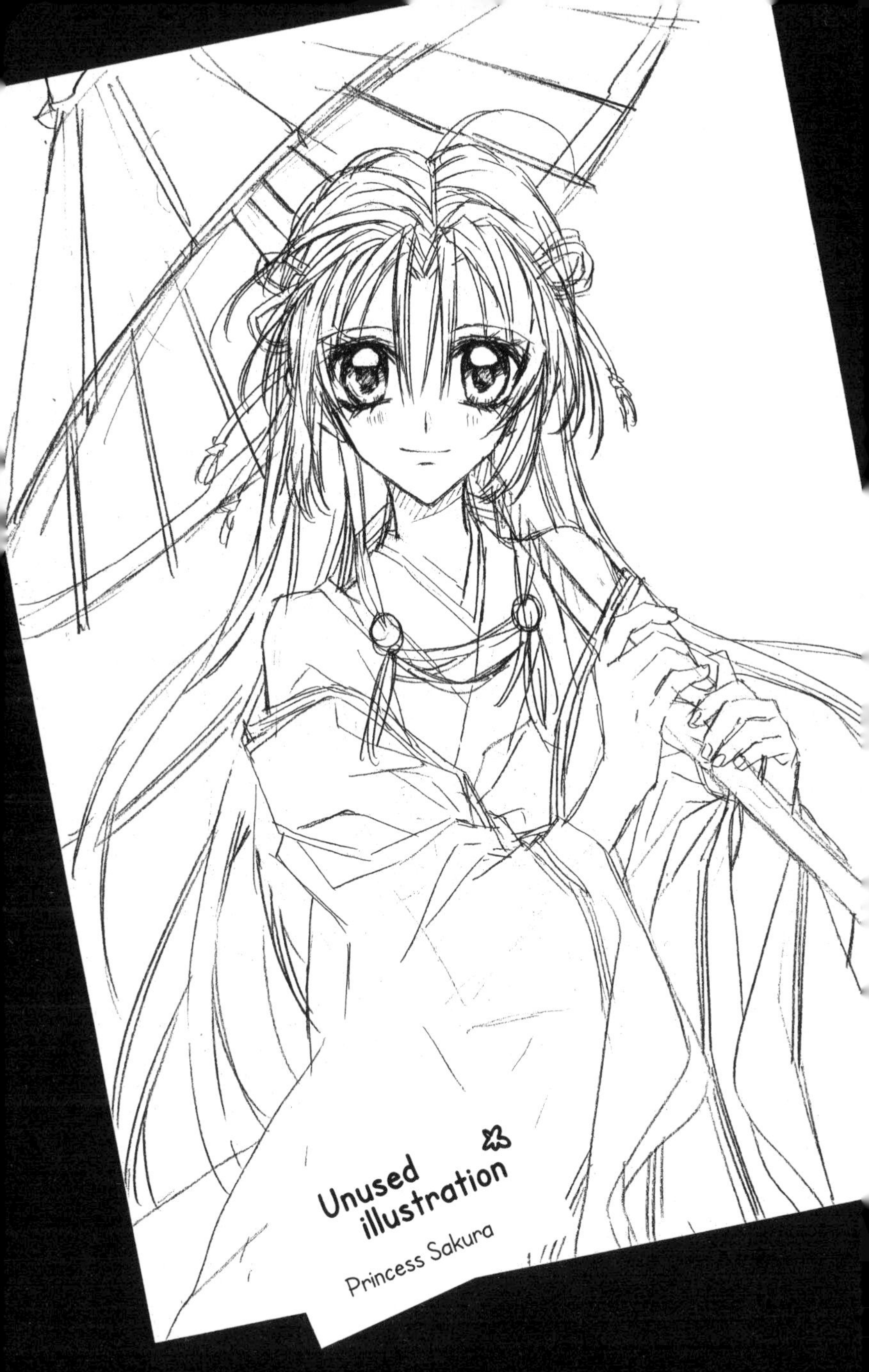
Unused illustration
Princess Sakura

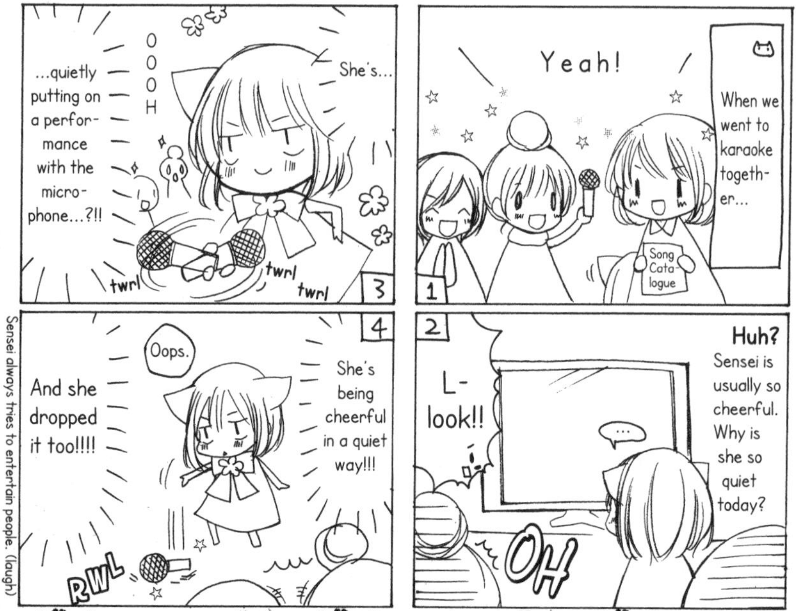
When we went to karaoke together...
Yeah!
Song Catalogue
Huh? Sensei is usually so cheerful. Why is she so quiet today?
L-look!!
...
OH
She's...
...quietly putting on a performance with the microphone...?!!
OOOH
twrl twrl twrl
She's being cheerful in a quiet way!!!
Oops.
And she dropped it too!!!!
RWL
Sensei always tries to entertain people. (laugh)

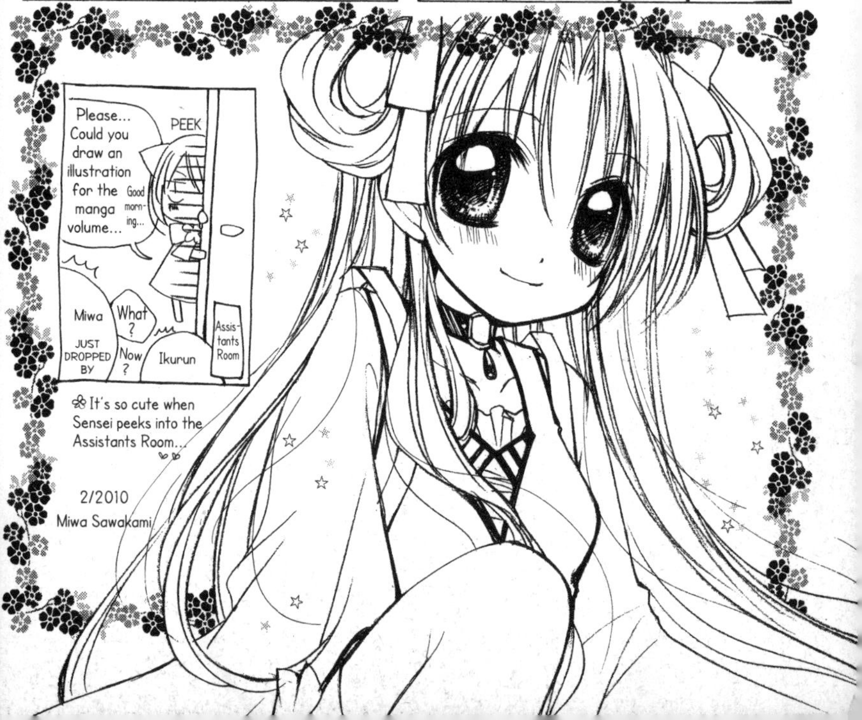
PEEK
Please... Could you draw an illustration for the manga volume...
Good morning...
Assistants Room
What? Now?
Miwa
JUST DROPPED BY
Ikurun
It's so cute when Sensei peeks into the Assistants Room...
2/2010
Miwa Sawakami

An illustration for
the furoku that
comes with the
magazine ✿

Sakura

ARINA TANEMURA

So the new story arc has started. In these chapters I was aiming for a shonen manga with lots of cool battles, but after I drew them, I was faced with the fact that it turned out differently than I had envisioned. So I realized that I had been aiming for a shojo manga after all. (Though I guess it is kind of swerving away from that genre as well...) It's a battle in which emotions rage and characters face their pasts and personal struggles. There may not be as many battle scenes in this as you expected, but I hope you will realize how all the characters are trying desperately to "live."

Arina Tanemura began her manga career in 1996 when her short stories debuted in *Ribon* magazine. She gained fame with the 1997 publication of *I·O·N*, and ever since her debut Tanemura has been a major force in shojo manga with popular series *Kamikaze Kaito Jeanne*, *Time Stranger Kyoko*, *Full Moon*, and *The Gentlemen's Alliance †*. Both *Kamikaze Kaito Jeanne* and *Full Moon* have been adapted into animated TV series.

Sakura Hime: The Legend of Princess Sakura
Volume 4
Shojo Beat Edition

STORY AND ART BY
Arina Tanemura

Translation & Adaptation/Tetsuichiro Miyaki
Touch-up Art & Lettering/Inori Fukuda Trant
Design/Sam Elzway
Editor/Nancy Thistlethwaite

SAKURA-HIME KADEN © 2008 by Arina Tanemura
All rights reserved.
First published in Japan in 2008 by SHUEISHA Inc., Tokyo.
English translation rights arranged by SHUEISHA Inc.

Printed in the U.S.A.

Published by VIZ Media, LLC
P.O. Box 77010
San Francisco, CA 94107

10 9 8 7 6 5 4 3 2 1
First printing, October 2011

www.shojobeat.com

www.viz.com